JEDEDIAH SMITH JIM BRIDGER
HUGH GLASS JAMES P. BECKWOURTH

These were some of the men who, between 1822 and 1834, carved a historic path through virgin wilderness. In these years before the beaver hat gave way to silk, men whose names are now almost legendary were leaving civilization behind, each for his own reasons, to face the rugged life of the mountains.

Jim Bridger, who was only seventeen when he started out, became renowned as a leader and guide through the unknown territory: Hugh Glass, mauled by a grizzly and left to die, returned to camp to astound his awe-struck fellow-trappers; James P. Beckwourth, champion liar, kept a journal indicating that he saved the day in every crisis that ever rose in the wilderness. These were the men who lived because they learned new skills and ways of life from the Indians, whose ebullience and courage survived a harsh, demanding life because they were where they wanted to be—in virgin territory where a man's life depended on the often cruel dictates of nature. And there were those who made fortunes on the work the trappers did—men like John Jacob Astor and Billy Subliette, fighting a different kind of battle, grasping for power and control of the fur trade.

There is no more exciting saga in the history of the West than Don Berry's magnificent account of the Rocky Mountain Fur Company—rich, vivid, and above all, true to the time and the spirit of the men who lived it.

To David/ Bonny/ Duncan

Contents

PART THREE

THE ROCKY MOUNTAIN FUR COMPANY
1830-1834

Author's Preface

An early Northwesterner—I've forgotten who it was—once took a hard look at his own journal and put down his considered opinion that it was "ill wrote worse worded and not well spelt."

I don't know how many gloomy hours I've spent contemplating that honest admission. A good many, I think, because long ago I came to feel a profound sense of kinship with that clear-sighted gentleman. He knew what he was about; this is the invariable impression given by that first terrifying look at the completed work. At times like that one regrets the passing of the old, engaging sort of Author's Preface that began "Gentle Reader . . ." It amounted simply to a plea for tolerance; be kind, it said, and forgive my transgressions; all errors herein proceed from a natural feebleness of mind for which I am not responsible. If there is a writer who doesn't feel the need for some such appeal to the reader, he's a braver man than I; and I hereby enter my official plea.

The bones and muscle of this book are the direct quotations from the original sources. I have merely supplied a little connective tissue, hoping to make the parts hang together more securely. In the process I've historian. Not, I hope, in competence; the day is long past when inadequate research might be excused, and we are well rid of it. The difference is in the matter of opinions. The amateur can afford to have them. Too often the academician has to endure the sidelong glances of his confreres if he expresses his own notions in language insufficiently academic, whereas I have cheerfully set down whatever happened to catch my fancy without making much attempt to phrase these personal observations in formal terms.

This, of course, gives the book a somewhat conversational tone, and if anyone is offended by the lack of dignity herein he has my regrets, and I wish him better luck elsewhere. Doubtless a good many of these hard-gained opinions are quite wrong; but all surmise is so labeled and shouldn't cause any confusion. For my errors I apologize, and invite the reader to form his own judgments from the facts as given. If the quotations seem to indicate conclusions different from my own, their evidence is much to be preferred.

The facts themselves may be dependent upon; every statement of fact in the book is documented. Where data has been newly plowed up in my own research, I've generally quoted the pertinent papers at sufficient length to demonstrate my point. This is also true on those occasions when I've been forced to differ from what has been written about the trade previously. The reader should not by any means take my comments on other historical opinions as disparaging to them; I've simply pointi~~~ ~~~~~~ where I h~~~ ~~~

PART ONE

ASHLEY AND HIS MEN

1822-1826

CHAPTER 1

"There to be employed"

TO

Enterprising Young Men

The subscriber wishes to engage ONE HUNDRED MEN, to ascend the river Missouri to its source, there to be employed for one, two, or three years. For particulars enquire of Major Andrew Henry, near the Lead Mines, in the County of Washington, (who will ascend with, and command the party) or to the subscriber at St. Louis.
Wm. H. Ashley

General Ashley was a careful man. His advertisement appeared in the *Missouri Gazette & Public Advertiser* on February 13th, 1822, and began to run in the St. Louis *Enquirer* two weeks later. Altogether it appeared in St. Louis papers for six weeks running.

By March 27 it had done its work; the general had recruited his men, opened a great era of American history, and ensured the permanence of his own name. He would not have been entirely pleased.

In fact, if someone had been able to tell him he would take his place in history as the author of that advertisement and its results, the good general might well have frowned. It was not that he minded going down in history. Not at all; he was quite prepared for that eventuality. But he had in mind a rather different approach to the matter.

William Ashley was an ambitious man, but the furthest ambition from his mind was to be known as one of America's great adventurers. The idea was ludicrous on the face of it. Ashley, now in his middle forties, was a man of slight build; his face thin, with a nose generously styled and a projecting chin. His ambitions were coming along nicely, but they had little to do with mountain adventuring. He was already lieutenant governor of the state of Missouri and a brigadier general in the militia. Then, too, there was a gubernatorial election coming up, and who could tell what might happen? Politics was his first love; his other ventures were simply means to that eventual end. Money is, after all, a requisite for even a dedicated office seeker, and the sad fact was that General Ashley needed it badly. One source estimates he was nearly $100,000 in debt. Nathaniel Wyeth, writing eleven years later, says, "At the time he [Ashley] engaged in this undertaking he was bankrupt, but was a person of credit, which enabled him to get the requisite means."

"A person of credit" covers many of the aspects of General Ashley's career. He was a man of excellent intelligence, and was highly respected. Wherever he went he gravitated into positions of responsibility, inspiring confidence in both his abilities and intentions. If his financial affairs had not gone as he might have wished, it had certainly not diminished the high regard in which he was held.

Most recently Ashley had been in the gunpowder business. When he first arrived in Missouri he had done some little exploring of the back country, armed with "a knowledge of surveying and a slight familiarity with geology." He had discovered, among other things, a large cave in Texas County, which was plentifully stocked with potassium nitrate. When the demand for gunpowder increased under the impetus of the War of 1812, Ashley built a complete plant at the cave for the extraction of commercial saltpeter. This he hauled to Potosi, some eighty miles away, where he had built a factory to complete the conversion of the saltpeter into gunpowder.

At Potosi, seventy miles southwest of St. Louis, Ashley probably met his future partner Andrew Henry for the first time. Henry also had been moved to wartime production; he was engaged in lead mining. He had not been actively engaged in the fur trade since 1811, but had kept some financial interest in the Missouri Fur Company.[1] [See Brief Calendar . . . , p. 403.] When the demand for gunpowder and lead subsided after the war, both men withdrew from their businesses. Henry—judging from the famous advertisement—remained in residence near Potosi, and Ashley returned to St. Louis. It was time to begin looking around for more profitable fields.

One was waiting for them, and it seemed ready-made for this particular combination of men. The fur trade was beginning to swing upward. The revitalized Missouri Fur Company under Joshua Pilcher was making up-river plans. Rumor had it, and rumor was correct, that John Jacob Astor's American Fur was at last planning to open an establishment in St. Louis.[2] Companies which had corporately survived the depression were increasing their capital and new partnerships were being formed.

It was the biggest news on the river; the trade was coming to life. St. Louis—always a trade town—shook herself and began to take an interest in life again. Her neighbors, many of them of French peasant stock who had come west when Britain took over the east bank, called her *Pain Court*, Short-of-Bread, because food sometimes had to be imported. St. Louis replied with a scornful *Vide Poche* applied to her sister agricultural communities: Empty-Pockets.

St. Louis: the hub, the center, the Rome to which all roads led, because there was only one road—the river. The river was the city's blood stream and its reason for existence. St. Louis existed by courtesy of the brown flood that swept past her doorstep. The shrewd trader Laclede picked this site, just below the confluence of the Missouri and the Mississippi. The great arteries of the interior funneled all their traffic down to the village; if you wanted to go anywhere you had to go through St. Louis. South? Down the river. East? Up the Mississippi and across by the Great Lakes route. West? The Missouri offered the only decent access to the interior of western America. Wherever you chose to go in the continental vastness, St. Louis was on the route.

Here was a safe channel near shore; a bank high enough to protect from the floods, but not too high for unloading vessels; a broad shelf of land extending back from the river for the village. In 1764 Laclede predicted "one of the finest cities in America" would rise on his site of St. Louis, and he would not have been disappointed.

The tradition goes that news of Napoleon's cession of Louisiana to the United States arrived at nearly the same time as the news of Spain's cession to Napoleon. In order to fulfill the treaty with France, her flag must yield to the Stars and Stripes. But there wasn't a French flag flying; it was still

Spanish. Hence, on May 9, 1804, the Spanish flag was lowered and the French run up; on May 10 this was replaced by that of the United States, making St. Louis the only city in American history to exist under three sovereign flags in twenty-four hours.

It may not have happened; this is a traditional account. If it didn't happen, it should have, because the tradition is a beautifully apt symbol of St. Louis' cosmopolitanism. The population (4,000 in 1820) was as varied as could be found anywhere. At the time of our narrative the French character of the city was still highly evident. There were still log cabins of the early French settlers, their logs vertical and planted in the soil. This was beginning to change; the local boosters bragged that a third of their buildings were brick. They were beginning to pave the streets, to the immense annoyance of farmers whose wooden cart wheels broke on the paving. These people, the original French stock, were well content with things the way they had always been. As one historian observed: "The enterprising spirit of the Anglo-Saxon had no charms for them." But the city was always in flux, and they simply had to get used to it or leave.

Her streets were a kind of perpetual pageant; a continuous parade of all kinds and colors of men. Travelers of all dispositions, European nobility, Kentucky woodsmen, honest merchants and dishonest ones. Buckskin and homespun, lace kerchiefs and silks from China, blankets and paint—Indians were all over the town, some permanent, others perhaps making a respectful visit to the house of their red-haired friend General William Clark. They called it Red-Head's Town, and you could usually find a party of Sioux or Poncas or Minnetarees around someplace.

And if the cosmetic paint of the Indians palled, you could wander back from the waterfront past La Rue Principale to La Rue de l'Eglise and look at another kind, better applied. The new cathedral had on display for the glory of God a few daubs by nonindigenous painters: Veronese, Rubens, Raphael.

Back to the waterfront, and look at one of the unique classes of the American continent: the rivermen, the boatmen. The waterways of North America, from the Gulf of Mexico to the Arctic Circle, have always belonged to the French, to the *voyageurs*. In Canada they were the canoemen, those of the flashing paddles and endless songs, the red feather in the hat, the braggadocio and strut, the men who could carry three "pieces" for ten hours a day, plus whatever they thought they needed in the way of personal possessions. A piece weighed about ninety pounds, and some of the portages were longer than you'd care to think about. Here, in St. Louis, the rivermen were still French, but a slightly different breed. They were the keelboatmen, who pushed, pulled, and generally muscled a fully loaded keelboat a thousand miles or more up one of the most treacherous rivers known to man. The effort was fantastic; it astonished every traveler who saw it for the first time; it seemed only barely possible. For the rivermen—*eh, bien, il faut qu'on manger, tu sais?* It was how they made their living. They shared with their *frères du nord* their roistering gaiety and coxcombry, their ruffling and strutting, and also their reputation for absolute and unequivocal cowardice. Time and again in the literature of the trade, American and Canadian, it comes up; you can't depend on the *voyageurs* in a fight, particularly with Indians. There were exceptions, but they appeared seldom.

For all that, they were masters of the river, and absolutely essential to any project involving water travel, which—at the time—meant any project at all. These men were the custodians of communication; the history of the West at this time depends upon them. It should be needless to add that, if they were conscious of any responsibility at all, it did not weigh too heavily on them.

II

St. Louis, then, late in the month of March, 1822. Ashley is here, slight, well-spoken, a man with an excellent name, fine political connections and, above all, "a person of credit." Andrew Henry has come down from Potosi to take charge of the expedition. For the time being he has laid aside his violin and books to take up a rifle. Tall and slender, with dark hair and light eyes, Henry is an experienced and knowledgeable man in the trade; a few years later his type will be known as the "mountain man" but the term with that specific meaning doesn't exist in 1822. Henry hasn't yet invented the breed.

Ashley got his men in response to the advertisement; some of them had probably been waiting for it. There had been rumors of this expedition as much as five months earlier, and evidence exists that Ashley and Henry had been putting supplies together as early as September, 1821, seven months before.

There is a slight ambiguity in accounts of the destination of this first party. Contemporary newspaper accounts mention the Three Forks area, noting that it contained "a wealth of furs not surpassed by the mines of Peru." They also note that the expedition "would very likely penetrate to the mouth of the Columbia." A grandiose ambition; more likely the product of an editorial writer's fertile imagination than any part of Ashley's immediate plan.

In a letter to Joshua Pilcher, Thomas Hempstead of Missouri Fur Company notes the departure of Henry's party and adds that they intend to establish a fort at the mouth of the Yellowstone. Chittenden says the original intention was to build a post at the Falls of the Missouri, but this is highly unlikely. Henry knew exactly where he was going; he had been there before. He was well aware that the Falls were in Blackfoot country, and would not be likely to build squarely in the middle of the same tribe that had chased him out once before. [Brief Calendar . . . , p. 403.]

This is the most probable arrangement: From the number of horses Henry took (probably about fifty) the likelihood is that he was contemplating overland travel. Where? Well, there are two ways to get to the Three Forks area. The first is by following the Missouri itself almost 800 miles beyond the mouth of the Yellowstone. This route passes directly through Blackfoot territory. The second way is to ascend the Yellowstone to the area of present Livingston, Montana, then across the pass to Three Forks, which would require horses. It is probable that Henry's intention was to build a sort of depot at the mouth of the Yellowstone (not a trading post, as has generally been assumed by historians) and to trap the Three Forks area by means of the Yellowstone route. His main base would thus be out of the extremely hostile area and on the direct route back to St. Louis. Ashley, the business end of the firm, would remain in St. Louis to handle the problems of outfitting the field parties, merchandising the catch, and juggling the dozens of factors incident to keeping a productive party in the field.

In organizing this expedition Andrew Henry wrought some major changes in the fur trade. Previous to this time trappers operating out of trading posts were *engagés,* hired employees working on salary. Henry's men were not. They had gained a degree of independence unknown to the *engagé,* and it is important to note that this first expedition contained the elements of a coming revolution. In this connection, the letter from Hempstead to Pilcher, as quoted in Dale Morgan, *Jedediah Smith and the Opening of the West:*

> Genl. Ashley's company starts this day with one boat and one hundred & fifty men by land and water they ascend the Missouri river to the Yellow Stone where they build a Fort the men are all generally speaking untried and of evry description and nation, when you see them you will judge for yourself, the Company will be conducted by honourable men I think, but I expect they will wish nothing more of us than to unite in case of difficulty. my opinions as regards the manner that those men are employed might differ with yours, but I think it will not, they are engaged in three different ways I am told the hunters and trapers are to have one half of the furs &c they make the Company furnish them with Gun Powder Lead &c &c, they only are to help build the fort & defend it in case of necessity, the boat hands are engaged as we engage ours, the Clerks are also the same but of those are the fewest number. I do think when men are engaged upon the principals of the above, that regularity, subordination, system, which is highly necessary to have on that river should be the first object of any company to establish but pray let me ask you in what way it can be done under those circumstances Should the hunters wish after they get above to leave them in a mass in what way will they prevent them, this kind of business of making hunters will take some time and much trouble.

Hempstead didn't think much of the idea, obviously. It did take some time and trouble, but it paid off. These men of Henry's first party were the beginnings of the free trapper. Not quite yet—the true free trapper of later years, the elite of the mountain men, bought their outfits where they pleased and sold to whatever company bid highest at the rendezvous. Henry's men were still indebted to one company for their equipment and obliged to dispose of their catch there. (The later equivalent would be known as a "skin trapper.") But the vital element of initiative had been introduced; the men were paid directly according to their hunting success.

Henry's party got off from St. Louis on April 3, 1822 (the date of Hempstead's letter). A bit prematurely, it may be noted—their license didn't come through until a week later, April 11. No matter; General Ashley was the good friend of General Clark, of the great Senator Tom Benton, both stanch supporters of the trade. It was only last month that Benton's powerful efforts in Congress had at last achieved that *summum bonum* of the trader, the overthrow of the government factory system (see Appendix A, p. 405).

It was on a Wednesday that Henry left, early spring, 150 men and some horses and one boat, "to ascend the Missouri river to its source," as advertised. It takes no time at all to read that phrase—"ascend the Missouri river to its source"— and this may be the clinching argument for the superiority of art over life. Because the reality was something quite different; not nearly so easy to glide over as the phrase.

III

The great river was, in fact, something of a bitch. Petulant, treacherous, impossible to understand, sometimes seeming almost human with her concentrated malice. In other moods she was a psychopathic child, playing with her giant's toys and not caring where they landed.

The trip upriver is routine in the literature. I suppose it may even have gotten to be routine in reality, but it's difficult to see how. It was an unhappy circumstance of the trade that their year began in the spring, with the breaking of the ice on the upper rivers. This was the time when supplies had to be sent up, the new parties put into the field. While the keelboat was toiling up the river the men at the posts would be setting out on the spring hunt, wading into streams still bone-jarring cold to set their traps by beaver runs and slides. The boat would arrive on the upper river in early fall, with luck, in time to unload her provisions, stocking the post for the severe winter to come, outfitting the men for another year; turn around and return to St. Louis with the previous fall and spring catch. (Of the two annual hunts, spring was the more important. The winter cold improved the pelt; summer, though some trapping was done, was not so good. Pelts tended to be scraggly. Fall fur was good, but not as good as spring.)

Spring flood on the Missouri, and half the continent seemed to be moving downstream in bits and pieces; it was the natural order of things. Mankind, of course, was going the other way. Henry's boat left the St. Louis waterfront on April 3, and by the end of the day was probably at the mouth of the Missouri proper. Here it began; here the boatmen had to loosen their shoulders and put themselves to it.

The keelboat was, like St. Louis, a product of the river, the river designed it. Or advised in the design, rather, by destroying those that didn't meet her fancy. Over a period of years the form of the keelboat was standardized, and by the time of this narrative all were built to roughly the same pattern, with variations in size.

Henry's boat was probably anywhere from sixty to eighty feet long. Larger ones are on record, but that was about average. Her beam was about a quarter, say sixteen to eighteen feet. A heavy keel ran from bow to stern, and the hull was framed and planked. The cargo box was the *raison d'être* of the keelboat, and there was no mistaking it. The entire deck, except for short spaces at bow and stern, was cargo box about five feet high; the boat was simply a box on a hull. Slightly forward of center stood a high mast. Running fore-and-aft on either side of the cargo box was the *passe avant*, a narrow walkway of about sixteen inches with cleats spaced along it for purchase. Five or six pairs of sweeps, near the bow, would give her the aspect of an ungainly water bug when in use. Except that water bugs skim, and a keelboat was not known to skim, ever.

There were four ways of propelling a keelboat upriver, of which one was tolerable. A clumsy, square sail could be hoisted on the mast, and if the wind was at your back you would move, as long as the current wasn't too stiff. Glance at a map, at the course of the Missouri River. It will give you an idea of how often the wind was from behind, and how long it could be expected to remain there. With every twist and turn of this twisty, turny river you would lose your wind. However, the sail was used whenever possible, and the *voyageurs* could then afford high spirits for a few miles. In the day-to-day inching up the river, a few miles of relative leisure meant something; perhaps half a day.

The other three methods were poling, the sweeps, and the cordelle. The poles were of varying lengths, with a ball at one end that fitted into the hollow of the shoulder. The boatmen would face aft along the *passe avant*, equally divided on each side. They would plant their poles in the river bottom and lean into them, taking the thrust through the ball socketed at their shoulders. Then they would trudge, bent almost horizontal, back along the *passe avant*, throwing all the weight of their bodies into the pole, feeling for the cleats with their feet. Reaching the aft end, each man would free his pole and return to the bow, hurrying to get his "set" again before the current caught and stopped the boat, causing the loss of all his work. He reset, threw forward, and started along the *passe avant* again, with the sweat rolling down and burning in his eyes and the ball threatening to tear his shoulder off. Over and over and over, to the patron's *"A bas les perches! Levez les perches! A bas! . . . Levez! . . ."*

Even getting a set was not simple. Your pole could hit a rock and slip; sink deep into the loose mud; catch a snag and break; all of which would throw you off balance and possibly overboard. In which case you would probably not be worrying about the ball in your shoulder any more. It happened surprisingly seldom on the river; the boatmen were enormously skilled in their craft. A good boatman could feel bottom with his pole, find a solid set and lean into it with one motion that looked to the unskilled as though he just plunked the stick down in the water.

When the water was too deep for poling, or the bottom too bad, the sweeps could be used. These were the least resorted to; the piles of junk flooding down the river could snap an oar without warning and drive the shaft at the rower with enormous force.

Last, there was the cordelle, and this was probably the most frequently used. The principle of the cordelle is very simple. You drag a fully loaded 70-foot boat against the current. Cordelling was accomplished by means of a long line attached to the mast. It went through a ring at the bow, the ring itself being on a short length of line. From the bow, the line passed to shore, where it was shouldered by however many men were available for the job. Marching along the bank, they dragged the heavily laden boat after them.

"Along the bank" is a euphemism. Half the time when cordelling the men were up to their waists in the muddy swirling water somewhere in the general vicinity of the bank. The bottom here was no less treacherous than anywhere else, and you didn't want to slip. When they were on dry land they were more often than not scrambling through thick, ripping underbrush, where the steadily burrowing midwestern woodtick hitched a bloody ride and masses of mosquitoes gave each man his personal black halo. In many places along the flooded river a man wouldn't be quite certain whether he was wading or walking; whether this was thick water or thin soil he was plodding through.

This was the life of a boatman, taken note of by no less an organization than the United States government, which— while prohibiting all other liquor in the trade—still allowed each boatman four fluid ounces per day of the journey. (This ruling, incidentally, led to the presence of a truly incredible number of boatmen on each trading expedition, including those which traveled entirely overland.)

To the *voyageur* the keelboat was an inert mass, whose sole aim in life was to go downstream. To the *patron*, in charge of the vessel, it was something else again: a precious treasure, which the river was trying to snatch away from him. The *patron* had his own problems; his was the responsibility for the boat. In a small operation it might well represent the total of his worldly goods and future hopes. And though his problems might not be as strictly physical as the boatman's they were quite as real and the river was behind every one of them.

The logs that came plowing down the river were not so bad; you could at least see them. Usually they could be avoided if seen in time. The particular dread of the *patron* was the danger that lay unseen, just below the surface. Sawyers: great uprooted trees revolving in the current. At any second the smooth surface ahead might be broken by the wheeling roots or branches of a gigantic tree that came sweeping down on the boat. Or it might be lying just under the surface, massive and relentless, waiting to rip the guts out of the boat or overturn it completely. Planters: trees fixed to the bottom, but out of sight. Plain snags, and waterlogged debris that came down almost submerged, and might be overlooked or underestimated. The water, muddy and opaque, made seeing the bottom impossible. You didn't know shoal water until you were in it, and probably aground. Then it was everybody over and heave and tug until she comes free. And if, in coming free of a sandbank, the boat's prow was caught by the current, that was the end of it. A keelboat broadside to the current was helpless, swept downriver out of control with virtually no way of turning back into the stream and no means of control. Once abeam of the current, the chances were that she'd be swept under, or at least capsized.

Meanwhile, separated groups would be roving the banks

on foot. Hunters for the party would be trying to make meat. Passengers, endlessly bored with the painstaking, snail-like crawl, would be wandering around for no better purpose than to be off the boat for a few hours. The naturalists who occasionally ascended with early trapping parties would be the happiest people aboard, for on the banks of the Missouri were as many unclassified species as a man could want. At night the boats tied up along shore and camp was made. The daily wounds were licked, plans discussed, the boatmen did a little obligatory bragging before dropping into the sleep of utter exhaustion. The sound of the river was always with them, the rush of the current and whipcrack snaps of limbs broken, the slow crashing as a log was driven into foliage along the shore, the crackling of distant driftwood grinding itself to powder.

In the morning it began all over again. The best long passage on record averaged eighteen miles per day. You were lucky to average twelve, very lucky. Manuel Lisa's accomplishment of seventy-five miles in one 24-hour period is incredible.

This—almost four months of it—is what was meant by Ashley's advertisement: "ascend the Missouri river to its source, there to be employed."

IV

Henry's party passed Franklin, Missouri, on April 25, twenty-two days out of St. Louis. If these reported dates are accurate, Henry had been having hard going; he was making about nine miles a day. Franklin was in the Boone's Lick country; on the opposite bank from Franklin a small collection of shacks dignified itself with the name Boonville. At this time Franklin was the farthest west outpost of civilization, 205 miles above the mouth of the Missouri. Beyond this were only occasional posts, and the newcomers could consider themselves in the wilderness now.

Early in May, Henry reached Fort Atkinson, the army post a little north of present Omaha, and stopped there briefly. Farther upriver some of the men—"generally speaking untried"—began to lose heart. Deciding the life was not for them, they began to desert in small numbers, trickling back down the river. Henry may have asked for it; as was customary, he took few provisions aboard the boat, relying on his hunters to provide for the recruits. But 150 men were a lot to provide for, and apparently it was necessary to go on short rations. This was discouraging enough to lead to the desertions.

In August he passed the Mandan villages (near Bismarck, North Dakota), and the course of the river trended to the west. This was good; the Mandan villages were only about 250 miles from the mouth of the Yellowstone, and the better part of the trip was over.

Then he ran into trouble. A little above the Mandan villages he encountered a roving band of Assiniboines. Henry was aboard the boat, the horses and land party probably out of sight somewhere on the bank. The Assiniboines got off with "forty or fifty" horses.[8] This was a serious blow to the party, particularly in view of the fact that intensive overland travel was probably planned to reach the Three Forks.

The party moved on, arrived in due time at the mouth of the Yellowstone and began building their post. Henry chose the narrow point of land between the two rivers, just above the confluence. He set up his palisades, log pickets from twelve to sixteen feet long planted vertically, and probably—following the usual design—crude blockhouses in diagonally opposite corners of the rectangle. The walls of these corner enclosures projected beyond the picket wall, and made it possible for riflemen to cover the whole outside wall. (It is possible that the post Henry originally set up was not this complex; it may have been of a more temporary nature.)

In St. Louis, General Ashley, too, was running into difficulty of an expensive sort. First, the departure of the expedition's second boat, the *Enterprize,* had been delayed. Too many firms, new and old, were drawing heavily on St. Louis' resources that spring; men and material were hard to come by. Ashley had to wait, specifically, for guns, and may even have had trouble obtaining the *Enterprize* itself. The various companies were snapping up boats all up and down the river, as far as 150 miles from St. Louis.

Berthold, Pratte and Chouteau, the "French Fur Company," were organizing a party which, while not directly competitive with Ashley in area to be worked, was certainly competition in purchasing supplies. A new company, Columbia Fur, made up of Americans and ex-Nor'westers from Canada, was planning to work around the Mandans, approaching from the east via the Mississippi and Minnesota Rivers.

But the biggest threat to the new organization was Missou-

ri Fur. Under the new leadership of Joshua Pilcher, Missouri
Fur intended to work the mountain veins, too. This was
formidable competition, and no mistake. Pilcher had been
preparing the party for almost a year, and it was going under
two of the company's best partisans, Jones and Immel. Henry
had counted coup by getting into the field ahead of the
competition, but how long this advantage could be
maintained was dubious. Henry's men were, remember, new
to the trade; Jones and Immel's were veterans.

The *Enterprize,* under command of Daniel Moore, got off
for the mountains over a month after Henry's boat, on May
8. The personnel of this first expedition, counting both boats,
cannot be determined with complete accuracy. It is certain
that it was the fledgling flight for a number of the major
figures in the narrative that follows. Jim Bridger was there,
eighteen years old; David Jackson, Jedediah Smith, Tom
Fitzpatrick, and possibly Etienne Provost. Bill Sublette may
have been along, but this is doubtful.

The *Enterprize* plodded up the river without incident until
sometime late in May, probably the 30th or 31st. Then,
twenty miles below Fort Osage (or about sixty miles below
present Kansas City), the boat was lost. Chittenden says by
hitting a snag, Dale Morgan says the mast caught an overhanging tree and the boat swung broadside to the current.
Either would have done the job. Ashley and Henry had made
a votive offering to the big river of about $10,000 worth of
boat and material. The crew, miraculously, were saved.
Moore returned to St. Louis with the news, arriving on the
2nd or 3rd of June; the June 3 *Enquirer* carried the story.

Ashley, in spite of the obvious difficulties, had another
boat and material. The crew, miraculously, were saved.
assumed command himself. The *Enterprize* survivors were
picked up en route, having in the meanwhile spent about
three weeks communing with nature on the banks of the
Missouri. (Daniel S. D. Moore has retired into the mists of
obscurity, having never been heard from in the trade before
or after.)

Ashley was a businessman, and politician, not a mountaineer. In the present case, this turned out to be a blessing.
Being something of a *mangeur de lard*—the common term
for a greenhorn—himself, he did something few experienced
men would have done: he stocked up heavily on provisions,
bacon and hardtack mostly. Considering the inexperience of
his men, hunters included, this was a stroke of genius, and a

more charitable observer than I might chalk it up to superior management. Whatever the case, Ashley thereby avoided the loss of men through desertion.

At Fort Recovery (on Cedar Island, a mile below present Chamberlain, South Dakota), Ashley stopped to make his peace with the Sioux. Fort Recovery was one of Pilcher's Missouri Fur Company forts, probably named because it was rebuilt after having been burned in 1810.

Here the pork-eaters would make their first acquaintance with the undomesticated American Indian. "Sioux" was not their name; it was either Dacotah, Lacotah, or Nacotah, depending on the dialect. (The currently accepted "Dacotah" was from the Santee dialect, "Lacotah" from the Teton group, "Nacotah" from the Yanktonais.) They were known— as were in fact a great many tribes—by an uncomplimentary term applied to them by their enemies, in this case the Chippewas. "Sioux" is a Canadian-French corruption of the Chippewa *nadewessioux*—meaning enemy or snake—and dates back to the time when the Sioux lived farther east.

They were a warlike tribe, particularly the Yanktonais branch, but not wholly unreasonable about it, as were the Blackfeet. During the War of 1812 they still raided the Aricaras every chance they got, of course, and you wouldn't want to take a really weak party through Sioux country. On the whole, though, if a man weren't downright stupid about customary precautions he could get along with them all right by the year of our narrative.

So the Sioux were passed and the boat was lighter by the amount of presents necessary to prove the white man's heart was good. The Aricara (Rickaree, Arickaree, or just plain Ree) were next. Ashley reached the Aricara villages on the 8th of September. These were a little above the mouth of the Grand (or Big) River, almost at the present North Dakota border.

Ashley was received here with reasonable cordiality, considering the fact that the Ree villages had been fortified not long before. This was because of recent nettling by the Sioux, and it was expected that the Aricaras were about to turn nasty. They did, the next year, but now they talked and smoked and appreciated Ashley's presents and traded him a few horses.

At this point, conscious of the growing lateness of the season, Ashley decided to take a party on foot with the horses ahead of the boat. He took charge of the land group himself (according to Jedediah Smith, who was along) and they proceeded up as far as the Mandan villages along the river. There they turned west, and went overland to the mouth of the Yellowstone and Henry's new fort, where they arrived on October 1.

The boat got in two weeks later, and they had made it; the Ashley-Henry expedition was in business. The topography around was still as plainlike as ever, but they were officially in the mountains now. It had cost them fifty horses to the Assiniboines, presents to the Sioux, Rees and Mandans, and $10,000 worth of boat and goods to the gluttonous river. But they were here.

Sometime within the next couple of weeks the Jones and Immel party from Missouri Fur stopped off at the new fort, inspected it, and ascended the Yellowstone to the mouth of the Bighorn, where they built their own. The competitor's brigade had made it without incident, and it must have been discouraging to Ashley and Henry, after their own losses.

Ashley returned to St. Louis and began preparing next spring's expedition. Henry dispatched his parties on the fall hunt.

CHAPTER 2

"Being completely Parylized"

IT HAD cost them about $10 a mile to get where they were, counting only outright losses; saying nothing of time and wages and expenses which actually produced something. The nature of the trade was such that other losses might be expected at any time. What was it all about? What could be worth this prodigal expenditure of time and money and men's lives we call the fur trade? In a word—beaver. For when we speak of the fur trade, we mean the beaver trade. Other furs were handled; others—notably the rich sea otter—were more valuable by far. But the beaver was the root and core of the trade.

An innocuous animal, the beaver, unusual only in his building of dams and monogamous marriage. But, like the Greek dramatic figures, the beaver was born with a tragic flaw: the hairs of his rich underfur, called "muffoon," were microscopically barbed, and because of this the species was almost wiped out. Many men died, a continent was explored, an indigenous race degraded and its culture crushed; all because beaver fur, with its tiny barbs, felted up better than any other. Felt is made without either weaving or adhesives, and depends for its substance on the matting qualities of the fibers. In felting, the underfur of beaver is unsurpassed, and for this reason the finest felt hats were "beavers." While the fur hats were in vogue, this inoffensive little mammal was assured of a high death rate.

He was, so said the Indians, the wisest of all animals. Trappers on occasion agreed, because when the beaver of an area were "up to trap," you might as well go elsewhere. You weren't going to get any fur, and stood to lose a few traps. The folk tales of the beaver's sagacity are many and imaginative, and quite a number have a certain currency today.

Osborne Russell, a trapper whose mountain journal is one of the best, mentions a belief widely held among trappers—that the beaver practiced a form of population control. The story was that a female birthed from two to six at a litter, then killed all the kittens but one male and one female. Russell didn't question the fact; but he was interested in establishing whether the male or the female did the killing.

The beaver does not, as often claimed, control the direction of tree fall. The trunk is girdled completely around, and the tree falls in the direction in which it is tilted. Near a stream the trees generally incline slightly toward the water, and this is responsible for the beaver's presumed precision. They make a lot of mistakes, as any naturalist can tell you.

Beaver seem to have an irresistible impulse to stop flowing water; modern beaver placed in an artificial pond promptly dammed the input stream with the unfortunate consequence of killing by flood the neighboring cottonwoods on which the colony depended for food. Under normal conditions the beaver dam provides a pool of deeper, calm water and creates a marshy area of some extent around the pool. This gives a colony their "territory," which they further mark with piles of mud on which they secrete a yellow glandular substance known as "castoreum." The beaver lodge, like his dam, is made of twigs and sticks plastered up with mud. The entrances are, of course, underwater. Inside, raised about twelve inches above water level, is the main chamber. This may or may not be supplemented by other small chambers; sometimes a water rat will build his own nest in one corner. Here the young are born and nursed, and here the beaver spends the winter, never having to go farther for food than his doorway.

In the active seasons the beaver is constantly engaged in one of two projects: architectural repairs or food gathering. When trees are felled, he chops off branches and drags them to his pool. Taking them under, he plants one end deep in the mud outside the entrance. Gradually, he builds up a large stock of these branches with their soft bark, sometimes weighting them down with rocks or mud. Russell claims as much as a half cord of wood per adult, but this is probably high. At the bottom of the pool, the food is safe from freezing, and the lodge is supplied for the winter.

The repairing work—enlarging the lodge or fixing the dam—is apparently compulsive in nature. A colony placed in a pool whose dam was made of stone and mortar spend the entire summer "repairing" it with sticks and mud, just as if it were one of their own.

Trapping the little animal called—and calls—for considerable skill and knowledge. Traps could be placed at strategic places on the beaver's route, at the base of slides, for example, or beside the drag path along which the beaver hauled his wood. This was only moderately successful, because a beaver is extraordinarily perceptive and wary.

The best way, and most often practiced, was to make the animal "come to medicine." Castoreum, the beaver's own glandular secretion, was the medicine. (Trappers used both terms.) It was carried at all times, in either a little wooden box or a stoppered vial of horn. Castoreum is an extremely musky, pungent substance; its biological purpose is to attract attention. Being used to it, the trapper didn't mind the smell. It did, however, tend to make his relations with townsfolk a bit strained.

The traps were heavy, five pounds apiece, worth $12 and up, mountain price. His line consisted of perhaps half a dozen of these traps, carried in the trapsack.[1] When he had decided on his spot (on the basis of "sign": cuttings, stripped twigs, dams and so forth) the trapper waded into the stream some distance down, so as to cover his smell, with the trap already set. He placed it in shallow water by a bank, anchoring it with a stick driven through the ring and into the stream bed. He dipped a stripped twig into his "medicine" and planted it on the bank where a beaver would have to stand up to sniff it. (A good trapper could set to catch front or back paw, as he desired.) Then he waded back downstream and moved on, scattering water over his trail where he emerged.

"Coming to medicine" is not a sexual phenomenon, as later historians have carelessly assumed. While the glandular secretion was probably of service in the mating season, it was principally a device used in regulating the social life of the beaver, and marking its territory.

When the beaver emerged from his lodge, two or three hundred yards away, he smelled the medicine and went to investigate. Rising to examine the stick, his foot was caught. Generally his impulse was to head for the bottom. If the trapper had placed properly, this put the animal into water too deep to surface, with the trap and stake holding him down. He drowned there. When the trapper came to check his line, he would sometimes find that the beaver's struggles had wrenched the stake loose. (An adult can hit sixty pounds and is enormously muscular.) In that case the "float stick" attached to the trap would show where the animal was. The beaver had to be drowned, because if he reached land he would chew his leg off to escape. More than one trapper found himself with only a sprung trap and a bloody paw to show for his carelessness.

The skins were scraped clean of flesh, stretched on circular hoops, and dried in the sun. When sufficiently cured, they were made up into packs weighing ninety to a hundred pounds and stored until they could be taken back to market. This "pack" was the basic unit of the trade. (The American companies calculated their beaver by the pound and by the pack; the British by individual pelts, which would average around one and a half pounds apiece.)

This, then, is the animal and the process. When Andrew Henry's men set out in the fall of 1822 from their new fort, this is what they were going for.

II

It was too late in the year to do much about the Three Forks area. The rivers would be closing up soon (in about six weeks, as it turned out) and they were still hundreds of miles away from the Forks. It would not be possible to reach the valleys before the harsh northern winter froze them into camp, much less do any trapping and return.

The horses were gone with the Assiniboines, and this was the most serious problem. Nothing could be done about it until next spring, when Ashley would presumably send more with the outfitting party. So, for the time being, Henry's party was restricted in its movements, and he was probably contenting himself with a general survey of the area.

This winter of 1822 saw two camps of Henry's men established. Roughly half his party wintered at the new Fort Henry (at the confluence of the Yellowstone and Missouri). Another group made a tentative exploration farther up the Missouri and decided to winter at the mouth of the Mussel-shell River, some 180 miles away on an air line. (As a matter of minor interest, the term "on an air line" was in use long

before there was any air travel. See N. J. Wyeth's letter of
Nov. 3, 1833, in *Sources of the History of Oregon,* [Eu-
gene, 1899].) This detached camp settled in around November 1. The river froze solid shortly after, and the party was
treated to one of the great pageants of the trade—the
buffalo. Smith's journal:

> . . . we were astonished to see the buffalo come pour-
> ing from all sides into the valley of the Missouri and
> particularly the vast Bands that came from the north
> and crossed over to the south side on the ice. We
> there fore had them in thousands around us and
> nothing more required of us than to select and kill the
> best for our use whenever we might choose.

One of the members of this wintering camp on the Musselshell was Mike Fink, Riverboatman. The capital on the
title is because Fink has become one of America's storied
folk heroes. This man, a lying, sadistic, foul-mouthed brag-
gart, a treacherous and murdering psychopath, has been
translated by the genteel art of bowdlerizing into a fit and
heroic subject for children's literature.

What he was doing on this expedition nobody knows, but
with him were two compatriots concerned with his last adventure, Carpenter and Talbot. At the winter camp, so the
story goes, Carpenter and Fink got into a brawl (which is
likely) over a woman (which is not; there were none around).
It was made up, but broke out afresh when they returned to
the Yellowstone fort the next spring. Made up again; in
testimony of their friendship, Fink proposed that he and
Carpenter resume one of their old friendly games, one shooting a cup of whiskey off the other's head. A flip of the coin
decides Fink shall have first shot; Carpenter informs Talbot
he is about to die, marches bravely out to face Fink. From
here I quote Morgan's version:

> Mike paced off the usual range and leveled his rifle,
> then lowered it to say with a smile, 'Hold your noddle
> steady, Carpenter, and don't spill the whiskey, as I
> shall want some presently."
>
> Again he raised the rifle. With the sound of the
> shot Carpenter pitched forward on his face. . . . He
> had been shot in the center of his forehead, an inch
> and a half above the eyes. Mike set the breech of his

gun on the ground and, putting his lips to the muzzle, blew the smoke out of the barrel. Finally, he said, "Carpenter, you have spilled the whiskey!"

A little later Talbot shoots Fink in retribution, and is himself drowned trying to swim the Teton River. There are more complete versions of this edifying little moral tale around, notably in a biography of Fink by Blair and Meine, *Mike Fink, King of Mississippi Keelboatmen*.

The river did not break until April 4, 1823. Eleven trappers of the Musselshell winter camp left on the 6th, and continued the ascent of the river in two canoes, headed for Three Forks. The rest returned to Fort Henry at the Yellowstone, including Fink and friends.

The canoe party worked up past Judith River and Marias River, trapping as they went. By the middle of May they had reached the mouth of the Smith River (about twelve miles upstream from present Great Falls, Montana).

A party of only eleven men, penetrating the very heart of Blackfoot territory; this was tempting the Fates a bit too much, and it is surprising that Henry permitted it, in light of his own earlier experience. The Blackfeet responded with characteristic promptness. They jumped the party somewhere around the mouth of the Smith and killed four men, taking what pelts they had already gathered. The remaining seven fled back down the Missouri to Fort Henry, a downstream trip in the neighborhood of 450 miles.

At about the same time the Missouri Fur Mountain Expedition was having its own troubles. Immel and Jones had passed Fort Henry the previous October (1822) shortly after it was built. They and their men, forty-three of them, had proceeded up the Yellowstone and built their fort at the mouth of the Bighorn, which put them nearly 250 miles closer to the rich Three Forks area than Henry's men. They also had enough horses to make the overland journey between the Yellowstone and Three Forks practicable.

By May 16 they had completed a 20-pack hunt and were ready to return to their post. They were still on the Jefferson, probably about twenty-five miles southeast of present Butte. The party had been reduced by winter desertions to the number of thirty. (It may well be wondered how any sane man could decide to desert in the middle of the winter in the Bighorn country; it is a question I cannot answer.

According to the records, thirteen of Immel and Jones's men did it. Nine of them even survived.)

On May 18 the party encountered a band of Piegans—one of the three divisions of the Blackfoot tribe, and the least bloodthirsty. The Piegans were peaceable enough, and the headman Iron Shirt even carried a certificate of good conduct from a British trader across the border. However, the Missouri Fur brigade immediately began a concerted drive to get back across the mountains to their base at the Bighorn, in safer Crow country.

Unfortunately, the Piegans had been talking to some of their less amiable confreres, the Bloods. On May 31 Jones and Immel walked into an ambush within ten miles of a friendly Crow encampment. Jones, Immel, and five trappers were killed; four were wounded. Horses, beaver, equipment— all were lost. And so, too, were the hopes of Missouri Fur on the upper river. Most of their resources had gone into outfitting the Immel-Jones party.

Joshua Pilcher wrote later:

> This our second adventure to the mountains had surpassed my most sanguine expectations; success was complete and my views were fulfilled in every respect . . . [But now] the flower of my business is gone; my mountaineers have been defeated, and the chiefs of the party both slain.

Anti-British feeling was still running high, and Pilcher placed the blame for the Immel-Jones massacre directly at the doorstep of the British traders across the line. In another letter relating to the event, Indian Agent O'Fallon said of the British:

> Like the greedy wolf, not satisfied with the flesh they quarrel over the bones. They ravage our fields and are unwilling that we should glean them. . . . Alarmed at the individual enterprise of our people, they are exciting the Indians against them. They furnished them with . . . the instruments of death and a passport to our bosoms. Immel had a great experience of the Indian character, but (poor fellow!) with a British passport they at last deceived him and he fell a victim to his own credulity; and his scalp, and those

of his comrades, are now bleeding on their way to the British trading establishments.

Slightly exaggerated; the scalps were not, but the furs eventually turned up at the Hudson's Bay post on the Saskatchewan. The factor there, to his great credit, apparently offered to return these furs to Missouri Fur, something that, as we will see, no American company would have done.

Shortly after this there was more bad news on the upper river. Henry received an urgent appeal for help from General Ashley; it seemed the general too was having trouble with some Indians.

III

General Ashley had spent only a short time at the mouth of the Yellowstone the previous fall (1822), returning to St. Louis almost immediately to outfit the next year's expedition. It is highly likely he had no intention of ascending the river at all, but was forced into it by the circumstance of losing the *Enterprize*. (Ashley was not then, and never became, fond of the mountains. He was, remember, primarily a politician and businessman.)

Sometime in the early spring of 1823—before Blackfoot trouble materialized on the upper river—Major Henry had sent an express downriver with the young hunter Jedediah Smith. Neither the date nor the contents of this message are accurately known; students of the trade have assumed it was a request for horses to replace those stolen by the Assiniboines. This seems unlikely, because Ashley was at the Yellowstone fort *after* the theft and was well aware of this need.

Whatever the message, Smith was with the party that came up the river in the spring of 1823. Outfitting had been difficult for the general; men were harder and harder to obtain as the revived trade picked up momentum. Another advertisement, this one offering the excellent salary of $200 per year, wasn't entirely successful. Ashley appointed the Virginia mountaineer James Clyman as a sort of informal recruiting agent. Clyman worked the time-honored fields of the desperate recruiter, the taverns and bawdyhouses. The completed party was—to put it charitably—somewhat various in composition. Clyman's own considered judgment: "Falstaff's Battalion was genteel in comparison."

Ashley outfitted two keelboats, the *Yellow Stone Packet*

and *The Rocky Mountains,* which left St. Louis on March 10, 1823. There was no accompanying land party. Ashley was planning to buy horses and dispatch an overland group at the Aricara villages.

The Aricaras ... A man approaching the Aricaras would probably be doing a little fast figuring, in the wistful hope of being able to predict his reception. To recapitulate their record briefly: 1804 and 1806—friendly to Lewis and Clark; 1807—hostile to a party under Manuel Lisa of Missouri Fur; 1811—hospitable to the Astorians; 1816—attacked a party of whites; 1820—attacked and robbed two Missouri Fur Company posts; 1822—very friendly to Missouri Fur Company President, Joshua Pilcher, and to Ashley himself.

This year, 1823, "them rascally Rees" had been unfriendly again. A party had wandered down into Sioux country, beaten and robbed some Missouri Fur Company *engagés* who were trading there. A few days later the company's post at Cedar Island was attacked by a strong party of about 115 Aricara warriors. Two Indians were killed, and the Rees were touchy about it. When the keelboats reached the Aricaras on May 20, General Ashley thus had a fair notion that the situation was a delicate one.

The Aricara settlements consisted at this time of an upper and a lower village on the right bank of the river, about 300 yards apart. Each village contained about seventy mud lodges. When Ashley arrived, they had been newly picketed; reinforcement against the recent harrying of the villages by the Sioux. Indian pickets were not a uniform palisade, but consisted of a variety of sticks, poles and logs stuck upright in the ground. These of the Aricara villages were, by Ashley's report, from twelve to fifteen feet high and about six inches thick. A shallow ditch circled the village just outside the pickets, and a similar one inside.

The river channel in front of the villages was very narrow, being compressed between the bank and a sand bar. Here, too, the river made a loop, with the Indian villages on the convex point. Opposite the end of the sand bar the Rees had built a breastwork of timber which effectively commanded the passage through the narrow channel.

Ashley anchored the boats in the channel, as far away from the beach as possible. This, unfortunately, was not very far. (Chittenden says ninety feet.) He went ashore himself in a skiff, and was met on the beach by two of the Aricara chiefs, Gray Eyes and Little Soldier (Gray Eyes' son was one of those killed at the Missouri Fur post.) The general demonstrated that his heart was good with presents, and the Rees seemed pleased. Ashley tentatively brought up the subject of the recent trouble and made it plain he was in no way connected with the Missouri Fur Company, regretted the incident profoundly, and hoped the Aricaras were not going to be unreasonable about it.

Nothing could have been further from their minds. As far as the Aricaras were concerned, Ashley was told, all white men (particularly Ashley) were the good friends of all Indians (particularly Aricaras). Everybody's heart was very good indeed, and what did the general have in mind in the way of trade?

So far so good. Trading began with the lower village on the next day. Ashley secured, by his own account, forty or so horses, though other accounts say the number was closer to twenty. Late in the afternoon Ashley was invited to the lodge of Bear, one of the principal chiefs. He went, accompanied by the experienced interpreter Edward Rose. When they arrived at Bear's lodge they found several other Aricara chiefs waiting for them. All were markedly friendly, and whatever suspicions Ashley may have had were apparently dispelled by their actions. The conference was short, and the general returned to his boat in the evening.

Somewhere about this time Rose advised Ashley that the Aricara, despite peaceful appearances, were drumming up trouble. The general, however, chose to disregard the interpreter's advice. He retired for the night leaving all the horses and forty men camped on the beach below the Aricara villages.

It was an expensive choice. About 3 A.M. Ashley was wakened by the bad news; one of his men had been killed in the village. The details are not accurately known; presumably the man, one Aaron Stephens, had gone into the village to take advantage of the Aricara hospitality. Like the Mandans above, the Rees were not averse to turning a bit of clear profit on the intangible qualities of their wives and daughters.

Confusion ensued, undisciplined preparations for defense were begun and a demand was made by some of the men for the return of Stephens' body. One of the Aricaras shouted an offer to do so, if he could be given a horse. Unfortunately, he came back to report, Stephens' eyes had been put out, the body decapitated and "otherwise mangled" so badly it was not worth the effort. This news doubtless did little to improve the morale of the party isolated on the beach.

By now it was almost dawn. The Aricaras opened intensive fire from behind the palisades as the sun rose. They raked the exposed beach, and in a few minutes most of the horses had been killed and many of the men, The remainder found what shelter they could behind the corpses of the animals, and tried to return the fire.

Ashley, seeing the almost-instantaneous devastation of the party, ordered the keelboats to shore to take them off. The boatmen refused, "being," says Clyman, "completely Parylized." In desperation Ashley dispatched the skiffs. By the time they arrived, however, the beach party had changed its mind; they stubbornly refused to retreat, and continued to throw what they could at the picketed village. Only seven men, two of them wounded, returned to the keelboats. The larger of the two skiffs returned again, but the oarsman was shot as he approached the beach and the boat swirled downstream in the swift current.

Now the Aricaras piled out of the village and worked down to the end of the sandy beach. The shore party was forced back into the river. Some were picked off as they entered the water, others sank as they attempted to swim to the tantalizingly near keelboats. Still others were caught by the current and swept past the boats, leaving them no choice but to take to the shore again a little downstream. Getting aboard what men he could, Ashley weighed anchor and began to drift downstream. The cable of the other boat was cut, and it followed.

They dropped back down the river as far as the first grove of timber (probably the head of Ashley Island, a short distance below) and made a landing. Now Ashley tried to restore things to order and make sense of the confusion. The final score was thirteen dead and eleven wounded. The boatmen were completely demoralized and refused to do anything.

Ashley's apparent intention was to get the party back into some semblance of coherent organization and make another attempt to pass the villages, probably at night. This was flatly rejected. They made camp and bedded down for the night.

In the morning Ashley appealed again for a reorganization and another attempt, and was "told by the men (with a few exceptions) that under no circumstances would they make a second attempt to pass without a large reinforcement."

Many of them, the boatmen in particular, would not even try again with a larger party; only a total of thirty were even willing to wait for reinforcements, and the remainder intended to get back downriver any way they could. Seven of those who volunteered to stay were wounded, and could be of only limited use.

Ashley was left with very little choice. He kept one of the keelboats, *The Rocky Mountains,* and took his small crew of volunteers on board. The other he dispatched downriver with the unneeded goods and the men who would not stay with him. He sent with this boat a letter describing the attack, dated "25 miles below Aricara towns, 4th June, 1823." This was to be delivered at Fort Atkinson, in the almost-forlorn hope that the military might take action. He ended up by stating his intention to "remain between this place and the Aricara towns, not remaining any length of time in one place, as my force is small, not more than twenty-three effective."

Ashley had little confidence that he could expect help from the military establishments. He had to rely for reinforcements on his own men, and they were at the mouth of the Yellowstone. He sent Jedediah Smith and a French-Canadian—both volunteers—to Major Henry with an appeal for help.

Shortly after this he apparently decided he was still too close to the Aricaras and retreated another seventy-five miles down the river to the mouth of the Cheyenne, where he settled in to wait for help.

IV

As news of the various events on the upper river trickled down to civilization, it began to form an alarming picture. *Within a two-week period every major trapping party on the upper river had been assaulted—and worse, overwhelmingly defeated—by the Indians.*

The seriousness of this sequence went far beyond the twenty-four white men killed, the many wounded. If this could happen, the fur trade itself was finished; the economy of the western frontier completely destroyed; and the only point of peaceful contact with the Indian nations obliterated. This was not the sporadic skirmishing that occurred from time to time; things were assuming the proportions of a full-scale uprising among the Indians—the tribes involved were a thousand miles apart.

The importance of Ashley's defeat was, of course, immediately realized by every man involved with the fur trade; and there were few on the western frontier whose lives did not to some extent revolve around it. The need for decisive, effective action was clearly apprehended by whites and Indians alike. I emphasize this in order to point out that this was a critical juncture in Indian relations and that both sides were completely aware of it at the time.

After Ashley's defeat, Major General Gaines wrote an urgent letter to Secretary of War Calhoun, emphasizing the extreme importance of disciplinary action and pointing out the "evils that must inevitably result from our being forced to recede from the position we have taken." He further pointed out that "tLe trade forms *rein* and *curb* by which the turbulent and towering spirit of these lords of the forest can alone be governed." He went on to explain the unique position of the trade with respect to international affairs: "To suffer outrages such as have been perpetrated by the Ricaras ... to go unpunished, would be to surrender the trade, and, with it, our strong hold upon the Indians, to the British."

And the lords of the forest? The tattered remnants of the Immel-Jones expedition, coming downriver, stopped off with the traditionally friendly Mandans. They noted there was no other topic of conversation among the Mandans, Minnetarees, and other upriver groups. The Mandan chiefs held a council on July 10. The result was to offer the protection of the Mandan villages to their traditional enemies, the Aricaras. There was "reason to apprehend," wrote Gaines, that the other Upper Missouri tribes would unite with the Aricaras if they succeeded in pushing back the whites. Reason indeed, when Mandans offer sanctuary to Rees.

In the early summer of 1823 most of the men of the western United States—brown or white—were watching the two mud villages near the mouth of the Grand River.

The summer of 1823 ... Why then? What was causing this enormous wave of Indian hostility?

The British, of course, came in for their share of blame. There were—then and later—many men who considered everything that went wrong part of the British plot. These were not only the hotheads, either. Many individuals of considered opinion resented the influence of the British traders on the northern tribes. It had been a serious matter during the War of 1812, and the specter of British intrigue still hung heavy over the upper Missouri. Gaines, in the same letter of July 28, 1823, estimates that without British competition America would not need "1/10 of the force and expense" to preserve the peace effectively. (But under later direct questioning by a Congressional committee, even inveterate Britain-hater Joshua Pilcher admitted he had no reason to believe the Aricara attack was sponsored by them.)

There was another view, but the blame it placed was not acceptable to as many people as the "British intrigue" theory. Backtracking a year, to the spring of 1822:

Major Benjamin O'Fallon, Indian agent at St. Louis, wrote a deeply concerned letter to the Secretary of War. O'Fallon understands a license has been issued to Ashley and Henry to trade, trap, and hunt on the upper Missouri. He "expresses a hope that limits have been prescribed to their trapping and hunting on Indian Lands, as ... nothing is better calculated to alarm and disturb the harmony so happily existing between us and the Indians."

Through William Clark, Secretary Calhoun assured Major O'Fallon that the license granted "confers the privilege of trading with Indians only, as the laws ... do not contain any authority to issue licenses for any other purpose."

But, as we have seen, both Henry's party and the Immel-Jones party fully intended to trap the country for themselves, licenses or no. Thus, even the dubious benefits of trading were to be taken away from the tribes and their lands hunted without compensation. The government factory system having been overthrown in the spring of '22, actual *trade* would dwindle to nothing. The fur hunters had figured out a more efficient way; go in with self-sufficient parties.

So at least a year before the Aricara affair, the Indian agent at St. Louis was upset by the possibility of trapping and hunting on Indian lands, realizing the probable reaction of the tribes.

The Indians themselves were perfectly aware of the shift of techniques; their communications were excellent and their information somehow flawless. For example, the thirty-eight Piegans who spent the night with Immel's party were quite familiar with the company's intention to set up a post. They also knew the approximate size, and the exact position, of Henry's party, which they had never seen.

It is my contention, based on the above reasoning, that the much-debated "wave of hostility" in the spring of 1823 was the direct result of the change in technique which the trade was undergoing; that is, the abandonment of trading in favor of independent trapping.[2]

There is no evidence that the British Hudson's Bay traders directly instigated any of the attacks; on the other hand, it is morally certain they didn't actively *discourage* what hostility to Americans they found among the Indians. And they were no whit reluctant to provide guns and ammunition as per usual; as long as the furs came in, the inventory of the British posts was for trading. What the Indians did with the guns was their own business, unless it reinvolved the Hudson's Bay Company.

The above digression from our narrative was for the purpose of setting the stage; because what follows deserves to be seen in its clear historical significance. The Aricara campaign of 1823 was undertaken as a direct result of Ashley's defeat at the villages. Conducted by Colonel Henry Leavenworth, it was the first military campaign ever mounted by the United States Army against Indians west of the Mississippi. As such, it was invested with dignity and significance and importance to the nation. A slapstick comedy was not called for.

CHAPTER 3

"The honor of American arms"

WHEN Ashley dispatched Jedediah Smith to bring help from
Henry, he expected to receive it in "twelve or fifteen days."
Considering the length of the necessary journey—the exact
route is not known, but must have been 300-400 miles—this
is a most unrealistic estimate, explainable only through Ashley's inexperience. He was out of his element in the field; his
handling of the Aricara trading venture was marked by
uncertainty, vacillation, and imprudence. He had lost control
of his men at the critical point and was thus unable to
redeem his previous error of judgment.

When Smith arrived at the Yellowstone with the news of
Ashley's defeat, Andrew Henry took action immediately. He
was still smarting from the Blackfoot victory over his trapping party, and the spring hunt had not been good. If Ashley
were delayed too long, the necessary supplies for the fall
hunt would be too late and the whole year's take jeopardized.
Their St. Louis creditors would not view such a situation
optimistically, and it began to look as if the whole Ashley-
Henry enterprise were on the verge of cracking.

Leaving a crew of twenty to man the fort, Henry immediately embarked the rest of his men, numbering about fifty, in
canoes. When passing the Aricara villages, they were greeted
with a friendly waving of buffalo robes, the customary invitation to a parley; a hospitable gesture which impressed Henry
not at all. He sailed by, and joined Ashley's waiting party at
the mouth of the Cheyenne.

Now a conference was held and their position evaluated.

Henry probably gave his opinion that it would be foolish to attempt to pass the Aricaras again, even with the addition of his men. Only one keelboat was available, *The Rocky Mountains*, and many of their supplies had been sent back down the river on the *Yellow Stone Packet*. If they *did* reach their fort they would still be short of supplies for the fall hunt and winter camp.

The alternative was to abandon the river entirely and try to outfit overland parties, perhaps for the Crow country. Since the Three Forks and Great Falls areas had proved so inhospitable, it would be better to make the fall hunt in areas where such vicious opposition might be avoided.

All very well, but there were no horses for such a venture. They would have to be obtained from the Sioux. The augmented party dropped back downriver to the mouth of the Bad River (present Pierre, South Dakota), but no luck. Leaving the main camp where they were, Ashley descended still lower, past the Grand Detour, looking for some Sioux with horses to dispose of. When he reached Fort Kiowa, just below Grand Detour, it was the 19th of July, 1823, the summer well advanced. Here he received some pleasant and unexpected news, in the form of a letter from Indian Agent O'Fallon, written a month before: the military was on its way, an expedition had been organized and was coming to discipline the Aricaras.

Ashley immediately abandoned the plan of buying horses for an overland expedition and left Fort Kiowa the same afternoon, hurrying back to his camp with the joyous news.

Though the general didn't know it, the military had almost caught him. The grandeur and majesty of the United States Army was only thirteen miles below Fort Kiowa, at Fort Recovery.

The retreating keelboat *Yellow Stone Packet* had arrived at Fort Atkinson on June 18, two weeks after leaving Ashley. Ashley's letter was presented to Colonel Henry Leavenworth, commanding, and augmented by the accounts of the boatmen. (Quite ferocious accounts, no doubt, in order to explain how they happened to be going downriver when the action was upstream.)

If any military action were to be taken, Colonel Leavenworth would have to do it on his own responsibility; getting orders from below would require an unconscionable delay. Leavenworth made his decision the same day, and six companies of the 6th Infantry were alerted to march. Word of the expedition was sent to the proper authorities.

O'Fallon called on Joshua Pilcher for some additional help, and it may have been a call of desperation. No one had a very high opinion of Leavenworth's ability to deal with Indians; he was a good officer, but his experience with Indians was negligible. Pilcher's expert knowledge could mean a great deal on the expedition.

It was decided to round up what allies they could among the Sioux, and Pilcher was appointed subagent to accomplish the job. This was, naturally, an appeal to the public spirit of the man, since arrangements for compensation were missing. "Great will be your sacrifice in a pecuniary point of view," O'Fallon wrote Pilcher, but, on the other hand, "you will soon be amply compensated in the bosom of the richest fur country in the world."

O'Fallon then made an impassioned plea to Ashley's defectors, the "Forty three men who deserted Genl. Ashley." He referred to his own mortification at their desertion, and General Ashley's—"he is my friend, he is your friend, he is the people's friend"—and recruited about twenty of them to serve as Leavenworth's boatmen. It may have been his comment to the effect that the murdered men's "spirits have pursued, shedding tears in your tracks." That kind of thing is hard to take, even for a cowardly *voyageur*.

Leavenworth's party, numbering about 220 officers and men, left Fort Atkinson on June 22, 1823. The *Yellow Stone Packet* and two other keelboats transported supplies, artillery, and part of the expeditionary force. Pilcher followed with two boats of his own, and a brigade of Missouri Fur Company men.

After a bad voyage, which included the complete loss of one of the army keelboats, the party reached Fort Recovery on July 19. While the military paused there to refit, Pilcher picked up a small band of Yankton Sioux and sent out messengers to other bands in the vicinity. Within a couple of days there were bands of Saone Sioux (under Fire Heart) and Hunkpapa Sioux to the number of 200 ready to join the expedition.

In a letter to O'Fallon, Leavenworth expressed his intentions: "If the Aracaras and Mandans unite, I shall proceed to the Mandans; and if they keep the Aracaras in their village, I shall attack them. . . . The honor of American arms must be supported at all events."

The expedition moved on from Fort Recovery on July 22 and joined Ashley's full party eight days later. Here the last formalities of organization were arranged: Ashley's men (about eighty) were divided into two companies, respectively under Hiram Scott and the young hunter who had been proving himself so useful, Jedediah Smith.[1]

Pilcher's Missouri Fur men and the Indian allies were lumped together under Pilcher, who was now a nominal major. Pilcher never did relinquish his majority, though Leavenworth says: "These appointments were merely nominal, and intended only to confer the same privileges and respect on them as were paid to our own officers of the same grade." Ashley was a brigadier general and Henry a major in the militia already, and this was considered adequate.

Now everybody had proper military titles, and the expedition could proceed, secure in the essential rightness of its organization. The whole conglomeration of trappers, Indians, and military was given the name and style of the Missouri Legion, which has a nice martial ring to it.

By August 8 they had reached a point about fifteen miles below the Ree towns. There they disembarked and made ready for the assault to begin the next day. Leavenworth had borrowed forty rifles from the traders, which helped make up for the loss of those on the wrecked keelboat. The Sioux were given strips of white muslin to tie around their heads for identification.

Meanwhile, word of Leavenworth's punitive expedition had reached the government, and was taken very seriously. While the colonel's superiors endorsed his action, they were aware of the dangers involved should the party be set back. They were deeply concerned that this first foray against trans-Mississippi Indians should be completely successful. In one letter Major General Gaines makes the flat statement that "premature effort, on our part, will but ... enhance the evil we thus attempt to correct."

In all the letters discussing the coming battle, there is a note of optimism; the phrase "I have but little doubt of [Leavenworth's] success" recurs frequently. Nevertheless, the prudent General Gaines took the more concrete precaution (on July 26) of ordering up six companies of the 1st Infantry, to begin marching immediately to St. Louis. Also, "should it be advisable," he suggests four more companies of the 7th Infantry and provisions to secure "if necessary" a battalion of mounted riflemen from the governor of Missouri. These troops were to be supplied with provisions for up to nine months. General Gaines was taking no chances; he intended to be sure.

The importance of the whole affair was summed up in a letter from General Atkinson of July 15, 1823. It was a matter of utmost necessity to "impress the Indians in that quarter with a just idea of our capacity to chastise every outrage they may commit."

In view of all these expectations, precautions, and concerns, the ensuing fiasco appears even more dismal.

II

Saturday, August 9, 1823

In the morning the boats were put in command of Major Wooley, one of Leavenworth's officers. Pilcher's party was set to man them, presumably because Leavenworth had no intention of trusting Ashley's small group of deserter-*voyageurs*. Four boats were left, and there were ten men to a boat. They were ordered to proceed upstream (bringing with them the artillery), while the remainder of the force went on by land. By now Leavenworth's command had been swelled by new Sioux recruits to about a thousand men.

When the Grand River had been crossed and the Ree villages were only five or six miles ahead, Leavenworth dispatched an advance party of Sioux under Pilcher. These were under instruction to attack the Aricaras if feasible, but principally to prevent their running away. Leavenworth's plan required them all neatly stacked into their picketed villages.

The Sioux set out with such enthusiasm that they quickly outdistanced the bulk of the party by more than Leavenworth had intended. But this, after all, was what the Sioux had come for; a little roughhouse with the Rees.

Pilcher came back to hurry up the main body; the Sioux had gotten a full hour ahead and were engaged with the Aricaras on the plain about a half mile from the villages. There were between six hundred and eight hundred warriors in the village, quite enough to give the relatively small advance party trouble.

Leavenworth hurried, and shortly afterward the main force of the Missouri Legion came out onto the plain where a full-scale Indian battle was swirling. The noise was incredible, and the sight itself must have shocked Leavenworth's neat military sensibilities.

Intertribal warfare was not conducted along strategic lines; it was just one big free-for-all, to the accompaniment of the maximum possible noise. There was no particular plan of attack. There they were and here you were; mix it up.

Mix it up they did. Screaming and caterwauling, the Indians engaged in their own simple variety of warfare, making the plain look, according to Clyman, "more like a swarm bees than a battle field they going in all possible directions." Leavenworth formed a good military line at the edge of the plain.

Now it was discovered that the distribution of white identifying bands for the Sioux was more useful in theory than in practice. The allies' were so inextricably mixed with the enemy that there was no possibility of differentiating between them, white muslin headbands or not. Leavenworth's line dared not fire.

Seeing the reinforcements coming up, the Aricaras broke for their village, now badly outnumbered. The Sioux followed gleefully. Leavenworth moved up behind, finally taking a position just out of gunshot from the villages, about three or four hundred yards away. The Aricaras were now securely pegged in the villages, and stage one of the master plan had been accomplished. Leavenworth's men sat down to wait for the artillery and watch the aftermath of Indian warfare.

Thirteen or fourteen Rees had been left dead. The Sioux had lost only two, and had seven wounded; a massive victory in Indian terms. The battle had probably been fought by eight hundred to a thousand men; to our more civilized perceptions it would seem that a vicious hand-to-hand fight among that many men should yield a more satisfactory rate. But we are more sophisticated in these matters, and if Indian war seems woefully inefficient to us we must remember it was a different age; they had not our advantages.

Whatever his inefficiencies in mass-number killing, it is undeniable that the Indian made more complete use of the casualties than we are accustomed to do. It was this spectacle to which Leavenworth's men were now treated.

Postbattle activities served several important ends. Scalping, for example, was only the beginning; the scalper accrued prestige. Later he would perform a more formal ritual of counting coup, detailing before the tribe his exact actions in the battle, how he took the scalp, and probably as much of his life history as he could remember, with emphasis on feats of warlike valor. This was on the personal level.

The defeated tribe was also humiliated and derided. The bodies of the vanquished were generally mutilated if the victors had time, and this was usually done by squaws. In the present case of the Aricaras, one of the Sioux chiefs brought his squaw up to a Ree corpse near the village wall. With a war club the woman began to smash the body to a pulp, while the chief taunted the Aricaras with their weakness and cowardice. As far as the tribe's humiliation was concerned, it genuinely made little difference that the man was already dead. (The same kind of thing was done even when the vanquished tribe was absent, and in the victor's eyes the ceremony was quite as effective as if the defeated had been watching.)

Other braves were dragging dismembered pieces of the Aricara warriors around the plain. This, too, was a sort of informal humiliation procedure, and also derived from plain malice.

The making of medicine was seldom observed immediately after a battle; it was generally reserved for a more formal triumphal occasion, the tribal celebration of the victory. On this occasion, however, one of the Sioux—of the "grizzle Bear medicine," according to Clyman—did perform a magic ritual directly on the battleground. Walking on his hands and feet, "snorting and mimican the bear in all his most vicious attitudes . . . with his teeth tore out mouth fulls of flesh from the breast of the dead body of the Ree."

Evening came, and the keelboats with the artillery arrived about sundown. The guns were unloaded and disposed along the line in preparation for the next day's attack. Then the troops settled down for the night.

From inside the Ree villages came the blood-chilling mourning wails of the squaws; outside, the Sioux were still noisily celebrating their triumph, guns firing, men yelling and shouting and running. The village dogs, upset, were in full voice, and the mules and horses of both sides added their harsh sounds to the general melee. The dead horses and men were beginning to raise a stench, according to Clyman, and the whole scene might have been drawn from the *Inferno*. It is doubtful that the men got much sleep that night, in particular those whose first experience this was.

Sunday, August 10, 1823

In spite of the unpleasantness of the night, the morning of the 10th dawned with a decisive victory in view. The Aricaras were pinned in the villages and all that remained was to pound them with artillery, either destroying the villages or driving the tribe out to face Leavenworth's vastly superior force.

Captain Bennet Riley and his company of riflemen were sent to the upper village. The Missouri Fur group, under Henry Vanderburgh, also was stationed there, and one of the cannons was set for the bombardment.

The remainder of the force, including Ashley's two companies, completed a quarter-moon around the Ree villages on the inland side, pinning the Indians against the river.

The assault began shortly after A.M., with the artillery at the lower village firing the first shot. The infantry, including Ashley's men, moved forward and fired a volley "to discharge their guns which had been loaded for some time."

At the upper village the artillery had meanwhile been pouring a murderous barrage into the river. The six-pounder was placed too high, and Sergeant Perkins assiduously plunked balls over the village and into the water until he was stopped. "Though this was presently rectified," writes Morgan, "the effect on the Rees was not remarkable."

This went on all morning without any evident effect. The infantry sat and waited for the Rees to be driven out, occasionally plopping a shot at the stockade. The Sioux, bored with this effete siege warfare, had wandered off into the hills, where they were methodically gorging their way through the Ree cornfields and waiting to see how things turned out.

This was obviously an unproductive beginning for the day. Leavenworth decided to make an infantry assault on the upper village, using Captain Riley's company of riflemen and possibly backing them up with some of the Sioux irregulars. He sent Pilcher to bring the Indians up. Ashley's companies were detailed to create a diversion at the lower village. The trappers accordingly scrambled into a ravine within "20 paces" of the lower village and began firing.

Pilcher came back and said the Sioux weren't much interested. The cornfields suited them fine for the time being, and, in any event, they hadn't been impressed with the whites' warlike prowess. Convinced the charge would fail without the co-operation of the Sioux, Leavenworth called it off.

This infuriated Captain Riley, who had been enthusiastic about the plan, and he demanded the privilege of making the assault anyway, "stating that they had been laying at garison at Council Bluffs for 8 or 10 years doeing nothing but eating pumpkins and now a small chance for promotion occurred and it was denied him and might not occurr again for the next 10 yeares."

This kind of talk, one may note, is hardly to be tolerated from a subordinate, and must be counted an unfortunate indiscretion on the part of Captain Bennet Riley. The charge, Leavenworth repeated, was off.

Where force fails, guile may prevail. Leavenworth, according to Chittenden, then concluded he would "try a stratagem." Pilcher said he had better try *something*, because the Sioux were getting disgusted with the way things were going; at the present rate, Pilcher did not know how long they would stay around. His opinion of the stratagem was that it "could do no harm, at any rate."

Leavenworth's stratagem was to send the Aricara interpreter, one Simeneau, to tell the Indians they "were fools that they did not come out and speak with the whites." This, by Leavenworth's sly reasoning, would at least give the whites an "opportunity to examine the works."

It did no harm, but it did no good either, as it failed to come off.

Discouraged with his efforts at the upper village, Leavenworth then returned below, contemplating an assault on the lower village instead. Arriving there, he discovered that Lieutenant Morris had enthusiastically used up all but thirteen of his round shot; at which Leavenworth ordered the bombardment abandoned. He then drew all troops back to a camp opposite the boats, a half mile away from the villages.

The withdrawal of the massive white force left the Sioux in the cornfield exposed. Leavenworth warned them of their danger, advising them to withdraw to "save their stragglers from the tomahawks of the Aricaras."

Since the Sioux had done most of the fighting so far—had, in fact, won a victory over the Rees—this kindly advice was not taken in the intended spirit. As far as the Sioux could tell, they had opened the campaign well and the whites had failed to follow through. Now they were counseled to "save their stragglers." It was too much. They disappeared entirely that night.

By the time the withdrawal had been completed it was past 3 P.M. "Orders were given to senior officers of corps to have their men obtain some refreshment as soon as possible, and then to form their corps and march to the enemy's cornfield to obtain some corn for the subsistence of our men, several of whom, and particularly General Ashley's men, had not had any provisions for two days." Leavenworth retired to his cabin on the boat for a late lunch.

After lunch the colonel emerged to take counsel with Ashley and Pilcher. While discussing future operations, they saw an interesting group gathered on a hill beyond the upper village; some Sioux and Aricaras, having a little parley. Leavenworth had been afraid for some time—and with some cause—that the Sioux were about to switch sides and unite with the Aricaras. Also, what with the artillery shot almost exhausted, this seemed a particularly auspicious time to consider a peace treaty. Accordingly, Leavenworth and Pilcher hurried to join the Indian parley on the hill.

The Aricaras, it seemed, were interested in peace, too. They told Leavenworth that Gray Eyes, who had been the cause of all the trouble, had been killed. They were most abject, and begged for pity. Leavenworth magnanimously informed the Ree delegate that he had not come to fight (which was probably obvious by then) but to bring peace. He would, however, have to speak with persons of authority. The Aricara returned to his village, Leavenworth and Pilcher returned to the boat to await the delegation of chiefs. Pilcher was thoroughly disgusted by now, realizing that any treaty entered into at this time would simply be letting the Aricaras off. He was not convinced of the extent of damage claimed, nor of the abjectness of the Rees.

Soon ten or twelve Aricaras emerged from the villages and made their way toward the boats, among them Little Soldier. Leavenworth greeted them warmly, embracing Little Soldier affectionately; which act further infuriated Pilcher. He later wrote that the gesture "done credit to the goodness of your heart; but did not in my humble opinion, comport with the dignity of the *Legion's chief.*"

Ceremonial buffalo robes were spread, the Indians and some of Leavenworth's officers sat to parley. Leavenworth required, as conditions of peace, that Ashley's stolen property be returned, that the Indians behave well in the future, and that they give him five hostages to take to Fort Atkinson as surety for this last condition.

The Aricaras said they would be happy to return what they still possessed, but that the Sioux had made off with a good part of it and killed many of the horses as well. Leavenworth then expounded at some length on the majesty and power of the United States Army, to which dissertation the Indians apparently listened without smiling. They would return what they could, the Aricaras said again, and made other expressions of their good intent.

"Considering my small force," writes Leavenworth, "the strange and unaccountable conduct of the Sioux, and even the great probability of their joining the Aricaras against us—and also the expense and trouble of a long Indian war, and the importance of securing the Indian trade, I thought it proper to accept the terms."

The peace pipe was duly produced. Pilcher refused to smoke, being in goodly rage by this time, nor would he shake hands. He "got up and walked back and forth in great agitation, telling the Indians that they could look out for him on the morrow" (Chittenden). Since the Aricaras had been informed that Pilcher was the most important white in the expedition, "his manner produced a bad effect upon [them]." As well it might.

Leavenworth finally persuaded him to smoke, but Pilcher flatly refused to condone any other part of the inadequate agreement.

While Leavenworth was picking out his hostages from among the nervous Indians, something occurred to upset them. It is not known precisely what this was, but it ended in the Indians' refusing to go. Several shots were fired in the excitement, but no one was hurt. The Aricaras scampered back to the villages and the first negotiations for peace ended.

Monday, August 11, 1823

In the morning the Sioux allies were gone. So were seven of Ashley's horses, six government mules, and an unrecorded percentage of the Aricara cornfields.

Shortly after sunup the minor Aricara chief Little Soldier appeared again. He explained to Leavenworth that his people were very much disturbed by Pilcher's attitude. They wanted to know what the fiery Missouri Fur leader was going to do.

Leavenworth guaranteed that Pilcher would be bound by any treaty made; that he would have no choice in the matter if he, Leavenworth, made peace. Thus reassured, Little Soldier proposed that he bring some chiefs out to negotiate a treaty and that Leavenworth in turn send a few whites into the village, probably as a guarantee of the chiefs' safety. Agreed, but who of Leavenworth's command had that much nerve?

Edward Rose the interpreter, qualifying as a white by the accident of employment, volunteered to go in alone and look things over. Without any doubt, Rose was the best man for the job. He had lived with the Aricaras for three years and they were "very much attached to him." Rose also had a ferocious reputation among Indians; he was known as Five Scalps by the Crows, commemorative of a famous solo battle.

Rose went into the village and returned with the report that the fortifications were not nearly so strong as had been thought and that the Indians were quite humbled. Other officers among the whites then went in and confirmed Rose's report.

The Aricara "chiefs," however, turned out to be men of no particular responsibility. They were sent back (probably by Pilcher) and eleven others came out. Pilcher was still not satisfied, and claimed none of the Indians present had any authority. Nevertheless, the second group were the signers of the treaty.

When it came to the drawing up of the treaty itself, Leavenworth ran into another snag. He requested Pilcher to draft it. (Not in order to shift responsibility, as some scholars have claimed, but because such a treaty was clearly the job of the ranking Indian agent present; and this was Pilcher.)

Pilcher, of course, flatly refused. Leavenworth was finally reduced to drafting the treaty himself, which he did very simply. It consisted of four articles. The first, and most important, provided for the return of "the arms taken from Ashley's party and such other articles of property as might remain in their hands which were obtained from Genl. Ashley in exchange for horses." The second article consisted of promises that the navigation of the Missouri be kept unobstructed and that authorized traders would be treated civilly. The third and fourth articles were pledges of enduring mutual friendship between the Indians and the United States.

The treaty was signed by the eleven Indians, Leavenworth,

five of his officers, and Ashley, at whose request the expedition had been formed.

The Aricaras then returned to the villages to gather together what goods of Ashley's they could find.

All they could seem to locate was three rifles, sixteen robes, and one horse. This was not sufficient, and they were sent back for more.

Tuesday, August 12, 1823

By the afternoon of the 12th Little Soldier finally came back with the report that no more of Ashley's goods could be found. He pointed out again that Gray Eyes was dead, though what this had to do with Ashley's property is somewhat vague. The upper village refused to contribute anything at all, claiming that they had not been involved in the original attack on Ashley and could not be expected to donate valuable goods.

Leavenworth told Little Soldier he would have to attack the village if the first article of the treaty, the most important one, were not complied with. He was apparently more confident since their inspection had shown the weakness of the village defenses. (Lieutenant Morris had somewhere found more round shot, which doubtless added to Leavenworth's confidence.)

The threat of another attack agitated Little Soldier considerably, and he inquired if he might change sides. He could be of considerable value to the whites, which point he illustrated by giving a bit of logistic advice. He pointed out where the village might best be attacked, and suggested that the cannon be aimed lower, because everybody in the village would be lying on the ground when they fired.

This was all very interesting, and possibly even useful, but it still didn't settle the problem of Ashley's goods. Once having made the threat of attack, many men might have felt compelled to carry it through if the treaty were not honored. Leavenworth did call his officers, and it was agreed to everyone's satisfaction that a general assault should begin the next day if the goods were not forthcoming.

Edward Rose went back into the village and managed to squeeze a few more robes out of the Rees, but that, they declared, was the absolute limit. He brought the robes back, and also information to the effect that the Indians were intending to desert the towns.

This was what Leavenworth was afraid of. He could deal with the Aricaras all right as long as they stayed in their villages but would be completely helpless if they scattered over the prairie. The desertion of the Sioux cut his force from 1,100 to about 350. His previous statement—to the effect that he would follow to the Mandan villages if necessary and attack them there—was not repeated at this time. Instead, he called his officers back and announced that the proposed attack was called off.

Little Soldier, said Leavenworth in effect, had done the very best he could. "I have therefore determined to abandon the charge and dispense with that article of the treaty." It being noteworthy that this article was the only one not wholly vague and theoretical.

Leavenworth, like Little Soldier, was doing the best he could. He was apparently convinced he had done his job: "For my own part I felt confident that the Indians had been sufficiently humbled, fully to convince them of our ability to punish any injury which they might do us, and that they would behave well in future if we left them undisturbed in their villages." He also thought his word to the Aricaras would be sufficient, and took no special precautions to prevent their desertion of the villages.

Wednesday, August 13, 1823

On the morning of the 13th the human population of the Aricara towns had dwindled to one; that one being the ancient mother of the dead malefactor Gray Eyes. There were still some dogs, however, and a rooster, by one account. But no Aricaras. Leavenworth hopefully sent out a patrol to look for them.

Thursday, August 14, 1823

The patrol came back. Still no Aricaras. Leavenworth then wrote the following plaintive little note, which I give in its entirety:

Ricaras Towns August 14,1823
Colonel Leavenworth, commanding the 6th regiment, to the chiefs and warriors of the Ricaras nation of Indians,
Greeting:
Ricaras:

You see the pipe of peace which you gave to me, in the hands of Mr. Charlonnan, and the flag of the United States.

These will convince you my heart is not bad. Your villages are in my possession; come back and take them in peace, and you will find everything as you left them. You shall not be hurt if you do not obstruct the road or molest the traders. If you do not come back, there are some bad men and bad Indians who will burn your villages. Come back, and come quickly. Be assured that what I say is the truth.

H. Leavenworth
Col. U.S. Army

They then left Gray Eyes' mother in complete possession of the Ree towns, supplied her with provisions and water, and departed at 10 A.M. on the 15th of August.

Behind them, as if to prove Leavenworth's absolute veracity, the towns burst into flame. The colonel was convinced some of Pilcher's men had done the dirty work—quite correctly, as it turned out—and addressed Pilcher: "The Colonel commanding, is extremely mortified to say, that he has too much reason to believe, that the Ricaras towns, have been set on fire by [men of your] company . . . ; with such men he will have no further intercourse."

His offical report, two weeks later, when he had returned to Fort Atkinson:

If the nation has been deprived of the advantages which might have resulted from the magnanimity of her troops toward a fallen and an humbled enemy, it is chargeable to that company, or to those individuals, who set those towns on fire. Had not this been done, there is no doubt that the Ricara Indians would in the future have behaved as well toward our countrymen as any other Indians on the river. It is now my deliberate opinion that those Indians will be excited to further hostilities if in the power of the Missouri Fur Company to effect it. It is understood that the company have withdrawn their trade from above the Sioux country . . .

He goes on to imply that Pilcher's intent is to hamper the activities of Ashley and Henry; and to laud the latter organization for their cooperation.

> Our officers and men [Leavenworth concludes] have returned in fine health and spirits and it is well; for those left here are nearly all sick . . . Our spring wheat has done well, and all our crops are very good.

The only white battle casualties of the entire campaign were two men slightly wounded. Far and away the greatest loss was occasioned by the wreck of the keelboat on the way up, which had drowned seven men. No wonder they returned in fine spirits.

Chittenden estimates that the Aricara campaign cost $2,000, and most historians have followed him. However, there is another cost that can be charged to the campaign: that of moving the supporting troops which were never used. By September 5 there were six full companies encamped a short distance above St. Louis. For the movement of these troops, Major General Gaines issued a request to the quartermaster for an additional $12,000, which makes the campaign seem a good deal less a bargain.

The most amazing part of the campaign was that Leavenworth was convinced he had done his job. In the set of "Orders" issued to his men immediately on return to Fort Atkinson, he says:

> The Colonel commanding is happy to announce to his command that the objectives of the late expedition against the Ricaras Indians have been effected. The blood of our countrymen has been honorably avenged, the Ricaras humbled, and in such a manner as will teach them, and other Indian tribes, to respect the American name and character.

This was so far from the truth as to be a classic example of the monstrous fictions possible to the military mind. The Aricaras now became more murderous than ever, massacring several trappers near the Mandan villages immediately after. Even the long-time friends of the whites, the Mandans themselves, were involved in several attacks that fall and winter. For several years it was not safe for a white man to show his face on the upper Missouri. The Sioux had been completely alienated by the ineffectual show and henceforth had an extremely low opinion of the Great White Father and all his aides.

So unpopular was Leavenworth that the two men he excepted in his indictment of the Missouri Fur Company—Vanderburgh and Carson—wrote to their boss Pilcher that they were "extremely mortified at having been selected as the object of his approbation and praise."

The truth was much closer to Pilcher's hotheaded accusation:

> I am well aware that humanity and philanthropy are mighty shields for you against those who are entirely ignorant of the disposition and character of Indians, but with those who have experienced the fatal and ruinous consequences of their treachery and barbarity these considerations will avail nothing. You came to restore peace and tranquillity to the country, and to leave an impression which would insure its continuance. Your operations have been such as to produce the contrary effect, and to impress the different Indian tribes with the greatest possible contempt for the American character. You came (to use your own language) to "open and make good this road"; instead of which you have, by the imbecility of your conduct and operations, created and left impassable barriers.

The greatest burden under which Leavenworth labored was undoubtedly his appalling ignorance of Indians. He was consistently dealing with some strange figment of his own imagination rather than real people. He treated the Indians not only as children but as retarded children. It is quite amazing that a man in charge of a military force on the American frontier could refer to "advantages [resulting] from the magnanimity of her troops toward a fallen and an humbled enemy." This is a rather romantic view of warfare, and certainly one the Indians did not comprehend at all. For "magnanimity" any Indian would read either "cowardice" or "weakness." They were not conversant with the European concept of gallantry.

Leavenworth naturally had to consider how his action would appear to his superiors. In the civilized East, having slaughtered their own Indians, people were developing a strong conscience about what the West did with theirs. It is possible this was a factor; he had, after all, taken a large body of men on a punitive expedition without authorization and did not know that this would be approved. If it ended in the obliteration of the Aricaras, he might well have a great deal to answer for. There is very little justification, however, for his failing to insist on the observance of the treaty, once signed.

The conduct of the campaign became a sort of *cause célèbre* of the day and was widely debated. On the Missouri there was more or less unanimous agreement that the expedition had been a complete failure.

In spite of this, Leavenworth and the military continued to regard the campaign as an unqualified success (if it hadn't been for the rascally Missouri Fur Company). Leavenworth wrote glowing recommendations for all his officers, including those who didn't do anything but showed by their general attitude their bravery, loyalty, and other desirable military qualities.

Gaines himself wrote to Secretary of War Calhoun: ". . . if the President of the United States should be pleased to confer any token of his approbation on either of the officers engaged in the late expedition. Colonel Leavenworth himself has a well founded claim to the first notice."

An aide-de-camp, however, informed Gaines that "the President . . . deems it inexpedient to confer any brevets for services on that occasion."

CHAPTER 4

"A Verry unfavourable account"

THE Missouri Legion was disbanded at the mouth of the Grand River, just a few miles below the Aricara villages. Rancor and bitterness within the party were the rule; Leavenworth gave Pilcher and his Missouri Fur men dishonorable discharges—nominal, presumably, as were their ranks—and Ashley's men received honorable ones.

For Ashley the consolation was a small one. The campaign, far from restoring his losses, had cost him seven more horses. His men were half a thousand miles from where they should be, sitting on the wrong river with no supplies. It was past the middle of August—the trappers should have been preparing for the fall hunt—and unless 1823 was to be a complete loss some men had to be gotten into the field immediately. If they folded now, it was for good; even a "person of credit" can push his financial luck only so far. The losses already sustained by accident and Indian were enough to disillusion the most optimistic of backers.

There had been some hope—precampaign—that they could get back up the river before the fall season began. Now, as far as the trappers were concerned, the river was effectively closed as transportation to the field. They had no choice but to revert to the notion discussed when Henry came down from the Yellowstone: overland expeditions. And not into Blackfoot country either.

The best idea seemed to be for Henry to close up the Yellowstone post completely, get out of the upriver country. Move down, say, to the Bighorn, in good, substantial Crow territory. Send a party over to the Snake, and see what could be found there. In any event, get moving immediately.

All the supplies were downriver at Fort Kiowa, left off by the retreating *Yellow Stone Packet*. With those goods, and a few horses, one party could be gotten off within a couple of weeks. This would be Henry, who could move up to the mouth of the Yellowstone, close out the post, and ascend the Yellowstone itself to the Bighorn. In the meantime Ashley could be outfitting another party to proceed directly across toward the Snake. The two could get together in the mountains.

So it was decided. They dropped back downriver to Fort Kiowa, picked up the supplies left there and a few horses, and sent Henry off. Outfitting an expedition for the mountains was not a simple process in the best of times, and to do it on such short notice would have required herculean efforts. But Henry got off with a small party early in September. He had too few horses, heavily burdened, and the men would simply have to walk. This they did, following the Missouri back up to the mouth of the Grand. There was no telling where the Rees had gone, but it was a safe bet they were in an ill humor and nobody wanted to risk meeting them. Henry left the Missouri and followed the Grand, heading almost due west across the barren plains of present South Dakota. The country was flat, stale, and unprofitable. Vegetation was scrubby and dwarfish, interspersed with tangled thickets of brushwood.

Meat was a problem. Several hunters were kept constantly ahead of the party, combing for game and provision. One of these was a man known as Old Hugh Glass, a crotchety, querulous, insubordinate, completely independent hunter—in short, a mountain man. The epithet "old" in the mountains didn't necessarily have anything to do with age; most of the men who carried it were under thirty. It was meant a man had been around long enough for people to get to know him. There's some evidence, however, that Glass really was old by this time; but we know very little about him. He'd been with Ashley when the Aricaras snapped at him the first time and had been wounded there. But that was months ago, and Old Hugh was not the kind of man to let a little thing like a bullet slow him down. Watch Glass as he forages ahead of the party; he is about to become one of the legends of the trade.

Thrashing and cursing his way through a brushwood thicket, he suddenly broke into a tiny clearing. The floor was covered with sandy soil and a grizzly bear; a she-bear with cubs. Before Glass could decide whether to shoot or go blind, grizzly had him. She grabbed him by the throat and smashed him to the ground. Ripping out a mouthful of flesh, she gave it to her cubs and started back to work the man over more thoroughly.

The main party heard Glass scream and now broke into the thicket. The grizzly abandoned the inert form of Glass and chased two of the newcomers into the river. The repeated volleys of the hunters finally brought her down.

They now returned to the thicket, where Glass was lying. The man was impossibly mangled, his throat torn open, his body claw-ripped, arms and legs lacerated. He was, somehow, still alive.

Incredibly, he remained alive all through the afternoon and by evening Henry was faced with an ethical problem. Glass, obviously, could not be taken on. There was no doubt that he was about to die; no man could be so badly mangled and live. There was, of course, no medical care available. They were a week out from civilization, and it seemed dubious that he could survive even under a surgeon's care.

But the party could not wait. They still didn't know where the Rees might be, they still had to get to the post, and certainly the whole expedition couldn't be abandoned for the sake of one dying man. Henry asked for volunteers. They were to wait until Glass died, bury him, and come after the main party. (Or until Glass could travel, Henry added—Old Hugh was conscious.)

It was a lot to ask of them. They were in hostile country, and the vigil must have seemed nothing worth risking your own life for. But a purse was finally made up as inducement— some say $80—and two reluctant volunteers stepped forward, John Fitzgerald and a greenhorn on his first trip, name of Jim Bridger.

The next morning Henry moved on. Glass was not the only casualty of the trip. Late in September, while camped for the night, Henry's party was fired on by an unseen war party. Two men were killed and two wounded. Two of the precious horses were lost. The white party fired back blindly and scored, almost by accident. Not daring to leave their position, they remained alert all night, and when morning came the war party had disappeared, leaving behind one of their number. It was a Mandan. Roving very far from home, this war party, and it was uncomfortable knowledge. The Mandans were the friendliest of all tribes on the Missouri, traditionally hospitable, traditionally co-operative. Now— abruptly—this. Very uncomfortable knowledge.

Henry continued, his party getting smaller. He made it to his fort at the Yellowstone without any further losses, only to find more when he arrived. Twenty-two of the horses he had left there were gone. Seven more were stolen after he arrived. Men, equipment, and animals were gradually being picked off; the incredibly consistent process of mountain and other "fixens," and come to the fort.

A few days later Fitzgerald and Jim Bridger pulled in, to report Glass dead. He had lasted five full days and gone under at last. They had buried him, collected his gun, knife and other "fixens" and come to the fort.

Local Crows brought the further heartening news that the Blackfeet were deliberately out to hunt down and destroy any trapping parties in their country. Henry quickly set about the business of abandoning the fort. He made a cache for some of the goods and embarked the rest, with all the men, on the Yellowstone. They were able to make it up that river until they reached the Powder, where they had to go ashore because of the rapids. They were roughly 125 miles up the Yellowstone from the mouth, not quite halfway to their destination, the mouth of the Bighorn.

Here, near the mouth of the Powder River, Henry had the first luck that had come his way all year. He met a band of friendly Crows, and secured forty-seven horses from them. With these he outfitted a trapping party and sent them on ahead to the Bighorn. They were to trap their way up that river as long as they could, and then winter where they had to. (Possibly some previous arrangement had been made to meet the party that was expected to depart from Fort Kiowa after Henry. But as yet he didn't know if that party had been able to get off.)

The remainder of the men he would keep with him; he would need a fair-sized force to get a post readied before winter closed in.

Here at Powder River he lost three more men, but not to Indians. Fitzgerald had been considerably shaken by the overland trip from Fort Kiowa. What with Hugh Glass and Indian attacks and the prospect of more in store, Fitzgerald decided he had had enough of the trapper's gay life to suit him. He wanted to go back to civilization and do something a little safer. (What he had in mind was joining the army, which he did.) He and two others took their leave from Henry's party and started down the river in a canoe. With various mishaps along the way, the three finally arrived at Fort Atkinson on December 18 and there made a report of activities on the upper river to Colonel Leavenworth. A few months later Fitzgerald enlisted.

After the departure of the three men, Henry moved on to the mouth of the Bighorn. He may have used the remnants of Manuel Lisa's old Fort Lisa or built a new one himself. Probably he took over the abandoned post and rebuilt. By the end of December, just in time to welcome in the new and hopefully more prosperous year of 1824, he and his party were well installed. In spite of the late season, he had sent a small party off to trap the Yellowstone tributaries.

According to the tradition, the staff at the post was celebrating the new year. Whiskey was flowing, spirits and spirit content high. Spirits, in fact, were the order of the day, because Hugh Glass walked in and joined the celebration. He was looking for John Fitzgerald and James Bridger.

II

No one will ever know why Fitzgerald and Bridger abandoned Hugh Glass. Speculation is virtually useless, because the whole drama is something quite beyond our comprehension. It has been fictionalized in several ways and explained in several others. I have no theory. They did it, and there began an ordeal that remains one of the most incredible feats of the human animal ever recorded.

They left him alone, without a rifle, without knife, without even the fixens from his possible sack. He woke, still in the brushwood thicket where the bear had mangled him. Unable to walk, he somehow dragged himself to a spring that was close; even this much must have cost him almost everything. But he reached it. There were berries by the spring, wild cherries and buffalo berries in the thicket. Glass lay beside the spring, keeping himself barely alive for ten days.

At the end of that time Glass decided he'd better be moving on. How he had strength enough to stand, let alone walk, is simply one of the many questions that can never be answered. He started to walk back to civilization; the nearest post, Fort Kiowa, was over a hundred miles away, across the desolate Dakota plains. There was nothing he could do about his wounds. Many of them he couldn't even reach. They must have broken open frequently when he tried to move, and the consistent loss of blood would have been enough to kill a lesser man.

Before he had gone far he had a piece of luck. A pack of wolves had cut down a buffalo calf. Waiting until they had fed enough to make them less irritable, Glass moved forward and scared them away from the carcass. The decaying buffalo corpse was his home for the next few days. He lay in the lee of it—the fall nights were cold, and certainly the smell would have been better than the wind—and ate. Meat's meat, in the mountain saying, and in the circumstances it would matter very little that he had no knife to cut it or fire to cook it. He ate as much as he could, for as long as he thought he dared to stay in the same place. Then he moved on again, stumbling across the arid plains, living on what berries he might find, what scraps of meat the wolves and buzzards left when he came up—anything.

The details of this crawl across South Dakota are impossible to determine. Somehow he did it, but there is an uncertainty about where he ended; several reports say he actually made it to Fort Kiowa. Beause of the dates and time span involved, this does not seem likely. He was abandoned in September; and even allowing for early September, it is improbable that he could have made it to Fort Kiowa by October 10. On that date, or near it, a six-man party left Kiowa on their way upriver. By the time they reached the Mandan villages the party numbered seven, and one of them was Hugh Glass. It is most likely that Glass made his way to the Missouri in the vicinity of the Bad River. This is a much shorter distance from the place he was left, and allows five more days for him to make it. On October 15 the small party was about thirty miles below the mouth of the Teton. (This is the only date we are certain of in the whole story; one of the trappers, apparently none too optimistic about approaching the Aricara country, felt called upon to make out his will on that date.)

This party, under one Langevin, plodded upriver, taking about six weeks to reach the Mandans. During this time Glass must have been recuperating from his ordeal at an unbelievable rate. When they reached a point ten miles below the Mandans, Glass was put ashore. He was already hunting for the other members. While their boat worked its tedious way around a bend of the river, Glass was to hunt on the point, going straight across and meeting them on the other side.

He stumbled on a Ree war party, who immediately started after him. The Aricaras had purchased a dirt village from the Mandans after their own had been burned and some of the tribe was living there. It was from this new settlement the war party came. Running for his life, without one chance in ten thousand of winning, Glass suddenly encountered a Mandan brave on a horse. For some reason the Mandan saved him, swinging him up on the horse and galloping away from the infuriated party of Aricaras, now cheated of one slightly shopworn scalp.

The Mandan took Glass to his own village, where there was a temporary post of the Columbia Fur Company.[1] So far this company had maintained an uneasy peace with the Mandans, though shortly after this the Rees killed the trader and the post was abandoned.

As it turned out, there was no use in Glass's waiting for the Langevin party. The angry Ree warriors had found and massacred them all. Once more Glass had escaped by the narrowest of margins.

He set out again the next day, headed for the mouth of the Yellowstone and Henry's fort there. He walked. He took the east bank of the Missouri and walked from the Mandan villages to the Yellowstone in two weeks, meeting not one human being.

It is not possible to explain the drive that kept him going. By any sane standard, he was going in the wrong direction. He should have been heading toward civilization and help, instead of which he was walking straight back to the mountains, all alone.

When he reached the Yellowstone fort, it had been abandoned. So he walked down the Yellowstone itself, headed for the Bighorn and Henry's new fort. The dramatic version of Glass's story says he was motivated by the unquenchable desire to find and kill Fitzgerald and Bridger. It may be. Whatever drove him, when he reached the Bighorn in time for the New Year celebration he didn't kill anybody.

Bridger was still there, and the boy must have been paralyzed with fear. Even after it had been demonstrated that

Glass was a living human being, they found it difficult to persuade Bridger to come near him.

Glass—this again has been explained in various ways—did apparently forgive Bridger.[2] One version of the story records the following unlikely monologue from Glass:

> I swore an oath that I would be revenged on you, and the wretch who was with you, and I ever thought to have kept it. For this meeting I have braved the dangers of a long journey. . . . But I cannot take your life . . . you have nothing to fear from me; go,—you are free;—for your youth I forgive you.

III

Having spared Bridger for indeterminate reasons, Glass still had a notion to see Fitzgerald. The opportunity came up in February, 1824. Major Henry had a dispatch of considerable importance to go downriver to General Ashley. What this was we don't know in detail; he had enough news, certainly. The loss of the additional horses—another $2,000 worth—the establishment of the Bighorn post, the dispatching of trapping parties. By this time, too, he may have had the news of Jedediah Smith's arrival in the mountains (see Chapter 5), which Ashley would be glad to hear. In view of later events, it seems likely that Henry also had some news to impart which the general would distinctly *not* be glad to hear: that Henry was quitting the mountains, leaving Ashley without leadership for the field end of the business.

Whatever the content of the express, Henry thought it important enough to detail five men for the delivery, reducing his effective trapping force by that much more. Hugh Glass was one of these; the names of the others were Dutton, Marsh, Chapman, and More. The initial stage of their journey (up the Yellowstone, Powder, and overland to the headwaters of the Platte) was made without recorded incident or difficulty.

Soon after they reached the Platte the river ice loosened and broke. The trappers decided to try their luck with a bullboat. The bullboat was a kind of coracle of the western rivers. It was simply made, nondurable, virtually uncontrollable, and could carry a truly fantastic amount of freight—with a 2½-ton load, the draft was about six inches. It was simply a framework of willows, covered with buffalo hides sewed and tallowed at the seams with varying success. It ranged in form from nearly circular, five feet in diameter, to a roughly boat-shaped version which might be as long as thirty feet and as wide as twelve. It was propelled with a short paddle with which the rower reached out as far as he could, then pulled directly in toward the boat; otherwise it simply rotated downstream. When a nearly-round bullboat took to spinning in the current, it was hard to stop. The sight of Indian families (horse Indians used them constantly for ferrying purposes) whirling in the impromptu merry-go-round of a bullboat was one that afforded a good deal of merriment in the mountains. A bullboat was a craft entirely born of expediency; thrown together for short trips downstream, then abandoned without regret. Boats of the same type are still used in Tibet, and a reed-woven version in present-day Iraq.

In this most primitive of boats Glass and his four companions embarked on the spring floodwaters of the North Platte. The current swept them down to the mouth of the Laramie (about fifty miles upstream from present Scottsbluff, Nebraska). There they found a Pawnee village of almost forty lodges; were cordially hailed and invited to a feast. The trappers accepted the invitation happily and disembarked; untrapperlike, all but Dutton left their guns in the boat. In the midst of the pleasantries, according to Chittenden's version, Glass perceived that the squaws were "carrying away their effects." As it turned out, the band of friendly Pawnees were neither friendly nor Pawnee. They were Rees, drifted all the way from the Missouri River into Wyoming after the burning of their towns. The band was led by Elk Tongue (Langue de Biche), second warrior in the tribe after the dead Gray Eyes. The other group of displaced Rees, near the Mandan villages, were probably a thousand miles away by any travelable route; Hugh Glass had run into both bunches within six months. This kind of coincidence begins to wear a man down.

The trappers piled out of Elk Tongue's lodge and made for their boat. It was still there, strangely, though their guns were gone. They scrambled into the little skin tub and made it across to the opposite bank, while the river behind them swarmed with swimming Aricara warriors. On reaching shore the trappers scattered. Dutton, being still armed, wasn't pursued; Marsh apparently outran the Indians, later got together with Dutton and the two proceeded down the Platte together.

Hugh Glass watched as the Aricaras caught More and Chapman and butchered them; one within a few yards of where he lay hiding. The Rees kept up the search for the hidden Glass all day. When night came they returned to their village on the opposite shore, and Glass could move again.

The *Missouri Intelligencer* reports him saying:

> Although I had lost my rifle and all my plunder, I felt quite rich when I found my knife, flint and steel, in my shot pouch. These little fixens make a man feel right *peart* when he is three or four hundred miles from any body or any place—all alone among the painters and wild varments.

Thus "rich" in his own terms Glass was off again on another solitary overland trip. This time he angled off northeast, diagonally across Nebraska and South Dakota. Since it was very early spring, he had no trouble catching newborn buffalo calves at first; the northwest corner of Nebraska, through which he was passing, was a fertile buffalo prairie. But as Glass walked the year grew older and so did the calves. They were faster, harder to catch, and for the last part of the trip he was back to his familiar diet of bark and buds and roots.

Finally he was picked up by a Sioux hunting party. They carried him the rest of the way to Fort Kiowa, where he arrived early in June (1824). After resting briefly, he dropped back down the Missouri to Fort Atkinson at Council Bluffs. There he discovered that Marsh and Dutton had survived, and beaten him to the fort. He also found Fitzgerald, but was faced with a problem. Fitzgerald was now in uniform, under the protection, such as it was, of his commander, Colonel Leavenworth.

The episode was finally ended with the restitution of Glass's rifle (which Fitzgerald had appropriated), and Leavenworth provided the old trapper with enough other possibles to fit him for his trade again.

Shortly after, Hugh Glass joined a Santa Fe caravan, deciding to try his luck in warmer weather perhaps. He got back to the northern mountains again, eventually, and was finally killed in the winter of 1932-33 by his old acquaintances, the Aricaras. Whichever Ree finally took the scalp of Old Glass could count coup in a big way; he was one of the great ones.

IV

Back to September, 1823, at Fort Kiowa. After Henry's party got off, General Ashley turned his attention to outfitting the second group. This brigade was to move directly overland—across South Dakota and Wyoming—to the Bighorn basin, where they would meet Henry's men swinging back down from the Yellowstone post.

Two new hands were put in charge of the second party, but at least one of them had already proved his worth on an overland trip—Jedediah Smith. Tom Fitzpatrick, another name that would become important in the trade, was Smith's second-in-command. With this party (estimated variously from eleven to sixteen men) were also Edward Rose, Bill Sublette, and James Clyman. Three other names are recorded, Eddie, Stone, and Branch, but these men were never to achieve the stature of the others. On Clyman's journal we depend for most of our information concerning the party.

The Smith party got off in late September, probably three weeks after Major Henry. Horses were still in very short supply; the party, in fact, could not be outfitted on the Missouri. They were forced to set out with horses borrowed from an obliging factor of the French Fur Company (Berthold, Pratte, & Chouteau), who also lent them a guide.

Smith's party set out in a southwesterly direction, marching all day through the arid, rolling country of central South Dakota to the valley of the White River, where they made first camp.

After several days' march along the valley of the White they left the bank to cut directly across a wide U curve, expecting to reach a water hole the next day. Dark caught them in the midst of a huge tract of prickly pear, whose thorns could rip apart the best moccasins in no time. They had barely room to spread their blankets, and it was a bad night. When they reached the expected water hole at noon the following day, it was dry.

They had now been twenty-four hours without water, and the horses were beginning to fail. The worried company picked up its pace, in order to reach the river again before nightfall. The French Company guide soon got far ahead and

James Clyman was not far behind. Smith himself took the rear of the line, which was now spread out well over a mile. The men slanted off to left and right of the line of march in search of water, and soon were so dispersed there was nothing that could be called a main party at all.

Jim Clyman had a knack invaluable to a mountain man; he could almost always find some kind of provision. He did in this case, finding a good water hole shortly before sunset. He threw himself in (he reports having fired a signal shot first, but one wonders), came out, and fired off (another) shot.

The other members of the party began coming in at full tilt, and soon the hole was filled with men and horses companionably soaking up the water. Three men were still missing at nightfall, among them Smith. He finally came in, reporting that the other two had given out. He had buried them in the sandy soil with only their heads showing in an attempt to conserve as much moisture as possible by lessening the rate of evaporation. After he had been able to recuperate a little himself, Smith took a horse and went back after them, returning later in the night.

Continuing upstream next morning—this time carefully staying close to the river—they came to an encampment of Bois Brule[8] Sioux. Here they were able to secure some horses and return those borrowed from the French Fur Company.

Now they left the river and veered off to the northwest, striking for the south fork of the Cheyenne. For a few days the going was good. This—except for the prickly pear—was easy country, and they met sufficient buffalo to provide them with at least one meal a day. Falling in with a band of Oglala Sioux they traded a few more horses and got rid of their "more ordinary."

Shortly after this they entered a country as weird as any found in North America, the South Dakota Badlands.

These gullied, desolate tracts of land, the *Mauvaises Terres* of the French traders, are some of the bleakest and most inhospitable terrains in the world. Endless vistas of eroded and twisted lumps of earth; deep ravines, with multicolored spires and pinnacles jutting up; razorback barren ridges that twist and crawl off toward the horizon. These hills are ashy and sliding, and the soil when wet is an oily, slippery muck. There is no vegetation here; the earth will not support it. The land is devastated as if by some unimaginable catastrophe, deep scars gashed across the face of it and grotesque, tumescent swellings sprouting like cancerous growths from the flat plains. The land might be a nightmare made reality, the dream of a sickened mind given substance.

Clyman observes, with his characteristic calm understatement, "it looked a little remarkable that not a foot of level land could be found."

He also remarks on the "remarkably adhesive" qualities of the loose soil; and out of experience:

> ... there [came] on a misty rain while we were in this pile of ashes and it loded down our horses feet in great lumps ... the whole of this region is moveing to the Misourie River as fast as rain and thawing of Snow can carry it.

Soon after this dismal passage the party reached the Black Hills. This was better country by far than the Badlands, but presented its own problems for the traveler. Streams here formed narrow ravines, unsuitable for traveling. Near the end of one day the party got itself so far into one of these that the horses had no room to turn around, and the men were caught by darkness. The imperturbable Clyman, with two others, got down over some slippery rocks into a "nice open glade whare we killed a Buffaloe and fared Sumpiously that night while the rest of the Company remained in the Kenyon without room to lie down."

After the standing night in the Kenyon, they tried the ridges. Here they could move more easily, but food for the horses was scarce, and their animals began to weaken. Smith thought it likely that the western slope of the Black Hills was drained by the Powder River. Probably acting on this assumption, which would have meant they were in Crow territory, Smith sent Edward Rose off to find fresh horses among his adopted people. (The assumption was incorrect; the Black Hills are drained on both slopes by the Cheyenne, whose northern and southern forks almost encircle the short range.)

After Rose's departure, the main party continued on for another five days. Then, in a narrow, brushy ravine between two ridges, they ran into trouble. The men were picking their way through the brush with Smith in the lead. Suddenly, from the slope at their side, a massive grizzly came charging down, almost running into the line of men. The bear wheeled and ran beside the column toward the head. Smith raced for

open ground, hearing the shouts behind him, and just as he
broke out into the clear met the bear, apparently head on.

"Grissly," says Clyman, "did not hesitate a moment." He
clouted Smith on the head with one of his huge paws, sending
him sprawling in the clearing. The bear continued to attack
Smith until driven off by the arrival of the other men.

Smith had several broken ribs and was badly cut about the
head. The other men of the party stood around their mangled
captain in a paralysis of uncertainty. "What was to be done
one Said come take hold and he wuld say why not you so it
went around."

Clyman finally asked Smith himself, who was still conscious, what to do. Calmly the twenty-four-year-old captain
gave him instructions: to get some water and, if anybody had
a needle and thread, sew him up. Simple as that.

The job fell to Clyman. When he had cleaned away the
blood from Smith's head he found

> the bear had taken nearly all his head in his capcious
> mouth close to his left eye on one side and clos to his
> right ear on the other and laid the skull bare to near
> the crown of the head ... one of his ears was torn
> from his head out to the outer rim ... after stitching
> all the other wounds in the best way I was capabl and
> according to the captains directions ... I told him I
> could do nothing for his Earse ... O you must try to
> stitch up some way or other said he.

Clyman did, "laying the lacerated parts together as nice as
I could with my hands."

The mountain moral: "this gave us a lisson on the charc-
ter of the grissly Baare which we did not forget." -

Like Hugh Glass, Smith could not be taken on immediately. They made camp near a stream and pitched their only
tent for Smith's comfort. According to Clyman's version, the
whole party remained there until Smith was able to travel
again—in ten days. By another account, two men were left
with him, and five of the most-tired horses, taking the opportunity of letting the animals recuperate as the captain did. By
this last version, which I am inclined to accept, Tom Fitzpatrick took charge of the main party and went on.[4]

While Smith and the two others were in this semiperma-
nent camp, a white party suddenly appeared and joined
them. This was a brigade of Pilcher's Missouri Fur Company

led by two survivors of the Immel-Jones massacre of the previous spring, Keemle and Gordon. (Gordon was also a survivor of Colonel Leavenworth's wrath; he was one of the men who set the Ree villages on fire.)

The mountains were not so exclusively the bailiwick of Henry as he had supposed; Pilcher had decided to have a go himself, at least at the Crow trade.

Competitors or not, Smith and the others were probably happy to see the Keemle company; they could go on to the Bighorn together, forming a larger and safer company.

When Smith was able to travel again, the combined parties moved on. They came up with Fitzpatrick's party at a village of Cheyennes, with whom they probably stayed for a day or two.

Now they crossed from the deceptive drainage system of the Cheyenne to the headwaters of the Powder, a fairly short overland hop by mountain standards. A few days later Edward Rose found them. He had with him fifteen or sixteen of his Crow friends, and a few extra horses. These helped out greatly, and the party entered the last lap of the year's trip.

Rose and the Crow warriors took what they could pack and went on ahead. The Crows had hospitably offered Smith's party the chance to winter with them, and Smith accepted. It was now November, and the mountain cold was beginning to be difficult for a traveling party. Snow flurries were beginning, and wisdom dictated finding a wintering camp very soon.

The Smith party came on behind, traveling slowly and even doing a little trapping. They skirted the southern end of the Bighorns and followed the Crow trail up and over the Littlehorns (now known as Owl Creek Mountains). On the south side of the Littlehorns was the valley of the Wind River, the major source of the Bighorn. (The Wind was often called the Bighorn by the trappers.)

They almost delayed their passage too long. Winter was gripping the mountains in an icy fist by the time they came to the Wind River valley and men and horses were almost frozen. They ascended the valley almost to the source of the river and found the wintering village of Crows.

There they settled in.

CHAPTER 5

"A more pitible state if possible than myself"

THE mountain men of this and later times recognized two divisions within the Crow nation: Mountain Crows and River Crows. The territory of the River Crows was (in a very general way) the lower Yellowstone, roughly the southeastern section of present Montana, to the confluence of the Yellowstone with the Missouri. This division was known to the Crows themselves as the Dung-on-the-River-Banks band. There were two bands comprising the Mountain Crows. The largest was called the Main Body (*acarahō: Where-the-Many-Lodges-Are*), the smaller was the Kicked-in-Their-Bellies (*erarapī'o*).

The Smith-Fitzpatrick party almost certainly spent this winter of 1823-24 with the Kicked-in-Their-Bellies, who customarily wintered in the Wind River valley. In the spring they would rejoin the Main Body, but for the time being they existed as a separate unit of the Crow nation.

The Crow's name for themselves was Absaroka (variously spelled). It indicated, according to the squaw man Leforge at a later date, "a peculiar kind of fork-tail bird resembling the blue jay or magpie." Crows told Robert Lowie (whose account, *The Crow Indians* [New York, 1935,] I generally follow here) that it was a bird no longer seen in the country. Early translators—almost inevitably—rendered it as *gens de corbeaux*, crow people, and so we have it.

Their language was Siouan; a fact of virtually no significance to anyone but a trained philologist. A Crow could certainly not understand the language of the Dakota proper.

67

Their closest relations, both linguistically and by descent, were apparently the Hidatsa of the upper Missouri, with whom the Crows had once formed a single nation. At the time of our narrative they made frequent social visits to the Hidatsa and the neighboring Mandans, and sometimes referred to themselves as a single people.

The Crows enjoyed life enormously; it was the national temperament, as horse thievery was the national sport. They were inordinately fond of practical jokes, puns, and general game-playing of all kinds. The language being very complex, there was much opportunity for sophisticated wordplay, and a man clever with the language was respected for it. (The Crow tradition had it that no foreigner was ever able to learn the language. It isn't true, but the Crows liked to think so.)

There was even a special joking-relationship. One who was your joking relative (ī'watkusu a) had the privilege of joking you at any time and under any circumstances. Anger or resentment was not permitted; you simply had to wait your chance to get even. While the duty of the clan was always to protect the individual from insult, the jokers held it *their* duty to humiliate and insult and jeer at him in public. Any shortcoming of a man (or woman) was sure to be picked up immediately by his jokers and made great sport of. If he had not actually performed any objectionable deed, the chances were his jokers would invent some. This could get rough, as in the case when a young man returning from burying his mother was twitted unmercifully by his jokers for being an orphan (a terrible anguish and humiliation for a Crow). If the joking became too much to bear, there was one way to stop it, but it was considered quite serious. A man might cut off a lock of the joker's hair. This was a considerable disgrace, and the cutter generally had to compensate with the gift of a horse. When hair was cut, the two ceased to be each other's jokers. Woman jokers never cut hair.

The Crow fondness for verbal byplay extended to the point of formal tongue twisters, of which the best known to contemporary Crows is *basakapupe'cdec akapupapa' patdetk:* "My people who went to the Nez Perce are not wearing Nez Perce belts." Lowie recounts how he once took the phrase down from an interpreter, "carefully memorized it, and then fairly staggered an old Indian by quickly and correctly reciting it."

On the more serious side of Crow life were the Crazy

Dogs. These were men—Crazy-Dog-wishing-to-die was the full title—who for one reason or another had decided that they were anxious for death and set about to court it. (One recorded reason was grief over the death of a man's father.) A Crazy Dog wore special trappings and had unique songs. He "talked crosswise"—said the opposite of what he meant—and expected to be spoken to in the same way. He was absolutely without fear, and incredible exploits of Crazy Dogs in warfare are recorded. He also had something of a privileged status in the band, for the good and sufficient reason that no man was anxious to dispute with a Crazy Dog. A Crazy Dog who lived out a full season was considered to have made a fool of himself, the notion being that if a man genuinely wants death, it isn't that hard to find.

Most Crows, however, found life well worth living. They found it quite incomprehensible that people should want to be anywhere else than in their own country, Absaroka. In Washingtons Irving's *Captain Bonneville* he records a speech made by the famous chief Rotten Belly (Arapooish) to Robert Campbell. While the language is Irving's, the sentiment rings true as Crow:

> The Crow country ... is a good country. The Great Spirit has put it exactly in the right place: while you are in it you fare well; whenever you go out of it, whichever way you travel, you fare worse.
>
> If you go to the south you have to wander over great barren plains; the water is warm and bad, and you meet the fever and ague.
>
> To the north it is cold; the winters are long and bitter, with no grass; you cannot keep horses there, but must travel with dogs. What is a country without horses?
>
> On the Columbia they are poor and dirty, paddle about in canoes and eat fish. Their teeth are worn out; they are always taking fish-bones out of their mouths. Fish is poor food.
>
> To the east they dwell in villages; they live well; but they drink the muddy water of the Missouri—that is bad. A Crow's dog would not drink such water.
>
> About the forks of the Missouri is a fine country; good water; good grass; plenty of buffalo. In summer it is almost as good as the Crow country; but in

winter it is cold; the grass is gone; and there is no salt weed for the horses.

The Crow country is exactly in the right place. It has snowy mountains and sunny plains; all kinds of climates and good things for every season. When the summer heats scorch the prairies, you can draw up under the mountains, where the air is sweet and cool, the grass fresh, and the bright streams come tumbling out of the snow-banks. There you can hunt the elk, the deer, and the antelope, when their skins are fit for dressing; there you will find plenty of white bears and mountain sheep.

In the autumn, when your horses are fat and strong from the mountain pastures, you can go down into the plains and hunt the buffalo, or trap beaver on the streams. And when winter comes on, you can take shelter in the woody bottoms along the rivers; there you will find buffalo meat for yourselves and cotton-wood bark for your horses; or you may winter in the Wind River Valley, where there is salt weed in abundance.

The Crow country is exactly in the right place. Everything good is to be found there. There is no country like the Crow country.

Considering the frequency of starvation rations and the bitterness of mountain winters, Arapooish's statement must be considered a reflection more of Crow attitude than geographic description. Which is not by any means to demean or discredit his eulogy of Absaroka. The deep love-of-place it represents is one of the faculties we are perilously near to losing, and man is poorer without it.

The inveterate horse thieving of the Crows is a prominent feature in personal journals of the trade. From the white man's point of view it was very nearly their only vice; for they killed seldom, and the Crow women were considered both attractive and obliging. But horse stealing was a matter of honor. The fact that few whites were killed by Crows was indeed explained by one Crow as resulting from the horse stealing: If the whites were killed they wouldn't come back to Asaroka with more horses to steal. It would be ridiculously bad policy to cut off all that potential horseflesh. "Trust to their honor," said Robert Campbell, "and you are safe; trust to their honesty, and they will steal the hair off your head."

All in all, relations between trappers and the Absaroka peoples were pretty fair, as long as it was understood about the horses.

Shortly after the Smith-Fitzpatrick party pulled in at the Wind River camp, exhausted and half frozen, they were joined by another of Henry's parties, under Captain John H. Weber. (The "captain" was from his seafaring days; he'd come to America after the Napoleonic Wars.) This was the trapping party dispatched by Major Henry from the post at the mouth of the Bighorn, and there was very likely some prearrangement for the two to winter together.

Dating from this winter camp in the Wind River valley is another story reflecting discredit on Edward Rose, the interpreter. As with most of them, the authority for it is flimsy. When Washington Irving was writing his books on the trade— *Astoria* and *Captain Bonneville*—he took a dislike to Rose and took particular pains to paint him darkly. It was easy enough to do; Rose had a mysteriously bad reputation with whites. And yet I have not found a single instance of Rose's duplicity in the contemporary literature. Rumors, apprehensions, and what not; but never facts. As Chittenden observes: "If judgement were to be passed only on the record as it has come down to us, he would stand as high as any character in the history of the fur trade." Most later writers, however, have sung in the key of Irving, who describes Rose as "withal, a dogged, sullen, silent fellow, with a sinister aspect, and more of the savage than the civilized man in his appearance ... [who was denounced by a secret informer as] a designing, treacherous scoundrel."

In *Bonneville* Irving states that Rose had left the Crows earlier because of internal feuds and general dislike of him. He reportedly used his position as interpreter with Smith and Fitzpatrick this winter of 1823-24 to restore himself to popularity through the simple expedient of distributing the trappers' goods with a lavish hand, taking advantage of the fact that he was the only man who spoke the language of their hosts.

Whether or not this is true, it is certain that Rose's skills as an interpreter would have been called upon frequently in the snowbound months that followed. What the mountain men wanted was information: What was on the other side of the range? How to get there? That and refitting.

Crow women were unexcelled in the housekeeping arts, the

making of moccasins and leggings, general stitching up and repairing of the trappers' accouterments. For this reason, they became in later years among the most desirable of Indian wives: clean, efficient and fast. And for the wife of a mountain man there was always enough to do.

Making new moccasins would be a big part of it; there were never enough. The Smith-Fitzpatrick party would by now have discarded (or simply worn out) what of the town they'd brought with them: boots, woolens, and such. Moccasins were more efficient in the mountains, and not the least of advantages was their replaceability. They were also easier on the feet when you got used to them; before that they could cripple you in a day's march. You had to learn to toe in very slightly as you walked, and forget about the heel-down-first clump of boots. Walking in moccasins you put nearly the whole length of the foot down simultaneously, which produces something closer to a glide than a walk.

The men would be picking up new leggings too. These, like those of the Indians, would generally reach to the hip and were fine for turning the brush. (If they were lucky, much of this clothing would have been made of skins saved from last year's lodges. Smoked day after day for a year, this was the softest and most flexible stuff available.)

Buckskin had its disadvantages, though, particularly for a trapper who had to be in waist-deep water to practice his trade. A pair of buckskin breeches first goes soggy and develops a permanent sag; then hardens stiff as a board and shrinks around the leg like an iron clamp. For this reason most trappers, particularly in the coming decade, stagged their buckskin breeches at the knee and added leggings of cloth. (Moccasins were subject to shrinking too, and there didn't seem to be any way around it. They had to be worn to bed or they'd shrink up so you couldn't get them on the next day. More than one mountain man wakened from a dream of having his feet clamped in a vise to stagger over to the stream and soak his moccasins so they'd loosen up and he could get back to sleep.)

The upper garment would usually be buckskin too: a long, loose, tunic-like affair, with a broad overlap in front, reaching down almost to the knees. There were no pockets in these Indian-made clothes, of course, and the various articles to be carried were either tucked into the loose flap at the front of the tunic or in the small leather bag known as a possible sack. When a trapper was actually working his line, the traps were carried on his back in a large sack, often burlap.

Blanket capotes were very much in demand when available; an over-covering similar to the buckskin, made from a Hudson's Bay Company blanket. (Wool was excellent clothing and much to be preferred despite our tradition of the buckskin-clad trapper. But after a year or so away from a source of supply, wool would generally have been ripped, torn, and worn so badly that it had to be replaced.) A superb visual record of the trapper's appearance and daily life is available in *The West of Alfred Jacob Miller,* published by the University of Oklahoma Press. These paintings were made firsthand in the 1830's and constitute one of our most reliable sources. For a verbal description, here is Frederick Ruxton (from *Life in the Far West,* also published by the University of Oklahoma Press). Ruxton is describing Old Bill Williams, but the description may be taken as general:

> . . . Williams always rode ahead . . . his keen gray eyes peering from under the slouched brim of a flexible felt-hat, black and shining with grease. His buckskin hunting-shirt, bedaubed until it had the appearance of polished leather, hung in folds over his bony carcass, his nether extremities being clothed in pantaloons of the same material (with scattered fringes down the outside of the leg—which ornaments, however, had been pretty well thinned to supply "whangs" for mending mocassins or pack-saddles). . . . In the shoulder-belt which sustained his powder-horn and bullet-pouch were fastened the various instruments essential to one pursuing his mode of life. An awl, with deer-horn handle . . . hung at the back of the belt, side by side with a worm for cleaning the rifle; and under this was a squat and quaint-looking bullet mould, the handles guarded by strips of buckskin to save his fingers from burning when running balls, having for its companion a little bottle made from the point of an antelope's horn, scraped transparent, which contained the "medicine" used in baiting the traps.

While the snow whirled outside, the trappers would be pouring bullets, stitching up breeches and moccasins (or watching a hired squaw do it), knifing a dollop of meat out of the always-boiling pot, and otherwise fortifying themselves against the trapping season to come.

(Their knives—"scalpers"—were garden-variety butcher knives. The trapper's famous Green River knife did not come until later. Contrary to accepted opinion, these knives were *not* stamped "GR" in imitation of a British knife; nor did the Green River name refer to the trapper's stamping ground in Wyoming. They were made—beginning in 1834—by John Russell on the Green River in Greenfield, Massachusetts. The British Sheffield works later imitated Russell's stamp on their own knives. To drive a knife in "up to Green River" meant all the way to the hilt; to the factory stamp. The factory is still in production.)

Traditionally, time in winter camp was also improved by a certain amount of judicious lying and some reading.

One of the most famous stories in the annals of the trade was probably polished to its final form in this camp of the Kicked-in-Their-Bellies: the famous "putrified forest" tale, with its putrified birds singing putrified songs, and even the law of gravity putrified so a man could make a fantastic leap across a canyon.[1] (Clyman found it, a grove of petrified trees in the south ranges of the Black Hills on their way out.)

Jedediah Smith would be spending what time he could with his Bible; this twenty-four-year-old brigade leader was the most devout man ever seen in the mountains, and so remained until his death. Smith was a haunted man; his letters to his family constantly reiterate his tremendous feelings of guilt in religious matters. Five years after this—and from about the same place—he wrote:

> God only knows, I feell the need of the watch & care of a Christian Church—you may well Suppose that our Society is of the Roughest kind, Men of good morals seldom enter into business of this kind—I hope you will remember me before a Throne of grace—

And to his brother, on the same day:

> As it respects my Spiritual welfare, I hardly durst Speak I find myself one of the most ungrateful, unthankful, Creatures imaginable Oh when Shall I be under the care of a Christian Church? I have need of your Prayers, I wish our Society to bear me up before a Throne of Grace.... It is, that I may be

able to help those who stand in need, that I face
every danger—it is for this, that I traverse the Mountains covered with eternal Snow—it is for this that I
pass over the Sandy Plains, in heat of Summer, thirst-
ing for water, and am well pleased if I can find a
shade, instead of water, where I may cool my over-
heated Body—it is for this that I go for days without
eating, & am pretty well Satisfied if I can gather a few
roots, a few Snails, or, much better satisfied if we can
affo(r)d our selves a peice of Horse Flesh, or a fine
Roasted Dog, and, most of all, is it for this that I
deprive myself of the privilege of Society & the satisfaction of the Converse of my Friends! . . .—Oh My
Brother let us render to him to whoom all things be-
longs, a proper proportion of what is his due   I must
tell you, for my part, that I am much behind hand,
oh! the perverseness of my wicked heart! I entangle
myself altogether too much in the things of time—
I must depend entirely upon the Mercy of that being,
who is abundant in Goodness & will not cast off any,
who call, Sincerely, upon him; again I say, pray for
me My Brother . . .

Jedediah's piousness was a quality somewhat foreign to the
mountain milieu. Most trappers, forced to consider why *they*
"traversed the Mountains covered with eternal Snow," etc.,
would have come up, at best, with a more mundane reason.
Smith's evaluation of the general moral level was accurate,
even understated. Any number of the mountain men were
fugitives from civilization, legal or social. Many of them were
men who just couldn't seem to get along in town; the winter
lodges with the Crows or Shoshones were more to their taste.
On the other hand, there were men like Smith, men like
Major Henry with his taste for reading and the violin. A little
later, reasonably educated men like Osborne Russell appeared
in the mountains, and the institution known as the Rocky
Mountain College, gradually formed itself in the long winter
evenings around a lodge fire. Joe Meek, for one, got all the
education he had at the Rocky Mountain College, having
left the comforts of civilized life before he had learned to
read. Old Bill Williams, the dirtiest, toughest, most cantankerous loner in the trade, had been a preacher before
he was a trapper, and they said he'd preached out all the

religion he knew in civilization and so arrived in the mountains with none at all.

This is getting ahead of our narrative. Here we are watching the birth of a whole breed, because Major Henry's men were the first of the true mountain men: Bill Sublette, twenty-four. Tom Fitzpatrick, also twenty-four. Jim Bridger is at the post on the Bighorn, and won't be twenty until March. Jedediah Smith is almost elderly; he'll be twenty-five in January.

II

Thirteen years earlier, in the fall of 1810, Andrew Henry had found good trapping in the valley of the river since known as Henry's Fork of the Snake. When the Blackfeet drove him out of his post in the Three Forks area, Major Henry had moved directly south, crossing the continental divide which, at that point, runs east-west. In all probability Henry's present intention was to have his detached brigades work the same area. The problem now facing Smith and Fitzpatrick was access to the rich area; Henry had approached over a relatively easy pass from the north, and they were due east of it. To reach the valley of the Snake (known to the mountain men by the name of its parent river, the Columbia) they had to cross the very spine of the continent.

One pass was definitely known. Union pass, the route of the overland Astorians in the fall of 1811, lay almost at the northern end of the Wind River valley. Early in February, which was rushing the season, a party set out to see if passage was possible. It wasn't. The snow was deep and impassable. From the top of the pass they could see the Teton Range directly between them and the valley of the Snake; and that is not a very encouraging vista for foot travelers, however beautiful it seems to modern eyes.

Back to the winter camp for more talk with the Crows. There was, so said the Indians, good beaver country just the other side of the Wind River Mountains, on the Seedskeedee Agie, the Prairie Chicken River (a traditional translation; the actual meaning is debatable). So good, in fact, that a man didn't really need traps. He could walk along the streams with a club. The Crows also told them of a pass that would get them over the mountains to the south.

It was probably mid-February when the party set out again, following the Wind in a southeasterly direction, then up the Popo Agie. Near this stream, a little east of the Wind River Mountains, the trappers came upon one of the natural curiosities that became a fixed feature of the trade: an oil spring. (In later years the oily substance oozing from the ground here was regarded as a sort of mountain pharmacy; every mountain man liked to have a little with him, to tend to his horses' pack sores, and maybe even his own rheumatic twinges. Its medicinal properties were highly regarded.)

The party soon found they had started too early in the season. The wind was razor-sharp and incessant, and the temperature well below freezing. It was strong enough to blow away the fires they kindled, and their campsites were raked with granular, frozen snow. Sublette and Clyman were lost on a hunting foray, making their way back to the main party exhausted and half frozen.

By now they had reached the valley of the Sweetwater; according to the Crows they could follow it west—through a broad depression—and reach the Seedskeedee Agie. But travel was impossible; the near-loss of two of the best men made that clear enough. They would have to make camp and wait for the weather to clear a little.

At last a campsite was found that offered shelter: an aspen grove just below the canyon later known as Three Crossings (on the Oregon Trail). Here they were out of the main force of the wind, they had fuel, and mountain sheep in reasonable numbers. The party sat and waited it out until the second week in March. Finally they were forced to move again, the sheep becoming scarce. A cache was made for lead, powder, and other supplies, and the spot was designated as a rendezvous in case any of the party should be separated during the spring hunt. In any event, the entire group would meet here (or slightly below) at the end of the hunt, no later than the first of June. Then they moved west up the Sweetwater, looking for the low place in the mountain chain where the Crows told them they could cross.

One of the more popular sports among western historians is arguing about who first discovered South Pass: Etienne Provost? Fitzpatrick? Smith? And should we count the returning Astorians, who (possibly) traveled it from west to east? Or did Andrew Henry use it in 1811?

I'm not going to get into this marathon discussion, for the good and sufficient reason that I don't know who first wandered through South Pass. The importance of the pass itself can't be denied; it made the Oregon Trail possible by providing a route across the mountains along which wagons could be transported. But entirely too much convoluted reasoning has been spent to prove the contention of one man or another. Readers interested in seeing how much steam can be generated by diligent scholars working with inadequate data are referred elsewhere.

The effective "discovery" of the pass, meaning that crossing which brought it to public notice, was probably this one of the Smith-Fitzpatrick party, regardless of who was the first individual to set his moccasins on it. The pass is not a hidden crevice in a mountain chain, but a depression that ranges from twenty to thirty miles wide, which makes a good deal of the discussion about routes seem a bit beside the point.

In any event, this small trapping party probably crossed the continental divide on their sixth day out from the Sweetwater cache. Because of the gentleness of the terrain it was very likely another day or so before they could be sure they were now on the Pacific drainage slope.

This entire area of western Wyoming and southeastern Idaho is physiographically extremely complex. Here the drainage systems of the Missouri (Gulf of Mexico), the Colorado (Gulf of California), and the Columbia (Pacific Ocean) meet in a complicated web of overlapping tributary streams; it is a geographer's nightmare. Even the superb geographic sense of the mountain man barely sufficed in this country, until it became known to him.

Still striking westward, the party reached the Sandy, and followed that stream down to its junction with Green River, the Seedskeedee Agie of the Crows. (Take your choice: Seeds-kee-dee, SeetKadu, Seetskeeder, Seeds-ka-day, Siskadee, etc. The stream was already known as the Green River by the Spaniards to the south. The two names were in more or less concurrent use up to 1840, when "Green" won out. Most trappers referred to it as the Seeds-kee-dee.) They finally reached the river on March 19, 1824, the first American trapping party to set their sticks on the west side of the divide since Henry's short-lived and almost accidental venture of 1811.

Here on the Seedskeedee the party was split up. Smith took six of the men to descend the river to the south, Fitzpatrick, Clyman, and two others remained to trap the upper reaches.

III

There is no direct record of the spring hunt made by the portion of the party under Jedediah Smith. He is presumed to have descended the Green at least as far as Black's Fork and spent the ensuing two months trapping that stream and adjacent waters (between present Evanston and Green River, Wyoming). After the departure of Smith's party, Fitzpatrick's small force of four men moved north up the Green, trapping as they went. Much of the time was probably spent in the general vicinity of Horse Creek.

They encountered, and camped with, a band of Indians from another tribe who called themselves Shoshones, later known as Snakes. (The sign language gesture for their tribe was an undulating motion of the hand, probably indicating that they lived by the twisty river. This was apparently interpreted as being a snakelike movement: Snakes they became, and still later the river, previously known as Lewis' Fork of the Columbia, became the Snake too. At the time of this narrative it was known occasionally as Lewis' Fork or Lewis' River; more often simply as the Columbia.)

These Indians were very friendly, possibly due to the fact that Fitzpatrick gave them beaver to eat. (Beaver tail was an Indian delicacy, though the trappers ate it only when they couldn't get anything else.) But eventually the congeniality came to an end, as all things must, and the Shoshones departed (with Fitzpatrick's horses).

The beaver hunting was good in this area; so good that apparently Fitzpatrick's party made out very well trapping on foot. It has been suggested that the trapping was so good the mountain men scarcely missed their horses, but the reality is probably much closer to Dale Morgan's version: they couldn't figure out in what direction they'd gone.

At the end of the hunt Fitzpatrick cached furs and goods and set out for the Sweetwater rendezvous on foot, apparently intending to come back when he had gotten replacement horses. As it happened, it wasn't necessary. On the first day of their march to rendezvous they ran head on into a group of half a dozen Indians on their stolen horses. Making a rather brave show considering the size of his force, Fitzpatrick forced the Shoshones to take the white party to their encampment, which consisted of six lodges about a mile away. There he recovered his horses, finding it necessary to take one of the Indians as hostage and threaten him with immediate execution if the final remaining horse were not delivered.

They picked up their cached goods and hastily departed the Snake country, back through South Pass and down the Sweetwater. They arrived late at the rendezvous, probably around the middle of June. Finding their cache of the previous March intact, Fitzpatrick correctly assumed that Smith was even later than himself, and settled down to wait. In the meantime, it might be just as well to scout down the Sweetwater a little farther; a decent water route back to St. Louis would be a godsend in this country.

He and Clyman rode some distance downstream, and it looked fairly possible. Leaving Clyman to go farther down and find a campsite, Fitz returned to pick up the furs, powder, and what not. While he was packing up, Smith and his party arrived with a good catch; their section of the Seedskeedee had been as rich as Fitzpatrick's.

There was very little point, they decided, in the return of the whole party. Why make a round trip to St. Louis when two or three men could get the pelts down, leaving the rest free to get an early start on the fall hunt?

A bullboat was the answer, and Fitzpatrick (with two others, Branch and Stone) undertook the job of taking the catch downriver. It was the first real success they'd had, and spirits must have been high. While Fitz started work on the bullboat, Smith rode downstream to pick up Clyman.

At the mouth of the North Platte, Smith found Clyman's shelter, with wood gathered for a fire but no sign that one had been built. He also found evidence of the reason why no fire had been built: the area was crisscrossed with horse tracks. A large Indian party; a great confusion of riding to and fro; and no Clyman. The conclusion was too easily drawn for comfort.

Smith went back and helped Fitzpatrick finish the bullboat, and the loss of the redoubtable Virginian must have weighed heavily on the whole party.

When Fitzpatrick went back after their goods, Clyman had continued downstream looking for a suitable camping place from which they could load and depart, not realizing that the melting snow would soon deepen the river enough to make departure feasible from their present camp. He found a spot that satisfied him near the mouth of a river that joined the

Sweetwater from the south, made a shelter in a clump of willows, and gathered driftwood for a fire.

Before he had got his fire going, he was startled by the approach of a mounted war party on the opposite bank. There were more than twenty Indians and perhaps thirty horses. They made their own camp almost opposite him, at which point Clyman decided it was time to be someplace else. He scuttled back away from the river until he was out of sight of the Indian party. He mounted a high ridge, and there settled down to keep watch on his uninvited guests.

In the middle of the night, as the band was on the point of decamping, two of their horses broke loose and swam across the river to Clyman's side. Almost ten of the Indians were finally involved in the chase, all riding about the area where Clyman's camp had been, but in the darkness and confusion of the horse chase they missed his track. At last the war party rode out of sight, and Clyman caught some sleep.

The next day he climbed the cliffs overlooking the canyon that in later days was known as Devil's Gate, and was appalled at the speed with which the river roared through the narrow gap. As he watched, another party of about twenty Indians appeared on the banks below, this batch on foot. They rafted their goods across to the other bank and moved off in the opposite direction from that of the previous party, again without spotting Clyman. (About this time Smith was at Clyman's previous camp, drawing his own melancholy conclusions from the sign he found.)

Clyman returned to the ridge from which he had watched the first war party and settled down to wait for Fitzpatrick's return, not knowing that Smith had gone back to report the good probability that Clyman's hair had been lifted. He waited on the ridge for eleven days, by his own testimony. On the twelfth day he started to walk back to civilization.

The story of his trek is another of the amazing evidences of what a mountain man down on his luck could accomplish. There is no space here to detail it, but he had somewhat better luck than Hugh Glass. (At one point Clyman's hopes were raised by finding an abandoned bullboat on a sand bar; perhaps his interpretation would have been different if he'd known that the bullboat was the one from which the displaced Rees had driven Hugh Glass.)

He starved and crawled and walked and fought his way across the better part of present Wyoming and all of Nebraska, finally arriving at Fort Atkinson sometime in the month of August, ragged and so weak that when he saw the American flag over the fort he "swoned emmediately." And when a man like Clyman swones, you know he's had some hard traveling.

Ten days at the fort, or thereabouts, and: "Mr Fitspatrick Mr Stone & Mr Brench arived in a more pitible state if possible than myself."

Fitzpatrick, too, had been having troubles; this was the season for unhappy men to be tramping down the Platte, it seemed. After all the arrangements had been made for meeting again, Fitzpatrick and the two others set out down the Sweetwater in their brand-new bullboat. This careened along swimmingly until Devil's Gate, where it naturally swamped and sank, with all the furs of a rich spring hunt aboard.

Somehow or other, the three miserable trappers managed to dive up most of them and get them dried out. They made a cache a few miles below Devil's Gate at the huge monument that became known to travelers on the Oregon Trail as Independence Rock. (Some say this cache was made on July 4; hence the name.) And then *they* started walking down the Platte for Fort Atkinson, arriving, as noted, about ten days after Clyman and in just as bad condition.

While regaining his strength at the fort, Fitzpatrick probably either wrote or relayed a report on the year's activities to Ashley in St. Louis. Then he borrowed some horses and returned to Independence Rock for the furs he had cached. By October 26, 1824, he was back at Fort Atkinson and had brought in the fur.

Ashley was by this time at Fort Atkinson, and he needed the good news; he hadn't had much that summer. First of all his true love—politics—had proved as fickle a mistress as her reputation. All spring and most of the summer he had conducted a campaign for governor of the state. And lost.

About the same time Ashley's political hopes were crushed (end of August) Major Henry appeared in St. Louis with news that nearly killed Ashley's hopes for the fur trade: Henry was bowing out, quitting, leaving the mountains. Except for the news of the rich trapping ground on Green River, things were not going well for the general. He was left without a field captain and would be forced to go into the mountains himself. His credit was now virtually nil, owing to the losses incurred in the previous two years. (Henry would also have brought the news of the robbery of the Yellowstone

cache and the death of six more men, four on the Yellowstone and two on the Missouri.) There was much talk going
on about his responsibilities and debts. So much talk that one
of his best friends felt obliged to write that he, for one,
stoutly believed Ashley "solvent & honest."

In the meantime the one man left in the field, Jedediah
Smith, had crossed the divide again and run head on into the
real giants of the fur trade. A company with 150 successful
years behind them instead of two miserably inadequate ones:
The Governor and Company of Adventurers of England
Tradeing into Hudsons Bay.

Known more simply as HBC; a description occasionally
decoded as Here Before Christ.

CHAPTER 6

"Whom I rather take to be spies"

WE HAVE no firsthand account of the movements of Henry's trappers in the summer of 1824. Clyman—the sole chronicler of this phase—was back at Fort Atkinson (or, more accurately, on his dreary way there). The account that follows is inferred from the impact made by this group on others; largely the journals and records of Alexander Ross, one of HBC's brigade leaders.

Apparently the trappers remaining in the mountains moved back to the Green River shortly after seeing Fitzpatrick off in his rickety bullboat. There they split up. Jedediah Smith himself, assuming more and more responsibility, took the smallest (and thus most hazardous) party. This consisted of six men besides himself; for his second-in-command he had Bill Sublette, now a ripe old twenty-five and beginning, like Smith, to show the fiber that would make him one of the most famous of the mountain men. The larger group, probably twenty-five men, was under Captain John Weber, and included Jim Bridger.[1] This means the Bighorn post, if manned at all, had only a skeleton crew.

The disposition and status of the third group operating that summer is not so clear. It was led by Etienne Provost, with his partner Leclerc. (There was a goodly swatch of Leclercs in the mountains from time to time, and we don't know certainly which one this was.) Provost's outfit seems to have been semiautonomous; in any event he wasn't directly connected with Ashley-Henry partnership, as were Smith and Weber. It may have been that Provost had made some kind of arrangement with the Ashley-Henry bunch for sale and transportation of his pelts back to St. Louis, thus making it unnecessary to weaken his own force. This later became, in the case of individuals, one of the standard procedures of the trade. The "free trapper," bounden to no company, made an arrangement in advance to sell his catch to a given company and was usually supplied by them for the year's hunt. In all probability this was how Provost was operating, though acting for his whole band rather than just himself. (There is also a possibility that, having entered the mountains from Taos by the southwest route, Provost had simply outfitted himself from Henry's party. However this may be, his fortunes and misfortunes are so closely linked with those of the Ashley enterprise that we must consider them jointly.)

Smith and his six men moved north up the Green, working the same area Tom Fitzpatrick had found so profitable in the spring. Sometime during the summer they crossed the ridge between the Green and the watershed of the Snake. (In some places the distance between the Green and streams that enter the Snake is less than five miles, not much obstacle for the trappers.) They moved slowly up the Snake and reportedly had cached 900 beaver by October. This is probably not true, but there is little doubt they were getting a lot of pelts. (One wonders about the quality, though. Much of this would have been summer beaver.)

In the meantime the might of the British Empire was approaching from the north, in the person of the HBC Snake Country Brigade under Alexander Ross. Ross is of considerable importance in the history of the trade, principally because of the books he wrote about it: *Adventures on the Oregon* (the Astoria venture), *Fur Hunters of the Far West* (with the Northwest Company and Hudson's Bay), *The Red River Settlement* (where he went when he retired). In his nonliterary capacity as brigade partisan he was not always up to beaver. He made errors of a rather remarkable obtuseness—one is coming up very shortly—and had what seems in retrospect a strangely beclouded vision of his own importance in the scheme of things.

Ross was not a happy man as he approached his historic meeting with Jedediah Smith. He had left Flathead House—a principal post of HBC, in western Montana—in the dead of winter with his brigade, which numbered about fifty-five. It consisted, according to Ross, of "two Americans, seventeen

Canadians, five half-breeds from the east side of the mountains, twelve Iroquois, two Abanakee Indians from Lower Canada, two natives from Lake Nepissing, one Saultman from Lake Huron, two Crees from Athabasca, one Chinook, two Spokanes, two Kouttanois, three Flatheads, two Callispellums, one Palooche, and one Snake slave. Five of the Canadians were above sixty years of age, and two were on the wrong side of seventy." There were also twenty-five women and sixty-four children, families of the married men.

Ross, very simply, couldn't handle this motley bunch. It is questionable whether anyone could have, though some did better than Ross with no better material. (But this was a constant problem of HBC; how to handle the unruly band of *engagés* and freemen they always had. Their Snake Country Expeditions were notorious for this.)

Ross had been nervous from the start. In April his journal notes sadly:

> Monday 19th. As we are on dangerous ground, I have drawn up the following rules.
> (1) All hands to raise camp together and by call.
> (2) The camp to march as close as possible.
> (3) No person to run ahead
> (4) No person to set traps till all hands camp
> (5) No person to sleep out of camp
> These rules which all agreed to were broken before night.

On top of this the spring hunt was not what it should have been. A May notation:

> Thursday 6th. On a rough calculation all the beaver in camp amount to 600 skins, one-tenth of our expected returns.

During the spring he had constant trouble keeping his Iroquois in line. Several times they had petitioned him to let them trap independently. Old Pierre Tevanitagon was the spokesman. His notion, as Ross recorded it, was that the large party was making it impossible for individuals to do much good. They were all deeply in debt to the company (the routine condition of HBC freemen) and saw no way to reduce it while traveling in such an ungainly body.

By what he considered adroit management, Ross managed to sidestep this issue until June. Several of the Iroquois deserted, however, and hoping to nip that sort of thing in the bud Ross pursued them. "[One] in particular would neither lead nor drive, and we threatened to drag him back at one of the horse tails before he consented to go. Back however we brought them." The next day they ran into a party of Nez Perces, and a couple of the Iroquois traded off their own guns. Ross notes a solemn piece of advice for brigade leaders: "Such improvident and thoughtless beings as Iroquois should always be restricted to their hunting implements: all the rest goes in traffic among the natives, to no purpose."

Finally, early in June, the harried bourgeois gave his consent, and a party of the Iroquois under Pierre Tevanitagon wandered off after being outfitted. Ross heard no more of them for four months, until October 14. He continued, and the trapping improved considerably. On the 14th, however, his journal entry reads:

Today Pierre and band arrived pillaged and destitute. . . . They passed the time with the Indians and neglected their hunts, quarreled with the Indians at last, were then robbed and left naked on the plains. The loss of twelve out of twenty trappers is no small consideration. With these vagabonds arrived seven American trappers from the Big Horn River but whom I rather take to be spies than trappers. . . . The quarter is swarming with trappers who next season are to penetrate the Snake country with a Major Henry at their head, the same gentleman who fifteen years ago wintered on Snake River. The report of these men on the price of beaver has a very great influence on our trappers. The seven trappers have in two different caches 900 beaver. I made them several propositions but they would not accept lower than $3 a pound. I did not consider myself authorized to arrange at such prices. [Ross was paying his own freemen 60 or 70 cents a pelt (about 1½ pounds) and that in merchandise at 70 per cent advance on prime cost.] The men accompanied us to the Flatheads. There is a leading person with them. They intend following us to the fort.

That last calm line—"They intend following us to the fort"—must have caused some hair-tearing when it was read by Ross's superiors.

The British were acutely aware of the impending American competition along the continental divide. Because the question of sovereignty in the Oregon country was so difficult to untangle, the governments had been obliged to defer any final decision at all. This they did by the joint-occupancy provision of the Convention of 1818, which involved the territory west of the Rockies between 42° and 49° latitude. This agreement was to expire in 1828. The British, however, were apprehensive about this provision; a great many Americans regarded the area as American in all but name and took a stiffly proprietary view toward British "interlopers." South of 42° was Spanish territory, but the nationality of what is now the American Northwest was unsettled.

The diplomatic situation was a touchy one; the commercial aspects scarcely less so. The Governor and Committee of HBC, writing from London as early as September, 1822, had expressed their alarm clearly. In a letter to the chief factors of the Columbia Department they enclosed an extract from an American paper stating that a party of 150 Americans had left the Missouri for an expedition in the direction of the Columbia. (This was the first Ashley-Henry party.) They had also heard there was some plan afoot by the Americans "to form a settlement at the Columbia," and called for information on these developments. The Governor and Committee closed with a none-too-gentle prod to the factors: "And we depend on your strenuous exertions to secure the Fur Trade to Great Britain."

As Governor of the area which included the Columbia Department, HBC had a man to whom strenuous exertions were a favorite form of relaxation. This was George Simpson, a peppery fireball of a man who never did understand why his people weren't as energetic as himself. Simpson had authorized the outfitting of the Snake Country Expedition under Ross, principally because he couldn't find anybody else. ("The Snake Country Expedition has hitherto been considered a forlorn hope the management of it the most hazardous and disagreeable office in the Indian Country—no volunteer could be found for it among the Commissioned Gentlemen.") This was in 1823, and Simpson made a very specific point that "Ross ... should be cautioned against opening a road for the Americans."

By the fall of 1824 it had become obvious that the Americans were steadily pushing west; the trapping parties reported in the joint-tenancy territory were only the beginning. They were, in the correct opinion of Simpson, the forerunners of settlements. If Americans should colonize the area, their claim to it would be so much the stronger and the chances were good that Great Britain would lose all rights. In an attempt to discourage American expansion across the Rockies, Simpson set forth a plan which reversed the usual HBC policy of trapping; he intended to destroy the Snake country as hunting ground. Where HBC tactics generally called for conservative trapping and employed intelligent principles of conservation, the Snake country was to be denuded of beaver. Then, if the British were evicted diplomatically, they would have the fur.

Simpson sets forth this idea in explicit terms in his journal (I quote this particular entry at length, because it also gives an interesting picture of Simpson's attitudes):

> [Referring to the employed freemen] ... when such a worthless and motley crew are collected together laying idle for Four Months on end they are forming plots and plans quarrelling with the natives and exposing themselves and us to much trouble and danger. This band of Freemen the very scum of the country and generally outcast from the Service for misconduct are the most unruly and troublesome gang to deal with in this or perhaps any other part of the World, are under no control & feel their own independence they therefore require very superior management to make anything of them but I regret to find that Mr Ross has not that talent and that his presence among them has been attended with little good.
>
> [Referring to the Snake country] If properly managed no question exists that it would yield handsome profits as we have convincing proof that the country is a rich preserve of beaver and which for political reasons we should endeavour to destroy as fast as possible.

Simpson then outlines a proposal to put the crack partisan Peter Skene Ogden in charge of the Snake Brigade, and wipe out the country as a source of fur.

Simpson was too late, by about two weeks. As he made that entry on October 28, the Americans were being given a guided tour through the rich country on the west slope of the Rockies, courtesy of Alexander Ross.

II

The seven Americans who brought Pierre Tevanitagon home were, of course, Jedediah Smith and his trappers. Encountering the "pillaged and destitute" Iroquois somewhere near present Pocatello, Idaho, Jedediah made some kind of bargain with them. (He told Ross it involved the exchange of 105 beaver for an escort back to Ross's party.) Pierre, on the other hand, had a story of being robbed by a war party of Snakes, losing 900 beaver (!), 54 steel traps, 27 horses, 5 guns, and most of their clothing. He made no mention of paying in beaver for the escort of the Americans.

This difference in stories eventually led Ross to conclude that Pierre and party had been seduced by promises of high prices from the American company and had left their furs *en cache* with those of Smith. The more likely version is that of Smith: that the Iroquois, being in hostile territory, had offered the beaver for armed protection.

We will never know what possessed Ross to accept the company of Smith and his men on the return trip to Flathead House. It was certainly in direct contradiction to his orders. While the phrase "opening a road for the Americans" was probably intended metaphorically, Ross made a literal reality of it. On their return trip Smith got the first American look at the Snake country and the operations of HBC there. He also had ample time during his month's sojourn at Flathead House to make a thorough inspection of the British system of trading with northwest tribes.

It was a windfall for the American trappers, the kind of good fortune one could not rightly expect.

The Snake Country Brigade, together with its interested American observers, arrived back at its home base on November 26, 1824. A few hours before they came in, Peter Skene Ogden had arrived to take over command of the field party for HBC. Ross, rather typically, chose to regard this as promotion for himself; at any rate his journal notes it thus: "Mr Ogden handed me a letter from the Governor appointing me in charge of this place for the winter. Mr Ogden takes my place as chief of the Snake expedition."

That Simpson was not concerned with the promotion of Ross is fairly well established by his own journal comments on the management of the Snake operation:

> ... This important duty should not in my opinion be left to a self sufficient empty headed man like Ross who feels no further interest therein than in as far as it secures to him a Sal^y of £120 p Annum and whose reports are so full of bombast and marvellous non-sense that it is impossible to get at any information that can be depended upon from him.

Thus the judgment on the man of letters by the man of action.

After separating from Smith in early summer, the main body of American trappers moved in the opposite direction, that is, south, following the Green River downstream. Sometime in the late summer they crossed over into the valley of the Bear River and made the principal part of their fall hunt on the Bear and its tributaries. (During this fall there occurred a minor drama, of which we know only through a curt report made several years later. In the official list of "Deaths of men caused by accidents and other causes not chargeable to Indians," Smith notes briefly: "1824 Thomas, a half breed was killed by Williams, on the waters of Bear river, west of the mountains.")

Where Captain Weber's party reached it, the Bear is flowing almost due north (exactly opposite to the Green, which they had just left). It flows north past Bear Lake, makes a hairpin turn around the northern end of the Bear River Range, and changes its direction of flow to south. By the time they made camp for the winter Weber's party was on this south-flowing stretch, known as Câche Valley. (Early references sometimes call it Willow Valley, but this name quickly lost currency.) During this winter camp another man—one Marshall—was lost, "not chargeable to Indians."

Tradition has it that the perverse flow of the Bear led to a dispute among the trappers that winter, which is quite likely. The winter camp offered time enough for arguing, and geography, after all, was in many ways the livelihood of the mountain man. In order to settle a bet, Jim Bridger with an anonymous companion was dispatched to find out where the river led.

He returned from the expedition with the somewhat unlike-ly advisement that the Bear River flowed directly into the Pacific Ocean. The water, Bridger claimed, was salt, and furthermore no end to the vast expanse could be seen. Thus, to settle a bet among the mountain men, the Great Salt Lake was discovered. In the next year or so this general area was to be thoroughly traveled, both by the Americans and the Ogden-vitalized Snake Country Brigade, but at the moment it was new, and this vast expanse of salt water must have caused some little confusion in the geographic ideas of Weber's trappers.

While there is no space here for a full discussion of the contemporary notions of western geography, a few major points may be mentioned.[2]

Reports of a huge lake in the Great Basin had led to the inclusion of such a lake on maps of the period. Generally called Laguna de Timpanogos, this was (according to Morgan) a cartographers' combination of Utah Lake—reported by two Franciscan friars in 1776—and the Indian rumors of Great Salt Lake. To the mapmakers it seemed reasonable and necessary that such a large body of water should have a direct outlet to the Pacific Ocean, so they gave it one. This outlet, Rio Timpanogos, theoretically emptied into San Francisco Bay.

The Mulnomah River (present Willamette) was consistently overestimated by early cartographers. Almost invariably they show this river as giving access far into the interior of the continent, which it does not.

One other mythical river had considerable importance, the Buenaventura. (The name was also given to the Sacramento-San Joaquin.) This ran south of Rio Timpanogos and parallel to it, having its headwaters along the continental divide with the Snake, Rio Grande, Bighorn, and Arkansas. The Buenaventura also emptied directly into the Pacific, and along its length (somewhere) was another large lake variously called Buenaventura or Salado; probably another confusion of reports of the Great Salt Lake.

From this it may be seen what the mountain men expected to find on the west slope; any one of several rivers that emptied directly into the Pacific or, in the case of the Multnomah, into the Columbia and thence to the Pacific. The Green River, Seedskeedee, might be either the upper portion of the Rio Colorado of the West (which is correct) or the Buenaventura.

To the modern reader, with present-day maps, these points may be assessed as quaint, archaic little errors. But it should be remembered that geography and physiography were of more than academic interest to the fur traders; they were, without exaggeration, matters of life and death. With modern forms of transportation we have become more or less independent of geography; unless it happens to be of scenic interest, we virtually ignore it. But the establishment of accurate ideas of tributary systems and watersheds was of vital importance to the mountain men. Generally speaking, particularly in the thirties and forties, the available maps were of virtually no use to a trapper; the head of any given individual contained more accurate geography than all the universities in the world. Those who survived knew the country; it was as simple as that. This is one of the reasons so many superannuated mountain men were used as guides, both by the government and by immigrant trains, in the years following the decline of the trade. Some of the men who were, in the own minds, chiefly trappers, achieved their national reputations through their strictly geographic feats as guides. Jim Bridger, for one, and Tom Fitzpatrick and Old Bill Williams; the latter two served as guides for the famous Frémont explorations. The best known, of course, was Kit Carson, another trapper whose later service as guide and scout immortalized him. Beginning with the movements of the Ashley-Henry parties, the mountain men came to have a conception of western geography that was not overtaken by the cartographers for another fifty years or so.

But this knowledge was also one of the tools of the trade, and as such it was not bandied about lightly. If a company had a Jim Bridger on the payroll, the maps he carried in his mind were of inestimable value in plain dollars and cents. There was a good deal of understandable reluctance to provide accurate information to competing companies, and a stock of special knowledge was quite likely to be hoarded as carefully as the location of a fur cache.

Inroads into the still "semimythical" area had been made that year from three separate directions (if, as seems most probable, Etienne Provost had started from Taos).

The HBC Snake Country Brigade worked down the west slope of the continental divide, while on the other side (though not at the same time) Major Henry's men from the now-defunct Bighorn post examined the Bighorn basin. Both of these parties came from the north, working in a general southerly direction. Smith and Fitzpatrick reached the area from due east. From the Spanish settlement of Taos, Etienne Provost's band came up through the Uinta Mountains.

Since a normal corollary of trapping operations was the sending of small exploratory parties at tangents along the route, this three-pronged assault on the Rockies very quickly made the general geographical features known.

This vicinity—Western Wyoming and the adjacent regions of Idaho and Colorado—became the pivot of the trade, and so remained for two decades. From the early twenties to the early forties was the Golden Age of the American Fur Trade, and this territory was central to it.

It was also the pivot around which revolved the sensitive relations between the United States and Great Britain, though there's an ironic cast to the consideration of Peter Skene Ogden and Jedediah Smith as ministers without portfolio.

III

At the Flathead post Ogden whipped a brigade into shape in quick order; by the third week in December, 1824, he was ready to leave.

Ogden was, in many ways, the epitome of the brigade leader. Tough, competent, an extremely effective leader who commanded respect from the wildest of the freemen. (And with Ogden the cliché "commanded respect" takes on a very literal signification. In a journal entry for a later year he laconically notes that a potential deserter had "for his impudence received a drubbing from me" which settled the problem neatly.)

Ogden's superior, George Simpson, kept a private "Character Book," in which his opinions of his subordinates were set forth with pleasant frankness. Simpson's estimate of Ogden included:

> A keen, sharp, off hand fellow of superior abilities to most of his colleagues, very handy and active and not sparing of his personal labour. Has had the benefit of a good plain Education, both writes and speaks tolerably well, and has the address of a man who has

mixed a good deal in the World. Has been very Wild
& thoughtless and is still fond of coarse practical
jokes, but with all this appearance of thoughtlessness
he is a very cool calculating fellow who is capable of
doing anything to gain his own ends. His ambition
knows no bounds and his conduct and actions are not
influenced or governed by any good or honorable
principle. In fact, I consider him one of the most
unprincipled men in the Indian Country, who would
soon get into habits of dissipation if he were not
restrained by the fear of their operating against his
interests, and if he does indulge in that way madness
to which he has a predisposition will follow as a
matter of course ... likely to be exceedingly troublesome if advanced to the 1st Class as the Trade is
now constituted, but his Services have been so conspicuous for several years past, that I think he has strong
claims to advancement.

(It should be remembered that Simpson now and again
used the private "Character Book" to vent himself of a bit of
spleen. The casual confidence with which he asserts Ogden's
predisposition to madness—in the event of dissipation only,
of course—is really quite remarkable. But then Simpson was,
in his own way, quite a remarkable personage.)

Ogden departed Flathead post on December 20, 1824,
with what that post's brand-new factor Ross called "the most
formidable party that ever set out for the Snakes" (though it
consisted of fifty-eight men, only three more than Ross's own
party). Twelve of these were *engagés,* the rest freemen. Not
noted in Ogden's own compilation were his seven tag-alongs,
the American party under Smith. For some reason Ogden
chooses to ignore the Americans entirely, until well into the
spring of 1825; his journal contains no reference to them
until April 8, just before they were ready to separate.

Smith and his party remained behind when Ogden's
brigade set out, and did not join him until December 29.
Since Ogden's own journal (which was obligatory for a
brigade partisan and intended for the eyes of his superiors)
does not comment on their arrival, we rely for this information on the voluntary notations of Ogden's clerk, one William
Kittson.[3]

By the end of the year the brigade was just west of

Hellgate, the narrow canyon near present Missoula through which Clark's Fork flows. Said Ogden, reviewing:

> This ends 1824 & I shall only remark amongst the many Changes that have taken place none is less pleasing to me than the one I have experienced from a State of independency to *one* the very reverse.

Apparently the new-found responsibility of brigade partisan was not completely congenial to the lover of "coarse practical jokes."

The new year was seen in with considerable restraint for a trapping party. Ogden: "Bright & early all the Freemen paid me their respects in return they received my best Wishes for a good hunt & a long life. [The hunters brought deer] which enabled us to feast & be merry all quiet." Which Kittson amplifies: "They had no liquor to make them troublesome."

The British brigade moved south, following almost the same route Ross's returning party had taken the previous fall. Among other delays due to natural causes, the party had to stop twice for children to be born among the Indian women who were accompanying their husbands, legal or pro tem.

By the middle of January they were in the Big Hole Prairie, and Ogden was giving thought to the fact that they were "now in the Black feet Country of Wars & Murders [and] we must regulate our progress by the encampments we may find suitable for defense."

The first casualty had in fact already occurred, but it couldn't be attributed to the Blackfeet. Kittson's journal, entry for January 13:

> During the night a dispute took place between a Nez Perces and his wife, he struck her a blow with the but end of his gun on the head, she fell, and he thinking that she was dead, shot himself though the breast, he died soon after and the woman came to life. Traded a horse on that account in order to sacrifice some things to his memory.

On the 6th of February an Iroquois named Louis Kanitagan was accidentally shot and killed by his wife, causing

Ogden to remark with foreboding that "there is Certainly a fatality attending the Snake Country & all Snake Expeditions."

They crossed Lemhi Pass on the 11th of February, working down into the Lemhi valley. Normally this would be entering the final lap of their trip—"not more than Eight encampments" from the valley of the Snake. Here, however, Ogden decided to strengthen his horses in preparation for the "well known poverty of the [Snake] Country in grass."

There were buffalo in plenty in the valley, which made it a paradise for the freemen. Nothing appealed to the freemen so much as a good buffalo run, and they would desert traps, company, wife, children, and hope of redemption in the hereafter to chase a herd down. "The freemen in their glory in pursuit of Buffalo," says Ogden, ". . . many killed this day not less than 30 but not more than 300 wt. of meat Came in to Camp, the temptation of running Buffalo is too great for them to resist."

But what started as an intentional pause turned into something less to be desired—an enforced encampment. For the next six weeks the brigade moved by fits and starts across the Lemhi valley. The grass gave out and the horses, rather than gaining strength, rapidly weakened and began to die. Bitter winter weather kept them from crossing the passes out of the valley, and the scouting parties sent out to find their way could not plow through the heavy snows.

The freemen continued to run buffalo on their weakening horses, and between runs importuned Ogden to turn back. Blackfoot sign was seen around them in the mountains, and several encounters with war parties—one of them numbering sixty braves—kept the trappers on their toes.

By March 18 Smith and his six men had decided they could make better progress on their own, and Kittson's journal notes their intention "to leave us tomorrow and try to make their way to the snake river." The next day:

> The Americans traded some ammunition and Tobacco from us for Beaver at the same price as our freemen. About noon they left us well satisfied I hope with the care and Attention we paid them. For since we had them with us no one in our party ever took any advantadge of or ill treated them. One Jedidiah S. Smith is at the head of them, a sly cunning Yankey.

The departure of the American party went unremarked in Ogden's own journal, though he is suddenly moved: "I feel So anxious to proceed that I shall again Send a party to examine another Defile." Contemplating the possibility that they would be forced to return to the Flathead post without even having made a spring hunt, Ogden's frequent pessimism shows in his journal entry:

> how Cruelly mortifying after spending the winter in this dreary Country to loose the main object of our voyage when almost within reach of it, the Severe Winter the poverty of the Country in grass & my ignorance of the Country are the principal reasons for this failure.

Ogden then sent the clerk Kittson to see if he could find a way out of their imprisonment, but he was driven back to the camp by a party of some thirty Indians. Though Ogden's journal makes no mention of it, Kittson was also instructed to find, if he could, which way the Americans had gone. They had made a better choice of route than he, Kittson found, noting that their track was "to the Southward of our way."

Finally, on the 25th, Ogden's party got across the defile separating the waters of the Salmon River from those of the John Day River.

Ogden camped beside the John Day and sent out the Iroquois John Gray to find their way.[4] Gray returned to report that the snow made all trails impassable. Ogden very rightly concluded that "there is no dependence to be placed on the free men . . . the greater part do not appear over anxious to reach a Beaver Country or they would act differently."

He sent out Kittson again, and the doughty clerk's report was quite the reverse: the passes were negotiable. They raised camp again and on March 30 passed the site of a recent American camp (again unrecorded by Ogden). Another week went by in which Kittson occasionally remarks on passing the trail of the Smith party.

At last, on April 7, Ogden caught up with the Americans where they were in camp. The next day his journal acknowledges their existence for the first time on the trip; the occasion was worthy of note because it represented something of a victory for Ogden:

The seven Americans who joined Mr. Ross last Summer & accompanied him to the Flat Heads & have been since with us ... requested to trade & 'tho they found the prices high   say the Freemens Tariff but being in Want they were obliged to Comply & traded 100 Lar. & Sm. Beaver   this is some recompence for the Beaver they traded with our party last Summer.

Some recompense, indeed; HBC made a very neat profit, in fact, since the pelts were undoubtedly traded for ammunition at the customary 70 per cent advance on prime cost and Ogden would certainly have allowed well under a dollar apiece for them. This must have hurt; those skins were worth —to the Americans—around $3 apiece in the mountains and probably $5 in St. Louis. But Smith had been away from his own sources of supply ever since June, almost a year. His need was probably quite desperate.

In this transaction with Smith Ogden came out comfortably ahead; Smith had gotten 105 pelts from Ross's Iroquois and been forced to part with 100 of them. The exaggerated markup on trading goods would have ensured that a profit accrued to the company.[5]

Owing to the fact that the Ogden journals weren't published until quite recently, historians have made rather a large thing of Smith's earlier transaction with the Iroquois. It is, in fact, one of the classic anecdotes of the trade. But here we see that in reality HBC had well made up for this loss within a year. (Smith had also been forced to trade off some beaver at the Flathead post.) Rather than being victimized by the unprincipled American trappers (which has been the character given by students to this whole episode), HBC rather primly victimized them. It must be admitted that this was their general business practice with respect to their own freemen, so perhaps victimization is not the proper word. Still, the day was not far off when even the profit-minded George Simpson would be forced to admit their relations with the freemen were not of the best.

The next day Ogden was reminded that he had other problems than the Americans. Antoine Benoit was caught out by a party of forty Bloods. His companions found him on the 10th "naked, Scalp taken a Ball in the body one in the head & three Stabs with a knife ... he could not have Suffered long."

Ogden is now on the Blackfoot River, one of the direct tributaries of the Snake. After burying Benoit, he moved:

> ... 10 miles due East ... & encamped on a fine Spot for defence ... the Free men started with 100 Traps but they had not been absent an hour when two Came back full Speed Calling out Black Feet ... a party of 30 well Armed Started in pursuit of the Villains with orders to spare None but in the evening they all re-turned it proving to be a false report, for it proved to be the American party who had left us in the Night ...

Smith and his men hadn't been able to find a suitable spot to ford the river and so had changed their course, and precipitated a minor panic in the British camp. Ruefully Ogden notes "in Consequence of this false alarm [we have] but few traps in the Water."

For the next week the British and American parties played a game of mountain leapfrog, passing each other and being passed. Finally they separated for good on April 18; the Americans, according to Kittson, going back "to take the other route."

Late April brought Ogden's party to the Bear River, the very heart of the Snake country. The failures he feared had not materialized, and prospects were good for the spring hunt. Also, it looked a though he was rid of the Americans for good, since they were going the opposite direction, ascending the Bear as Ogden moved downstream. Though he makes little mention of it in his journal, Smith's presence was disturbing the British partisan. Enough so that he had detached a party of fifteen freemen in the middle of April to range ahead, trying to prevent Smith and his men from skimming the cream ahead of him.

Unhappy Mr. Ogden; on May 4th he was informed by seven Snakes that "a party of 25 Americans wintered near this & are gone in the same direction we had intended going if this be true which I have no reason to doubt it will be a fatal blow to our expectations."

This was Weber's party, who, having wintered in Cache Valley were now bestirring themselves about the spring hunt. As yet, Ogden had no idea of how many American trapping parties had reached the Snake country ahead of him. The worst of his anticipation was that the beaver would be scarce, and even this he considered a "fatal blow."

One wonders what his journal entry would have been if he had been able to see a few weeks into the future. Peter Skene Ogden was on the verge of the most humiliating experience of his career, one which drew him sharp reprimands from his superiors, embarrassed the British Empire, and caused the monolithic HBC to backpedal furiously.

He had three weeks of grace; then, on May 22, he was startled by the appearance of two of the deserters from a Snake Expedition of 1821. The next day, Monday, Kittson records the opening curtain:

> In the Afternoon Jack McLeod and Lazard the two Deserters came up to us with their camp consisting of besides them, 3 Canadians, a Russian, and an old Spaniard. This party under the Command of one Provost . . .

CHAPTER 7

"Do you know in whose Country you are?"

IN THE fall of '24 Etienne Provost had (probably) worked up the Strawberry River and across the Wasatch Range into the Great Basin. The latter part of his fall hunt was made on the Provo River, and by wintering time he had reached the valley of Great Salt Lake. While trapping a river subsequently identified as the Jordan he met a party of Snakes under the famous chief Mauvais Gauche (variously known in the trade by the English as Bad Left Hand, or by the bilingual compromise Bad Gocha).

After initial friendly overtures, the Shoshone chief induced Provost's men to lay aside their arms—claiming his medicine forbade him to smoke in the presence of metal objects. (The mountain men would have been respectful of any man's medicine.) It was simple treachery, and seven of Provost's men were killed in the attack that followed.

Provost's movements following this defeat are not certain, but by the spring of 1825 he was back in the Salt Lake area, probably with a new outfit from his partner, Leclerc, and a new batch of trappers to replace those lost to Mauvais Gauche.

On May 22 two of Provost's trappers had encountered an HBC freeman in the canyon of the Weber River and accompanied him to Ogden's camp. As it happened, the two were former employees of that esteemed organization themselves: Jack McLeod and the Iroquois Lazard Teycateyecowige. Having deserted HBC in 1822, McLeod, Lazard, and twelve others—most Iroquois—had made their way eastward, all the

102

way to St. Louis, where they drifted off with one trapping party or another.

McLeod and Lazard happened to be with Provost; arriving back in the mountains via Taos—and after three years—they had made full circle of a rather remarkable trip. Now they were happily reunited with their old family HBC, and what could be more natural than a little lying to liven up the occasion?

Such as the fact, noted by Ogden, that they were "15 days march from the Spanish Village," which was more fuel for the partisan's apprehension. (The "Spainish Village" meant Taos, which, though in Spanish territory, was already the place of outfitting and departure for American parties trapping the Southern Rockies.)

Flathead post was five full months of hard traveling behind, and if the Americans could reach this country in two weeks . . .

One of the two deserters promised to stay with HBC, and the other promised to pay his debt, which was at least an amiable gesture even if it wasn't strictly sincere. McLeod and Lazard departed on this friendly note, and hightailed it back to Provost's camp with the news.

The next morning Provost's entire party appeared at the British encampment. This was trouble enough for Ogden, but it was soon overshadowed by the arrival of the principal antagonists in the coming drama: "also in the afternoon arrived in Company with 14 of our absent men a party of 25 Americans with Colours flying the latter party headed by one Gardner."

II

Johnson Gardner appears spasmodically in the literature of the trade as a free trapper. (Strictly speaking, the caste system among American trappers—including "free trapper" at the top—had not yet developed; the term is not current, and is used here as a convenient description.) This year of 1825 he had some definite connection with Ashley, and had probably wintered with the Weber party. His appearance in Ogden's camp "with Colours flying" marks the first direct conflict of American and British trappers west of the divide. (Ogden's expression was quite literal; the party was conspicuously displaying a large American flag, though God knows where it had come from. Such was not standard equipment in the trade, though it did become more frequent later.)

After Jedediah Smith had separated from Ogden's party he somehow heard of the wintering party of Americans in Cache Valley. While the British brigade was trapping down the tributaries of the Bear, Smith found the Weber party and doubtless reported of his stay at the Flathead post.

In a fine burst of enthusiastic patriotism quite remarkable for men whose trade was based on a violation of federal law, Gardner and his party proceeded to Ogden's camp, about eight miles from their own. He raised his own camp a hundred yards from the British and set Old Glory to fluttering bravely in the face, metaphorically speaking, of HBC.

Gardner then entered the British camp and delivered a short speech touching on the various aspects of monarchy and democracy, and pointing out some of the advantages of the latter. Further, he informed his interested listeners that they were now in the United States territories. As a consequence of this fact, every man among them was quite free, whether indebted or engaged.

". . . & to add to this," says Ogden, "they would pay Cash for their Beaver 3½ dollars p. lb., & their goods cheap in proportion." Which may have been more to the point than the questions of freedom and geography.

Kittson adds Gardner's statement that

> whomsoever wished to go with him they were welcome. No man would dare oppose the measures they would take, he and his party were ready to stand by, any that wished to Desert Mr Ogden, Free or Engaged men were the same in this land of Liberty, and night coming on no more was said. Strick watch set for the night. Fair weather.

The next day Ogden's journal records:

> *Tuesday 24th.*—This morning Gardner came to my Tent & after a few words of no import, he questioned me as follows Do you know in whose Country you are? to which I made answer that I did not as it was not determined between Great Britain & America to whom it belonged, to which he made answer that it was that it had been ceded to the latter & as I had no license to trap or trade to return from

whence I came to this I made answer when we receive orders from the British Government we Shall obey, then he replied remain at your peril.

On this threatening note Gardner left Ogden's tent. However, instead of returning to his own camp, he walked over to the tent of the Iroquois John Gray. Seeing this, Ogden hastily followed.

The argument that followed took place mostly between Ogden and the Iroquois. Gardner contented himself with observing that "you have had these men already too long in your Service & have most Shamefully imposed on them selling them goods at high prices and giving them nothing for their Skins on which he retired."

Gray—Ross had described him the year before as "a turbulent black guard, a damned rascal"—then launched into a denunciation of the policies of HBC in general and the men of the Columbia Department in particular: ". . . the greatest Villains in the World & if they were here this day I would shoot them . . ."

He excepted Ogden himself from this denunciation, saying he had always treated his men fairly. However, he and all the rest of the Iroquois were leaving, "& all you Can Say Cannot prevent us . . . & if every man in the Camp does not leave you they do not Seek their own interest."

Gray then ordered his own lodge-mates to break camp. His example "was soon followed by others at this time the Americans . . . advanced to Support & assist all who were inclined to desert."

The Iroquois were striking their lodges quickly and the situation was getting out of hand. A potential deserter named Lazard "Called out we are Superior in numbers to them let us fire & pillage them."

At this he advanced on Ogden with his gun cocked and aimed. However, Peter Skene Ogden was not a man to be intimidated so easily. Having given up the vain hope of trying to prevent the Iroquois themselves from leaving, Ogden was furiously battling to prevent them from taking his horses. Lazard's threat failed to scare the partisans, and the deserter backed off.

Ogden was shortly joined by Kittson and McKay. They called for help to the *engagés,* and two of them reluctantly came. These five managed to secure the threatened horses "not without enduring the most opprobious terms they could think of from both Americans & Iroquois." There was a brief scuffle between Ogden and Old Pierre Tevanitagon about two horses which had been loaned to Pierre, and which Ogden wanted back. The Americans and Iroquois, of course, cheered Pierre on. One of the horses was returned, and the other paid for.

The Iroquois finally departed with their lodges and furs (amounting, according to Ogden's later report, to about seven hundred skins). The deserters (the spellings are from Kittson's journal):

Alexander Carson	Ignace Hatchiorauquasha
Charles Duford	(John Gray)
Martin Miaquin	Laurent Karahouton
Pierre Tevanitagon	Baptise Sawenrego
Jacques Osteaceroko	Lazard Kayenquaretcha
Ignace Deohdiouwassere	Joseph Perreault
	Louis Kanota

Alexander Carson was one of three who paid their debts to the company before leaving, but to compensate for this he stole a horse belonging to one of the remaining loyal freemen. Ogden dispatched Charles McKay to bring it back.[1] This almost precipitated another shooting. John Gray "wanted to fire at him, but on McKay's turning to face him he soon got quiet." McKay got back with the horse.

Ogden then put his camp into position for defense, having been informed (source unstated) that the Iroquois and Americans "intend to attack & pillage the Camp." He talked with his men and found those remaining "would assist in defending the Company's property in Case of attack."

A double watch was set, and on top of the rumors of attack came another wave saying more of the freemen were intending to desert. This was substantiated the next morning when five more men announced their intention of joining the Americans (including the man whose horse had been recovered for him by McKay). These new converts were Annance, Montour, Antoine Clement, Prudhomme, and Sansfacon.

Gardner showed up in camp again to offer a helping hand, accompanied by a mixed group of Americans and Iroquois. There was a brief flare-up between Gardner and Kittson, occasioned when the HBC man refused to permit Sansfacon to take horse and beaver.

Gardner immediately turns to me [Kittson] saying
Sir I think you speak too bravely you better take care
or I will soon settle your business. well says I you
seem to look for Blood do your worst and make it a
point of dispute between our two Governments. One
thing I have to say is, that you had better begin the
threats you so often make use of.

Gardner did not, however. The five men left, and Ogden
hastily decamped after absorbing Gardner's prediction that
HBC "will see us shortly not only in the Columbia but at the
Flat Heads and Cootanies as we are determined you shall no
longer remain in our Territory."

Ogden made his by-now familiar reply: that HBC would
leave the Columbia when so ordered by their government
and not before. He turned north and backtracked along
his incoming route, finally making camp on their previous
site of the 19th. It was an ignominious departure for the great
Ogden, and his journal, made out that night, reflects his
profound discouragement:

here I am now with only 20 Trappers Surrounded on
all Sides by enemies & our expectations & hopes
blasted for returns this year, to remain in this quarter
any longer it would merely be to trap Beaver for the
Americans for I Seriously apprehend there are still
more of the Trappers who would Willingly join them
indeed the tempting offers made them independant
the low price they Sell their goods are too great for
them to resist & altho' I represented to them all these
offers were held out to them as so many baits Still it
is without effect.

The memory of this defeat would hang over Ogden for
several years, filling him with a sense of foreboding every time
there was an American trapping party within a hundred miles
of him. A preliminary report to his superiors (written while
still in the Snake country) sums up all his feelings:
". . . that damn'd all cursed day that Mr. Ross consented to
bring the 7 Americans with him to the Flat heads."

In view of the geographical claims so freely bandied about
in this affair and the fact that much of the action revolved
around the question of territoriality, one fact is worthy

of note: neither of the gentlemen had the faintest legal right to be where they were. They were both in flagrant trespass on Spanish Territory, being somewhat below the 42nd parallel at the time.

III

Andrew Henry's return to St. Louis in August, 1824, had presented General Ashley with a serious problem. Henry's retirement left the whole conduct of the operation to Ashley, and it was an operation he was not particularly well suited to manage.[2] The general was in his element in cosmopolitan St. Louis; he had no love for the mountains and never, in the entire course of his operations, did he display any great degree of talent in field operations. This is not to his discredit; he was aware of his own shortcomings and made every effort to compensate for them by engaging as principal partners men who were fitted to handle that aspect of the trade in which Ashley himself had no interest.

The typical mountain man was a dealer-with-places; it was a temperamental predisposition absolutely necessary to his trade. Ashley, on the other hand, was a dealer-with-people; creditors and politicians and Indian agents and the like. It was what he enjoyed and what he was good at. The two types are oriented to the world around them in wholly different ways. In combination they could make of the fur trade a relatively efficient operation; either one alone was quite ineffective.

Eventually the two halves of the trade—the mountain and the city—became almost completely separated. This was the unique characteristic of American operations. The intermediary was the supply company, which outfitted trappers at the annual rendezvous and took their pelts in exchange. (And, in the process, took most of the profit ever made in the American trade.)

But in the fall of 1824 General Ashley had no choice but to assume control of the mountain end as well as his own more congenial duties. He had a party of trappers depending on him for supplies and there was nothing for it but to take them himself. The emergency was comparable to that of supplying Henry's Yellowstone post two years before. Then, too, Ashley had been forced to take charge of a supply party, on that occasion running headlong into the Aricaras.

This time his nemesis was to be geography rather than Indians, for he set out to make a winter crossing overland.

His new license was issued on September 24. (This, of course, gave him no more right to trap than had any previous one; it was strictly for purposes of trading with the Indians. The government was still making desperate efforts to regulate the fur hunters and prevent the chaos their activities were making of Indian relations. It was beginning to be obvious that the abandonment of the factory system had been an error of serious dimensions. The government efforts bothered nobody, however.)

By October 21, 1824, Ashley had outfitted a party and was at Fort Atkinson. On the 26th Tom Fitzpatrick and his small party arrived, having successfully recovered the furs left in the câche near Independence Rock. Ashley remained at Fort Atkinson another week, hoping Henry would change his mind and lead the supply party back into the mountains, but Henry's decision was final. Ashley was also somewhat apprehensive about the mood of the Indians along his course; there was some difficulty between Major O'Fallon, the Indian agent at Fort Atkinson, and a band of Pawnees, which the general hoped would be settled before he left. To a friend Ashley wrote on the 29th:

> These are matters of much importance to me, but there is little, or no probability of my wishes in either case being realized. I shall therefore have to accompany my party of Mountaineers to their place of destination.

Ashley sent the party off on November 3, himself remaining behind and overtaking it two days later. Fitzpatrick and Jim Clyman were there, and there were some new names that would become well known. Zacharias Ham, competent and experienced, was to lead one of the parties that separated later, putting him on a level with Fitzpatrick and Clyman. Robert Campbell, twenty years old, was with the party on advice of his physicians. This tubercular young man completely recovered his health and became one of the major figures of a later phase of the trade.

Also on Ashley's roster was a young mixed-blood named Jim Beckwith. Jim later suffered a mountain change—into something rich and strange; namely, James P. Beckwourth. This was when he was dictating his autobiography to an attentive amanuensis, T. D. Bonner. (This highly controversial document, *The Life and Adventures of James P. Beckwourth,* redounds very highly to the credit of James P. Beckwourth, making him the hero of every Indian battle and every dramatic rescue that ever happened in the mountains and quite a number that didn't. Jim was a great liar. Even the ordinarily charitable Chittenden says that "there is probably not a single statement in it that is correct as given." This is a just criticism, so far as Jim's heroics are concerned. Once in a while, however, Jim's attention seems to have wandered and there are several passages in the book that do not deal with Beckwourth-as-demigod. These check out very well with other sources.)

his
At the moment he is plain Jim X Beckwith, blacksmith, but
mark
in deference to his later dignity, he shall be known henceforth by the full style.

The whole party consisted of about twenty-five men, fifty pack horses, "a wagon and teams, etc." This wagon would have been an important one historically if we knew anything about it. This was the first attempt to take a wheeled vehicle across the divide, and was probably made by virtue of the information brought back by Henry and/or Fitzpatrick on the easy crossing at South Pass. Unfortunately, there is not a single further mention of the wagon in Ashley's own narrative, and we don't know what became of it.

The route and adventures of this supply party have been admirably detailed elsewhere (notably in Harrison Dale, *The Ashley-Smith Explorations*), and this account will be brief.[3]

The trip began miserably. Within a week the party was suffering from the weather and want of food; Beckwourth records the ration as a half pint of flour per day per man. (If this seems strange to a modern reader, it must be remembered that provisioning of these parties was customarily a day-to-day process; and any given day's bad hunting meant short rations.) Ashley had left Fort Atkinson "under a belief that I could procure a sufficient supply of provisions at the Pawney villages to subsist my men until we could reach a point affording a sufficiency of game."

Unfortunately, the Pawnees had deserted their villages two or three weeks earlier, moving up the Platte for their wintering grounds. Without these expected provisions, Ashley was forced to feed his men on horse meat and his horse meat on cottonwood bark.

It had begun to snow the day after the general joined his party, and after two days "with but little intermission" the ground was covered two feet deep.

> In this situation we continued for about the space of two weeks, during which time we made frequent attempts to advance and reach a point of relief, but, owing to the intense cold and violence of the winds, blowing the snow in every direction, we had only succeeded in advancing some ten or twelve miles ... cold and hunger had by this time killed several of my horses, and many others were much reduced from the same cause.

It was around this time that James P. Beckwourth had himself a moment of truth, a spurt of moral growth. When General Ashley ordered the best hunters out and afield, James P. Beckwourth naturally "seized [his] rifle and issued from the camp alone." Weak and near starvation. He spotted two teal ducks about three hundred yards from camp "and handsomely decapitated one."

"This," dictated the hunter some thirty years later, "was a temptation to my constancy; and appetite and conscientiousness had a long strife as to the disposal of the booty. I reflected that it would be but an inconsiderable trifle in my mess of four hungry men, while to roast and eat him myself would give me strength to hunt for more. [But] A strong inward feeling remonstrated against such ..."

Anyhow, after considerable mental to-and-fro, appetite won out on the moral grounds that it would strengthen him to "procure something more substantial than a teal duck." This—being refreshed and invigorated by the duck—he did, to the tune of one buck, a large white wolf, and three good-sized elk. The camp had "heard the reports of my rifle, and, knowing that I would not waste ammunition, had been expecting to see me return with game ... the game being all brought into camp, the fame of 'Jim Beckwourth' was celebrated by all tongues."

But the fiery pangs of conscience gnawed yet at the heart of James P. Beckwourth, in spite of the fact that the above list makes one teal duck seem rather small potatoes. He confessed all to his messmates (after they had eaten) and was gratified to find that

> All justified my conduct, declaring my conclusions obvious. . . . At this present time   I never kill a duck on my ranch, and there are thousands of teal duck there, but I think of my feast in the bushes while my companions were famishing in the camp. Since that time I have never refused to share my last shilling, my last biscuit, or my only blanket with a friend, and [the experience] will ever serve as a lesson to more constancy in the future.

Somehow General Ashley overlooked this incident in his own record of the trip; possibly because it has taken the art of the modern novelist to reveal that these moments of self-insight—the ethical leap, so to speak—are what make men out of boys. But where the modern novel goes, armed with psychiatric jargon, James P. Beckwourth has gone before with naught but his unerring aim and febrile imagination.

On December 3 Ashley's party caught up with the Grand Pawnees near present Kearney, Nebraska. They were now one month and roughly 180 miles out of Fort Atkinson. Since the 24th the going had been better, with the hunters able to keep them plentifully supplied with provisions, while "the islands and valleys of the Platt furnished a bountiful supply of rushes and firewood."

But here the news was bad. The friendly headmen of the Grand Pawnees told him that there was only one place between there and the mountains where he could find fuel, that being the Forks of the Platte, and "but little food of any description for our horses. They urged me to take up winter quarters at the forks of the Platt, stating that if I attempted to advance further until spring, I would endanger the lives of my whole party. The weather now was extremely cold, accompanied with frequent light snows."

Nevertheless, Ashley pushed on. A little farther upriver he fell in with a band of Loup Pawnees, who were headed for the Forks to make their own winter camp.

Indians and trappers traveled in company to the Forks, which they reached on December 12. Ashley remained here until the 24th, recruiting his horses on the good range provided by the valleys. The uplands still held "eighteen to twenty-four inches of snow," and the next 200 miles were described to him as being "almost wholly destitute of wood."

From the Loups he was able to buy twenty-three horses, "notwithstanding they had been overtaken by unusually severe weather before reaching their wintering ground, by which they had lost a great number of horses."

Up to this point the general has been retracing the route followed by Tom Fitzpatrick the previous summer, but here he diverges into country untraveled by any of his party. The Loups told him there was more wood on the South Fork, and Ashley decided to ascend that branch. He left the winter encampment on the 24th. A blizzard with violent winds came up the next day, and lasted through the night of the 27th.

> The next morning four of my horses were so benumbed with cold that they were unable to stand, although we succeeded in raising them on their feet. A delay to recruit them would have been attended with great danger, probably even to the destruction of the whole party. I therefore concluded to set forward without them. The snow was now so deep that had it not been for the numerous herds of buffaloe moving down the river, we could not possibly have proceeded.

The march continues in much the same pattern; snow and high wind and hard going, though he was able to welcome in the new year of 1825 with the happy discovery of an unexpected grove of cottonwood, providing much-needed food for the horses. (Peter Skene Ogden, far to the northwest, is noting in his journal his dissatisfaction with his new state of dependency.)

He crossed the continental divide itself the first week in April—after a good deal more "unusual labour"—via the depression later known as Bridger's Pass.

His welcome to the Pacific slope was the loss of seventeen horses to an itinerant party of Crows. A search party was unable to recover the horses, but their northward pursuit of the Crows brought them to the Sweetwater, thus giving Ashley for the first time an accurate picture of where he was.

Finally, on the 19th of April, the party reached the Green

River and camped about fifteen miles above the mouth of the Sandy.

> On my arrival ... [at the Green] ... I determined to relieve my men and horses of their heavy burdens to accomplish which, I concluded to make four divisions of my party, send three of them by land in different directions, and, with the fourth party, descend the river myself with the principal part of my merchandise.

Zacharias Ham took a party of six men "Westerly to a mountanous country that lay in that direction," i.e., to the Ham's Fork Plateau, just beyond which is the valley of the Bear River. On this journey Ham doubtless fell upon and named Ham's Fork of the Green, one of the important streams in the subsequent history of the trade.

Clyman "with six men to the sources of the Shetskadee," i.e., north, working the area covered by Tom Fitzpatrick and himself the previous year.

Fitzpatrick "with 6 men southwardly," paralleling by land Ashley's own water route down the Green.

Before dispatching these parties Ashley wrote out a detailed set of instructions for each of the leaders. These instructions dealt with "The place of rendavoze for all our parties on or before the 10th July next," and gave a list of signs which Ashley would make to designate the spot:

> Trees will be pealed standing the most conspicuous near the Junction of the rivers or above the mountains as the case may be—. should such point be without timber I will raise a mound of Earth five feet high or set up rocks the top of which will be made red with vermillion thirty feet distant from the same— and one foot below the surface of the earth a northwest direction will be deposited a letter communicating to the party any thing that I may deem necessary ...

Thus were the arrangements made for the first of the most famous of mountain institutions, the annual rendezvous. It is certain that Ashley had not yet realized how important the idea of the rendezvous was; it is equally certain that by the end of the first one he had been struck by the inescapable logic of it.

The rendezvous, when it became standard procedure, gave the American trapper an enormous advantage over the British brigades coming down from the north. In order to penetrate the mountains in time for the spring hunt a party had to leave their permanent base in the dead of winter, enduring the kind of hardship the vast winter had dealt both Ogden and Ashley. The time and energy spent in the simple transportation of a trapping party to its grounds were inestimable, and constituted the greatest expense inherent in the trade.

On the other hand, suppose the trappers remained in the mountains for the winter; didn't come back to civilization at all, but wintered on the spot with friendly Indians or in camps of their own. A supply party could reach them at a predetermined spot in the summer, when hunting was poor anyway, and take their furs back. The trappers themselves would have nothing to do with the eventual marketing of their pelts; that would be left to better businessmen than they; they would simply live in the mountains permanently but without permanent base, which suited most of them fine. This was the beginning of the mountain man.

But this first rendezvous, of 1825, was not conceived as a permanent fixture of the trade. It was simply a gesture of expediency, an attempt to round up Ashley's widely scattered bands of trappers.

From the 19th to the 21st of April they remained in camp on the Green while Ashley prepared for his voyage by water. A bullboat measuring sixteen by seven feet was constructed for his party and loaded with the merchandise he had brought with him and the furs taken en route. He would deposit these at "some conspicuous point not less than 40 or 50 miles from this place," and that would be the place of rendezvous. He intended to continue beyond this point himself, being anxious to find out where the "Shetskadee" went; it was not clear from the existing information whether this was a part of the Pacific drainage system or not, and the knowledge was essential.

He left camp on the 21st and began the first attempt to navigate the Green River.

IV

The bullboat made forty miles the first day, but the general discovered she was too heavily burdened, and clumsy. The next day was spent making a companion craft. On the 24th they got under way again, with goods and crew distributed between the two boats. While in this camp they were overtaken by the land party under Fitzpatrick, who supplied themselves briefly and went on ahead.

Ashley selected his rendezvous point on the 1st of May, but changed his mind a few days later when he reached Henry's Fork: "finding this a much more suitable place for a Randavouze I have made marks indicative of my intention to randavouze here."

He named the stream Randavouze Creek, but the name didn't stick; it became Henry's Fork. "So far," Ashley notes, "the navigation of this river is without the least obstruction."

It was an optimistic note, but didn't last long:

> we continued our voyage about half a mile below our camp, when we entered between the walls of this range of mountains, which approach at this point to the waters' edge on either side of the river and rise almost perpendicular to an immense height. The channel of the river is here contracted to the width of sixty or seventy yards, and the current (much increased in velocity) as it rolled along in angry submission to the serpentine walls that direct it, seemed constantly to threaten us with danger as we advanced.

He was now in Flaming Gorge Canyon. In spite of the ominous aspect the river was beginning to assume, they "succeeded in descending about ten miles without any difficulty or material change in the aspect of things and encamped for the night."

The next day Ashley entered Red Canyon, just over the border of present Utah, where the river turns east: "the navigation became difficult and dangerous ... at twenty miles from our last camp, the roaring and agitated state of the water a short distance before us indicated a fall or some other obstruction of considerable magnitude."

This fall is now known as Ashley Falls. The bullboats had to be unloaded and lined over the falls. The party camped for the night a mile below the falls. While here Ashley painted a famous inscription on the cliffs overlooking the river. It read, simply enough, *Ashley—1825;* virtually the same legend every schoolboy marks on some monument or other. Ashley wasn't marking a monument, however; he was making one. For many years after, during the period when

Ashley himself had been forgotten, this enigmatic note gave rise to much speculation as to who the writer might have been. It was certainly a shock to the travelers of 1849, who thought they were the first white men to see this canyon.

Things got worse and worse; the rapids more frequent and more violent, and the necessity for portages slowing them down. Finally, in Split Mountain Canyon, he tried to keep the boats in the water too long. They discovered "at the distance of about 4 or 500 yards . . . a verry great & dangerous fall." The smaller of the two boats, bringing up the rear, capsized, which turned out to be good fortune; it kept her where she was until word of this fall had been relayed.

Ashley's boat was ahead, and by the time they discovered the falls it was too late to land. "I discovered from the appearances of the rocks that our only way & that doubtful . . . was to lay the boat straight with the current and pass in the middle of the river."

Just after they entered the "heavy billows our boat filled with water but did not sink." Wallowing in the middle of the stream, the bulky craft was caught by the current and thrown against a rock near the base of the rapids. It swung off into an eddy, "two of the most active men then leaped in the water took the cables and towed her to land just as from all appearances she was making her exit with me with her for I cannot swim & my only hopes was that the boat would not sink."

James P. Beckwourth figures largely in this story, in spite of the fact that he was hundreds of miles away, and going in the other direction, to boot. In *Life and Adventures* he had saved the general from a wound-maddened buffalo only a page or so before, and in the shipwreck now rescues Ashley from the seething torrent. (In his account James P. Beckwourth does say the general was no swimmer, which the general's journal confirms. It should be admitted, however, that until Dale Morgan's identification of the Ashley diary historians had scoffed at the idea of Ashley's shipwreck entirely; but James P. Beckwourth was right and they were wrong.)

By May 16 Ashley had finished his passage through the Uinta Mountains and camped at the mouth of the stream since known as Ashley's Fork. There (apparently) he met two of the men from Provost and Leclerc's party, who gave him the intelligence that the country south of him was dangerous and barren of game. Nevertheless, the general decided to continue a little farther down, probably in hopes of contacting the main body of Provost's trappers.

He came upon Provost's winter camp at the mouth of the White River (two miles below the Duchesne). Nobody home. The trappers were out—on their way to the meeting with Peter Skene Ogden, in fact—but there was a note saying Leclerc was six miles farther down with goods. Back into the boats and downstream; but Leclerc wasn't there either, having been forced by the scarcity of game out on an extended hunting party.

Rations were short for Ashley too at this point. He detached half his party (three men) to scout for game, while he and the remaining three followed the river a little farther down to check on the unfavorable report of Provost's men. It was true enough, the country along the river being, according to his own notation, "a barren heap of rocky mountains."

The remainder of May was spent attempting to buy provisions and horses from the local Indians (Utes). It was not until the 7th of June that he made contact with his trappers again. By that time he was moving west toward the Great Basin, and encountered Etienne Provost, with a party of twelve men. Ashley now got the first direct news of his detached parties, and—what with the account of the desertion of Ogden's Iroquois—something more than that. For the first time the general learned of Jedediah Smith's international entanglement and his trip to the Flathead post; of the fact that Weber had wintered on the Bear River; and of the present whereabouts of both parties, now united.

On the 15th of June, after raising Ashley's cache back on the Green River, the combined parties set out again for the Great Basin, guided by Provost. There is no direct record of Ashley's reunion with his men, but the chances are it followed James P. Beckwourth's description closely: "The night was spent in general rejoicing, in relating our adventures, and recounting our various successes and reverses."

The recounting of successes and reverses was the winter night pastime of the mountain man, and the summer rendezvous had its fair share, too. A number of friends were reunited in June—Smith and Fitzpatrick and Clyman and Sublette—and the tales, without doubt, flowed freely. (It must not be supposed that, because I've made a certain amount of sport with James P. Beckwourth, he was the only "gaudy liar" in the mountains; a good liar was highly regarded around the fire and American mythology has been greatly enriched by these imaginings, not even excluding those of the redoubtable blacksmith.)

At any rate, all the parties were together by July 1, in two encampments about twenty miles from Ashley's designated rendezvous:

> when it appeared [wrote Ashley] that we had been scattered over the territory west of the mountains in small detachments from the 38th to the 44th degree of latitude, and the only injury we had sustained by Indian depredations was the stealing of 17 horses by the Crows ... and the loss of one man killed on the headwaters of the Rio Colorado, by a party of Indians unknown.

There on the Green River near the mouth of Henry's Fork, the first of the great mountain rendezvous was held, July 1, 1825.

CHAPTER 8

"Has indemnified himself for all . . . losses"

ASHLEY had two immediate points of business to conduct at the rendezvous, the first being naturally the collection of furs and distribution of supplies. (James P. Beckwourth comments that "The general would open none of his goods, except tobacco, until all had arrived, as he wished to make an equal distribution; for goods were then very scarce in the mountains, and hard to obtain," which is quite likely.) There were more at this rendezvous than the general had counted on; about 120 men, counting the twenty-nine who had, in Ashley's discreet phrase, "recently withdrawn from the Hudson Bay Company." And this does not count the wives and children who accompanied the deserters.

Wives and children. . . . This was a new concept for Ashley, and probably for his trappers as well. While the HBC brigades customarily moved about like a small village, the Americans were going in minuscule parties; just passing through, so to speak, and in consequently greater danger from Indians than the larger British parties.

The logic of permanent residence in the mountains must have occurred to many men during this rendezvous; it certainly occurred to Ashley himself, and probably through his conversations with the knowledgeable old Iroquois Pierre Tevanitagon. In talking with Pierre, a whole new picture of mountain operations must have been shaped in Ashley's mind. From our comfortable vantage point of a hundred-odd years we can see the final shape of the American fur trade beginning to crystallize here, and quite suddenly.

Ashley had brought with him the means of conducting a trade, a business: powder, lead, traps, knives, iron, a few trading trinkets, some coffee and sugar. But the notations he made on supplies for the next year included something else; it was not a list for supplying a trade, but for supplying a way of life. In addition to the necessities as above: combs and earrings and ribbons, soap and "slay bells" and sewing silk; there would be women involved in this new system. A breed of men was being born at Rendezvous 1825 whose way of life would set them apart from any other group in history: the mountain men.

Beaver was going for $3 a pound from the free trappers; $2 a pound from some others (probably those with a previous outfitting arrangement and its subsequent debt). The HBC deserters were paid at the going rate, and "Thyery" Goddin turned in 136 pounds.

These skins were paid for in merchandise at the following prices:

Butcher Knives . . $	.75	Powder . . . . $	1.50/lb
Lead	1.00/lb	Tobacco	1.25/lb
Coffee	1.50/lb	Sugar	1.50/lb
3 pt. blankets . . .	9.00	Scarlet Cloth	6.00/yd
Cloth	4–5.00/yd	Beads	5.00
Awls	2.00/doz	N. W. Fuzils	24.00
2½ pt. Blankets	7.00	Sheet Iron kettles .	2.25/lb
Square axes	2.50	Flour	1.00/lb
Alspice	1.50/lb	Raisins	1.50/lb
Common quality		Assorted Calicos .	1.00/yd
Flannel	1.50/yd	Thread assorted . .	3.00/lb
Domestic cotton .	1.25/yd	Vermillion	3.00/lb
Assorted beads . .	2.50/lb	Tin pans	2.00/lb
4th Proof Rum .	14.50/gal	Ribbons assorted .	3.00/bolt
Handkerchiefs . .	1.50/ea	Looking glasses . .	.50/ea
Buttons	5.00/gross	Copper kettles . . .	3.00/lb
Flints	.50/doz	Dried Fruit	1.50/lb
Fire Steels	2.00/lb	Shaving soap	2.00/lb
Washing soap . . .	1.25/lb	Steel bracelets . . .	1.50/pair
James River to-			
bacco	1.75/lb		

Large brass wire . . . . . . $ 2.00/lb
Traps ran $9.00/ea; and so forth.

The general ended with almost nine thousand pounds of beaver, a figure which probably includes forty-five packs *en cache,* which he picked up along his homeward route. At St.

Louis prices $40,000–$50,000 worth of beaver. This is well and good—the newspapers became almost ecstatic—but it might be well to look more closely at this figure, because it is the beginning of the legend of Ashley's mountain success. The general is paying $3 a pound; and selling at, say, $5 in St. Louis. For this profit it is necessary for him to outfit a major overland party (with the consequent great risk of loss to Indians) and make the complete trip to and from the mountains; this means paying men. With horses at a mountain price of $60—and sometimes unobtainable even at that—it doesn't take much bad luck to wipe out the profit. Later, the charge for simple transportation back to St. Louis was $1.12½ a pound for beaver. These factors cut the profit figure down to something a good deal less impressive.

But I think it was at this rendezvous that General Ashley first discovered exactly where the money was to be made in the fur trade; and the furs themselves were not the major factor. After all his subsidiary costs had been accounted for, the resale of beaver yielded perhaps 80–90 cents per pound (on a cash basis), which is fine, but not magnificent. The key to making money was in the merchandise with which the pelts were bought. In St. Louis, selling pelts, Ashley had to contend with businessmen of the acuity of Bernard Pratte and the Chouteaus. This alone would keep the profit made on furs to a relative minimum. But in the mountains . . .

It must have become obvious that in the mountains the supplier was king; the markup on merchandise was at his own discretion; who was to say him nay if he decided 400 per cent over prime cost was just the thing? The supplier was in a position to make a profit at both ends; but mostly at the mountain end, because in the mountains he was in the enviable position of being able to say exactly what a dollar was worth.

So, by virtue of the fact that he paid not in cash but in merchandise at his own valuation, the outfitter stood to make a good deal. And this is the way it fell out, eventually. With rare exceptions, the money made from the fur trade was made by the intermediaries, the suppliers. Later, in the early thirties, the advance on prime cost became quite ridiculous, and this was when there was stiff competition between rival outfitters. They competed to get to the rendezvous first, but the competition—Mr. Keynes to the contrary notwithstanding—didn't seem to give the trappers a break on prices.

At any rate, Ashley's return this year was not so impressive as has been made out. In terms of his financial affairs its major importance probably lies in the hint he received: leave the trapping to them as like it for their own peculiar reasons; buy and sell, buy and sell.

But that was in the future, and it must be noted that Ashley's prices were among the fairest in the land as long as he was supplying. He seems to have used the supplier's advantage in terms of security for his investment; increasing the certainty of making a profit rather than trying to amass a vast fortune overnight.

For now he was still in the trapping business—and by himself. He needed a field partner, a man to replace Major Henry, and he had a pretty fair field to choose from: James Clyman, Tom Fitzpatrick, Zacharias Ham, Jedediah Smith, Bill Sublette—any one of them could have handled the job. It is not known why he settled on Smith; though it is interesting that Smith, in the future, showed a willingness to invest his own money in a company, rather than spend it on foofarraw. Whatever the reason, Smith it was. For the next year the company was Ashley & Smith (though owing to its short duration this partnership has not been generally recognized).

With this final piece of business settled, Ashley was ready to depart for St. Louis with the year's catch; the first year of decent luck since he began. He decided to go by the Bighorn route; which is to say he crossed South Pass eastward to the valley of the Sweetwater, thence north to the headwaters of the Bighorn. He took with him a party of fifty men, including his new partner and James P. Beckwourth. Twenty-five of the party would accompany him all the way to St. Louis, the other twenty-five "were to accompany me to a navigable point of the Big Horn River, thence to return with the horses employed in the transportation of the furs."

Ashley's choice of the Bighorn route was probably dictated principally by factors of caution. He was not likely to try to navigate the Platte, not after Fitzpatrick's dunking the year before; nor could he return overland, through want of horses (those he brought were needed in the mountains). Also Ashley knew that a government party was scheduled to reach the upper Missouri late in the summer. This expedition, under General Atkinson and Indian Agent Benjamin O'Fallon, was on a treaty-making mission; in brief, trying to patch up some of the damage done by the unhappy Aricara campaign and alleviate some of the hostility caused by the fur hunters' encroachment on Indian lands. The protection of an adequate military force was certainly something Ashley would not have overlooked, and it is probable that he was making a deliberate attempt to contact the Atkinson-O'Fallon party.

With twenty men, Ashley detoured a few miles east of their route to pick up the cached furs, while the remainder of his party took a direct route. He raised the cache, and also a war party of sixty Blackfeet. Attacking at dawn, the Blackfeet stampeded Ashley's horses and made off with all but two. One of the trappers was wounded—which one is not certain, but James P. Beckwourth takes the honor to himself—and an attempt by the Indians to take the camp was repulsed.

The next night an express was sent to overtake the rest of the party and bring back horses; Ashley remained in camp for two days while waiting. When the horses arrived they set out and were attacked again on the first night, this time by a war party Ashley identifies as Crows. This attack

> resulted in the loss of one of the Indians killed and another shot through the body, without any injury to us. The next day I joined my other party and proceeded direct to my place of embarkation just below the Big Horn mountain, where I arrived on the 7th day of August. [The trappers consistently referred to mountain ranges in the singular; as in this case, where "mountain" means the whole Bighorn range.]

Bullboats were made, the party divided. Ashley, with the remaining half, set off down the Bighorn to the Yellowstone, which he found "a beautiful river to navigate," and down the Yellowstone to its confluence with the Missouri. He arrived here (at the site of his first projected post, abandoned by Major Henry) on August 19. Obligingly enough, the Atkinson-O'Fallon Yellowstone Expedition had arrived two days earlier.

II

Joining the Atkinson-O'Fallon party must have been a great relief to Ashley. Returning home with his first profit in three years of business, he would likely have been more than ordinarily apprehensive; not looking forward, for example, to the passage past his old friends the Aricaras. Now, however, he was as safe as anyone ever got to be; there were no fewer than 476 men in this party, transported by eight keelboats. (All the boats were named for fur-bearing animals of the Missouri: *Beaver, Buffalo, Elk, Mink, Muskrat, Otter, Raccoon,* and *White Bear.*)

The expedition is somewhat beyond the scope of this narrative, except as it touches General Ashley, and I will not attempt even a broad picture of it. It was, generally speaking, quite successful in its peacemaking aims, or, more accurately, its treaty-making aims. The technique was fairly simple, consisting almost entirely of military marching in full uniform, which "made an excellent impression on the Indians." Various tribes were treated to displays of rockets and artillery of various sorts, thus adding to an almost festive air: "Lieutenant Holmes threw six shells from the howitzer in the presence of the Indians. They exploded handsomely and made a deep impression."

By the time the expedition reached the mouth of the Yellowstone their work was nearly over. They had intended meeting the Blackfeet and treatying them, but from Ashley's information it seemed probable they were beyond the Falls, farther than the party intended going. Perhaps it was just as well.

On the off-chance of raising a band of Assiniboines, part of the group went another hundred miles or so upriver, and were accompanied by General Ashley. No sign was found, and they returned to the Yellowstone encampment on the 26th of July. The next day they began an uneventful descent of the Missouri, after loading Ashley's hundred packs of beaver aboard the *Mink,* the *Muskrat,* and the *Raccoon.* The *Muskrat* hit a snag on the way down, but the furs were recovered and no great damage was done.

The benefit of this meeting was not entirely one-sided; in the past two years Ashley's trappers had accumulated a good deal of important information. Atkinson listened attentively to Jedediah Smith's reports on the British trade and his own routes of exploration. Ashley promised Atkinson a topographical sketch of the newly explored country but it has never been located. (The covering letter, written December 3, is the source of most of the information in the previous chapter.)

The new partners arrived in St. Louis on October 4. According to James P. Beckwourth, when they arrived "at St. Charles, twenty miles above St. Louis, the general dispatched a courier to his friends, Messrs. Wahrendorff and Tracy, to inform them of his great success, and that he would be in with his cargo the next day about noon." (The Messrs. Wahrendorff and Tracy had more than a friendly interest in the general's arrival; they were his backers, and if they had become somewhat restive in the previous three years it was understandable.)

In St. Louis Ashley and Smith entered into a hectic month of outfitting; Smith for another trek into the mountains, Ashley for another up the aisle, his third. On October 26 Ashley was married to Miss Elizabeth Christy, of whom we know little more than the name. (She died five years later, and in 1833 Ashley was married for the fourth time, to an exceptionally talented widow, Mrs. Wilcox. Of his first two wives no record remains.)

On the 29th, less than four weeks after their arrival in St. Louis, Smith was off again with a full party. Contemporary newspaper accounts number his men at seventy; Smith, in a letter a year later, says sixty; his license to enter the Indian country names fifty-seven. Call it around sixty somewhere, together with 160 horses and mules. The value of his outfit was estimated at $20,000; it is certain Ashley didn't have that kind of cash, certainly not after paying his debts, so we can assume the silent hopefulness of Messrs. Wahrendorff and Tracy again, and this time with better cause.

Smith's record of this trip is typical of those he left concerning his movements. It says he left St. Louis with a party and "arrived at the place of destination in June." This, it will be observed, covers a good deal of ground in very few words. Whatever else Smith may have been, he was no scribbler.

Parts of his itinerary are disputable, but in general he must have followed the Platte route taken by Ashley. We are on equally uncertain ground when it comes to the movements of the trappers left in the mountains; the fall hunt of 1825 is a blank.

Bill Sublette was in charge of at least one brigade; there is some indication that he was in a position of loose authority over all the Ashley men remaining in the mountains for the winter. The fall hunt was made by scattered parties with unrecorded success, and as the mountain cold began to close in they drifted back to the designated winter camp in Cache Valley. Soon after all the parties were in, the camp moved en masse down toward Great Salt Lake; possibly because of the severe cold, but just as likely for some reason unknown to us. (According to James P. Beckwourth, this move was ordered by Bill Sublette; his statement is the evidence, such as it is, that Sublette was left in charge of the whole body of men.) Two camps were formed, one on the Weber River and one near the mouth of the Bear.[1] The combined camps were large, as a fair-sized band of Snakes—about two hundred lodges—attached themselves.

Shortly after settling down, and apparently before they were joined by the Snakes, the white encampment lost a batch of horses to a marauding band of Bannocks; eight, according to the gaudy liar, who tells it:

> On missing them the next day, we formed a party of about forty men, and followed their trail on foot.... I volunteered with the rest, although fortunately my horses were not among the missing. After a pursuit of five days we arrived at one of their villages, where we saw our own horses among a number of others. We then divided our forces, Fitzpatrick taking command of one party, and a James Bridger of the other.
>
> The plan resolved upon was as follows: Fitzpatrick was to charge the Indians, and cover Bridger's party, while they stampeded all the horses they could get away with. I formed one of Captain Bridger's party, this being the first affair of the kind I had ever witnessed. Everything being in readiness, we rushed in upon the horses, and stampeded from two to three hundred, Fitzpatrick at the same time engaging the Indians, who numbered from three to four hundred. The Indians recovered a great number of the horses from us, but we succeeded in getting off with the number of our own missing, and forty head besides. In the engagement, six of the enemy were killed and scalped, while not one of our party received a scratch. The horses we had captured were very fine ones, and our return to the camp was greeted with the livliest demonstrations.

(Remember, Beckwourth is dictating this in 1855, long after "a James Bridger" had become "Old Gabe," most famous of the mountain men. He is perfectly aware of the irony of his reference.)

The winter camp broke up toward the last of February, splitting into several trapping parties. We have definite knowledge of three of them: one led by Smith, one by Fitzpatrick, and one by an unknown booshway which contained twenty-eight men, among them a number of the HBC deserters of the previous year. Naturally, it was this last party which stumbled on Peter Skene Ogden's Snake Country Brigade of 1826.

III

Ogden was understandably bitter when he left the Snake country in 1825. The defeat he had suffered at the hands of Johnson Gardner, the loss of his freemen, and—important to a man of Ogden's temperament—the taunts and imprecations he had been forced to endure left him with memories that rankled. One might expect that this would have led to an implacable hatred of the Americans, but such was not the case. Ogden's reaction is more complicated than hatred—he was an intelligent man—and possibly the editor of his journals, E. E. Rich, sums it up best when he observes that Ogden "Seems to have become allergic to them." A month after his encounter with Gardner, Ogden had written George Simpson with an uncommon savagery: "You need not anticipate another expedition ensuing Year to this Country, for not a freeman will return, and should they, it would be to join the Americans."

And the rebuke he received from his superiors would not have set well with the tough partisan; for it was, in effect, based on an error. Ogden's letter of July 10—his report of the incident to the Governor and Committee—was mistakenly dated "East Fork of the Missouri," indisputably American territory. The Governor and Committee informed George Simpson rather stiffly:

> We have repeatedly given directions that all collision with the Americans should be avoided as well as infringements upon their Territory ... [but] Mr. Ogden must have been to the southward of 49° of latitude and to the Eastward of the Rocky Mountains which he should particularly have avoided ... any inattention to this instruction ... will be attended with our serious displeasure ...

The confusion was eventually straightened out, but for the moment Ogden was deeply humiliated and in the bad graces of the company.

In the spring of 1826 Ogden was once again in charge of the Snake Country Brigade. Despite his own wishes, he was moving directly back toward the cause of all his troubles, the Americans. He had been hoping to make a spectacular hunt in compensation for last year's losses, but as early as March 20 he received Indian rumors that threw him into a characteristic depression: a party of Americans and Iroquois, not more than three days' march from his own camp:

> ... if this be the case which I have no cause to doubt our hunts are damn'd ... I dread meeting the Americans, that some [of the freemen] will attempt desertion I have not the least doubt.

To top off his depression, a few days later he received more word of the Americans (from the Snake band who had wintered on the Bear) and the beaver tasted bad:

> ... no want of wild himlock here and some dread of being *Ill* the Beaver have certainly a Strange taste different from any I have ever eaten.
> [The next day] . . . one of the Canadians seriously Ill attributed to the Beaver Meat he was suddenly seized with a violent pain in his Loins and from thence his head and shortly after entirely lost all motion of his Limbs.

(The mountain materia medicum yielded up a mixture of gunpowder and pepper in water, which for some indeterminate reason did no damage, and the man recovered.)

A little over a week later (Sunday, April 9, 1826) Ogden's forebodings were realized; about ten o'clock he was "surprised by the arrival of a Party of Americans and some of our deserters of last Year 28 in all." This was one of the parties from the Bear River camp.[2]

Now Ogden's journal speaks bravely, in contrast to his previous expression of dread: ". . . if we were surprised at seeing them they were more so at seeing us from an Idea that their threats of last year would have prevented me from again returning to this quarter, but they find themselves mistaken." So bravely, in fact, that it gives us pretty good

reason to believe that his entry for this day was not actually
written until after the event had been completed; because he
did much better this time.

On Monday, April 10:

> The Strangers paid me a visit and I had a busy day
> in settling with them and more to my satisfaction and
> the Companys than last year we traded from them 93
> Large and small Beaver and 2 Otters seasoned Skins
> at a reasonable rate and we received 81½ Beavers
> in part payment of their debts due to the Company
> also two notes of hand from Mr Montour for his
> Balance Gabriel Prudhommes and Pierre Tevanito-
> gans also we secured all the skins they had From
> what I could observe our deserters are already tired
> of their New Masters and from their manner I am of
> opinion will soon return to their old employers.

In fact, some of the deserters apparently promised that
they would return to the HBC Flathead post in the fall. This
was heady wine for Ogden, and he found time to muse "I
cannot conceive how the Americans can afford to sell their
Beaver so as to reap profit when they pay $3 per lb. for
coarse or fine but such is the case and Goods proportionately
cheap our hunt to Day 15 Beaver."

Ogden was not, we may infer, extremely concerned about
the profit accruing to Americans, but this appraisal sharply
defines the portrait of a man enormously relieved from
tension; musing complacently over trivia, unwilling to put his
exuberance on paper.

The next day Thierry Godin's son Antoine requested permission to join his father—relieving the old man's mortification, no doubt—and Ogden could afford to be generous. No
Johnson Gardner here, taunting and cursing, but Peter Skene
Ogden in control of the situation, a position to which he was
accustomed. He let young Antoine go, he "being a worth-
less scamp" anyway, and having paid his debt in full with the
assistance of three skins advanced by the Americans.

Thus Ogden was enabled to make a journal entry he had
probably never expected—and certainly not so soon: "not
one of our Party appeared the least inclined to leave us not
even a hint was given, so much to their Credit." A satisfactory contrast to his observation of a scant nine months before:
"you need not expect another expedition ensuing Year."

As for the rest of Ashley's men this spring we have even briefer notes. Tom Fitzpatrick's party was accompanied by James P. Beckwourth himself, and so, quite naturally, there was a good deal of heroism and Indian killing involved (which two activities are sometimes indistinguishable in *Life and Adventures*). They trapped the tributaries of the Bear and the Portneuf, bravely defended themselves against hordes of howling Blackfeet, and in general seemed to have a rather average spring hunt. The one event which .is documented beyond James P. Beckwourth was the accident which gave Cache Valley its permanent name; heretofore it had been Willow Valley. While digging a cache for the furs of their previous fall hunt, the bank caved in upon the diggers, killing one or two of them. (One named Marshall is listed in the casualty lists for 1825 as having been lost in the valley, and this is probably he.)

The spring hunt of Jedediah Smith's detachment turned out to be more in the nature of an exploration than a hunt. We have mentioned briefly the mythical geography of the transmontane West, and that one of the few consistent features was a variously named river flowing from the great lake to the Pacific Ocean. Smith was to lay this ghost at last, for he set out directly into the barren lands north and west of Great Salt Lake, probably with a company of around thirty men.

His itinerary is not definitely known, nor any events of the exploration. From rumors Peter Skene Ogden picked up from the Indians, it would seem that Smith crossed the Promontory Mountains and skirted the northern edge of the lake. How far around its edge he went there is no way of knowing; but far enough to convince him there was no beaver to be had. He turned back toward the Snake, beaverless and hungry. The Indians reported to Ogden in June that the Americans

> had made an attempt to reach [beaver ground south of the lake] ... but starvation had driven them back and they had crossed over from the entrance of Bruneau's River to the North side of the South Branch if in quest of Beaver they will find none and animals very scarce—when last seen they were destitute of both and were killing their Horses.

This American party was doubtless one detachment of the

Bear River winterees, and possibly led by Smith. This spring of 1826 another famous event occurred; and again we can be fairly certain of the event, but have to guess at the participants. The Great Salt Lake was coasted by four trappers in a bullboat, names unknown. At various times Black Harris claimed to have done it; Jim Clyman, Henry Fraeb (almost always spelled and pronounced Frapp), and Louis Vasquez (Vaskiss) have also been given credit. It may have been any or all of these, and there is not sufficient evidence to get excited about proving anybody's particular claim. Take your choice. Their purpose was to discover both the extent of this huge body of water and its outlet. According to a later commentary, they did not discover the outlet, but discovered the place they thought it might be. (If this uncertainty seems strange, remember that the mouth of the Columbia River itself was missed by numerous navigators, including the entirely competent George Vancouver. Geographical observation from water is a good deal more tenuous than we are wont to believe from our armchairs.)

As the spring wore on, the various bodies of trappers began to drift back toward Cache Valley, which had been agreed upon as the place of summer rendezvous. By July they were all there, awaiting the arrival of General Ashley with the supply train, lying to each other, graining pelts, and listening to some very interesting rumors that shortly proved out true.

In the meantime Ashley had departed from St. Louis on March 8, with a supply caravan consisting of twenty-five men and possibly including Bill Sublette. Presumably he followed roughly the same route as he had the year before; it was proving out pretty well, and by now the techniques of overland travel had been thoroughly worked out.

Let James P. Beckwourth tell of the arrival (a little breathless, perhaps; he has just beaten off 500 Blackfeet):

> The absent parties began to arrive, one after the other, at the rendezvous. Shortly after, General Ashley and Mr Sublet came in, accompanied with three hundred pack mules, well laden with goods and all things necessary for the mountaineers and the Indian trade. It may well be supposed that the arrival of such a vast amount of luxuries from the East did not pass off without a general celebration. Mirth, songs, dancing, shouting, trading, running, jumping, singing, rac-

ing, target-shooting, yarns, frolic, with all sorts of extravagances that white men or Indians could invent, were freely indulged in. The unpacking of the *medicine water* contributed not a little to the heightening of our festivities.

We had been informed by Harris, previous to the arrival of the general, that General Ashley had sold out his interest in the mountains to Mr. Sublet, embracing all his properties and possessions there. He now intended to return to St. Louis, to enjoy the fortune he had amassed by so much toil and suffering, and in which he had so largely shared in person.

And that was a fact. General William H. Ashley was quitting the mountains, having finally discovered how to make the fur trade yield a profit.

PART TWO

SMITH JACKSON & SUBLETTE

1826-1830

CHAPTER 9

"That I will not furnish
any other company"

THE document of sale between Ashley and the new firm hasn't been preserved—unless perhaps in a St. Louis attic—which is unfortunate, since it would have saved a good deal of printer's ink. Speculation about its terms has been a popular indoor sport of students of the trade, and estimates have ranged up to $30,000, payable in beaver at $5/lb.

Ashley himself (in a letter to B. Pratte & Co., which will be discussed in more detail below) said that he

> placed under the direction of three young men ... my remaining stock of merchandize, amounting altogether to about sixteen thousand dollars which (after deducting therefrom five thousand dollars which I paid Mr Smith on a dissolution of Partnership with him) they promised to pay me in Beaver fur delivered in that country at three dollars per pound.[1]

Or, alternatively, they could deliver the fur to Ashley, who would then transport it to St. Louis for $1.12½/lb., and deposit the net proceeds (after this deduction for transportation) in discharge of the debt.

This, then, indicates a total indebtedness to Ashley of $11,000. About $3,000 was paid on the spot, presumably on the same terms of beaver at $3 (say ten or twelve packs). Smith Jackson & Sublette gave Ashley a note for the balance.[2]

The total proceeds of the fall '25 and the spring '26 hunts

amounted to 123 packs, which Ashley then took back to St. Louis. James P. Beckwourth notes his parting address:

> "Mountaineers and friends! When I first came to the mountains, I came a poor man. You, by your indefatigable exertions, toils, and privations, have procured me an independent fortune. With ordinary prudence in the management of what I have accumulated, I shall never want for any thing. For this, my friends, I feel myself under great obligations to you. Many of you have served with me personally, and I shall always be proud to testify to the fidelity with which you have stood by me through all danger, and the friendly and brotherly feeling which you have ever, one and all, evinced toward me. For these faithful and devoted services I wish you to accept my thanks; the gratitude that I express to you springs from my heart, and will ever retain a lively hold on my feelings.
>
> "My friends! I am now about to leave you, to take up my abode in St. Louis. Whenever any of you return thither, your first duty must be to call at my house, to talk over the scenes of peril we have encountered, and partake of the best cheer my table can afford you.
>
> "I now wash my hands of the toils of the Rocky Mountains. Farewell, mountaineers and friends! May God bless you all!"
>
> We were all sorry to part with the general.

Along with the 123 packs of beaver, Ashley took back home a document which has survived, and one worth more to him than the fur: the Articles of Agreement[3] "made and entered into this 18th day of July 1826 by and between William H. Ashley of the first part and Jedediah S. Smith David E. Jackson and Wm. L. Sublett trading under the firm Smith Jackson & Sublett of the second part . . ."

The purport of the Articles is an arrangement for Ashley to supply goods to the new firm:

> . . . at or near the west end of the little lake of Bear river a watter of the pacific ocean . . . [it isn't] . . . on or before the first day of July 1827 without some unavoidable occurrence should prevent, but as it is

uncertain whether the situation of said Smith Jackson
& Subletts business will Justify the proposed purchase
of Merchandise ... it is understood and agreed that
[they] shall send an Express to said Ashley to reach
him in St. Louis on or before the first day of March
next ... the amount of merchandise to be delivered
... shall not be less than Seven Thousand dollars nor
more than fifteen thousand and if it is in the power of
said party of the second part to make further payment in part or in whole ... that they will do so.

The final paragraph of this document is the most interesting, in view of later happenings. This is the binding clause:

... and it is understood and agreed between the two
said parties that so long as the said Ashley continues
to furnish said Smith Jackson & Sublett with Merchandise as aforesaid That he will furnish no other
company or Individual with Merchandise other than
those who may be in his immediate service.

In effect, this arrangement would mean that every trapper
in the mountains—whether formally attached to Smith Jackson & Sublette or not—would be dependent on the new company for his supplies. As has been pointed out, the new
system of trapping meant that the control of supplies coming
into the mountains was virtually synonymous with control of
the trade. This would put the new firm on a very good foot-
ing, indeed, since it would give it a near monopoly on the
American mountain trade. In order to evade this, an unattached trapper would have to make his own arrangements
for supplies delivered—far too much trouble, danger, and
expense.

Or so it would seem. But a man does well to look long and
closely at a document of that kind, particularly when drawn
up by a man like Genl. Wm. H. Ashley.

The general arrived in St. Louis the last week of September, 1826, with 123 packs of beaver—roughly 12,000 pounds
—roughly $60,000 at St. Louis prices. Figuring his cost at $3
a pound plus $1 a pound transportation, this gives him an
estimated net return of about $12,000 or $1 a pound. Combined with the hundred-pack return of the previous year, this
set Ashley back on his feet financially and laid a very satis-

factory foundation for progress. He was, in short, in a position to supply the merchandise to Smith Jackson & Sublette on his own hook, or possibly with the aid of his backers, Wahrendorff & Tracy, if he wanted someone to share the risk. However, he did not choose to do this, and he was certainly not content with the "ordinary, prudent management" of what he had accumulated.

One of the first calls Ashley made after his return to St. Louis was on General Pratte, of Bernard Pratte & Co. This firm (sometimes known as Berthold, Pratte & Chouteau, or simply the French Fur Company) was an association of some of the most powerful and formidable businessmen in St. Louis; a dangerous source of possible competition in the mountain trade. Ashley shrewdly sought to close the barn door before the horse had even glanced in that direction. He had a long talk with Pratte, and a few days later—October 14—made a formal proposition to the firm, offering them a half interest in his new business (which he later suggested would be called Wm. Ashley & Company). The new business, however, was somewhat more extensive than one would expect from his agreement with Smith Jackson & Sublette:

> I contemplate [he wrote Pratte & Company] sending an expidition across the R Mountains the ensuing Spring for the purpose of trading fur and trapping Beaver, and from a conversation had with Genl. B Pratte a few days since, I am induced to propose to you an equal participation in the adventure . . . [There follows an account of his arrangement with Smith Jackson & Sublette, part of which was previously quoted].

> It is also understood between the said Smith Jackson & Sublett, and myself, that provided they order the goods as last mentioned, that I will not furnish any other company in that country with merchandize, except such as I may employ on my own acct

> The following are the prices . . .

The statement that he intended trapping beaver as well as supplying the new firm might well have been a manner of speaking, except that his intention is made perfectly clear in the closing paragraphs of the letter:

> The expidition which I propose sending in the Spring will consist of about forty Men one hundred

and twenty mules & horses, the Merchandize &c
necessary to supply them for twelve months and that
to be furnished Messrs Smith Jackson & Sublett, all of
which must be purchased for cash on the best of
terms.

So the general intended to have two strings to his bow
after all. Once in the mountains, his supply party would
become a trapping brigade, entering into direct competition
with Smith Jackson & Sublette; the latter firm being under
the formidable disadvantage of having to purchse their goods
from the competition. It is most probable that the phrase
"those who may be in his immediate service" in the Articles
of Agreement was understood by Smith and his partners as
referring to the personnel of Ashley's supply party; such is
distinctly the impression given when read in context. But the
loophole is plain, after the fact, and the general is offering
Berthold, Pratte & Chouteau the chance to crawl through
with him.

What he intends to accomplish by the partnership with
Pratte becomes clearer as the negotiations go on. The next
February—1827—he amplified his proposal by making attractive terms for the division of profit; proposing to furnish
horses at $25 and mules at $55; suggesting that he himself be
paid a salary of $250 a month, etc. This letter also contains:

Messers. B. Pratte & Co. will not suffer any person
trading for them at Taus or other place or places,
directly or indirectly to interfere with the business of
the proposed concern in any way whatever—or allow
them to persue a similar business in the same section
of the country.

The logic of this restriction is plain enough; he is trying to
prevent Pratte from doing to him what he is doing to SJ&S.
But why the specific mention of Taos?

I think—and it is a matter of personal opinion—Ashley
was trying to meet a direct and specific threat to his control
of the mountain business, in the person of Etienne Provost.
This conjecture is based on the following reasoning:

There were at this time only a handful of men who knew
enough about the mountain geography to operate effectively
there. Smith Jackson & Sublette certainly did, but it would

seem Ashley had them under sufficient control through the provisions of the Articles of Agreement. Andrew Henry was probably another, but he was completely out of the trade and there was little or no chance he would try to re-enter it. Which leaves Etienne Provost as virtually the only man in the country who was capable of giving Ashley serious trouble.

Provost had been working the southern reaches of the Rockies out of Taos, probably for four years. His knowledge of the geography of the Green River and the Colorado was probably more extensive than that of any other trapper, and he was certainly familiar with the Bear River-Cache Valley-Salt Lake area, which was proving out so rich. Through the inclusion among his trappers of some of the early HBC deserters, he had at least a secondhand knowledge of the Flathead and northern Snake Country.

Provost was now a loner, his partnership with LeClerc having dissolved in some unknown way.[4] After Rendezvous 1826, when Ashley sold out to Smith Jackson & Sublette, Provost returned to St. Louis, where he applied for some kind of position with Berthold, Pratte & Chouteau.

When Ashley put his original proposal to the St. Louis office of B. Pratte & Company, the partners there wrote Berthold, who was at Fort Lookout, and apparently included some mention of Provost's application. Berthold replied that he "dare not advise" concerning Ashley's proposition, but that

> it seems to me that it would be well for us to assure ourselves of Provost, who is the soul of the hunters of the mountains. . . . Even if it was only to hinder the meeting between him and the Robidoux I would say . . . he should be made sure of, unless you have other plans.

(The Robidoux brothers were another enterprising bunch, and this is clearly enough designed to keep a good man out of the competition's hands.)

This note was written two months before Ashley's letter mentioning Taos; and in the interim B. Pratte & Company had assured themselves of Provost. He was on the payroll and apparently going to be working out of his old base, Taos.

By the time of Ashley's second letter he must have been getting worried. The express from the mountains was due by March 1 and as yet he hadn't been able to swing B. Pratte & Company to his side. Still, they had not refused him either.

On the last day of February Ashley reiterated the points he had made concerning the agreement and stated that "should Genl. Pratte exceede to these propositions, it will be necessary immediately to enter into articles of agreement." Immediately indeed; the express from Smith Jackson & Sublette was due, quite literally, tomorrow. Ashley had to know where he stood.

This brings up two other puzzling points. Why did Berthold, Pratte & Chouteau stall so long—over four months—before giving Ashley a definite answer? (Their letters are equivocal in the extreme, vaguely saying it would be better to wait until all the partners were back in St. Louis—Chouteau was in Philadelphia, Berthold at Fort Lookout, and Pratte at St. Louis—where they could accomplish more in conversation than through masses of correspondence.) And why did Berthold, a senior partner, say that he "dare not advise anything about the project with Ashley"?

These facts are pertinent: During the fall of 1826, while Ashley was desperately trying to arrange a partnership, B. Pratte & Company was engaged in secret negotiations of considerably greater scope. They were about to become the Western Department of the titan: John Jacob Astor's relentlessly growing American Fur Company.

Astor had been putting insistent, if gentle, pressure on the companies of the Missouri for a long time. As early as 1811 an attempt had been made on behalf of Astor to buy into the reorganizing Missouri Fur Company; which was flatly rejected by the local operators, who wanted control to remain in St. Louis. Then the failure of the Astoria enterprise caused him to pull in his horns for some time. In February, 1823, Astor had taken in the small firm of Stone, Bostwick & Company, which acted as his Western Department and operated out of St. Louis. The agreement between them ran for three and one-half years, or until the fall of 1826. It was not then renewed. Instead, private negotiations began between Astor and Pratte.

This was what American Fur had wanted for years: an association with one of the old St. Louis houses, and one of the strongest. The advantage for B. Pratte & Company lay in having the incalculable power of American Fur behind them; and it was power they would need. Ashley's successes—though much exaggerated by report—had been attracting a good deal of attention in St. Louis, and a lively competition seemed to be shaping up between several of the local concerns. Though it had not yet begun in actuality, a mass drive to the mountains was clearly in the making.

Negotiations were concluded in December of 1826, and Bernard Pratte & Company officially became the Western Department of American Fur (though this new status was not made public immediately). Only after the merger was complete did B. Pratte & Company make their decision on Ashley's proposal. When an agreement was finally reached, Pratte was not acting for an independent firm, but as representative of American Fur. Ashley, through no fault or knowledge of his own, gave "equal participation in the adventure" to John Jacob Astor.

II

It has been necessary to go into these complex business arrangements in detail. The activities of the mountain men cannot be comprehended without taking into account the background against which they played out their roles. This background—the subterranean struggle for power in the trade—has never been treated adequately. The dramatic, the essentially romantic, character of the mountain trade has obscured the fact that the trappers were frequently pawns, being played in an elaborate and sophisticated game they knew nothing about.

It was not simply a matter of exploitation (though this, too, was characteristic of the trade). The critical struggles were of an almost political nature, and they took place in St. Louis, Philadelphia, and New York, between such persons as Ashley, Pratte, and Astor.

There is an aura of intrigue and mystery about many of these sub rosa arrangements that may never be dispelled. Often the details were not made public at the time—as in the present case—and the available data has had to be unearthed by students. This data is, understandably, incomplete. From those documents which *have* survived, it is possible to sketch in the outlines with fair assurance that the over-all picture will be accurate, even if the detail is obscured.

The ethics of the business manipulations were highly questionable, involving outright deceit and treachery. (This is, of course, a matter of personal judgment. It may simply represent a monstrous naïveté on my part.)

Nevertheless, it is clear enough that Ashley's proposal to B. Pratte & Company was contrary to the spirit of his agreement with Smith Jackson & Sublette. (Except for the extremely unlikely possibility that this had been discussed at the rendezvous and agreed to by the new firm; an agreement tantamount to cutting their own throats.) It is also clear what Ashley was trying to accomplish, though I may have been assigning him too grandiose an ambition in attributing to him a desire to monopolize the entire mountain trade. Still, if his arrangements had gone through according to plan, this is exactly the situation that would have obtained, at least for a few years.

Several factors intervened to prevent the Ashley empire from being established. The first of these was the equivocal position of his proposed partners, B. Pratte & Company. Until their merger with American Fur had been accomplished they were not in a position to undertake any agreement of such potential importance. Further, they were becoming simply the Western Department of John Jacob Astor's firm. Any decision of this scope would have to be made by a representative of the parent company, probably Astor's agent, Ramsay Crooks.[5]

Secondly, Ashley-as-Mountain-King was not an attractive image. His plan, as proposed, would put an enormous amount of power in the hands of a man almost obsessively ambitious. Any of the principals on the other side—Pratte, the crafty Pierre Chouteau, Crooks—would have been alive to the dangers inherent in giving Ashley too much authority.

In their correspondence, Pierre Chouteau neatly used Ashley's own reputation against him. His great skill, said Chouteau in effect, would be needed on the expedition itself. Ashley's personal presence as leader of the trip was made one of the prime conditions of agreement. This naturally reduced Ashley to the status of a brigade leader with some investment in the enterprise. It also got him away from the nerve center, St. Louis, where the matters of policy and power were decided. Chouteau became quite insistent on this point. Ashley *must* lead the expedition in person; B. Pratte & Company could handle the administration and business end very well, thank you.

This arrangement was contrary to Ashley's wishes and his capabilities. He was not well at the time—his letters make frequent reference to the unhappy state of his health—and furthermore he had no intention whatever of returning to the mountains in person. He wanted to be on the civilized end of the business, the profitable end. He wanted, above all, to be in a position to resume his interrupted political career and to enjoy the benefits of St. Louis social life with his new wife.

All these factors were probably contributory to the final arrangement. Ashley's original broad scheme was turned down. However, if he were willing to restrict his activity to a simple supplying party—omitting the trapping entirely—B. Pratte & Company (acting for John Jacob Astor) would take a half interest.

Ashley's dream of empire was thus converted into a much more limited project. A reasonable profit might be expected, but the elements of power and control implicit in his first proposal were gone. Ashley's ambition had run up against a stone wall: the business acuity of men like Crooks, Chouteau, Pratte, and Astor, compared to whom Ashley was a *mangeur de lard*. In this first venture the Big Guys had deftly shown him his place and the caliber of his competition. It must have been a chastening experience.

III

The involved business negotiations described above took place in St. Louis from the fall of 1826 until early spring of 1827. During this time, of course, Smith Jackson & Sublette were entering Year One of the company in the mountains.

When Rendezvous 1826 broke up, each of the new partners took a brigade and commenced the fall hunt. This was a critical time; their success—or lack of it—would determine whether or not the three-man partnership could remain in business.

Two of these men we have been able to watch since the beginning of this narrative. Jedediah Smith and Bill Sublette had gradually assumed an increasing importance in Ashley's parties, though both started as complete greenhorns. With the retirement of Andrew Henry they (and Tom Fitzpatrick) became the backbone of the field operations. But where did the third partner come from? The answer, such as it is, is simpler than most: I don't know. His name appears at the bottom of the Articles of Agreement, and this is the first hint we have of David E. Jackson's existence.[6]

Davey Jackson, like Andrew Henry, is a man without a biographer, and this is a most unfortunate situation for a historical personage. Jackson, however, has better compensation than Henry. Jackson's Hole, Wyoming, is named for him, and no man could ask better remembrance than that. It was probably around this time, say 1825-1827, that Jackson's Hole received its name, but no definite record exists. More than likely he was booshway of a brigade which trapped the Hole in these years.

Sublette and Jackson took their respective brigades north, to work the Snake and its tributaries. Of Jackson's specific itinerary we know nothing at all, of course. Somehow none of the literary men ever got into his brigades. Sublette had with him Daniel Potts, who had been with the Ashley-Henry venture from the beginning; from the first encampment at the mouth of the Yellowstone. Potts wrote two letters which have become of some importance in the literature of the trade. The first, from the rendezvous just ended, summarized his activities from 1823 to 1826, largely as a member of Captain Weber's brigade.[7] The second was written from Rendezvous 1827, and from it is drawn what we know about Sublette's movements this fall of 1826.

Leaving Cache Valley Sublette worked his brigade slowly up to the Snake, probably by way of the Blackfoot River or the Portneuf. There was no hurry, at least with respect to trapping; this was still summer, and the pelts were liable to be ratty. Up to the Forks, where he turned up Henry's Fork (of the Snake River; not the identically named tributary of the Green) for a distance of about thirty miles, which would put him a little above present St. Anthony, Idaho. From there he crossed over the Tetons, heading east, into Jackson's Hole, where he reached the main fork of the Snake again. This he followed north to its source past Jackson Lake. For most of this time he was being harried by roving bands of Blackfeet, though the party records no casualties this season. Following the Snake past Jackson Lake had swung them toward the east again; now they turned directly north and crossed the range separating Jackson's Hole from what is now Yellowstone National Park. (The most likely route for this would seem to be up Barlow's Fork and Heart Fork Lake.) Here, just a few miles from the continental divide, they came upon the Heart Lake Geyser Basin, and occasioned the first written description of the features that had made the area known to the trappers as Colter's Hell. Potts wrote that they found a crystal-clear lake, which he generously estimated at 100 miles long by 40 wide. (The actual dimensions of Yellowstone Lake, which Potts meant, are closer to 20 miles by 14.) At the southern edge of the lake there were:

a number of hot and boiling springs, some of water and others of most beautiful fine clay, resembling a mush pot, and throwing particles to the immense height of from twenty to thirty feet. The clay is of a white, and of a pink color, and the water appears fathomless, as it appears to be entirely hollow underneath. There is also a number of places where pure sulphur is sent forth in abundance.

The lake itself for some little time bore the name "Soubletts Lake," in honor of their worthy booshway, but this, as with many of the mountain given names, soon disappeared. Sublette's party then took "a circuitous route to the North West," according to Potts (which may or may not mean circling around by way of Targhee Pass and back down Henry's Fork). On their return toward Cache Valley, the brigade ran into more intermittent trouble with the Blackfeet, and still got off with hair unlifted.

It was late in the season when Sublette got back to Cache Valley. Jackson (having trapped east: on Ham's Fork and the Green? or the Snake below the Portneuf?) was probably already there. The fall hunt of both brigades had been good; certainly good enough to pay the remainder of their debt to Ashley, and to warrant the sending of an express to St. Louis with an order for merchandise. (Jedediah's movements this fall were the most important; and are treated more fully in Chapter 10.)

Sublette himself chose to make the express, taking with him only one man, Black (nee Moses) Harris. (Alfred Jacob Miller, the painter, wrote some years later: "This Black Harris always created a sensation at the camp fire, being a capital *raconteur*, and having had as many perilous adventures as any man probably in the mountains. He was of wiry form, made up of bone and muscle, with a face apparently composed of tan leather and whip cord, finished off with a peculiar blue-black tint, as if gunpowder had been burned into his face." See *The West of Alfred Jacob Miller* [Norman, 1951.]) Harris was very near the classic type of the mountain man. He appears again and again in the records of the time, sometimes for his version of the putrefied forest tale (see p. 74), just as often for the craft that became his specialty, the midwinter express, either alone or with one other man. This time it was with Bill Sublette, and it is the first appearance of Harris in the role.

The two left Cache Valley in the dead of winter, January 1 of the year 1827. The snow was heavy, and they could expect it all the way to St. Louis; which made horses out of the question. They left on snowshoes, their only provisions carried on the back of a dog. (Before the advent of the horse in the mountains, almost all Indians had been dependent on trained pack dogs. There were still a few of these Indian-trained dogs about, but they soon disappeared as the bands became entirely horse-oriented.) The record—as related by Sublette fifteen years later—says the dog was loaded with fifty pounds of provisions and the men carried dried buffalo meat on their backs.

The first few days they probably followed the course of the Bear up and around the northern end of the Bear River Mountains; then crossed the complex series of ridges separating Bear Lake from the Valley of the Green River.

So far prospects were not particularly encouraging; no buffalo sign and some Indian, which looked like Blackfoot. Instead of following up the Sandy, Sublette and Harris cut across the plains to the south of that river, in hopes of avoiding the Blackfeet. This reduced them to melting snow for their water, but there was plenty of that. By the middle of January they were descending the Sweetwater; the fifteenth day out they made camp for the night in the shelter of Independence Rock.

Moving on the next day, they had to plow their way through drifted snow, and the going was hard. It became worse the farther they went; no game, no firewood, and frequently not even a hollow in which they could protect themselves from the wind and cold. They were coming on starvin' times and there was still the danger of Indians. Finding some evidences that Pawnees were moving about on the North Platte, the men left that river for several days and stumbled along out of sight of the water.

Finally they found, and followed, the trace of another band of Indians, hoping to get some food from them. Their own provisions had given out (part of them lost somewhere on the trail, fallen from the worn dog-pack) and both men and dog were reaching what seemed to be the end of the road. After four days they overtook the camp, which were Omahas under the chief Big Elk. While they were friendly, they could be of little help; Indians fared no better than whites in a winter like this. Subsequently they met several other bands on the move, all of whom received them hospitably but were unable to give them anything in the way of food. With one of these Sublette was able to trade his butcher knife for a buffalo tongue, good at the time, but hardly enough to support two men and a dog for long.

A raven was shot near Grand Island but was small comfort. Fatigue and hunger were such that they couldn't tell "whether it was good or bad, or how it tasted."

By now the dog was lagging far behind each day, following their tracks into camp long after dark. Both men were so weak from hunger and their exertions they were barely able to make camp at night. One night, some forty or fifty miles below Grand Island, Harris had a proposition. Sublette that night had just brushed the snow away and fallen into his blanket exhausted; Harris had managed to kindle some kind of fire with broken branches. As they sat in the blind stupor of starvation, Harris suggested they kill and eat the dog.

According to Sublette's later story, he was at first reluctant, but was finally persuaded. (Both men were reportedly sick at this time; but in circumstances of that kind it is difficult to distinguish between sickness and health.)

Harris swung at the dog with his ax, but the animal crawled back to his feet; there was no strength behind the blow. Staggering up to the howling dog, Harris struck at him again, and missed. On the third time the axhead flew off the handle, and the dog wailed away into the night. The two men groped for it in the darkness, and finally found it. Harris stabbed it, and threw it on the fire to singe off the fur, in accepted Indian fashion; but the reflex convulsions of the animal kicked the fire away. Sublette, frantic, finally bashed in the crown of the dog's head with his own ax and stumbled back to his blanket.

Harris stayed on his feet long enough to roast the dog, saving some for Sublette, who was able to eat a little in the morning. What remained they packed with them. It lasted for two days.

They were able to kill a rabbit and four wild turkeys in later days, which took them to the Big Vermillion. A little beyond that river they stumbled into a Kaw village, where they were fed. Sublette was apparently somewhat better by this time, but Harris had sprained an ankle and could barely pull himself along. Sublette, by trading his pistol, got a horse for the remaining two-day journey to St. Louis.

They arrived on March 4, and it could not have been a

pleasant homecoming to discover that Ashley was brimming with plans to send a trapping party into the mountains against them.

IV

There is no written record of Sublette's reaction when he discovered Ashley's plans. He must have objected in the strongest terms, and his objections may have had some effect on the final shape of the expedition. Possibly he was able to convince B. Pratte & Company that their best interests for the future lay not with Ashley, but with Smith Jackson & Sublette. (This, again, is pure conjecture. There is no evidence.)

Almost immediately after Sublette's arrival in St. Louis, arrangements for the supply party were initiated. Pratte & Company appointed a business agent for the expedition, in the person of James B. Bruffee. Bruffee worked on a straight salary: $800. The booshway, the field captain, was apparently Ashley's choice. This was Hiram Scott, who had served as a nominal captain under Ashley in the Aricara campaign. Scott was paid a total of $280, a rate of $2 a day for the time the party was in the field.

On March 8, 1827, Ashley advertised in the St. Louis papers for fifty men. He had little trouble in finding them; the rumors of his successes the past two years (both true and exaggerated) had made the name of William H. Ashley synonymous with fortunes to be made in the mountains. (This was a dream that died hard, if at all.)

Most of the men hired on at $110 a year, according to a document now in the collection of the Missouri Historical Society. There are a few unexplained variations: Antoine Durmai got $120; Potette Dyerda (Dejarda) $130; and Antoine Janis was high with $165. By the end of the trip, paytime, these sums were somewhat reduced by advances en route of one kind and another; Augustus Gerarda, for one example, had only $27.20 cash coming. (All except for John Bowen, who had $109 left out of his $110; I'd give a lot to know what he spent that buck for in transit. It must have been a soul-rending decision.)

By April 11 the expedition was outfitted and ready to go. Their jump off point was Lexington, and on the 11th Ashley wrote to Pratte & Company:

I am preparing to pack my mules & will depart therefrom tomorrow morning—My party is in fine condition & will in my opinion so remain, which is truly a fortunate circumstance as my verry bad health prevents much exertion on my part—Messrs Bruffee & Scott appears alive to our interest. The latter is entirely efficient & if properly supported by the former will keep all Things in their proper Channel—should my health continue as it is at present I shall proceed but a few days with them after leaving this place.

(Along with this expedition went a historic piece of artillery—a four-pounder, mounted on a mule-drawn carriage, the first wheeled vehicle to cross the continental divide over the newly found South Pass. The ruts it left would be followed by thousands of other wheels, the Conestoga wagons of the Oregon Trail.)

Bill Sublette caught up with the party a little later; he had been picking up his younger brother Pinckney, a boy of fourteen or fifteen, taking him to the mountains to learn the trade, and paying a visit to General Clark to secure the formal trading license. It authorized Smith Jackson & Sublette to trade for two years "on the waters of a river supposed to be the Bonaventure. —Horse Prairie, on Clarks river of the Columbia, and mouth of Lewis' Fork of the Columbia." (This license is interesting in that the area it covers is mostly in the disputed, "joint occupancy" territory. The "mouth of Lewis' Fork" is the confluence of the Snake with the Columbia, and in the direct scope of HBC's Fort Nez Perces. Horse Prairie, too, was within a few miles of the British Flathead House. SJ&S were plunging into the British back yard.)

Rendezvous 1827 was set for the south end of Bear Lake (some fifteen miles into Mexican territory), and the scattered trappers began drifting in toward the latter part of June.

The usual fringe of Snakes were there, together with a camp of "Utaws." In the early stages of the gathering, a war party of 120 Blackfeet descended on the camp and killed a Snake and his squaw. This precipitated a battle, with Snakes, Utes, and whites (though only six of these) besieging the Blackfeet where they'd holed up: a "small concavity thickly grown with small timber surrounded by open ground."

Total casualties were three Snakes killed and three wounded; one white wounded; no Ute casualties, "though they gained great applause for their bravery." They found six Blackfeet dead, and a number were carried off by their compatriots. (Cf. James P. Beckwourth's accounting: "one hundred and seventy three (Blackfoot) scalps ... seven or eight (whites) wounded ... eleven (of the Indian) allies killed in battle.")

This was conversational material for the campfire when the rendezvous filled up, but the biggest news came from Jedediah Smith, whose party had been given up for lost. When the fall and winter passed without word, the natural assumption was that Smith had fallen victim to the hazards of the trade; Injuns, starvin' times, and what not.

Well, he'd had them, and more than that, when he pulled in on July 3. There were only two men with him, and he had no furs.

Jedediah, it seemed, had walked over to California. The rest of his men, plus the fall hunt's pelts, were still there—and he was going back after them.

CHAPTER 10

"I was looked upon with suspicion"

IT HAS been stated that the Southwest Expedition of Jedediah Smith was principally one of exploration; purpose being, according to this interpretation, to determine whether or not the fabled Buenaventura River existed. But the mountain men knew by now that there was no such river flowing out of the northwest reaches of Great Salt Lake, and the "coasting" party had not been able to discover a genuine outlet anywhere around the periphery.

Jedediah himself has two different statements; however, he was making a rather special case each time. To the United States plenipotentiary in Mexico he later wrote that he started "for the purpose of hunting *Ber*"—but it was to Smith's interest that the Mexicans be convinced of this. To General Clark he wrote that he went "for the purpose of exploring the country"—a motive which would have been the last thing he would admit to the Mexican government.

This is not mere quibbling; there is a real and rather important difference between hunting for beaver and exploring the country, though naturally the two were often entwined. To me, the most reasonable explanation for this incredible expedition lies in Smith's statement to the United States plenipotentiary; that he started for beaver, and "not finding them plenty enough to justify me in Stopping, I pushed on."

This for two reasons. First, the tenuous situation of the new partnership; it was, according to the Articles of Agreement, "uncertain whether the situation of [the] business will justify the proposed purchase of merchandise" from Ashley. That being the case, it seems extremely unlikely that the major partner of the firm would be detached on a trip primarily intended for exploration. They needed the beaver too badly; they could not spare the men for a possibly unprofitable fall season. Secondly, there is good reason to believe they had gotten reports (Indian?) of the existence of a rich beaver country to the southwest of Great Salt Lake. These rumors had reached as far as the HBC traders.[1]

(My view here contradicts Mr. Dale Morgan, Smith's biographer, who inclines to the exploration-for-the-Bonaventura theory. I must mention that disagreeing with Mr. Morgan regarding the fur trade is something a man should do only after long and careful thought, and then with some trepidation. I have found it necessary to differ with him at several points in this narrative; and have done so each time with a clear and present sense of contradicting my betters.)

Jedediah remained at Cache Valley a month after Rendezvous 1826 broke up, probably making meat and getting his party in order for the expedition. He was well aware from his spring hunt that he had a vast distance of gameless, beaverless country to go through. In consequence, he outfitted himself with 700 pounds of dried meat, probably hoping it would last until he reached the rumored richer ground, where his hunters could supply the party with fresh game.

The brigade got off around the 15th of August. It consisted of about fifteen men, including Smith himself and his clerk, Harrison Rogers.[2] It was a journey of heat and hunger, dry holes and no game, and endless trudging across barren lands. Under the vicious sun of late summer this small party tracked south through the desert country of western Utah. The men were restive and quarrelsome, and the expedition soon took on the aspect of an ordeal. The 700 pounds of dried meat Jedediah had prudently carried gave out too soon, leaving them without provisions in this "Country of Starvation—Sandy plains and Rocky hills once in 20 30 or 40 *m* a little pond or Spring of water with a little grass."

Smith traveled through this country and finally fell on the headwaters of the Virgin River, which he named the Adams, in honor of the President. (The name Virgin is probably from Thomas Virgin, one of the members of Smith's second expedition.) On this river he met "a nation of Indians who call themselves Pa-Utches," the Paiutes, who told him of a

marvelous cave of salt. He took a sample of this to send to
General Clark; salt was one of the principal concerns as this
nation expanded to the west, and a discovery of a good
source was of considerable significance.

He moved down the Virgin to its confluence with the
Colorado. Somehow he was able to identify the Colorado
with the river he called Seedskeeder, and found that his
earlier conception of its destination was correct; this was
indeed the "Spanish River" that emptied into the Gulf of
California.

Four days he followed the Seedskeeder-Green-Colorado,
and at the end of that time reached a tribe whose name he
rendered as "Ammuchabas": the Mojaves. Here he found a
higher standard than among the Paiutes; the Indians were a
handsome race, and, more to the point,

> They cultivate the soil, and raise corn, beans, pump-
> kins, watermelons and muskmelons in abundance, and
> also a little wheat and cotton.

The Mojaves received Smith's party with a reasonable
hospitality; and the whites were much in need of something
of the kind:

> . . . coming through this *coun* of Starvation . . . I had
> lost so many horses that we were all on foot—my
> men & the remainder of my Horses were worn out
> with fatigue & hardships & emaciated with hunger.

Smith stayed with the Mojaves for fifteen days, resting his
men and deciding what to do. He knew by now the country
he was in was nothing like beaver country—and, from what
the Mojaves told him, there was none around. The rumors
hadn't panned out, and a more unlikely spot for mountain
trappers than the Mojave country would be hard to find. He
was able to trade off his starved horses and even buy a few
more. These had come from the Spanish missions, stolen by
runaway Indians. One of the Mojaves spoke a little Spanish;
so did one of Smith's men, and in this tongue they made
what sketchy communication there was.

> . . . by this means I found that it was not far to some
> of the Missions of California & I detirmined (as this

was the only resort) to go to that place as soon as my men & horses should be able to travel.

He found two guides—runaways again, Indians from the missions who found the rule of Christ as practiced by the Mexicans a little too hard on their backs—and set out from the Mojaves on November 10, 1826.

On November 27 Harrison Rogers' journal begins, and it records:

> There came an old Ind. to us that speaks good Spanish, and took us with him to his mansion, which consisted of 2 rows of large and lengthy buildings, after the Spanish mode, thay remind me of the British Barracks.

This was the arrival of Smith and his party in the dead heart of Spanish territory, the San Gabriel Mission. They were nine miles from the Pueblo de Nuestra Señora de Los Angeles (which consisted—at this time—of about eighty houses and seven hundred inhabitants; almost as many as a fair-sized Snake encampment).

II

They had passed from the Country of Starvation into the Land of Plenty. A cow was butchered immediately, and "there was great feasting among the men as they were pretty hungry not having any good meat for some time."

Shortly after their arrival at the mission, they were greeted by the "2 commandants of the missionary establishment [who] had the appearance of gentlemen."

Smith went with these two gentlemen to the mission house, some four miles or so from their present location. Rogers and the rest of the company remained behind, savoring their good fortune.

The principal part of that good fortune was to come upon the Mission San Gabriel near the peak of its prosperity. The genial Padre José Sanchez was in charge here, and a more gracious host never set table. More than a thousand persons were employed at the mission in various capacities: "all kinds of macanicks," men to work the rich vineyards, and tend the lush orchards of apple and peach and orange and fig. Indian women wove "blankets and sundry other articles." There was a whiskey distillery—brandy, more accurately—and a mill where the mission grain was ground into flour.

> The situation is very handsome, pretty streams of water running through from all quarters, some thousands of acres of rich and fertile land . . . in view, and a part under cultivation, surround on the N. with a high and lofty mou., handsomely timbered with pine, and cedar.

Rogers said the mission had upwards of thirty thousand head of cattle, and slaughtered two to three thousand head at a time. The sale of the cattle was the chief source of monetary income for the mission, and they also sold great quantities of tallow and hides.

A little later, with the secularization of the missions, this great wealth would diminish; but for now Father Sanchez held sway over a rich community, ruling with the absolute authority of a medieval baron. Other aspects of the feudal age were present, of a harsher nature. The two guides who had brought Smith from the Mojaves were imprisoned—being runaways—and one of them died. The other was sentenced to death, and reprieved at the last moment.

Rogers several times records the beating of the Indians, and as to their general condition:

> The Inds. appear to be much altered from the wild Indians in the Mou. that we have passed. They are kept in great fear; for the least offense they are corrected; they are compleat slaves in every sense of the word.

> [On December 10] There was five Inds. brought to the mission . . . and sentenced to be whiped for not going to work when ordered.

> Each received from 12 to 14 lashes on their bare posteriors; they were all old men, say from 50 to 60 years of age, the commandant standing by with his sword to see that the Ind. who flogged them done his duty.

> [And January 3] There was five or six Inds. brought to the Mission and whiped, and one of them being stubborn and did not like to submit to the lash was knocked down by the commandant, tied and

severely whiped, then chained by the leg to another
Ind who had been guilty of a similar offence.

But Smith and Rogers themselves were treated to the shiny
side of the feudal coin: the feasting and good wine and a
pleasant comradeship. The day after Smith had gone to the
mission house to be interviewed by Father Sanchez—and
politely disarmed—he wrote Rogers that he had been "received as a gentleman and treated as such." Rogers was to go
back and look for a pistol that was lost, and join his captain
at the "mansion." The clerk arrived

> late in the evening, was received very politely, and
> showed into a room and my arms taken from me.
> About 10 o'clock at night supper was served, and
> Mr. S. and myself sent for. I was introduced to the 2
> priests over a glass of good old whiskey and found
> them to be very jovial friendly gentlemen, the sup-
> per consisted of a number of different dishes, served
> different from any table I was ever at. Plenty of
> good wine during supper, before the cloth was re-
> moved sigars was introduced.

And in the meantime an express had been sent to the
governor of Alta, California informing him of the strange
arrival of a party of ragged, starving Americans who claimed
to have crossed the Great Basin for no better reason than
hunting beaver.

The governor, to whom Smith also wrote, was José Maria
de Echeandia, a suspicious martinet of a man, tall and
gaunt.[8] For some little time the governor responded neither
to Sanchez' express nor Smith's letter. The booshway and his
clerk were treated to a procession of elaborate and luxurious
meals, accompanied with music. The men of the party, char-
acteristically enough, were not treated so hospitally; they
were on short rations until Smith mentioned the matter to the
padre. Then the trappers were immediately moved into better
quarters and given ample provision.

At the "ellegant dinner(s)," Rogers wrote:

> Mr. S. and myself acted quite independent, knot
> understanding there language, nor they ours; we en-
> deavored to appologise, being very dirty and not in a
> situation to shift our clothing, but no excuse would be

taken, we must be present, and we have been served at there table ever since we arrived at this place; they treat [us] as gentlemen in every sense of the word, although our apparel is so indifferent, we not being in circumstances at this time to help ourselves.

After the new regulations regarding food went into effect, the trappers of the party settled down somewhat, though

Mr. S. informed me [Rogers] this morning that he had to give [James] Read a little floggin yesterday evening, on account of some of his impertinence.

On the 1st of December, Smith and Abraham Laplant, one of his men, made a trip to the "parblo" of Los Angeles, and returned the next day with news that a Mr. Francisco (probably Martinez) had promised him to supply all the horses and mules he needed.

For the next week nothing happened. Smith and Rogers idled about the mission, watching the Indians, trying to keep their own men out of mischief. Rogers' journal in part:

[Dec.] 4th. Still at St. Gabriel; things much as usual. 5th. We are still remaining at the mansion of St. Gabriel, waiting the . . Governor's answer to a letter. . . 6th. Things going on as they have been heretofore; no answer from the governor as yet; we are waiting with patience to hear from the governor. . . 7th. No answer as yet from the governor of the province.

Francisco Martinez came over from Los Angeles on the 7th; he spoke English, and was sympathetic with Smith's impatience. His advice was to see the governor in person if no reply was forthcoming, and Smith began to entertain the idea of riding to the presidio at San Diego. But on the next day, December 8, the governor's reply came. It was short and to the point. Smith was to report before Señor Echeandia immediately.

The next day Smith departed for San Diego, in the company of one of his men and Captain William Cunningham of the ship *Courier*. Cunningham was at San Gabriel to arrange for hides and tallow, and the *Courier* was lying in San Diego. This gentleman and Smith seemed to strike up a considerable friendship in their short acquaintance. It is probable that, without Captain Cunningham's assistance, Smith's difficulty would have been much more severe. In a letter written while being held at San Diego, Smith said, "I have found in Capt Cunningham of the Courier a friend which I stand much in need of as I am destitute of almost every thing."

If he had expected from Echeandia the kind of courtesy extended by Father Sanchez, Smith was disappointed. The governor—"who appears to be very much of a Gentleman but very suspicious"—could not satisfy himself as to the truth of Smith's story. It seemed to him much more likely that he had a pack of spies on hand. He demanded Smith's journal (which was probably Rogers'), his license (why did Smith come with fourteen men when the license from General Clark listed fifty-seven? were the others hiding out somewhere?), Smith's ideas of the country (and why, if he was merely a fur hunter, should he be making maps?), etc., etc.

Worst of all, Echeandia seemed reluctant to make a decision on this strange interloper by himself. It might be necessary to write to Mexico, saddle someone else with the problem. In four days Smith was:

> Questioned & crossquestioned three different times by the *Gov* ... I have applied to him for Horses & endeavored to convince him of the truth that I was only a hunter & that Dire necessity had driven me here I am to call next tuesday for to know whether I can pass, or be detained here 3 months, for an answer from Mexico ... instead of thanking me for the information which I have given him & assisting me to pass on about my business he seems to be for detaing me untill he ascertains that I am no Spy—which will deprive me of making a valuable Spring hunt.

This letter was written on the 15th, the "next tuesday" being December 19. So for three days Jedediah remained in San Diego, virtually a prisoner, while the gloomy Echeandia presumably sorted it all out in his mind.

Meanwhile Rogers was still enjoying himself about the Mission San Gabriel, noting almost every day in his journal "Things much the same" and "Nothing of consequence has taken place today more than usual." He went out fowling a couple of times, and broke up a fight among his own men; observed that the priest played at cards both Sundays and "weak a days; when he has company that can play pretty expert." There was even a theological discussion: Rogers being a strict Calvinist did not believe in the ability of any man to absolve another for his sins, yet listened to the priest's explanation of Catholic doctrine and duly noted it all down in his journal.

December dwindled out to nothing, and still he had not heard from his captain. On New Year's Day, 1827, he delivered a long address to the reverend father on the subject of missionary history as recorded in the Old and New Testaments, the text of which is carefully recorded in the journal. Finally, word came through, on January 3. Smith wrote that the governor had signed his passports; and a grudging signature it must have been. It took the sworn statements of six American officers—three of them full captains—to induce Echeandia's pen to paper.[4]

Smith had originally requested permission to proceed along the coast northward. He wanted to go to the bay of San Francisco, and "follow up one of the largest *Riv* that emptied into the Bay cross the *mou* at its head and from thence to our Deposit on the waters of the Salt Lake."

This permission the governor refused. He gave permission for Smith to trade such supplies as he needed, and to depart. But not north; Smith was to leave the Mexican territory the fastest way, which was—to Echeandia's precise mind—exactly the same way he had come.

It may well be that permission to go back across the Great Basin, which had already cost him thirty-two horses, was greeted with something less than enthusiasm by the booshway. Still, it was better than waiting three months, or being sent under guard to Mexico.

And at San Gabriel, Rogers observes with true Calvinist spirit:

> The women here are very unchaste. . . . They think it an honnour to ask a white man to sleep with them; one came to my lodgings last night and asked me to make her a blanco Pickanina, which, being interpreted, is to get her a white child, and I must say for the first time, I was ashamed, and did not gratify her or comply with her request, seeing her so forward, I had no propensity to tech her. Things about the mission much the same.

III

There had been a certain amount of disaffection among the men of Smith's party from the beginning of the trip. Rogers observes at one point that "Our own men are contentious and quarrelsome amongst themselves and have been ever since we started the expedition." This was due in part, of course, to their circumstances; first the ordeal of the desert crossing, then to be plunged overnight into idleness. Even the generosity of the good Father Sanchez was little appreciated. (Among other things, he had given Smith sixty-four yards of material to make shirts for his men.)

The principal troublemakers in Smith's brigade were his blacksmith, James Reed, and Daniel Ferguson. Reed was plain cantankerous; the mentions of him in Rogers' journal draw the picture of a man much inclined to feel himself put upon. It rankled him that Smith and Rogers were accorded better treatment than the rest of the men, even though Father Sanchez had been quick enough to improve their condition when it was mentioned to him by Smith.

It was previously noted that Smith found it necessary to "give Read a little floggin . . . on account of some of his impertinence"; but Harrison Rogers was not the man to discipline that rowdy crew with his fists. Smith's long-extended absence while wrangling with Echeandia left Rogers in an ambiguous position: "I am at a loss how to act in [Smith's] absence with the company, as he left no special instructions with me when he left here." [Jan. 1, 1827, entry.]

Reed's belligerence came to a head on January 6. On this Epiphany day wine was issued "abundantly to both Spanyards and Inds." And also to the transient trappers, because Reed and Ferguson started a brawl. When the Mexicans tried to break it up, one of them hit another of the trappers, Arthur Black. This, naturally, changed the direction of the fight; Reed and Ferguson presumably forgot whatever fuzzy-headed grievance they had with each other and turned to face the Mexicans.

A battle with an international flavor was on the point of breaking out, which would probably have resulted in serious consequences. When Rogers heard what was happening, he hurried off to confront the prospective fighters, and arrived before any real damage had been done. Somehow he managed to talk their way out of the impending situation: "I went among them, and passified our men by telling them what trouble they were bringing upon themselves in case they did not desist."

Trouble indeed; fourteen men in the midst of what amounted to an armed garrison were in no position to be starting a battle royal. The Mexicans maintained at San Gabriel a strong force of soldiers and had eight pieces of artillery; "to protect them from the Inds. in case they should rebel." Had the fracas begun, Smith would probably have returned to San Gabriel—if at all—in chains. However, Rogers managed the affair with a good deal of skill for a man not accustomed to command. He must have painted the picture of possible consequences clearly enough, for "the most of them [the trappers], being men of reason, adhered to my advice."

James Reed, as might have been expected, was not satisfied with this outcome; and his resentment at the officers' special treatment was still hot, perhaps nearly as hot as the *aguardiente* that nurtured it. Later that night, while Rogers and Father Sanchez were having their customary quiet dinner, Reed paid them a visit.

He was still enormously drunk when he burst into the priest's dining room and demanded more "ergadent." Father Sanchez very politely invited the man to sit at the table with them, and ordered a plate of food to be brought for him. Reed ate a few mouthfuls, and sullenly set the plate back on the table.

He grabbed the decanter of wine and drank, "and came very near braking the glass when he set it down." Father Sanchez' innate good taste and hospitality prevented anything coming of this second disturbance. As Rogers dryly noted, "The Padre, seeing he was in a state of inebriety, refrained from saying anything."

For Rogers himself the events of the day were probably as much embarrassing as dangerous; the little clerk was almost wistful about the good life as lived at San Gabriel. He was profoundly conscious of the poor appearance he and his men made, ragged and dirty, amidst the more civilized finery at the mission. Several of his journal entries deal with his embarrassment:

> My situation is a very delicate one, being among the grandees of the country every day. . . . I make a very grotesque appearance when seated at table

among the dandys with there ruffles, silks, and broad clothes.

This is hardly the kind of concern one might expect of the mountain man; but then the label tends to make us forget the wide variety of men who made fur hunting their trade. Not all were James Reeds by any means. For Rogers the civilized attractions of San Gabriel held great appeal.

> I could see a great deal of satisfaction here if I could talk there language [he wrote] but, as it is, I feel great diffidence in being among them, knot knowing the topic of there conversation, still every attention is paid to me by all that is present, especially the old priest. I must say he is a very fine man and a very much of a gentleman.

Four days after leaving San Gabriel, Rogers, the Calvinist, wrote of the genial priest:

> Old Father Sanchus has been the greatest friend that I ever met with in all my travels, he is worthy of being called a Christian, as he possesses charity in the highest degree, and a friend to the poor and distressed. I shall ever hold him as a man of God, taking us when in distress, feeding, and clothing us, and may God prosper him and all such men.

Smith arrived back at Mission San Gabriel on Wednesday, January 10, having been brought back up the coast by his seafaring savior, Captain Cunningham of the *Courier*.[5]

The next week was a round of horse buying, mostly at Los Angeles. Smith purchased around fifty horses in the ensuing week; and even at the relatively cheap California prices, it is not clear where he got the money to pay for them. It is probable he had made some kind of arrangement with Cunningham. The horses, according to Rogers' vague comment, were to be paid for in merchandise, at the *Courier* (now at San Pedro).

By the 18th the party had been made up. They rose early and started out—Smith having received a final courtesy from Father Sanchez, in the form of an order for "all the supplyes we stand in need of" at the frontier settlement of San Bernardino.

(Rogers had a bit of difficulty with the name, within three days having it variously Bernado, Bernardano, Bernandino, Burnandeino. The last he used twice, which gives it a kind of official sanction.)

However, within a half mile of the mission Smith discovered his Mexican-trained horses were still free of spirit; they "started and run 8 or 10 miles before we stoped them." They encamped for the night in the neighborhood of present Santa Anita, and Smith and Rogers returned to the mission for a last farewell. Father Sanchez "Gave each of us a blankett, and give me [Rogers] a cheese, and a gourd filled with ogadent."

They stayed in this camp all the next day. Five of their best horses were missing, and part of the men were detailed to find them, while others tried to break those that remained, with only indifferent success. The hunters returned without finding the missing animals, and Smith decided to abandon them. They procured an Indian boy for a guide and started out the next morning, Sunday the 21st.

The party was one man short. Daniel Ferguson had apparently been as much taken with Mission San Gabriel as Rogers; in any event, he hid himself there so Smith could not find him when the brigade was ready to leave. Another man, John Wilson, had been "discharged" by Smith on the 17th, under unrecorded circumstances. Wilson, however, had not been able to get permission to remain in the country, and was now back with the party, though not on pay as yet.

For nearly a week they remained at their camp of the 21st; an Indian farmhouse about four miles from San Bernardino. During this time Smith was engaged in negotiations with the steward at San Bernardino, making final arrangements for goods, trading off the wildest of his horses while the men continued their efforts to break those he kept.

(Rogers' journal ends abruptly on January 27, while they were still encamped outside San Bernardino. The movements of the party are somewhat more conjectural from this point.)

When Echeandia had finally given Smith permission to leave California, it was with the provision that he return by the way he had come. It is equally certain that Smith had no such intention (see Note 5, p. 439). His plan was to head toward the north, probably hoping to intersect a river that would take him across the mountains; possibly even across the Great Basin. He knew there was nothing to be had in the latitudes he had covered; but farther north there was still a possibility.

Smith described his return route in the letter to General Clark previously quoted:

> I returned to my party and purchased such articles as were necessary, and went Eastward of the Spanish settlements on the route I had come in. I then steered my course N.W. keeping from 150 miles to 200 miles from the sea coast. A very high range of mountains [the Sierra Nevadas] lay on the East. After travelling three hundred miles in that direction through a country somewhat fertile, in which there was a great many Indians, mostly naked and destitute of arms, with the exception of a few Bows and Arrows and what is very singular amongst Indians, they cut their hair to the length of three inches; they proved to be friendly; their manner of living is on fish, roots, acorns and grass.
>
> On my arrival at the river which I named the *Wim-mul-che* (named after a tribe of Indians which resides on it, of that name) I found a few beaver, and elk, deer, and antelope in abundance. [Morgan identifies this as Kings River.] I here made a small hunt, and attempted to take my party across the [mountains] which I before mentioned, and which I called *Mount Joseph,* to come on and join my partners at the Great Salt Lake. I found the snow so deep on Mount Joseph that I could not cross my horses, five of which starved to death; I was compelled therefore to return to the valley which I had left, and there, leaving my party, I started with two men, seven horses and two mules, which I loaded with hay for the horses and provisions for ourselves, and started on the 20th day of May, and succeeded in crossing it in eight days, having lost only two horses and one mule.

Meanwhile the Mexican authorities were becoming disturbed about Smith's steady progress up the middle of California. It was reported that Smith, or some of his party, had induced the desertion of 400 converted Indians from the missions. (It was later discovered that these desertions had been caused by one of the Christianized Indians "using the specious pretext of the Americans," but for the time being the presence of Smith's party was regarded with a good deal of alarm.)

Jedediah learned of this from some of the Indians he encountered and was anxious that there be no more trouble with the authorities. On May 19 (just one day before he left his camp to cross the Great Basin), he wrote Narciso Durán, president of all the missions, at San José:

> Reverend Father;—I understand, through the medium of one of your Christian Indians, that you are anxious to know who we are, as some of the Indians have been at the Mission and informed you that there were certain white people in the country. We are Americans, on our journey to the River Columbia; we were in at the Mission San Gabriel in January last; I went to San Diego and saw the General, and got a passport from him to pass on to that place. I have made several efforts to cross the mountains, but the snow being so deep I could not succeed in getting over. I returned to this place (it being the only point to kill meat) to wait a few weeks until the snow melts so that I can go on; the Indians here also being friendly, I consider it the most safe point for me to remain, until such time as I can cross the mountains with my horses, having lost a great many in attempting to cross ten or fifteen days since. I am a long ways from home, and am anxious to get there as soon as the nature of the case will admit. Our situation is quite unpleasant, being destitute of clothing and most necessities of life, wild meat being our principal subsistence. I am, Reverend Father, your strange, but real friend and Christian brother.
>
> May 19, 1827
>
> J. S. Smith

Father Durán would not receive the letter. Instead, he had it sent to Monterey; Echeandia was now there, and perhaps Durán felt the temporal authority better equipped to deal with the problem. The governor ordered the temporary *comandante* at San Francisco, one Ignacio Martinez, to take Smith into custody. His passport, said Echeandia, did not entitle him to inspect the Mexican settlements, doubtless making maps for future mischief. Smith was apparently to be disarmed and held at San José until further instructions could be forwarded from Mexico; or until a ship came that would transport him directly to Oregon, without the necessity of his passing through any more Mexican territory.

However, by the time these orders had been issued and put into effect, it was too late. The Mexicans found Smith already gone, having left with two other men to make the trip back to Great Salt Lake.

What transpired at the American camp (which was probably on the Stanislaus River) is not precisely known; presumably Harrison Rogers was in command in Smith's absence. He must have talked well; and perhaps the soldiery were "men of reason" also. In any event, the trappers were left unmolested, waiting for Smith to return from the mountain rendezvous.

The two men who accompanied Smith on the eastward trip were Silas Gobel, the blacksmith, and Robert Evans. It was a journey of starvation and thirst, of heat and desperation. On the summit of "Mount Joseph" the snow was from four to eight feet deep. Repeated thawings and refreezings had formed crust on the surface, and the hoofs of the animals sank only from six inches to a foot; without this minor fortune of weather, the crossing would probably have been impossible. As it was, he lost two of the horses and a mule; considered himself lucky to get off so cheap, referring to the loss as "only two horses and one mule." It seems enough, as he started with seven and two, respectively.

The three men were eight days crossing the Sierra Nevada.[6] They came down the eastern slope near the end of May, and started the long trek across Nevada. The country was

> completely barren and destitute of game. We frequently travelled without water sometimes for two days over sandy deserts where there was no sign of vegetation and when we found water in some of the rocky hills, we most generally found som Indians who appeared the most miserable of the human race, having nothing to subsist on, (nor any clothing) except grass seed, grasshoppers, &c.

Smith's descriptive letter to General Clark says he traveled "twenty days from the East side of *Mount Joseph*" to reach Great Salt Lake, but this does not jibe with his own journal.

The journal records seeing "the Salt Lake a joyful sight" for the first time on June 27; thirty-eight days from his camp and thirty after the eight-day crossing of the Sierra Nevada.

The last stage of the trip was an agony of endurance. On the 23rd, after having passed salty and undrinkable springs during the day, he finally reached "water that was drinkable but continued on in hopes of finding better"—and there was none. They had to encamp without any. By this time the horses had dwindled down to three; the superior endurance of the mule was beginning to show.

The next day Jedediah climbed a hill, but the prospect was just the same: "sandy plains or dry Rocky hills." Fifty or sixty miles to the northeast he could see a range of mountains whose peaks were snow-covered—a reminder there were places in the world where water was not a problem. Descending, he was afraid to tell Gobel and Evans what he had seen; told them instead that he "saw something black at a distance, near which no doubt we would find water."

One of the horses had died while he was on the hill; now there were only two. The party took the best of the flesh and pushed on. Smith tried to keep up the spirits of the other two, but what could he say? To his journal he told the truth: "The view ahead was almost hopeless."

They trudged through the soft sand all that day, and about four in the afternoon came to a small sand hill where a cedar was growing, giving shade. They dug holes and buried themselves in the sand, as Smith had done with two other men four years before. They rested there for about an hour, then wearily started out again.

During the afternoon and evening Smith was tormented by the sight of turtle doves; birds he could never remember seeing more than a few miles from water. Desperately he spent an aimless hour trying to find it; and there was none. At ten o'clock they rested again, but:

> Our sleep was not repose, for tormented nature made us dream of things we had not. . . . In those moments how trifling were all those things that hold such an absolute sway over the busy and prosperous world. My dreams were not of Gold or ambitious honors, but of my distant quiet home, of murmuring brooks. . . . After a short rest we continued our march and traveled all night.

Twelve hours later, on the morning of the 25th, Robert Evans gave out. He "laid down in the plain . . . being able to go no further. We could do no good by remaining to die with him and we were not able to help him along."

Smith and Silas Gobel went on alone. A few miles later they saw two Indians headed in the direction where Evans lay dying "and soon after the report of two guns was heard in quick succession."

And then they found water—"to our inexpressible joy. . . . Gobel plunged into it at once, and I could hardly wait to bath my burning forehead."

Smith filled a small kettle with water and meat; wearily trudged back to the place they had left Evans. To Smith's great relief, Evans had not even seen the Indians. He had fired the shots himself, to mark his position. He could barely talk when Smith reached him; enough voice remained to ask for water. When Smith gave him the kettle:

> O says he, why did you bring the meat and putting
> the kettle to his mouth he did not take it away until
> he had drank all the water of which there was at least
> 4 or 5 quarts and then asked me why I had not brought
> more.

The water sufficiently revived Evans that he was able to follow Smith back to the spring, and the three men lay there for the rest of the day, alternately in and out of the water, letting their "wearied and emaciated bodies" soak up the moisture.

Two more days brought them to the Great Salt Lake, spurring up in Smith the sensations of a "traveler who . . . comes again in view of his home. . . . It had become my home in the wilderness."

Swinging around the southern edge of the lake, Smith found the Jordan River in flood stage. He made a raft of cane grass bundled together and towed it over by a cord in his mouth, with the two men hanging on behind: "Unfortunately neither of my men were good swimmers . . . and we were swept down a considerable distance."

He had trouble making the shore at all, being, as he wrote, "very much strangled." But it was done, the goods and men dried off, and the march commenced again.

By July 3 Smith reached the rendezvous at Bear Lake. Overjoyed at seeing him alive so long after he and his party had been given up, the trappers promptly loaded up the four-pounder and blasted the mountain air in salute. It was a good thing Ashley had sent the cannon up with the supply train; the welcome salute to Smith was its only recorded use.

CHAPTER 11

"I have acted honorable
and shall continue so"

END Year One for Smith Jackson & Sublette. When the partners sat down to take stock at Rendezvous 1827, the picture looked bright. In spite of the fact that Smith's entire catch of the preceding seasons remained in California, the other two partners had acquitted themselves very well indeed. They could deliver to Bruffee almost 7,500 pounds of beaver (at $3), plus odds and ends in the form of otter skins ($2 each) and castoreum—the always necessary "medicine"—which brought the same price as beaver skins.

In all, they turned over almost $23,000 worth. This was, of course, paid for in merchandise at the prices agreed upon in the Articles of Agreement of the previous July. (Part of the invoice for merchandise also included the note given to Ashley—almost $8,000—leaving them with about $15,000 worth of actual merchandise to start the new season.)

Since the partners were now in command of all the goods in the mountains, it seemed a judicious time to do a little price hiking.

The supplies delivered by Bruffee, acting as agent for the complex Ashley-B. Pratte-American Fur combine, didn't trickle down to the trappers themselves at quite the same prices. Daniel Potts sets down as prices—to trappers—at this rendezvous:

Powder	$2.50	Pepper	$ 6.00
Lead	1.50	3 pt. Blankets	15.00
Coffee	2.00	Calico	2.50

Tobacco	2.00	Scarlet Cloth	10.00
Vermillion	6.00	Blue Cloth	8.00
	Beads	5.00	

(For the prices at which some of these goods were delivered to Smith Jackson & Sublette in accordance with the Articles of Agreement, see page 111.)

All in all, a most auspicious beginning for a firm which had been, only a year before, "uncertain whether the situation ... [would] justify the proposed purchase of merchandise."

Rendezvous 1827 lasted about two weeks; until the middle of July. Messrs. Bruffee and Scott loaded up their supply caravan and left for the Missouri, to bring up supplies for the next year. This time, however, there was a change in operating procedure (which must have been worked out between Ashley and Bill Sublette in St. Louis during the winter). The returning caravan proceeded only as far as Lexington, Missouri. It was met there by Ashley (on October 1), who had next year's outfit already assembled and ready to go. The returning party simply delivered the furs, took on supplies, and headed back for the mountains immediately, after buying (for Smith Jackson & Sublette's mountain use) the horses and mules used in the caravan. Thus, instead of a delayed, next-spring delivery, the new goods would be in the mountains by the time the trapping parties had to settle in for the winter. There was, apparently, no supply train scheduled for the next spring at all, at least not by Ashley.[1] (And it may be that the partners were casting about for someone else to market their furs. Robert Campbell wrote his businessman brother Hugh from this rendezvous, asking him to check market prices in New York, Philadelphia and Richmond.)

If Rendezvous 1827 was good for Smith Jackson & Sublette, it was good for historians, too. Somewhere in the midst of the general rampaging, fighting, fornicating, drinking, singing, lying, dancing, eating, shouting, shooting—which is to say, somewhere in the midst of the mountain fun—Daniel Potts found time to sit down and scribble a couple of letters that briefly detailed his activities for the past couple of years. On these rests a large part of our information on the movements of the earliest of the Ashley-Henry expeditions.

Jedediah Smith, too, had a few communicative moments; though he would not have been hampered by the general gaiety, being more likely to be spending his time musing on the great burden of guilt under which each naked soul enters the world. On July 12 he wrote General Clark a report of his first Southwest Expedition. (This is the letter on which Chapter 10 of this book is largely based.)

He closed in haste:

"The company are now starting, therefore must close my communication."

And Smith was off to California again. For another round with the Mexican authorities and—a little later—one of the major disasters of the trade. He was gone from the mountains for two years, not returning until the early summer of 1829. Smith's journeyings for this period are better recorded than the activities of the other partners; Chapter 12 recounts them.

II

We have brief records of several of the other parties on the Fall '27 hunt. Bill Sublette headed north toward the Snake, having as one of the members of his party the redoubtable James P. Beckwourth. Sublette's eventual intention was probably to penetrate as far north as the Hudson's Bay Company's Flathead post; such is the implication of the license he obtained from General Clark, and it accords with the other account of the party in *Life and Adventures*. This push north is interesting on two counts:

First, it would take Sublette into Blackfoot territory around the forks of the Missouri; country which Americans had pretty much left to the HBC brigades since the hostilities of four and five years previous had decimated both the Missouri Fur and the first Ashley-Henry expeditions. The incessant warfare between the Blackfeet and the Flatheads was rumored to be at low ebb this year; a truce, in effect, though nobody could have said how long it would last. Further, the Blackfeet were interested in trading (giving some cause to wonder if the truce weren't necessitated by a lack of ammunition).

For whatever reason, the mountain marauders' disposition was on the sweet side for a change, and it would be well to tap their rich country while the tapping was good. This was probably Sublette's notion.

Second, taking a party into this area would mean a deliberate and conscious opening of direct competition with HBC;

the north was traditionally their stronghold. It seems likely that the Americans were growing increasingly confident of their ability to carry the competition to HBC and come out holding the clean end of the stick.

Smith Jackson & Sublette probably considered this impending clash to be purely a matter of commercial competition. HBC itself was taking a somewhat longer range view of these increasingly frequent clashes between rival trapping parties and was more alive to the political consequences and implications.

The Treaty of 1818 was due to expire in another year. It was becoming obvious from reports in the American press, and the attitudes evinced by her trappers, that the United States was considering the joint-occupancy territory to be her own; it would seem reasonable to expect some decisive action by America on expiry of the treaty in 1828. (This was not the case; the Convention of 1827 once again put the problem off by extending indefinitely the period of joint occupation, until either party should give notice of reconsideration. However, the results of the convention were not known in the mountains in 1827. The position taken by HBC was logical in the circumstances as known to them.)

Behind the buckskin of the mountain men HBC saw the homespun of the colonist. In this year George Simpson wrote to John McLoughlin that

> the first step that the American Government will take toward Colonization is through their Indian Traders and if the country becomes exhausted in Fur bearing animals they can have no inducement to proceed thither.

HBC, in short, saw the trappers as forerunners of a wave of colonization, much as we are able to see them from our vantage point of a hundred years' perspective. The British viewed the incursions of small bands of men into the disputed territory as instruments of what Bernard DeVoto a hundred years later called the "Continental Mind." Their answer was to establish a scorched-earth policy; wipe the country clean.

Instructions of the Governor and Committee of HBC—to Simpson—are specific: About the time Bill Sublette was getting his licence from General Clark, the Governor and Committee wrote

We can afford to pay as good a price as the Americans and where there is risk of meeting their parties it is necessary to pay as much or something more to avoid the risk of a result similar to that of Mr. Ogden. By attempting to make such expeditions too profitable the whole may be lost and it is extremely desirable to hunt as bare as possible all the Country South of the Columbia and West of the Mountains.

Such were the political implications of Bill Sublette's northern foray in the fall of '27—for those who had an eye to such things. Other eyes, other views . . .

James P. Beckwourth, for example, remembers it principally as the time he gained two wives, not to mention the adulation of almost everybody concerned:

It seems that Sublette, encouraged by Blackfoot tenders of good will, asked for a volunteer willing to risk his scalp by setting up a trading post among the Devil's Own. Who but James P. Beckwourth? And so it was.

The head chief of the Blackfeet, As-as-to, was so impressed with James P. Beckwourth that he offered his daughter to the gentleman in holy, such as it was, wedlock. Unfortunately, after a few days of married bliss—"hymeneal enjoyments," is Beckwourth's term—a war party came back into camp with a few white scalps. The sight of them, James reports, "made my blood boil with rage."

Accordingly, when the scalp dance was held, he forbade his wife to dance. But dance she would, and a great dancer she was, outshining all the rest. "This was a sting which pierced my heart," said James, and picked up his battle-ax. With said weapon he promptly clobbered his disobedient spouse on the side of her head, "which dropped her as if a ball had pierced her heart."

Before long, of course, "the whole Indian camp was in a blaze. 'Kill him! kill him! burn him! burn him!' was shouted throughout the camp in their own language, which I plainly understood. I was collected, for I knew they could kill me but once."

However, James's father-in-law interceded; made a very moving speech which quieted the fiery-hearted braves. Then he went to the tent where James P. Beckwourth was collecting himself with such admirable resignation and said, "My son, you have done right; that woman I gave you had no sense; her ears were stopped up; she would not listen to you, and you had a right to kill her."

Furthermore, the chief continued, he just happened to have in stock another daughter, more beautiful and equipped with both good sense and good ears. Said paragon he promptly presented, and James found her good; "far more intelligent and far prettier than her other sister, and I was really proud of the change."

But that night, while James P. Beckwourth and Mrs. Beckwourth were "quietly reposing, some person crawled into our couch, sobbing most bitterly." Sure enough, it was his first wife, having survived the mighty blow of James P. Beckwourth—something no other Blackfoot ever did—and now back pleading forgiveness and claiming her ears had been opened and her sense improved by the Beckwourth battle-ax.

James finally relented, inasmuch as "it really did seem as if her heart was broken" (to say nothing of her head). And so, in the morning, he found himself married to not one but two of the daughters of the head chief of the Blackfeet.

"I thought myself," he recalled, "now well supplied with wives."

III

With the exception of James P. Beckwourth, none of the writing men was out on the hunting parties of '27–'28. In order to follow the fortunes of the company in its second working year, we have to follow them through the sharp eyes of an old acquaintance, Peter Skene Ogden.

Ogden had conducted his third Snake County Expedition— Fall 1826 to Spring '27—in central and southern Oregon. Probably to his relief, he had not encountered any of the American trappers on that trip.

He left on the fourth Snake Country Expedition on August 24, while Bill Sublette and the fortune-favored James P. Beckwourth were wending their way north from Bear Lake. His first journal entry is characteristic and admirable Ogdeniana:

> August 24. Left Ft. Vancouver for the Snake Country with 28 trappers and hopes far from sanguine.

By September 25 Ogden was camped on the Snake opposite Weiser River, directly on the present Oregon-Idaho border. Here came the first intimations of his *bête noire*:
"Trappers report traps of strangers set along this river."

Shortly thereafter the strangers themselves appeared: in
the person of an American trapper named Johnson, who told
Ogden he and five others were working the stream. This
six-man brigade, furthermore, was only a small part of a
larger outfit of SJ&S consisting of forty men altogether and
a band of more or less allied Nez Perces. From what Johnson told him, Ogden could conclude that the main body was
working in the direction of the Sandwich Island River. (Now
known as the Owyhee. Ogden himself had sent a detached
party in that direction under Thomas McKay.)

His predictable response to this news:

"My sanguine hopes of beaver here are blasted." (He
seems to have forgotten his hopes were "far from sanguine"
to begin with.)

Forty men and a band of Nez Perces . . . Ogden himself—
after detaching McKay—was left with only sixteen. He was
in a strange position for a partisan of HBC, being caught
with the smallest brigade in the mountains. He immediately
decided to turn around and head back to the Burnt River.

But Peter Skene Ogden was a man who managed to
discharge virtually all his discouragement and pessimism in
the act of writing his journal; the decision to retreat was, for
him, almost always a paper decision. He does not turn back;
neither does he note the fact that he's changed his mind. He
simply moves on.

Apparently Johnson, together with a man named Goodrich, decided to go along with Ogden's party; follow him to the
Columbia, in fact, which seems to indicate they intended
joining HBC. Ogden told them he could offer no better terms
than he did his own freemen. "With this," he writes, "they
were satisfied."

He pushed on across southern Idaho. On the 17th of
October he camped on a fork of what he calls the Malade
River (probably Camas Creek) and found another encampment of Smith Jackson & Sublette men—five of them. They
were another party detached from the forty-man brigade of
which Ogden had heard.

There are no further journal entries for another week.
When he resumes, the British booshway is able to note with a
certain understandable satisfaction:

"The Americans being in want of supplies, applied for trade. They consented to take ¼ less than Indian tariff. . . . Since the Americans have been with us they have taken only 13 beaver and are discouraged. . . ." From this exchange Ogden got 32 beaver and 25 "musquash"; muskrat skins.

With the American party was one of Ogden's own deserters, Thierry Godin.[2] Godin was a deserter of '25 who still owed the Honourable Company a considerable debt. Ogden was able to collect from him 35 large beaver in payment, making a total of 48 large and 19 small beaver he had collected for virtually nothing.

Now, in late October, the bad weather was setting in. This winter of '27-'28 was exceptionally severe, and November was ushered in by storms which prevented the party's moving on. Ogden had made an arrangement to rejoin McKay and his eleven men on "Day's River," which may be the present Little Lost River. The recombined parties would then proceed together for the remainder of the season.

While in forced camp for the storm—November 2—Ogden notes:

> It is my intent to amuse the American party now with us so that McKay's men may have time to trap the beaver where the Americans purpose going. As they are not aware of this, it is so much the more in our favour.

This he succeeded in doing. But if Ogden's wits were in his favor, the fates were not. When his party reached the appointed meeting place, McKay was not there. More important, the expected "grass for our horses and buffalo for our support" also were missing. He left a note for McKay and moved back to the Snake River across the lava plains of southeast Idaho. By November 22 he was camped on an island just south of present Blackfoot, Idaho.

A few days later the Americans decided they'd better get back to their own side. (As well they might. They had been forced to trade with Ogden fairly regularly, and by now the total was over a hundred beaver. During the same period they had trapped only 26; with Ogden buying at "¼ less than Indian tariff," even the somewhat steep prices of Smith Jackson & Sublette must have looked good.) They left on Friday the 30th and must have had hard going of it. The next day was "a wild storm of wind and snow," which kept Ogden's own camp in place.

It was becoming obvious that the winter was going to be a bad one. The trappers were coming in covered with ice and nearly frozen. (They would, of course, have to follow the same procedure on the trap lines as usual, regardless of the weather; which meant they were up to their chests in the freezing water half the time.)

Ogden's first word of the absent McKay came from a disagreeable source: more of the SJ&S men. On the 20th of December a six-man American party under Samuel Tulloch came in. They told Ogden they had left McKay—at Ogden's previously appointed meeting place of Day's River—a few days before. The snow was so bad, and McKay's horses so weak, they couldn't cross the lava plains. (Tulloch's own party had been forced to trade forty-nine horses from the Nez Perce—at $50 each—and lost nineteen of them crossing the plains. Six had been eaten. Ten more were stolen by Shoshones.)

From hints in Ogden's journal it appears that at least one large body of Smith Jackson & Sublette men had moved west from the Bear Lake rendezvous, working the Owyhee River in eastern Idaho. They had reached the area before the British party and the two groups moved together—probably for the sake of mutual protection—up to the scheduled rendezvous on Day's River.

Tulloch—"a decent follow," says Ogden—was most amiable when he came for a visit on Christmas Eve. More amiable than truthful, in fact. He told Ogden that SJ&S "would readily enter into an agreement regarding deserters" and apparently made some sort of promise to bring back one of the principal partners to arrange such an agreement. This would have been a little difficult, as Smith was in California (just out of jail), Jackson was either in St. Louis or snowed in at Bear Lake, and Sublette was up in Blackfoot country. However.

Tulloch also made it plain that Johnson Gardner's conduct with respect to Ogden had not been approved by the company. Ogden was well disposed to believe it. "I shd certainly be shocked," he wrote, "if any man of principle approved of such conduct as Gardner's."

On New Year's Day, 1828, Tulloch and his men left Ogden's encampment, headed back for the Bear Lake rendezvous. Ogden hoped to see them again—with one of the partners—in two weeks, to arrange the terms of an agreement about the deserters. "This would be most desirable," Ogden comments mildly.[8]

There is a hiatus in the journal from January 5 to 16. During the interim, Tulloch had apparently been turned back by the cold and snow, and rejoined Ogden's party. Also, something had happened to Ogden's fine good faith in Tulloch's promises. From the amiable camaraderie of Christmas Eve, Ogden had, by the 16th, turned to a policy of deliberate intrigue against Tulloch and his party. And in this little game Ogden held all the cards. The Americans were not accustomed to traveling under the heavy snow conditions, and were completely unfamiliar with the use of snowshoes. For Ogden's trappers this was a matter of routine, and they had occupied their idleness during storms by making snowshoes for the season.

> Wednesday 16th. [Jan.] The Americans are anxious to procure snow shoes, and I am equally so they should not as I am of opinion they are anxious to bring over a party of trappers to this quarter. I have given orders to all not to make any for the Americans. This day they offered $25 for one pair $20 for another but failed. . . .
> Friday 18 Jan. . . . The Americans continue offers for snow shoes but without success. . . .

> Sunday 20th. . . . Tullock, the American, who failed to get thro' the snow to Salt Lake tried to engage an Indian to carry letters to the American depot at Salt Lake. This I cannot prevent. It is impossible for me to bribe so many Indians with my party. I have succeeded in preventing them from procuring snow shoes.

And if this were not enough, Tulloch received a bit of gratuitous bad news on Tuesday following. A Snake came into camp and informed the American that one of his caches—valued at about $600—had been found and looted by a band of Plains Snakes. (Ogden was of the opinion the messenger himself was one of the thieves and sympathized with Tulloch's loss.)

His sympathy, however, was on a more or less theoretical level and didn't noticeably affect his policy of obstruction:

Wednesday 23rd [Jan.]. The American is now very low spirited. He cannot hire a man to go to his cache nor snow shoes, nor does he suspect that I prevented. This day he offered 8 beaver and $50 for a pair and a prime horse to anyone who would carry a letter to the American camp. In this also he failed.

Word trickled in that the Americans all over the mountains were in trouble. Not situated as fortunately with respect to game as Ogden's camp, Smith Jackson & Sublette's various detached parties were falling on starvin' times. Even at the Bear Lake headquarters things were not much better:

. . . The Americans are starving on Bear River . . . no buffalo in that quarter, they are reduced to eat horses and dogs.

And again on January 25:

Snows and storms continue, a terrible winter . . . reports of fearful distress of the Americans. Horses dead, caches rifled.

Finally, in desperation, Tulloch and his men tried to make snowshoes for themselves, and Ogden observes smugly "wh. they ought to have done 2 wks. ago." In spite of his general confidence, and self-satisfaction at having blocked their progress, Ogden was worried. He was a man of expediency, and had never fully shared the company's attitude toward the use of liquor in trading. He was fully aware of the enormous advantages accruing to a trader with liquor, and this was his present concern. He tried sounding Tulloch out, but was unable to learn the American's intentions.

I dread their returning with liquour . . . I know not their intentions but had I the same chance they have, long since I would have had a good stock of liquour here, and every beaver in the camp would be mine. If they succeed in reaching their camp they may bring 20 or 30 trappers here which would be most injurious to my spring hunt.

Tulloch and one other man started on January 28. They were not encouraged in their departure by the return of a messenger sent by Ogden; he had been unable to penetrate very far. And this was a man well experienced in snowshoe travel. Tulloch and his companion were discouraged. "They are not sanguine," Ogden wrote. "They have an arduous task, wretched snow shoes and this is the first time they ever used them."

The trip went badly from the beginning. The river ice was thin, and one of them broke through. "He made a noble struggle for his life," says Ogden admiringly. In spite of the bad beginning, Tulloch and his unnamed partner struggled on, plowing through the drifted snow on snowshoes improperly made and improperly used. The result was predictable, and a week later they trudged unhappily back into Ogden's encampment. "Most agreeable to me," he admits, "but a cruel disappointment to them."

Still, Tulloch was of the mountain breed and not about to give up. Within a week they were off again, even though all of Ogden's own messengers had been turned back.

> [Ogden:] It is laughable, so many attempts on both sides and no success. Was it not I feared a strong American party here I shd undertake the journey myself and would succeed.

Tulloch and his companion took the same route as on their previous attempt, following up the Portneuf River. On their previous trip they had turned back from a point near the source of the Portneuf; reaching it on this second attempt, they were greeted by a strange sight for these mountains. Coming in the other direction was a dog sledge, of all things, and behind it the young Irishman Robert Campbell and two trappers from SJ&S. (Campbell—then witness to the original Articles of Agreement—was gradually coming into more and more responsibility in the company. He and Bill Sublette were very close friends, and it is remotely possible that Campbell was in a position at this time to act for the firm in an official way.)

Campbell was apparently on his way north into the Flathead country, possibly with some intention of meeting Bill Sublette there for the spring hunt. Tulloch told him of Ogden's camp (and the four trappers remaining there), and the whole party now swung back to the Snake again, where they arrived on the 16th.

They report a fight with the Blackfeet and old Pierre the Iroquois[4] who deserted from me 4 yrs. ago was killed and cut in peices. Pierre owes a debt to the company but as we have a mortgage on his property in Canada we shall recover.

Whatever his faults, Ogden could not be accused of being oversentimental.

Now there came an ironic reversal of roles. Johnson and Goodrich—the first two American trappers to meet Ogden this year—had remained with the camp. Campbell broached the subject to Ogden, who apparently took a very high tone about the whole situation.

Johnson and Goodrich, said Campbell, were heavily in debt to Smith Jackson & Sublette, and ought to pay off the debt or return to their service. "I replied," Ogden writes, "I had no knowledge of the same and that it was his duty to secure his men and debts also."

Which sounds remarkably like the kind of reasoning Ogden objected to in Johnson Gardner. Further, Ogden rather stiffly informed Campbell that his treatment of them was "far different from theirs to me four years since."

Campbell, too, regretted Gardner's actions, and explained that there had been, at the time, no "regular company."

... otherwise I shd. have received compensation [says Ogden]. It may be so. At all events, dependent on me, they cannot acknowledge less. I have acted honorable and shall continue so. [The matter of the snowshoes was not discussed at this time.]

Johnson and Goodrich did rejoin the Smith Jackson & Sublette party, and on the 23rd part of the now-augmented force left for the north, probably under Robert Campbell. (They were, Ogden complained, "very silent regarding the object of the journey." He had a notion they intended to move up to the Three Forks district, which would lend support to the idea that Campbell intended to meet Bill Sublette.)

Of the trappers who didn't accompany Campbell's group, two left for the rendezvous a few days later. The remaining five stayed with Ogden until the middle of March, whiling away the time by playing cards. (Eight decks had somehow gotten into Ogden's camp, in spite of the fact that his own men were not permitted to buy them.)

"... more or less starving," Ogden says of those remaining, "[they] do not attempt to take beaver but gamble from morning to night. May they continue ..."

The last of them left on March 26, and this batch, too, headed for Bear Lake. Their euchre luck must have been fair because, according to Ogden, they parted "on good terms." The next day an impromptu rescue party appeared, consisting of two trappers sent to help get the remainder of the Americans back to base. Finding nobody needing their help, they left immediately.

And that was the last of the Americans that Peter Skene Ogden saw on the trip.

In the last group of five men to leave Ogden's camp was the man who had started the whole thing off, Samuel Tulloch. Pinckney Sublette (younger brother of Bill), one "Batiste" (probably Baptiste Sawenrego, another of Ogden's Iroquois deserters), and Jeandrois Rariet are the others whose names we know. Three or four days out, on the Portneuf, this party was attacked by a band of about forty Blackfeet. Pinckney, Batiste, and Rariet were killed. Tulloch and the unnamed companion escaped.

Ogden had overestimated his own craftiness. Tulloch had his opinions as to why he could not purchase snowshoes but had prudently kept his own counsel while in Ogden's camp. With the attack of the Blackfeet on his small party, Tulloch developed the notion that Ogden was behind that, too. When he finally made contact with Bill Sublette again, Tulloch informed him of his suspicions regarding Ogden. Sublette in turn passed them on to Ashley; Ashley included them in a letter to Thomas Hart Benton, and Tulloch's suspicions ended up in the Executive Documents of the United States Senate.

To Ashley's credit it must be said that he found the story too much to swallow, at least as respects Ogden's personal responsibility for the attack. However, since his letter was intended to explain the situation existing between the British and American trapping parties (with a view toward legislation), Ashley states:

... the recent conduct of the Blackfoot Indians may in a great degree be attributed to the location of their [HBC's] traders among them. They may not advise killing, but no doubt hold out other inducements which amounts to the same.... Mr. Tullock further states that somé time after separating from Mr. Ogden & party, but while within fifteen miles of his encampment he was attacked by a large band of indians, supposed to be Blackfoot, the Result was the loss of four of Mr. T's party killed, about four thousand dollars worth of furs, forty horses & considerable amount of merchandise—not withstanding I can not believe that Mr. Ogden himself, would dictate such conduct to indians ... there is no doubt in my mind but the furs thus plundered were sold to him, or some one of his party, in the course, perhaps, of twenty four hours after taken by the indians, and the purchaser must of known from whence they came.[5]

Ogden did, in fact, find evidence of the raid; but among a band of Plains Snakes. His journal entry for May 10 includes:

They report 2 days since raiding a party of Blackfeet. In the loot were clothes, hunters hats shoes etc horses belonging to the Americans who wintered with us. The furs were left on the plains. A convincing proof the Americans have been murdered and pillaged, knowing how blood thirsty the Bl. are and how careless the Americans. The sight of this caused gloom in camp. We may be doomed to the same fate.

CHAPTER 12

"This man was placed in power
to perplex me"

THE trapping season of '27–'28 was a sort of unofficial international year for Smith Jackson & Sublette. While the various mountain parties were drifting in and out of Ogden's British camp, Jedediah Smith was once again embroiled with the Mexican authorities. And once again in the person of his old nemesis, José Maria de Echeandia.

When Rendezvous 1827 broke up in the middle of July, Smith had recruited for his second California expedition eighteen men and two women.[1] In the group was Silas Gobel, one of the men who had accompanied Smith back across the Great Basin. (The other, Robert Evans, disappears from the mountains for seven years, which argues his character as a sensible man.) The two women, of course, were squaws following their men to the field, but there is no record of which trappers were their husbands. Appropriately enough, the new party got under way on Friday, July 13.

Jedediah's route was, of necessity, a choice between two evils. Bad as his first trip to California had been—via a southern crescent from the mountains—it was still better than the direct crossing he had made on the return. The cross-Nevada route he considered flatly impassable for a party with loaded horses at this season, and probably at any season.

His general course on leaving Bear Lake was southerly, differing in some points from the path he had made the previous year. He avoided the valley of Great Salt Lake, possibly because he had found it "completely barren and destitute of game" or possibly he was simply taking a look at some new country.

In any case, he eventually reached the Utah valley, where he encountered the same band of Utes with whom he'd treatied on his first trip. They gave him the interesting intelligence of other white men in the country; a group of starving trappers had appeared from the south, headed for Taos. The New Mexico-based trapping parties were beginning to expand their horizons, though, from the report, they were not finding the expansion immediately profitable.

At one point on his further journey to the Colorado, Smith discovered that his previous trip had borne fruit. At that time he had encountered a band of Indians on the Lost River, who had immediately disappeared. He had left a few trinkets at their encampment and moved on. Now he was treated to the sight of the same Indians approaching his party without apparent fear, and quite friendly. They told him of the passing of some white men the previous year, who had left a knife and other gifts for them.

Part of Smith's plan was to rest men and horses for a few days at the friendly Mojave villages, as he had done the year before. (The presence of the "Ammuchabas" was probably a considerable factor in Smith's choice of route, since he knew he would be able to procure supplies and fresh horses there.)

He reached the first of the Mojave villages without having seen any of the Indians; as a result, they scattered as his party approached. However, "finding an opportunity to talk with one of them they soon returned and seemed as friendly as when I was there before."

He remained at the first village for a day, resting his horses, and then moved down to the next encampment. This time news of his coming had preceded him, and he was met by the cordial Mojaves some distance above their settlement.

Smith set up his own encampment at the point he intended to cross the Colorado. For the next three days the party remained there, building some rafts of cane grass and generally enjoying the hospitality of the tribe. Jedediah was able to exchange a few of his horses for fresh ones and trade for some of the Mojave agricultural produce. (Beans, wheat, corn, dried pumpkins, and melons are those he lists in his report to General Clark.)

It was a little after the middle of August—probably the 18th—when he was ready to depart. He loaded part of the goods aboard his rafts and, together with eight of his men, started the ferrying procedure. The remainder of the supplies, all the horses, and the rest of his party were to come across on subsequent trips.

Several hundred of the amiable Mojaves had gathered to watch the crossing, and as soon as Smith was well out on the river they butchered the party he had left behind. Almost before Smith had time to realize what the noise was about, the riverbank was strewn with the bodies of ten of his men.[2] The two Indian squaws were taken prisoner.

Now this friendly, agricultural people turned their attention to the small party that had already embarked. Smith and his men had hastily drawn up on a sand bar to take stock of the situation. Spreading out what goods they had—personal supplies and fifteen pounds of dried meat—Smith immediately threw everything sinkable into the river. The remainder was shouldered by the men according to their choice. What they did not want was strewn around, Smith hoping the Indians would squabble over it long enough to give them a start. Melanion and the Golden Apples, with the part of Atalanta played by a horde of screaming Mojaves.

They were less than a half mile from the river when the Indians closed in around them, making any further progress impossible. Jedediah and his eight men retreated to the bank, holing up in a cottonwood thicket. Quickly they chopped down some of the small trees; cleared themselves a place to stand in the middle of the thicket with the felled saplings forming a flimsy breastwork around them.

There were only five guns left for the nine men, and the others tied their butcher knives to light poles, "so as to form," said Smith, "a tolerable lance."

Some of the men asked Smith if he thought they would be able to defend themselves against the estimated four or five hundred Mojaves. Backed up against the river, with his attackers on the other three sides, Smith said, yes, he thought they would do all right. "But that," he adds in his journal, "was not my opinion." Smith was developing an easy facility in lying to his men about their prospects; and it was a talent he needed quite often.

He gave orders that "not more than three guns should be fired at a time and those only when the Shot would be certain of killing." This, of course, was standard practice; the first tactic of any Indian offensive was to lead the opponent into firing his guns; the first tactic of defense was to avoid firing your guns. As long as there was even one gun loaded, Indians were hesitant about storming a barricade. But a trapper caught with a ramrod in his hand was seldom seen with his hair again.

The Mojaves approached the little redoubt with great care, keeping well covered. Occasional warriors would scamper out and back again, just within long shot, in the usual tactic intended to draw fire. This, however, was a middling poor tactic to use on Smith's brigade, which had a far-reaching reputation for marksmanship. (The giant Isaac Galbraith was said to amuse himself by shooting off the heads of blackbirds at twenty paces.)

> [Smith] directed two good marksmen to fire
> they did so and two indians fell and another was
> wounded,

which rather cooled the Mojave enthusiasm for attack. They scattered—"like frightened sheep"—and the nine lonely trappers could breathe again. The Indians stayed clear of the impromptu fort and too-accurate occupants all the rest of the day. At dusk the trappers decamped and pushed directly into the desert, traveling all night. The next morning they reached a spring, where they encamped for the day.

Jedediah had decided he had no recourse in the circumstances but to "again try the hospitality of the Californians." He hoped to be able to use the beaver he had left with the first party for trade—"if the Governor would permit me to trade, and I could find any person acquainted with the value of furr." With this he could get provisions to carry him up the coast toward the Columbia. (His written intent was to "continue the business of the firm more northwardly so far as he supposed to be the U. States territory." His supposition, apparently, was that the joint-occupancy area was United States territory, since there was nothing else north of the Spanish line at 42°.)

The trek across the desert was made in nine and a half days, mostly traveling at night, trying to stay out of the searing sun in the day.

Smith arrived at the San Bernardino Valley (probably via Cajon Pass) near the end of August. He stopped there to make meat, killing several cows. The overseer of the San

Bernardino Rancho made him welcome and Jedediah traded him enough of his meager remaining supply of goods to get horses for all his men. Horses, in California, were cheap; a far cry from the $50 minimum in the mountains.

He remained encamped in the valley for five days, during which he wrote a letter to his former benefactor, Father Sanchez at San Gabriel, explaining his situation and thanking the padre for the cows he had just killed. He probably also pondered the sudden reversal in attitude of the Mojaves. While at San Bernardino he heard from the overseer that some of the Mojave chiefs had been talking about the defeat of a party of Americans; this party, Smith concluded, was probably the same one he had heard of among the tribes, and whose tracks he had seen. The Mojaves had not mentioned a battle, of course, but had admitted a mixed party of Spaniards and Americans had come past, "quarreled," and split up. Smith decided "that they were defeated by the indians, separated in two parties in the affray, and traveled different ways."

(This may have been a partial explanation of the Mojave hostility, but Smith was later to learn of another: after his first trip the governor had instructed the Indians not to permit the passage of any more Americans into Mexican territory. In his report of the affair to General Clark, Smith says: ". . . to this advice, Mr. S. leaves the entire cause of his defeat,—it undoubtedly was, for any man acquainted with the savage and hostile habits of Indians, cannot judge the matter otherwise.")

At San Bernardino Smith lost another two men of his party, though in a less violent way. Isaac Galbraith, the giant who was later to bequeath his skeleton to a physician friend, apparently decided he liked the climate of San Bernardino. He wanted to stay. Thomas Virgin had been wounded by a Mojave war club and was to stay at the ranch recuperating until he could join Smith near San Francisco.

Jedediah then set out to make contact with the remnant of his first expedition, still encamped in the valley of the Stanislaus River (again following Dale Morgan's geographic identification, as I do throughout), which Smith called the Appelaminy.

It was not the happiest of meetings. Jedediah's intent to replenish the men for trapping had been abruptly short-stopped by the Mojaves. "I was there at the time appointed," he says, "but instead of Bringing them the expected supplies I brought them intelligence of my misfortunes."

Just a sad story, in short, with which it is practically impossible to trap beaver. The men at the Stanislaus camp had fared a good deal better than their booshway, having passed a "pleasant Summer not in the least interrupted by Indians. . . . They spoke in high terms of the climate." There was game around in plentiful supply: elk, antelope and deer, so food—for once—was not a problem.

Smith learned now of the visit of Mexican officials to the camp just after his own departure, and notes optimistically: "They appeared satisfied with the reasons Mr Rodgers gave for his being in the country."

His optimism, however, did not extend to the point of downright foolhardy expectations; he knew he was going to have to deal with the saturnine Echeandia again. He warned Rogers of possible difficulties, and suggested that in the case of official trouble he (Rogers) should take the party in to the Russian post at Bodega, north of San Francisco.

Smith remained at the Stanislaus camp for two days, doing what organizing he could to get the brigade ready to trap again. For a man whose profession was catching beaver, Smith had done a great deal of walking and very little trapping in the past year. A large part of the trapping strength of Smith Jackson & Sublette had effectively been taken out of circulation, and their loss could pose a threat to the survival of the company itself. It was necessary to do something to make up for the pitiful returns of his party for the year. He had on hand fifteen or sixteen packs of beaver and ten otter skins. If these could be swapped off for enough gear to outfit a real trapping brigade, it was more than possible he could make up the losses on the way north to the Columbia.

II

The problem was, as he had predicted, finding someone "acquainted with the value of furr." The idea of trapping beaver was, to all appearances, completely beyond the Mexican comprehension. In describing Smith's activities, the closest equivalent they can find is a fishing party. Thus we find a crack trapping brigade of Smith Jackson & Sublette referred to in the Mexican documents as "Smith, the fisherman's company." No amount of explanation—and there was of necessity a great deal—ever sufficed to make it clear just exactly what Smith did for a living. Writers have the same problem, but are not automatically assumed to be foreign spies, as was Smith.

After putting the Stanislaus party in as good shape as possible, Jedediah secured two Indian guides, who took him to the Mission San Jose, seventy miles away, to begin the dreaded wrangle with the Mexican authorities.

Smith greeted the two padres who met him there (one of them Narciso Durán), explained his purpose in the country, and requested permission to travel through the province to the governor's seat (at Monterey): "The reverend fathers appeared somewhat confused by my sudden appearance and could not or would not understand me."

In fact, they took him to "a dirty hovel which they called a guard house ... horses seized and taken away, and only allowed the privilege of writing to the Captain of the Upper Province."

There he remained for two days, unable to communicate and with "No provision whatever ... for my subsistence." He could not even establish the terms of his imprisonment, since "They would neither put me in close confinement nor set me at liberty."

Finally, through the intercession of an American named William Welch, Smith was granted an interview with Padre Durán, which eventuated in the sole piece of information that an official would be along directly to inquire into Smith's case.

Said official—Lieutenant Ignacio Martinez—arrived in due course. (Martinez was temporarily in command of the company at San Francisco in the absence of the *comandante*, Luis Arguello.) Smith was then treated to the rather startling intelligence that he was about to be tried, not only as an intruder but for "claiming the land" on the San Joaquin!

This, it turned out, was the report of an Indian. Lieutenant Martinez convened an impromptu court, and in the presence of Durán questioned both Smith and the Indian carefully. Durán himself was obviously anxious to have Smith convicted, "for what reason I know not unless perhaps it might be that he was apprehensive of danger to the *true faith*."

Martinez, after listening to both stories, decided Smith was innocent, at least in respect of claiming Mexican land, and ordered the Indian flogged: "which perhaps he did not deserve," adds the charitable Smith.

Martinez told Smith he would not be able to go directly to the governor at Monterey but would have to wait at San José until an express could be delivered and return. After inducing Father Durán to provide the American with a room and a semblance of regular feeding, Martinez departed, leaving Smith in the tender care of the padre for the next two weeks.

The only break in the prison monotony was the visit of an American, Captain John Cooper, who lived in Monterey. Cooper stayed at San José for two days, and expressed his willingness to help Smith in any way possible. This, to some extent, "relieved the anxiety of mind attendant on the uncertainty of my situation." Cooper was, in fact, called on for help a little later.

Finally a letter came from Echeandia: a "polite note from the Governor to pay him a visit." And as a possible suggestion that the visit was not entirely social, Echeandia sent along an armed guard, which stripped Smith of his arms and escorted him to Monterey. They arrived in the middle of the night, and Jedediah was promptly deposited behind bars.

His new-found ally, Captain Cooper, arrived with his breakfast and such encouragement as he could offer. Sometime later in the morning, Smith was summoned before Echeandia; but there was no interpreter available immediately, and the discussion was postponed.

Disconsolate, Smith was allowed a limited freedom of the town (under the sponsorship of Cooper) and encountered two of the men from his first expedition: Ferguson, who had remained behind at San Gabriel, and the discharged John Wilson.

Finally the talks with Echeandia got under way, and the issues were fairly clear-cut, at least to the dour and suspicious governor.

Smith was almost certainly a spy, as had been Echeandia's original contention, and was without doubt a liar—though being "much of a Gentleman" Echeandia did not phrase it in quite those terms. Near enough, though, as to make little difference.

Why was Smith back? To relieve his Appelaminy party. Then why had he come by such a circuitous route; why had he not gone directly to them, particularly after he had described his first route as almost impassable? Well, Smith had *tried* the direct route on his return, and found it even worse. Why had Smith not notified Echeandia immediately when he came in near San Gabriel? Smith had written a note to Father Sanchez, which he expected to be forwarded to the governor immediately.

And so it went. For each of Echeandia's questions there was an answer, which is not to say a satisfactory answer. Echeandia was far from satisfied; and it must be admitted that Smith's story is not a logical one to a man comfortably seated in the pleasant town of Monterey. To Echeandia it must have been almost incomprehensible that this man had crossed the Great Basin—on foot—three times in the past year; twice within the last six months. And all in pursuit of a small and insignificant animal whose name Echeandia barely knew. It was beyond all reason; *ergo,* there was more to this mysterious "fisherman" Smith than met the eye; Echeandia would have to think it over.

Echeandia, in common with most bureaucrats before and since, was of a contemplative turn of mind; which, freely translated, means he hated to take any action on a problem. What Echeandia really wanted was to forget about the whole thing, in hopes it would sort of wisp away. So he meditated on the problem of the fisherman's company at great length, without discernible result.

For his part, Smith would have liked nothing better than to evaporate like the morning dew, redepositing himself and men somewhere out of Mexican territory. Unfortunately he couldn't do it. Therefore, there was nothing for it but to badger the governor incessantly until he did something. This was most annoying to Echeandia.

Under Smith's prodding the governor finally decided he couldn't decide. Smith would have to go to Mexico. Fine, said Smith in desperation, the sooner the better. Echeandia agreed.

A few days later, Jedediah learned of an English whaler bound for Acapulco. He broached the subject to Echeandia, and that gentleman most graciously granted him permission to sail with the English ship. However, says Smith:

> I soon found that he was not disposed to put himself to any trouble about it. I asked him if he intended that I should go to Mexico as a prisoner and at my own expense. He said most certainly, if I had the privilege of going in a foreign vessel, but if I

would wait two or three months a Mexican Vessel
would be going to Acapulco when he might perhaps
as a favor from the Capt get a passage for me.

It seemed that this man was placed in power to
perplex me and those over whom he was called to
govern. That a man in possession of common sense
should seriously talk of making a man take himself at
his own expense to prison. That he should talk to me
of waiting 2 or 3 months for a passage to Acapulco. I
plainly told him that on such conditions I would not
go.

Echeandia's reaction to this is not recorded but is reasonably easy to guess.

Finally an idea arose which seemed to promise some
solution to this quandary. It was possibly Hartnell, the interpreter, who suggested it. In British law there was a provision
for dealing with emergencies among her travelers in foreign
lands where there was no official representative of the government. It permitted any four shipmasters in a foreign port
to appoint a sort of pro tem consul, who would act in that
capacity until the government could be advised and the
official opinion recorded. It was suggested that something of
the sort might apply here. Echeandia was agreeable to the
notion, and Smith now called on the proffered aid of Captain
Cooper. The ship captains who were requested to appoint an
agent "were not perfectly satisfied of the legality of the
proposition, but thought the urgency of the case would justify
the proceding."

It was done, and Cooper, as the most logical choice, was
appointed agent of the United States government. He forthwith accepted responsibility for Jedediah's behavior until such
time as he and his men left California.

Echeandia wanted Smith's party to come in where he
could keep an eye on them. There were some fantastic stories
circulating about them in the Mexican territory, mostly
revolving around their marksmanship; it would be just as
well, thought Echeandia, to have such a group under surveillance. What he had in mind by way of surveillance was
heavily armed guard. Accordingly, Smith was to write them,
ordering them into San Francisco.

I therefore wrote to Mr Rodgers that it was the
Governor request that they should come in, and at the

same time hinted at the treatment I had received. This I knew was sufficient for Mr. Rodgers, who from what had passed between us would go in to Bodega.

This, of course, was hardly subtle enough for Echeandia. After mulling over the translated letter for a couple of days he

> said he was afraid to send such a letter, for I had not ordered Mr. Rodgers positively to come in and that I had discouraged him from coming in from the manner in which I had spoken of the usage I had received . . . I told him I thought what I had written very reasonable.

He offered to write again. After extracting Echeandia's promise that the men would be well treated—that is, "not be imprisoned and should be furnished with provision," Smith wrote Rogers a more straightforward directive to put in to San Francisco.

Smith was then to be permitted to remain unmolested in California until word came from Mexico; or he could leave at any time he liked as long as he did no more "fishing around the country," as Durán had called it. In other words, if he could find a ship to take him off he could go. But no more spying.

This was impracticable, and another impasse seemed in the making. Through the generosity of Captain Cooper somewhat more lenient terms were arranged. In effect, Cooper mortgaged all he owned against the good conduct of Jedediah's party in leaving Mexican territory, the terms being that "they should make the best of their way out of the Mexican dominions, without staying to hunt within the territory, and on these terms Mr. S. left for San Francisco."

The route Smith was to take was clearly specified in the bond given by Cooper; the salient point here being that he was to cross the Bay of San Francisco at the Straits of Carquinez and proceed directly north. He was allowed two months to outfit the party and get them out of California:

> . . . under no condition will he delay on the way a longer time than is necessary . . . he will make no hostile excursion, and make no trip toward the coast

or in the region of his [Salt Lake] establishment south of the 42nd parallel.

Echeandia further refused to permit him to recruit more men to reinforce his party, though Smith "found several willing to engage, both Americans & English."

Sometime during his enforced stay at Monterey, Jedediah learned that Thomas Virgin (left at San Bernardino recuperating from a head wound) had been arrested and thrown in the "Callibozo" at San Diego. He succeeded in getting permission for Virgin to be released, to rejoin the party that was now at the San Francisco Presidio.

There now remained the problem of getting the trappers outfitted for the journey.

Smith's resources consisted of some 1,600 pounds of beaver, in the possession of the party at San Francisco. With another of the friendly sea captains—which breed provided Jedediah with all the help he got on either California trip— he arranged to sell these skins at $2.50 a pound. Considering the circumstances, this was a good price; he was very far away from any situation where they would bring more, and the (roughly) $4,000 they would bring would go a long way toward outfitting his party.

On Thursday, November 15, the last of the Monterey arrangements were concluded, about a month after negotiations had opened. Echeandia had apparently become suspicious again, and at the last minute Smith was obliged to sign a note binding himself for the sum of $30,000 "for the faithful performance of a certain Bond, given to the Mexican Govt dated at Monterey."

This, together with Captain Cooper's bond, reassured Echeandia to the extent that he forthwith issued the passport, permitting passage of the party and their goods, together with "a total of one hundred mules and one hundred and fifty horses."

In the early afternoon of the 15th Smith found himself a comparatively free man. He sailed for San Francisco on the *Franklin*, whose captain was to purchase his furs on arrival there.

III

The *Franklin* put in to San Francisco on the 17th, and Smith saw Rogers and his men for the first time since he had left them in September. (It had taken him about four months to make his trip back and forth across the Great Basin; and almost half that long just to get permission from Echeandia to leave.)

Smith reported to General Clark that when he finally reached his party he had

> found them in St. Francisco in a very deplorable state
> and [they] would have suffered immensely for
> want of victuals and clothing, was it not for the
> timely assistance of Mr. Vermont,[3] a German
> gentleman who happened to be trading on the coast,
> to whom Mr. Smith is under many obligations.

Luis Arguello was now back in his position of *comandante* of the San Francisco garrison, and to him Smith reported. Arguello approved the passport, and gave him permission to garrison himself at San José, a favor Smith probably requested because of the expense of living in San Francisco.

The furs were sold aboard the *Franklin* on the 18th (1,568 pounds at $2.50 a pound=$3,920, plus ten otter skins at (probably) $1.50–$2). For the next week Smith scurried about San Francisco getting supplies. Finally, on the 26th, the whole party moved off for Mission San José, "presenting," notes one observer, "rather a formidable appearance."

The horses that had been with the party had not fared any better in San Francisco than Rogers and the men. Smith arranged with Father Durán, his old accuser, to use the mission blacksmith shop, and nearly a month was spent getting the horses back in shape and making final preparations for departure.

Isaac Galbraith came in on December 6, apparently having decided not to remain in California. There is, after all, only so much a man is willing to put up with for the sake of a pleasant climate. A week later Thomas Virgin arrived, considerably the worse for wear. While in prison he had been "frequently without anything to eat and strictly forbidden to speak to any one. and abused in almost every way. . . . He was much rejoiced to see us and I am sure I was quite glad to see the old man again."

Arguello was not lax in the matter of escorts; a military detail of ten men was to ensure that the American trappers did not somehow become lost while making their way out of

California. Smith had discovered there was no boat to take him across at the Straits of Carquinez; and it was entirely too wide to swim. Reasonably enough, he expected Arguello would not object to his moving farther up until he could find a place to "swim my horses and carry my goods over on a raft which could not be done at the mouth." A gross optimism:

> ... he would hear nothing of this proposition but insisted that I should cross at the particular place directed by the Genl. I then told him to furnish the boat and I was ready to cross. This he could not do but said I must wait untill the Genl. could be advised of the situation of things and give further instructions.

Smith left, finally fed up to the teeth with the petty buck-passing of Mexican officialdom. He stormed back to San José; wrote the American minister in Mexico complaining of his treatment; wrote both Echeandia and Arguello, informing them, in effect, that the game had gone on long enough. He was going home, and if his route differed in some respects from the one they outlined—it was just too bad. But he was going.

On December 30—Samuel Tulloch is sitting in Peter Skene Ogden's tent a thousand miles away—Jedediah and his men finally got off from the Mission San José into a miserable, dreary rain, heading north for another point of international friction: the HBC post at Fort Vancouver.

So Smith began to trudge out of what his biographer has called "the California quagmire." The party saw the new year of 1828 ushered in through curtains of rain.

His purchase of so many horses and mules was a shrewd investment. They would serve not only as transportation back home, but as negotiable goods. The California price would have run around $10 a head; low mountain price anywhere from $50 to $60, and mules higher still. He had a sizable, self-propelled payload in his cavalcade; $5,000 worth in the mountains at an absolute minimum. If he could manage to get even half of them through alive, he would be more than amply paid for the beaver. On his present intended route—north to the Columbia, then east on his return to the mountains—he had no reason to expect the terrible attrition of a desert crossing. After he reached the Columbia he would be following fairly well-traveled routes; those taken by the HBC trapping parties based at Fort Vancouver. There was a reasonable hope of making it without too severe losses. Disregarding, for the moment, the viciously bad luck that had been dogging him ...

The prospects were better than fair, as they set out. On January 2 he crossed the San Joaquin River; goods carried on rafts, and the horses swimming across without a single casualty. A good beginning. Furthermore, beaver were plentiful on the tributaries of the San Joaquin.

Since Smith had set out on a new course, as his own man, he apparently felt that the "no trapping" provision of his passport was null and void. He spent almost the entire month of January trapping on the San Joaquin, and the hunt was good. In a two-day period he took forty-five beaver. If he was concerned that his hunting might endanger the man who had become personally responsible for him—Captain Cooper —there is no indication of it. Beaver was his business, and that was what he was after.

It wasn't all smooth going. The weather remained consistently foul as they turned north. Mud was deep and gummy, and the horses' progress was pitifully slow. Two men—the long-time troublemaker James Reed and one Louis Pombert ("Pompare," whose presence is a mystery)—deserted while on a trapping foray, taking their eleven traps with them. This was a serious blow, because Smith was extremely short on traps. These represented almost a quarter of his remaining supply, and their loss imposed a severe handicap. On the other hand, he was rid of James Reed at last, and it may be that was some small compensation.

The Indians at first had been remarkably friendly; more so than any other groups he had met. But the farther north he pushed the more frightened the bands became. He came to encounter more and more frequently the complete desertion of lodges in the face of his parties, and that was a bad sign.

He constantly had to make rafts to cross the "slous"; the whole area seemed to be a great bog. By late February he was on the American River (which he called the Wild). Here he had his first Indian trouble.

Toussaint Marechal and John Turner were about four miles from the camp, checking their traps, and "seeing some indians around their traps who would not come to them but attempted to run off they fired at them and Turner killed one and Mareshall wounded another. I [Smith] was extremely sorry for the occurrence and reprimanded them severely for their impolitic conduct."

The severe reprimand took the form of forbidding them to set traps, at least temporarily.

He held no high opinion of the Central California Indians, finding them, in fact, inferior to the beaver, "either from indolence or from a deficiency of genius." This surprised him; he thought the California country had been blessed with "a more than ordinary Share of ... bounties" and seemed "rather calculated to expand than restrain the energies of man."

But if the energies of man had been restrained in California, the same could not be said about the bears he met. *Their* energies, at least, had been expanded. On the 8th of March, while hunting, Harrison Rogers had his mountain baptism from a bear, being badly mauled. The party had to remain in camp until he was able to travel again, while Smith dressed his wounds with another unlikely combination from the mountain apothecary: cold water and a salve of soap and sugar.

A month later Smith had two encounters himself. (He wears his hair long, now, covering the mutilated ear he received in his first encounter; one brow is still disfigured and scarred.) Being intimately acquainted with the character of the bear, Smith cheerfully plunged head first into a creek; a little later another bear grabbed the tail of his horse. The horse departed, with Jedediah hanging on. The parade continued for forty or fifty yards, with the frightened horse setting such a pace that the bear could not close with him. At last the bear let go, and Smith notes in his journal that he was well satisfied to "get rid of his company on any terms."

During the first few months of the trip Jedediah had been trending generally north and northeast, trapping up the Sacramento valley on the eastern side. By the end of March the party had turned west again, reaching the Sacramento River. The valley here was about fifty miles wide; ahead and to the north the mountains seemed to close in around them. (They were nearing the head of the Sacramento valley.) Unable to cross the Sierra Nevada to the east, he was forced to slant off toward the coast, again in direct contradiction to his permission.

The party crossed the Sacramento in the second week of April, about thirty miles below present Redding. From here he angled northwest; his route was probably roughly parallel to US 299.

The Indians he met now were no longer meek and friendly; nor were they, apparently, much in awe of the white party. The hostility of the tribes through which they passed had increased as they neared the present Oregon boundary.

On April 15 there was an outright attack. The Indians followed parallel to their course all the next day, making a tremendous amount of noise, which did little to improve the morale of the trappers. The country was much rougher now; they were moving into the coastal mountains. The combination of hard travel and the constant menace of the Indians wore hard.

After he made camp for the night of the 16th—still to the Indian chorus—Jedediah took out a small party to see if he couldn't improve the situation. As best he could he tried to communicate to the howling band that his intentions were friendly and that he meant them no harm. The Indians were about as receptive to his communication as Mexican official-dom had been. They wouldn't listen. They kept up the constant din, standing with their bows strung, and refused to approach in answer to his overtures.

Finally Smith fired on them, "to intimidate them and prevent them from doing me further injury." Two were hit; the remainder scattered, leaving some of their goods. The trappers moved on.

Traveling through the mountainous country was becoming an ordeal. Several hundred head of horses and mules had to be gotten across streams and through canyons and ravines, negotiated along the edge of cliffs, steered through the brush, scrabbling on rocky slides, with inadequate feed—a few miles a day was good, and drained the last drop of energy from both men and animals.

Smith was following the Trinity River—which he called the Indian Scalp—by late April. Following where the steep and rocky ravines would permit, at any rate—moving steadily toward the coast, where he hoped the nightmare would end.

The minor skirmishes with the Indians continued, with the necessity of firing on them. This he hated, though not necessarily through his normal Christian inclination. As a practical matter it was dangerous. If the result was intimidation, fine. If it was an increase of hostility, not so fine. There was no way to know, but he had little choice in the matter.

He began to see evidence of white tools: trees on which axes had been employed; lodges of split pine. He was now among the Hupa peoples. The Hupa were the far-southern fringe of a whole cultural complex that extended northward as far as present Alaska: the Northwest Coast culture. They were farthest from the center—which was along the British Columbia coast—and the least highly developed of the Northwest Coast people. Still, they were more vigorous and with a higher technological achievement than the Indians he had left in the valley.

The Hupa were also the southern edge of another sphere of influence: HBC's. Trade goods from Fort Vancouver would trickle down to the Hupa through the customary intergroup Indian trading. HBC's trapping parties came down nearly this far on their Southern expeditions under Alexander McLeod. (They were shortly to push even farther, into the "Bonaventura" country: the Sacramento valley.)

By May 10 Smith was camped on the Trinity in the vicinity of present Burnt Ranch. On an air line, he was now about forty miles from the coast at Eureka.

On that date the second journal of his clerk, Harrison Rogers, begins. He lists the nineteen-man party (including Smith) and adds a musing sentiment on their diversity:

> *Many men of many minds, and many kinds of many,*
> *Kinderate of God's creation.*
>
> *When young in life and forced to guess my road,*
> *And not one friend to shield my bark from harm,*
> *The world received me in its vast abode,*
> *And honest toil procured its plaudits warm.*

Honest toil they had in sufficient quantity, though as yet the plaudits were virtually inaudible. Rogers' first entry may be taken as typical:

> ... The travelling very bad, several very steep, rocky and brushy points of mountains to go up and down, with our band of horses, and a great many of them so lame and worn out that we can scarcely force them

along; 15 lossed on the way, in the brush, 2 of them with loads; the most of the men as much fatigued as the horses.

On May 16 Marechal and Turner were sent ahead to survey the route. They came back the next day with heartening news: the party was within "15 or 20 miles of the North Paciffic Ocean; they report game plenty, such as elk and deer; they report the traviling favourable to what it has been for 30 or 40 m. back."

CHAPTER 13

"Murderers of your people &
Robbers of your property"

ON MAY 19 the party camped within sight of the ocean, only six miles away. "A fair view," said Rogers.

But there is a vast difference between a fair view from six miles away and actually reaching it. This they could not do. They were not able to move from this camp until four days later, owing to the lameness of their horses and bad weather. Heavy fogs had set in, and they were unable to find their way. Horses became lost, men detached to look for them came back empty-handed. During the period they were in this enforced encampment, Rogers and Thomas Virgin rode out toward the ocean. Although they "got within 80 or 100 yards of the beach," they were unable to ride down to it because of the steep rocky banks and brush. On their way back to camp Rogers pursued some elk, lost them, and went after a "black bare."

While Rogers was gone, Virgin remained with the horses, and was attacked. The Indians shot several arrows into one of the horses; Virgin shot and killed one of the attacking party.

When they reached the encampment

there was 7 or 8 Inds. at camp when we got there, and I [Rogers] made signs to them that we were attacked by some of there band, shoot at, one of our horses wounded, and we had killed one; they packed up and put off very soon.

On June 8, they reached the sea at last. They found grazing for the horses near the coast, and the hunters brought in game. "The men," Rogers notes, "appear better satisfied than they do when in a state of starvation."

On the 11th an incident occurred which threw its shadow into the future, though, naturally, little was thought of it at the time. When they were preparing to leave camp, the party discovered that their "fellin axe and drawing knife was missing, and the Inds. had left the camp."

Smith and five men went to the nearby lodges. They caught one of the Indians, tied him, and led him about two miles in this state, by way of persuasion. He finally revealed the ax, buried in the sand, and was released.

On the 20th they crossed Smith River; on the 23rd they were over the 42nd parallel and beyond the authority of the Mexicans. They were not aware of it; and Mexicans were, by this time, the least of their worries. It is remembered in Rogers' journal as the day the ammunition mule was temporarily lost, and not found until near nightfall.

They continued working up the coast, staying near the ocean, losing horses in the brush and rocks, drowning them crossing streams. Indians became less and less friendly; horses appeared in camp with arrows in them; it was impossible to open any kind of communication because the Indians could not be induced to come close enough.

Most of the men had been enlisted a year before, on July 2; when their time expired Jedediah reengaged them at a dollar a day. The next day they picked up an addition to the small party, though he could hardly be called reinforcement. Marshall brought a ten-year-old Indian boy into camp, whom they promptly named Marion. He was a slave, captured from one of the Willamette valley tribes, and not particularly averse to joining this odd, roving tribe of white men. His previous owners had all run off and left him, anyway. Rogers gave him some beads and dried meat, and he was "well satisfyed."

Now they began to encounter Chinook speakers; the great *lingua franca* of the Northwest Coast, universally used as a trading jargon. It was not Old Chinook, the tribal dialect, but a composite language. Starting from Chinook and Nootkan, the Jargon picked up words here and there from Salishan and other language groups; and when the whites came, it adopted French and English with equal ease. At its peak the Chinook Jargon was spoken by as many as 100,000 people of all colors and races, from California to Alaska and from the coast to the Rocky Mountains.

From two of these Chinook speakers Smith learned on July 5 that they were only "ten days travell from Calapos on the wel Hammet, which is pleasing news to us."

Meaning the Kalapuyan tribes of the interior Willamette valley. And pleasing news it was, because it meant they were within easy reach of "civilization"; defined as being the sphere of HBC. Once into the Willamette valley they could descend that river to Fort Vancouver with little expected difficulty. It began to look as though the end were in sight. In spite of the terrible difficulty traveling, the trapping had been good. Smith had nearly 800 beaver, 40 or 60 otters, and had managed to bring through 228 of his horses and mules (according to the later report of HBC's, factor at Fort Vancouver, John McLoughlin).

On Friday, July 11, they camped at the mouth of a large river, the Umpqua. They traded with the Indians they found there; fish and berries, though Rogers notes they were forced to pay "a pretty dear rate." The Indians themselves, however, appeared friendly, and several of them stayed overnight at the encampment.

The next day there was more trouble with petty thievery. One of their overnight guests stole an ax. Smith employed the same means of recovery as before; the man was caught and bound. According to Rogers, Smith "put a cord round his neck, and the rest of us stood with our guns ready in case they made any resistance, there was about 50 Inds. present but did not pretend to resist tying the other."

A little later, a minor chief mounted a horse and was parading around camp. Arthur Black forced him to dismount, and the stage was set for the Umpqua massacre.

II

On the night of July 13, 1828—exactly one year out from the Bear Lake rendezvous—Smith and the company were camped near the confluence of the Umpqua and Smiths Rivers, not far from present Reedsport, Oregon. The Indians had told them they should ascend the Umpqua fifteen or twenty miles inland; from there they would have easy going to the Willamette, and by that River to Fort Vancouver.

They were now to leave the coast, most probably to join the Coast fork of the Willamette. The country here—by

Smith's account to General Clark—was "very swampy in the lowlands and woody in the mountains." With John Turner and Richard Leland, an Englishman recruited in San José, Smith set off up the Umpqua in a canoe to examine the banks and see if they could find a passable road for the party. They were paddled by one of the Indians.

They went upriver only a short distance. Possibly they had found an easy route and were returning for the remainder of the party. As the canoe was nearing their encampment, another Indian of the band (who called themselves Kelawatsets) appeared on shore. He said something to Smith's guide, who immediately grabbed the white man's rifle and dove overboard.

The Indians on shore at once opened fire on the unprotected canoe. Smith and his companions paddled to the opposite bank and took to the woods. According to John McLoughlin's report to the Governor and Committee of HBC, "he ascended a Hill from whence he saw his Camp distinctly, but seeing none of his people & from none of them coming forward when he was fired on though within reach, he naturally concluded they were all cutt off."

Smith, Turner, and Leland then struck off for the coast, which they followed north to present Tillamook Bay. There Smith was able to get the Tillamooks to guide him across the coast range to the waters of the Willamette, which he followed down to Fort Vancouver. He arrived at the HBC post on August 10; the whole journey north from the massacre site had taken almost four weeks. At Fort Vancouver Smith discovered that news of the defeat had preceded him, in the form of the sole survivor of the camp party, Arthur Black. Black had beaten Smith to Fort Vancouver by two days, and from him Jedediah was able to learn for the first time the circumstances of the attack.

When Smith left camp on the morning of July 14 he had given Rogers instructions not to let many of the Kelawatsets into the encampment. This not through apprehension, since they had given him no reason for fear, but simply as a matter of mountain prudence. For one reason or another Rogers didn't observe this precaution. (Possibly he was not able to prevent the Indians' coming in, but it is much more likely that he was not concerned about the problem.) They had, after all, manifested a good deal of friendliness (and Rogers, it may be noted, had not been among the Mojaves when their friendliness turned to murder.) His journal entry of the night before—the last he ever made—was hopeful: "Those Inds. tell us after we get up the river 15 or 20 miles we will have good travelling to the Wel Hammett or Multinomah, where the Callipoo Inds. live."

Perhaps this prospect, coming after the dreary months of vicious travel and hardship, was enough to deaden his sensitivity to danger. In any case, there were nearly a hundred of the Kelawatsets in camp. As Arthur Black told the story to John McLoughlin:

> . . . a short time after Mr. Smiths departure, their being about a hundred Indians in the Camp & the Americans busy arranging their arms which got wet the day previous, the Indians suddenly rushed on them, two got hold of his [Black's] Gun to take it from him, in contending with them he was wounded on the hands by their Knives & another came with an axe to strike him on the head, which he avoided by Springing on one side & received the blow on the back. He then let go his Gun & rushed to the woods, as he was coming away he saw two Indians on one Virgil [Virgin], another, Davis [Daws] was in the water & Indians were pursuing him in a Canoe, a third was on the ground & a band of Indians were butchering him with axes.

After escaping from the encampment, Black had wandered in the woods for four days, and finally made his way back to the beach. The first Indian he met tried to take his knife away from him, but Black was able to keep him off. Shortly after this he ran into a party of seven, who "stripped him of all his clothing except his Trousers." These were soon joined by another party, and an argument developed; about himself, Black thought. He took advantage of the diversion to scamper into the woods and escape. He saw no more Indians until he reached the "Killimaux" villages, at present Tillamook Bay, then Murderer's Harbor, about 150 miles up the coast. ("Tillamook" was variously spelled, but always with the "k" sound until 1852.) There he secured a guide—as did Smith a day or so later—who took him inland to the Willamette and thence down to Fort Vancouver. He arrived about 10 P.M. on the 8th of August.

At daybreak the next day McLoughlin dispatched runners to the Willamette valley chiefs, requesting them to send out parties in search of survivors and bring them to the fort, if found.

Nothing came of this, of course, because the day after runners had been sent Smith, Leland, and Turner arrived, "to our great joy," says McLoughlin.

Now, for the third time in two years, Smith was again at the tender mercies of a foreign power, and this time it was Britain, which had very good reason for wishing Jedediah Strong Smith had never seen the light of day.

III

The use of the terms "American" and "the Americans" in HBC documents gives a faulty air of anonymity to their relations; almost as though HBC considered "the Americans" a rather odd tribe, and thought of them not as individuals but as a whole. This was far from the case. HBC took a strong interest in individual personalities connected with the American fur trade. They—and by this I include the Governor and Committee in London—were conversant with the name and activities of every American trader of any importance. In this respect they were far more knowledgeable than their opposite numbers on the American side, who viewed HBC simply as a monstrous, menacing corporate entity.

HBC's interest was due in part to the fact that it had a much less myopic view of the fur trade than did the American companies, and could afford the long view. From the solidity of its corporate structure HBC was, in effect, immortal. This is in sharp contrast to the outlook of the principals in this narrative. The American traders were individual mortal men, figuring what they could take out of the trade in the next six months, or year, or—at a maximum—five years. The British wanted a steady, stable return over a period of ten or twenty years, and they were profoundly concerned with the condition of the country in fifty years. They had, after all, been in business for 160 years by this time, and youthful impetuosity, if it ever existed, had long since faded sweetly away.

Despite the presence of highly colorful, powerful individuals in the ranks, the activities of HBC are comprehensible only when viewed as the actions of this immortal entity. Their standing policy of conservation, their reluctance to use liquor in the Indian trade, their discretion in clashes with American parties—all are directly attributable to this long view. And for the same reason the HBC factors tried to keep themselves informed about the principal American traders.

Thus, when Jedediah Smith appeared at Fort Vancouver, John McLoughlin was fully aware that "the American" was a chief partner of the major firm then operating in the Rocky Mountains; a firm which had given HBC some restless moments recently. (In the previously quoted letter, McLouglin identifies Smith as "this is the same that came to the Flat Heads 1824/5 and also whom Capt. Simpson saw last Jany. at St. Francisco.")

McLoughlin was a fiery man, six feet four with a seven-foot temper. When Ogden's freemen deserted to Johnson Gardner in 1825, McLoughlin had responded angrily: "we are justified in resisting to the Utmost of our power" any assumption of authority on the part of the American companies. He even wanted to send a party into the Snake country the following year for the express purpose of throwing the gauntlet back in the face of Smith Jackson & Sublette: "to defy them to put their threats in Execution."

Considering the situation as outlined above, it is reasonable to expect that Smith would be received rather coolly, if not treated to a display of outright hostility that would make even Echeandia wince.

Such was not the case. That it was not is to the eternal credit of HBC and the two men through whom the company acted, John McLoughlin and George Simpson. Never did HBC more thoroughly merit its sobriquet, "The Honourable Company."

When the survivors arrived at Fort Vancouver, McLoughlin was in the process of fitting out one of the "Southern Expeditions," under Alexander McLeod. The party was headed for an area not far from the site of the Umpqua massacre, and McLoughlin was only waiting the return of some men from Okanogan to dispatch McLeod.

Immediately on receiving news of the disaster, McLoughlin altered the purpose of the expedition to include recovery of Smith's property and disciplining the Indians who had plundered it. Until McLeod's party could get off, a matter of several weeks, McLoughlin sent Michel Laframboise to see what he could find out. Laframboise was a French Canadian who had been in the Oregon country for nearly twenty years; ever since the Astoria enterprise. He traveled freely and alone where even heavily armed angels feared to tread.

(According to one source, this was because he had a wife in almost every tribe he was likely to run across.)

It was September before McLeod's party—with Smith accompanying him—could get off. They took the Willamette south, and on the second day met Laframboise returning. The news was not particularly encouraging. The stolen property had been scattered around the country in various bands; it wasn't likely that much could be recovered. As to further survivors—there was a rumor that four of the men were alive and in the custody of the "Cahoose" Indians (probably either the Milluck Coos or the Manis Coos). But it was just a rumor. Laframboise had apparently talked to some of the Indians involved, and they had offered the ironic excuse that they had not taken Smith's party to be the same people as HBC.

Laframboise continued down to Fort Vancouver, carrying letters from McLeod and Smith to McLoughlin. Part of Smith's letter said:

> . . . should you think it necessary for the benefit of
> your Company to punish these Indians you would
> confer a favour on your humble Servant to allow him
> and his Men to assist.

McLeod was probably requesting instructions, now that there seemed to be no likelihood of recovering any of the American property without enormous effort.

Michel was back within a week, carrying replies to both men. Smith's offer of assistance[1] was appreciated, but McLoughlin wanted the American to understand his motives:

> I beg to assure you that in this case I am actuated
> by no selfish motives of Interest—but solely by feel-
> ings of humanity . . . in our intercourse with such
> barbarians we ought always to keep in view the future
> consequences likely to result from our conduct as
> unless those Murderers of your people & Robbers of
> your property are made to return their plunder, as we
> unfortunately too well know they have no horror or
> compunction of Conscience at depriving their fellow
> Man of life—If strangers came in their way they
> would not hesitate to murder them for the sake of
> possessing themselves of their property, but as it
> would be worse than useless to attempt more than our

forces would enable us to accomplish and as Mr. McLeod knows those Indians & knows best whether we can effect any good, he will decide on what is to be done.

To McLeod, the chief factor admitted that:

Mr. Smith's affair has a more gloomy appearance than I expected & it seems to be in that state, either that we must make War on the Murderers of his people to make them restore his property or drop the business entirely.

It was a difficult decision to make. McLoughlin's letter to McLeod reviews the pros and cons of the situation. On the one hand lay the danger of leaving the Indians unpunished, and thus incurring the danger of possible repetitions in the future. Against this was the dubious authority of HBC to make war, and the even worse consequences if they should undertake any action against the Indians that they were not able to carry through. McLoughlin wanted no Aricara campaign on his hands in the Columbia Department. All this they had gone over before, during the three weeks before McLeod's party was ready to move out:

it is unnecessary after the various conversations we have had for me to say any thing further on this subject—You know those Indians you know our means ... & as you are on the spot—you therefore will decide on what is best to be done.

Considering the possible consequences of a decision either way, this put Alexander McLeod in an unenviable position. It is characteristic of McLoughlin's compassion and understanding that he closed his letter thus: "whatever that decision may be at least as far as I am concerned every allowance will be made for the situation you are placed in."

McLeod's decision was to play his part by ear. Accordingly he continued down the Willamette, hearing rumors all the way that the Umpquas planned to ambush him. The party crossed over the mountains in the vicinity of present Cottage Grove and began to descend the Umpqua to the sea. As they moved down this river, the Indians scattered before them, until those with the brigade were able to reassure them this was not, strictly speaking, a war party.

McLeod had a chief of the Umpqua tribe in for a conference on October 11; the chief showed up leading eight horses from the massacred party. McLeod reassured him that the whites had no present intention of making war, but merely intended to restore Smith's property and "Establish Peace and Quietness."

McLeod could get nothing from the chief respecting survivors, though he did learn that the tribes were quite astonished that an HBC party should be upset about the massacre.

Some of Smith's party, apparently, had told the Indians "something about territorial Claim, and that they (the Americans) would soon possess themselves of the Country." The Indians' surprise was that HBC should interfere "in aiding and assisting People that evinced evil intentions toward (them)."

McLeod notes that this political talk

> makes the Natives about us very inquisitive not having heard such a thing before, and we avoid giving them any information, and treat the subject with derision. Mr Smith when told of this, observed that he did not doubt of it, but it was without his knowledge and must have been intimated to the Indians through the Medium of a Slave boy attached to his Party, a Native of the Wullamette.

The Umpquas on the upper river got together a few more of the animals—a total of twenty-six—and the party moved on. Ten days brought them to the Kelawatset village. It had rained incessantly throughout the journey, and they reached the village in a virtual cloudburst.

The Kelawatsets offered no trouble; they turned over 588 beaver skins, 43 otter, and 4 sea otter. Sundry articles were also returned: beads, traps, guns, and what not.

After about a week, during which the goods were trickling in, McLeod turned his party downriver again, to the mouth of the Smiths River and the site of the massacre. Here were eleven skeletons. In his movements around the country, this gentle Christian Smith was leaving behind him too many deposits of this kind.

Of the missing four there was no sign; and they were never able either to confirm or to discredit the rumor that said they were in custody among the "Cahoose." Whatever the case, none was ever heard from again.

Aftfer burying the remains of Smith's party, the HBC brigade moved north up the coast, collecting various other articles from the bands they met. The final total was near 700 beaver skins and 39 horses; the great majority of skins, but only a pitiful remnant of the herd of animals Jedediah had hoped to sell in the mountains.

On November 10—back on the upper Umpqua on the return journey to Fort Vancouver—McLeod picked up a few more trivia; including, by some indeterminate miracle, the journals of both Smith and Harrison Rogers. Why the natives had preserved these for five months is impossible to say; perhaps they thought there was medicine involved in those odd worm trails across the paper. If there was, it was a historian's medicine, because without these papers our knowledge of Smith's activities would rest on his laconic reports to General Clark; a prospect almost too abysmal to contemplate.

IV

McLeod's returning party, with the recovered plunder, reached Fort Vancouver sometime during the week of December 14–22. Smith found an interested observer newly arrived on the scene: George Simpson, governor-in-chief of all the territories of HBC in America.

Simpson (who was thirty-six at the time) was in charge of one of the largest commercial enterprises in existence. While naturally subject to the policy decisions of the Governor and Committee, Simpson's authority in the field was unchallenged. He was the boss; he knew it, liked it, and did a good job of it. He was no glad-hander, no one-big-happy-family man. When Simpon's hand came out you didn't extend your own, you ducked. This whirlwind of energy was presently engaged in the process of revitalizing the entire Columbia Department; a complex organization of posts and activities that extended from the Rockies to the Pacific and from the 42nd parallel north to anywhere you want to name.

When the McLeod-Smith party came in, their welcome was not entirely wholehearted. John McLoughlin was, in fact, astonished to see his brigade leader back. The intention had been for McLeod to continue south on a trapping run toward the "Bonaventura." Now he was back—in the middle of

December—and the fall hunt of the Southern Expedition was nonexistent. This was directly attributable to Smith, of course, for whose sake the brigade had gone off chasing willow-o'-the-wisps on the coast. Mr. Smith's appearance had proved decidedly expensive, through not only the use of the party but the loss of all expected returns for the season.

The Honble Co^y would remain Honble about it, of course. But they didn't have to like it. Simpson took over the handling of relations with Smith, and on December 26 put down on paper, in the form of a letter, the gist of previous discussions: "in order to guard against any misapprehension . . . our communications . . . should be in writing instead of Verbal."

Simpson reviewed the circumstances of dispatching Mc-Leod's party and managed to imply that there was good reason to believe Smith's party had brought the disaster on themselves. (McLeod had been told by the Indians that they had received reports of the American party "conducting themselves with hostility" toward the tribes they met coming north, ". . . for which," Simpson remarks, "it appears there were some grounds.")

He then explained that the loss of the Southern Expedition's fall hunt had subjected HBC "to an expense of exceeding £1000 independant of the loss of Profits we had reason to calculate on."

> Had you been in the condition of discussing terms with us we should as a matter of course have insisted on your defraying the expenses, that the recovery of your property might have occasioned to us, but you was not in that condition consequently nothing was said on the subject, and altho' we are well aware that either in Law or Equity we should be fully entitled to Salvage, we make no claim thereto, on the contrary place the property which we have recovered at your disposal without any charge or demand whatsoever.

Smith, in one of their previous conversations, had made several proposals regarding the disposition of the recovered goods. One of these related to thirty-eight horses, which had been left at a camp on the Umpqua. Smith proposed to turn these over to HBC. In return they were to provide him with an equal number at their Walla Walla post upriver. He proposed to leave horses and furs at Walla Walla while he

returned to the mountains to meet his partners at the 1829
rendezvous. During the summer he would then return to
Walla Walla and pick up his goods.

This arrangement was not possible; according to Simpson,
they had no horses at all, and would need five times as many
as they had any hope of collecting. As an alternative, Simpson said:

> . . . in order to accomodate you we are willing to take
> [them] off your hands at 40/St^g head, which is a
> higher price then we ever pay for Horses and the
> same we charge to our Servants & Trappers, but if
> you are not satisfied with that price, they are still quite
> at your disposal.

He strongly advised against Smith's notion of proceeding
immediately to Walla Walla with his furs, because of the
danger involved:

> We altho' perfectly acquainted with every Indian . . .
> rarely venture to send a party even with Letters, and
> with property never less than from 30 to 40 men;
> such a measure on your part would therefore in our
> opinion be sporting with Life or courting danger to
> [the point of] madness; which I should not consid-
> er myself justified in permitting without pointing out
> to yourself and followers in presence of witnesses the
> desperate hazards you would thereby run.

In this passage, I think, lies the key to this entire exchange: the not-quite-casual phrase "in presence of witnesses."

With this phrase, Simpson almost inadvertently reveals his
major preoccupation in the affair. Despite his protestations of
pure concern for Smith's welfare, Simpson is even more alive
to the political implications of the situation. He is profoundly
aware of the tendency of the American trappers to blame
every conceivable misadventure on HBC.[2]

With this letter to Smith ("to guard against any misapprehension")—Simpson is also guarding against any possible
future accusation against HBC. In part this is also responsible
for his constant reiteration of the great sacrifices the company has made on Smith's behalf.

This is surely an exaggerated concern for American good

will; it is doubtful that HBC was terribly worried about the opinion American trappers had of them. But, again, we encounter here the long view so characteristic of the Honourable Company. This same winter Simpson wrote London that he was confident HBC had nothing to worry about in the way of settlers in the Oregon territory. (This was because Smith's trip had revealed so many obstacles in the way of travel.) In Simpson's opinion the main factor was the huge outlay of capital, which he thought no one would risk for such a tentative return. He felt, in short, "perfectly at ease unless the all grasping policy of the American Government, should induce it, to embark some of its National Wealth, in furtherance of the object."

It seems to me reasonable, however, that a man of George Simpson's acuity would be perfectly aware of a strange national characteristic of Americans: our easy ability to become emotionally inflamed over an objectively unimportant event, even to the point of considering it sufficient cause for war. A righteous indignation has always been our national pleasure, much as horse thievery was among the Absaroka. Given a *cause célèbre*—that is, an injury to one of our citizens which captured the national imagination—the American government might well be pressured into embarking some of that National Wealth.

It would be ridiculous to suppose that Simpson sat down and considered the situation in those terms and wrote his letter accordingly. (I make no such supposition here, and the above musings are not by any means to be attributed directly to Simpson.) But two puzzling questions—the exaggerated concern for Smith's welfare and the insistence on witnesses and records—are partially explained by such a hypothesis. I think it highly likely that Simpson was motivated by a clear understanding of the possible consequences should Smith be ill-treated, and was aware that those consequences might well be out of all proportion to the event itself.

Whether the above conjecture is correct or not, it is certainly true that Simpson's arrangement with Smith was generous in the extreme. On first examining these letters one is misled as to the actual extent of Simpson's generosity by the terms in which it is phrased. He simply cannot deny himself the pleasure, as Dale Morgan has it, of "rubbing Jedediah's nose in that generosity":

You are well aware that we have already experienced much inconvenience incurred many sacrifices, and exposed the Concern to heavy loss through our anxious desire to relieve, assist and accommodate you we are willing nevertheless to do whatever else we can without subjecting ourselves to further loss or expense. . . . I shall now suggest what I conceive to be the safest course you can pursue. . . .

Your Beaver which is of very bad quality the worst indeed I ever saw, having in the first instance been very badly dressed & since then exposed to every storm of Rain that has fallen between the Month of April & the 22nd Inst. [December] consequently in the very worst state of Damage, I am willing to take off your hands at 3 Dollars p Skin payable at 30% sight[3] on Canada, which I conceive to be their full value at this place, and your Horses I will take at £2 St[g] p Head payable in like manner. But if these terms are not satisfactory to you the Furs may be left here until you have an opportunity of removing them & the Horses are at your disposal where you left them [on the Umpqua].

In either case yourself and followers shall be made welcome to a continuance of our hospitality while you choose to remain at our Establishment—and if agreeable you shall be allowed passage free of expense to Red River Settlement with me in the course of next Spring & Summer from whence you can proceed to S[t]. Louis . . . or you may accompany our Snake Country Expedition next Autumn by which means you will in all probability have a safe escort until you fall in with your people.

Jedediah received this letter, replied the same day, and had further conversations with Simpson. Even though his own letter has been lost, the contents are easily inferred from Simpson's reply to it:

I beg it to be distinctly understood that we do not lay claim to, nor can we receive any remuneration for the services we have rendered you, and indemnification for the losses we have sustained in assisting you, nor any Salvage for the property we have recovered for you, as whatsoever we have done for you was in-

222   *A Majority of Scoundrels*

duced by feelings of benevolence and humanity alone
. . . your distressed situation . . . the lamentable &
melancholy fate of your companions . . . [etc.] I beg
to assure you that the satisfaction we derive from
these good offices, will repay the Honble Hudsons Bay
Comp^y amply for any loss or inconvenience.

Smith accepted Simpson's offer of passage to HBC's Red
River settlement, and a little later, also accepted his offer to
buy the furs.[4]

Simpson then drew on the company's agent at Lachine for
£550. 2s. 6d. Halifax currency payable to the firm of Smith
Jackson & Sublette. For some reason this draft appears to
have been canceled and a new one issued in March, 1829, for
£541. 0s. 6d. Halifax currency, or $2369.60.[5]

Smith spent the remainder of the winter as the guest of
Fort Vancouver. Many Americans were to be cast in this
role in years to come, but as yet it was a novelty. From
Smith the HBC officials were able to garner a good deal of
information, about both the terrain through which he had
come and sentiment in the United States. They liked the
report of Smith's journey better than he had liked the traveling; the enormous physical barriers seemed to preclude any
emigration from the States.[6]

The problem of possible American emigration to the Oregon territory was occupying more than one person in this
narrative; and, strangely, though they were on opposite sides
of the fence, their statements were nearly identical and nearly
simultaneous.

In a letter to his superiors in London Simpson referred to
the problem and said that Smith had, on his present journey,
"discovered difficulties which never occurred to their minds,
and which are likely to deter his Countrymen from attempting that enterprize."

At almost the same moment, General William Ashley was
writing his own opinion to Senator Benton:

Three or four thousand people are ready to emi-
grate to the country as soon as a military establishment for Their protection is made. . . . I feel assured
it will be an act of humanity to suppress any Thing of
the kind at this time. They have not the least concep-

tion of the misery they would lead their families to by such an act.

Two thousand miles apart, the Britisher and the American were reaching similar conclusions. But the first surgings of the tide of emigration were beginning to be seen, and in another fifteen years the tide would begin to flow.

The exchange of information was not one-sided, of course. For the second time in four years Jedediah Smith had the free run of an HBC post; and moreover, the main depot of the entire Columbia Department. While enjoying the hospitality of Dr. McLaughlin, Smith was able to pick up a tremendous amount of valuable data simply by using his eyes.

It was obvious to him that Fort Vancouver was no temporary trading depot: "every thing," he writes, "seemed to combine to prove that this fort was to be a permanent establishment."

And this was the old Fort Vancouver; before Smith left in the spring he watched the beginning of work on a new post some 200 yards from the river (the old one was three quarters of a mile away).

A year after his return to the mountains, Smith wrote a complete description of the fort as he had seen it. In part:

Twelve pounders were the heaviest cannon . . . The crop of 1828 was seven hundred bushels of wheat; the grain full and plump, and making good flour; fourteen acres of corn, the same number . . . in peas, eight acres of oats, four or five acres of barley, a fine garden, some small apple trees and grape vines. The ensuing spring eighty bushels of seed wheat were sown; about two hundred head of cattle, fifty horses and breeding mares, three hundred head of hogs, fourteen goats, the usual domestic fowls. They have mechanics of various kinds . . . (a list follows) . . . a good saw mill . . . a grist mill. . . . They had built two coasting vessels [the *Broughton,* sloop, 30 tons, and the *Vancouver,* about 60 tons], one of which was then on a voyage to the Sandwich Islands. No English or white woman was at the fort, but a great number of mixed blood Indian extraction, such as belong to the British trading establishments, who were treated as wives, and the families of children taken care of accordingly.

It is interesting to note a difference between this and other Smith Jackson & Sublette communications to the government: whereas their previous notes of information on the West had been addressed to General William Clark, as superintendent of Indian affairs, this one was not. The recipient was the Honorable John H. Eaton, Secretary of War.

The purpose of the report becomes manifest in its closing sections:

> The inequality of the convention with Great Britain in 1818 is most glaring and apparent, and its continuance is a great and manifest injury to the United States. The privileges granted by it have enabled the British to take possession of the Columbia river, and spread over the country south of it; while no Americans have ever gone, or can venture to go on the British side. The interest of the United States and her citizens engaged in the fur trade require that the convention of 1818 should be terminated, and each nation confined to its own territories [the implicit assumption here being that the joint-occupancy territory belongs to the United States] . . . there are other considerations requiring the same result. These are, the influence which the British have already acquired over the Indians in that quarter, and the prospect of a British colony, and a military and naval station on the Columbia. Their influence over the Indians is now decisive. Of this the Americans have constant and striking proofs, in the preference which they give to the British in every particular. . . .
>
> As to the injury which must happen to the United States from the British getting the control of all the Indians beyond the mountains, building and repairing ships in the tide water region of the Columbia, and having a station there for their privateers and vessels of war, is too obvious to need a recapitulation.

And if the letter seems a bit belligerent, Jedediah had at least the good grace to acknowledge his treatment:

> . . . it is an act of justice to say, also, that the

treatment received by Mr. Smith at Fort Vancouver was kind and hospitable; that personally, he owes thanks to Governor Simpson and the gentlemen of the Hudson's Bay Company, for the efficient and successful aid which they gave him in recovering from the Umpqua Indians a quantity of fur and many horses, of which these Indians had robbed him in 1828.

During the spring word came to Fort Vancouver that there were American parties wintering near the HBC Flathead House, in northern Montana. This changed Smith's mind about going east with Simpson's party. He decided to make his way to the American winter encampment on his own.

Accordingly, he left Fort Vancouver almost two weeks before Governor Simpson, on May 12, and proceeded up the Columbia. The journey, despite Simpson's dire misgiving, was uneventful. (Actually, no such journey was really uneventful. This is a historian's conceit, the meaning of which is that we don't have any record of what happened.)

Smith had with him only one man—Arthur Black—of his surviving party. Another, John Turner, had elected to remain behind in Oregon. The third, Richard Leland, disappeared into the same obscurity from which he had come. The only information about him at all is the tantalizing note written by McLoughlin the following summer: "Thomas Petit and Richard Layland are on their way to Canada there are heavy accusations against them, you will please keep them in confinement and if you apprehend any chance of their making their escape you will put them in Irons." So presumably the little Englishman had an eventful spring of one kind or another.

Jedediah made contact with a party under his partner Davey Jackson sometime during the summer, exact date not known. This probably happened somewhere on the Flathead River, between Flathead House and Flathead Lake. They set out for the south, to rejoin the balance of the scattered crew of Smith Jackson and Sublette.

CHAPTER 14

"We dashed through the ranks of the foe"

SMITH had been gone for two years; it is now the summer of 1829. For the mountain activities of those two years we have to backtrack to the spring of 1828, while Smith and his party were still trudging miserably up the west coast toward the Umpqua massacre.

After Robert Campbell's short visit with Peter Skene Ogden, he took his party north. Though they were "very silent regarding the object of the journey," Ogden had his own private ideas about where they were going: "American party left for the Flat Heads and perhaps the Kootenays. I believe they intend trapping the forks of the Missouri."

If so, and it seems likely, Campbell's party was probably working slightly to the north of Bill Sublette who trapped both flanks of the Tetons and the Pierre's Hole area. Campbell did a fair trade with the Flatheads, turned around in late spring and started back for Bear Lake. On the way he picked up a small detached party of Sublette's men, including no less a personage than James P. Beckwourth, and was accompanied the rest of the way by them.

When within fifteen miles of Bear Lake, Campbell's party was attacked by a band of (reportedly) two or three hundred Blackfeet. The trappers broke for some nearby rocks, making it with the loss of one man; "being an inactive man, [Lewis Boldue] was overtaken and killed before he had reached the rocks."

Campbell had with him a Flathead Indian who spoke the language of the Blackfeet. Through this interpreter, Campbell informed their attackers that they were within a few miles of the rendezvous where, in addition to the white men, there were several bands of Indians hostile to the Blackfeet.

While this discussion was going on, "the Indians saw two men, mounted on fleet horses, pass through their lines, unhurt, to carry the information of Mr. C's situation to his friends."

This report, which may be taken as fact, is from a letter by Ashley, who was told by Sublette. For what it's worth, here is James P. Beckwourth on the same subject:

> To risk a message [to the camp] ... seemed to subject the messenger to inevitable death; yet the risk must be encountered by some one. "Who'll go? who'll go? was asked on all sides. I was wounded, but not severely ... I said, "Give me a swift horse ... [etc.]
>
> "You will run the greatest risk," said they ... [etc., etc.]
>
> Again we dashed through the ranks of the foe before they had time to comprehend our movement. The balls and arrows flew around us like hail ... [etc., etc., etc.].

Somebody did do it, though, even if not James P. Beckwourth. The Blackfeet, seeing the couriers get through, scattered rapidly. Campbell and his party marched into camp, and it began to look as though a pattern were shaping up. Last year, too, rendezvous had been preceded by a battle with Bug's Boys, as they were known to the mountain men (signifying, according to one source, the Devil's Own). If that sort of thing was going to go on, rendezvous could get to be pretty unpopular after a while.

Eighteen twenty-eight was a bloody year for the trade, though the mountain partners had not yet heard of the two largest massacres: Jedediah Smith and the Mojaves, Jedediah and the Umpquas.

Aside from these dramatic mass killings, the mountains were taking their toll in bits and pieces. Sublette had lost a man—Joseph Coty—to the Blackfeet. Tulloch lost three, including Bill's little brother Pinckney Sublette. Two others were lost on the Bear River, "while attempting to pass from one American camp to another:" John Johnson and A.

Godair. (Probably Thierry Godin, as Antoine—his son—shows up at the battle of Pierre's Hole, revenging his father's death.) Blackfeet got the credit for them, too, and for Old Pierre Tevanitagon.

Four others—Logan, Bell, Scott and O'Hara—wandered off together and were never heard from again. They could have gone under in either the fall of '27 or the spring of '28. A footnote in the contemporary casualty list says, "The fate of these men is not known, but the conclusion is hardly doubtful."

Counting Smith's losses—ten to the Mojave, fifteen to the Umpqua—this comes to thirty-six men. A bad year from the point of view of personnel.

But when the partners settled down at Rendezvous 1828 to count up the year's catch, things looked pretty fair. The trappers had brought in better than seventy packs of beaver—7,107½ pounds; 49 otter skins, 27 pounds of castoreum, and 73 muskrats. Since their supply train had come up the previous November, they would have to get the furs down to St. Louis on their own. That was all right, too. By doing their own transporting they would be getting St. Louis prices for the fur; and the difference was significant. Mountain price was still about $3 a pound; in St. Louis the beaver brought $5, the otter skins $3 each, the castoreum $4 a pound, and even the muskrats added 25 cents each. The grand total was $35,810.75.

To be sure, Smith Jackson & Sublette were still in debt to General Ashley by about $20,000 (including a note for $9,010.40 for the balance owing on the Fall '27 supply party.) But after all debts and charges had been made, Ashley was still able to enter on his books a "Ballance due S J &S this 26th day Octr 1828" amounting to $16,000. This was not all profit, of course. They still had to outfit a supply party for 1829. But this cost less than $10,000, leaving the partners free and clear and $6,000 ahead of the game.[1] The returns of the absent partner Smith were unknown, but Jackson and Sublette had managed to get the company out of debt without him, though it had taken the first two years of the partnership to do it. (About the time of Rendezvous 1828, Smith's party was being decimated by the Umpqua; had the mountain partners known of this, their optimism might well have been tempered.)

Bill Sublette was put in charge of the expedition down, and

he reached civilization around the first part of October, 1828. He disposed of his furs to Ashley at the prices noted above. The previous year he had returned immediately to the mountains with the new supplies; this time, however, Sublette was to remain in St. Louis for the winter of '28–29. The partners had in mind a strengthening of their trapping force, and Sublette was to recruit the new men and organize the supply train for the following spring.

(An old friend of ours also left Rendezvous 1828 on a mission of some importance: Old Hugh Glass. It is unlikely that Sublette and Jackson knew about Hugh's trip; it boded ill for them. Hugh, by way of the Bighorn and Yellowstone, made his way down to the spanking-new Fort Floyd [soon to be known as Fort Union] at the confluence of the Yellowstone and Missouri. Here Glass talked to one of the shrewdest men ever seen in the fur trade, the formidable Kenneth McKenzie, now working for John Jacob Astor and American Fur. Glass was a delegate without portfolio from the free trappers at Rendezvous 1828, who had apparently conceived the notion that prices might be lowered by a little competition. McKenzie was invited to bring supplies into the mountains after the spring hunt of '29, and the free trappers would consider the merits of his outfit. This trip casts a long shadow in the history of the trade, as it is the first stirring of the terrible competition that was about to descend. How McKenzie came to be at the mouth of the Yellowstone in an American Fur Company fort is a complex story, which will be dealt with a little later in the body of this narrative.)

During his stay in St. Louis Sublette gave Ashley as complete information as he could about the state of the trade. Including the anecdote of Tulloch and Ogden, and as much data on the operations of HBC as he had. Much of this Ashley worked into letters; and usually for the purpose of demonstrating the evil influence of HBC in the West.

Ashley was profoundly involved with the politics of the country's westward expansion. Through his contacts in the trade, such as Sublette in this winter of '28–'29, he was kept informed of happenings in the mountains and came to be regarded as the principal source of news from the territory west of the Missouri. He wrote frequently to another great advocate of the West, Thomas Hart Benton, including with his factual information various detailed recommendations for action to be taken by the government. His principal concern at this time was military protection for possible migrants to

Oregon. Ashley felt there was no possibility of making a successful mass move to the west until the government was able to set up—and maintain—a sufficient military establishment to offer her citizens protection against the Indians en route and the avaricious British forces already established in the Oregon country. By which he meant, of course, HBC. From the mountain grist Ashley's mill ground out a remarkable flow of propaganda, which probably had a somewhat greater effect on the attitude of the United States toward Oregon than it has generally been credited with.

II

While Sublette was in St. Louis disposing of the company's furs, the Fall '28 trapping parties were out. To some extent we can follow two of these.

Davey Jackson took a brigade up the west slope, into the Flathead country. He had with him Tom Fitzpatrick and an unrecorded number of men. For four months this party worked slowly north, probably following Henry's fork of the Snake, crossing the divide to the Three Forks area, and ending at last on the shores of Flathead Lake. They reached the lake by the first part of December, and settled in for the winter. Apparently the returns of the hunt had not been good. By the time they reached Flathead Lake—within the sphere of two HBC posts: Flathead House and Fort Colvile—the party was low on provisions, and they had to trade half their meager catch to HBC.

On his way north Jackson was followed by Joshua Pilcher. Pilcher, with nine men, was making one last attempt to stay in business. Rendezvous 1828 had not been profitable for him, naturally, since so many of his goods had been lost (see note 1, ch. 11). Two of his principal partners, Vanderburgh and Fontenelle, had returned to St. Louis in company with Bill Sublette's 75-man caravan; as far as they were concerned, the partnership was bust. (Vanderburgh apparently combined with another of the erstwhile Pilchermen, Drips, for a short time, but it didn't last. All three of these men later entered into an arrangement with American Fur.)

Pilcher later wrote that he left Rendezvous 1828 on a "tour to the northwest, with the view of exploring the region of the Columbia river, to ascertain the attractions and capabilities for trade."

By the time he reached Flathead Lake Pilcher had conceived a new idea; potentially profitable, if not entirely above-board. We know of this notion only through the reception it met. On December 30—the day after Jedediah Smith finished his arrangements at Fort Vancouver—Pilcher wrote Governor George Simpson. Simpson's reply of February 18, 1829, makes Pilcher's idea clear:

> I am aware that the Country watered by the sources of the Missouri, usually known by the name of the "Black Feet Country" is a rich preserve of Beaver, and that a well organized Trading and Trapping Party would in all probability make valuable returns there-in. . . . [I] would therefore readily entertain your prop-osition . . . if a difficulty of a formidable character did not present itself, which is the Territorial rights of the United States Government to that Country. These rights, we as British Subjects cannot infringe openly, and although the protecting Laws of your Govern-ment might be successfully evaded by the plans you suggest still I do not think it would be reputable in the Honble Hudsons Bay Co^y to make use of indirect means to acquire possession of a Trade to which it has no just claim. Under those circumstances I cannot fall in with your views and as regards Mr Ogden he cannot without acting in direct opposition to his in-structions cross the height of Land.

The winter of '28-'29, what with one thing and another, was a most honorable season for the Honourable Company.

The second traceable party was that of Robert Campbell, now a knowledgeable and experienced mountain man of twenty-four. Campbell had left St. Louis with one of Ashley's early parties, as previously noted here, and his star had been rising now for three years. His mountain sojourn restored his health, and he managed to stay on for ten years. Campbell's background was somewhat different from that of most of the mountain men. He had behind him an Irish estate of some considerable extent and a family lineage he could well be proud of. His brother, Hugh, was a respected Philadelphia merchant; judging from his correspondence, a most urbane and polished gentleman in whom the family ties were ex-tremely strong. His letters to Robert are warm and affec-tionate, and through them all runs one consistent thread:

leave the mountains and come home. For all his mountain
time Robert was entreated by various members of his family
to return to civilization and take up respectable life again.
Still he managed to put it off for one reason or another, even
though he professed to be anxious to return.

Among the thirty trappers Campbell commanded in the
fall of '28 were Jim Bridger and James P. Beckwourth. From
the latter of the Jameses we learn that Campbell's party was
organized to work the Powder River area, which had been
relatively untouched in recent years. After the first of the
Bear Lake rendezvous, Smith Jackson & Sublette had pretty
much confined their operations to the western slope of the
Rockies; or at any rate no farther east than Wind River.
But this, as noted, had proved expensive. Bug's Boys were
depressingly energetic in that area and all the way north. The
eastern slope of the divide, on the other hand, was generally
Crow territory; as such the trappers might be in danger of
losing their horses, but their lives were considerably safer.
This may have been one of the reasons for the slight shift
eastward. Another possibly persuasive argument was that the
Snake country was being trapped out. Between HBC's deliberate effort to wipe it clean and the less-purposeful but
equally effective American depredations, the Snake country
was losing its appeal. There may have been smaller detached
parties working west from Bear Lake, but the major movements were Jackson's—due north—and Campbell's—northeast.

Campbell's brigade probably moved east across South
Pass, skirting the southern end of the Wind River Mountains.
From there they worked up to the Wind River, which they
reached by the first of the new year. Moving north down the
Bighorn they reached the Yellowstone proper, followed it
downstream to the Powder, and made their spring '29 hunt
on the upper reaches of that river.

The only date and location we can be sure of is January 6,
when they were on Wind River. During this month Smith
Jackson & Sublette lost the services of one of the greatest
heroes ever seen in the mountains, but there seems to be
some difference of opinion as to just how it happened. This is
the story, in the version given by James P. Beckwourth
himself:

It seems that one of the trappers, Caleb Greenwood, had a
Crow wife. This being the case, it devolved upon Mrs.
Greenwood and spouse to tell the Crows all about the great

victory over the Blackfeet preceding Rendezvous 1828. By James P. Beckwourth's account, Greenwood eventually "became tired of so much questioning" (which strikes a true note; the Indian curiosity about such things was absolutely insatiable, and Greenwood could have been expected to act out every single incident of the battle, and make up those he didn't observe directly).

In order to relieve his boredom, Caleb invented a little tale to amuse himself and the Crows, to wit: Once upon a time the Cheyennes kidnapped the baby son of a Crow chief ... raised the child as a great warrior ... heroic feats, etc. ... bought by the whites ... heroic feats, etc. ... and when the Crows were sufficiently open-mouthed about the whole thing, Greenwood let them have it. That little boy, he said, grew up to be none other than James P. Beckwourth.

This was great stuff, and the Crows immediately demanded James P. for their very own. This was declined, and the Indians went back "to spread their tale of wonderment" throughout the tribe.

Now, on the Wind River, comes the action for which Greenwood's fabrication merely set the stage. It seems that Bridger and Beckwourth, out on a hunt, separated to set traps on two forks of a stream. While thus alone, James P. suddenly found himself "among an innumerable drove of horses":

> . . . I could plainly see they were not wild ones. The horses were guarded by several of their Indian owners, or horse-guards, as they term them, who had discovered me long before I saw them. I could hear their signals to each other, and in a few moments I was surrounded by them, and escape was impossible.

They were Crows, naturally, and James P. was taken to the village where he was subjected to what he calls (in italics) the "*examining committee.*" At last he was identified positively as the missing prince, so to speak, by a mole on his left eyelid. There was great rejoicing, since James P. Beckwourth's fame was well known all over the mountains and the Crows considered themselves fortunate indeed to have acquired such a mighty warrior. He was welcomed "with a public reception fully equal in intensity, though not in extravagence, to that accorded to the victor of Waterloo on his triumphal entry into Paris."

Sufficiently extravagant, however, that he was provided with twenty fine war-horses, complete equipage, four unmarried "sisters"—very attractive young ladies, too—who competed bitterly to serve him, and a new wife. "I could not," he writes, "find it in my heart to undeceive these unsuspecting people and tear myself away from their untutored caresses."

Nor could most of us if we'd be honest about the matter.

Thus James P. Beckwourth begins his long career as a Crow chief, which was marked by great success and a general prospering of the tribe. He did, in actual fact, join the Crows this winter, but there is a suggestion that his departure from the company might not have been so precipitate as all that. The terrible mourning of his fellow trappers (who thought he'd been killed) is, unhappily, a figment. They knew where he was going when he left. And Robert Campbell, furthermore, made him put his mark on an IOU before he let him go. Dated Wind River, January 6, 1829, it was for $275.17½—"which I promise to pay in good merchantable Beaver Furr at Three Dollars per pound." A somewhat more prosaic departure from Smith Jackson & Sublette; but, after all, a promissory note is far too banal a thing to be found in a book like *The Life and Adventures of James P. Beckwourth.*

Campbell lost four other men this spring, and these went the hard way. On the "Bad Pass of Big Horn," according to the casualty lists, Blackfeet took Ezekiel Abel, Peter Spoon, one Adam, and one J. Larime (Lariour). There was an Indian report some time later that these four had been killed by Snakes, but the original assumption of Blackfeet seems to be more likely.

It isn't certain whether these men were lost going to the Powder or on the return trip; Campbell almost certainly came back by way of the Bighorn, since Rendezvous 1829 was scheduled for some point on the Popo Agie.

Dale Morgan suggests that this may not have been a general rendezvous but simply an arranged meeting between Campbell's detached party and Bill Sublette, coming up from St. Louis with the new outfit. Whatever the actual scheduling had been, that was how it worked out. Davey Jackson did not reach the Popo Agie. His expedition to the Flatheads had been only moderately successful from the point of view of furs; but there he had been joined by the long-absent Smith, and now the two partners were making their way south along the western slope.

Sublette met Robert Campbell on the Popo Agie around the 1st of July and found his hunt had amounted to about forty-five packs of beaver.

Campbell decided to take the catch down to St. Louis himself. For the past four years the entreaties of his brother had become increasingly persuasive. Further, there was trouble at the Campbell estate in Ireland, and Hugh could not see to it. (The management of the estate was in the hands of "Long Andy," Andrew Campbell, and he was not doing too well, being somewhat inclined to get himself and family in debt over their heads. Hugh claimed that Andy had always had "the evil genius of the family.") Robert's presence was needed to put things in order, and he was probably happy enough to get a brief respite from the mountain rigors. Family feelings ran deep in the Campbells, and he had not seen his mother, sister Anne, or Hugh for four years. It is sometimes hard to remember that the mountain men were so young; Robert had left the comforts of a civilized life when he was barely twenty-one; he had already spent a fifth of his life among what his brother called "those Black Footed Black Headed & Blk hearted savages."

Campbell arrived on the Missouri late in the summer of '29, and arranged the sale of the beaver through Ashley, as usual. The price was a little higher this time: $5.25 a pound. Robert had 4,076 pounds of beaver, 7 otter skins (at $3) and 14 pounds of castoreum (at $4). The total was $22,476; a good catch, if you ignore the four men it had cost. The company had a balance on Ashley's books of $6,684 (left over from Sublette's transactions last fall), which was now raised by Campbell's take to $28,160. This, like the profits of the previous year, would have to be applied toward a new party; and, as it turned out, would not quite cover expenses.

After completing his transactions with Ashley in the winter of '29–'30, Robert left for Ireland to see what could be done about the estate and renew some of the old family ties. The mountains drew him back, but by the time he returned there was no firm of Smith Jackson & Sublette.

III

When Bill Sublette left St. Louis in the spring of '29 he knew what he was doing. Over the past four years the mountain men had gradually been working out the technical procedures of overland travel, until they were now in the form which they retained pretty much throughout the history of the American West. Ashley began it in '25, with the supply party destined for the informal Green River rendezvous. This caravan, led by the unhappy general himself, was the first of a long series to follow nearly the same course—the Platte route—and meet similar problems. This route became the road to Oregon, with all its famous landmarks: Independence Rock, Scott's Bluff, Devil's Gate on the Sweetwater, etc.

Since that '25 caravan, one or more large parties had made the trip every year. Gradually the procedure of march became standardized, and after this point one description will do for all. The first wheel ruts had been made on the Oregon Trial by Ashley's cannon; all that remained was to transport a body of wagons along this road, and even that was not far off.

A party consisted of anywhere from sixty to eighty men. The first place in line was taken by the booshway, as he was known to the American trappers. (From the French "bourgeois." The HBC brigade chiefs were more frequently known as "partisans.") The rear of the column was brought up by the company clerk, or little booshway (e.g., Harrison Rogers, Tom Fitzpatrick, etc.). Between these two the entire party stretched out, frequently over a distance of half a mile or more.

The booshway rode on ahead, searching out the road, encountering whatever problems might be in the line of march. Beside him was a mule, "chosen for its qualities of speed and trustworthiness," which carried panniers containing the necessary papers: company records, journals, the articles of agreement with the men, and what not.

The pack animals of the column were loaded in a conventional way with three packs. Loading these required—and still requires, for that matter—the patience of Job, the strength of Samson, and the wisdom of Solomon. The miserable, terrifying, and frustrating job of packing the animals was entrusted to a number of the men designated campkeepers. These were usually new recruits; greenhorns on their first trip, signed on by the company at a low wage, and responsible for all the mechanical trivia of march and camp. Each campkeeper was responsible for three animals.

Aside from the pack animals proper, with general goods and supplies, each trapper had two or more animals of his own: one to ride, the others for carrying his personal equipment such as traps, furs, and foofaraw for his squaw.

On departure, each member of the caravan was issued such goods as were considered necessary (which included his animals) and every disbursed item was entered in the company's account books by the little booshway. (One slightly ludicrous example was Harrison Rogers' notation on the agonizing first trip to California: the regular issue of shaving soap to Jedediah Smith, and him only.)

Organizationally, the entire column was divided into messes, consisting of eight or ten men. Each mess was represented by one spokesman, who made known to the booshway the complaints and desires of his particular mess. These messes formed the discrete units out of which the whole party was made.

When the booshway had determined their camping place for the night he stopped and let the rest of the column come up to him. The camps were generally laid out in a square, or rough circle, containing enough area for all the horses to graze within the perimeter, each horse being allowed a grazing range thirty feet in diameter. When camp was made by the side of a large watercourse, which was often the case, the water itself was made one side of the square, ground permitting. A position for each mess was designated, the animals unloaded, and a breastwork formed of the packs, packsaddles, etc., as protection against possible night attack.

The animals were then put on light halters and entrusted to the horse guards, who led them outside the camp to graze. At sundown, or slightly before, the animals were returned inside the ring. The horse guards then placed the stakes, or picket pins, thirty feet apart, and the horses were duly picketed for the night. If the presence of hostile Indian parties was suspected they were sometimes also hobbled.

While the horses were grazing outside, the men remaining within the camp circle would be seeing to the condition of their equipment, repairing the damage of the day's march, cleaning their guns, etc. All during the time of march a semimilitary discipline was observed. The booshway made inspection rounds of the camp before nightfall. Disciplinary procedure was (slightly, very slightly) indirect.

A booshway, finding a man with a dirty gun, seldom even spoke to him. The gun was found wanting; the booshway turned to the nearest man and said, "Can you do this right?" "Yes," said the man. "I'll give you ten dollars to do it," quoth the booshway, who then entered a $10 debit in the account of the offender. This was big money, and the mistake was seldom repeated. The firing of a gun in camp was one of the worst offenses possible, and seldom forgiven. Only under the extreme provocation of a direct Indian attack could a gun be fired. Internal disputes had to be adjudicated by means of fists or knives.

Throughout the day hunters ranged ahead and to the sides of the column. By dinner time there was—with fortune—a pile of game stacked in front of the booshway's lodge. Division of the game was the responsibility of the little booshway. He butchered the animals—or had it done—and the first man who happened to pass was given the job of distribution. He turned his back to the pile of meat, and the little booshway selected a piece at random. "Who is this for?" "Number ten," said the man, also choosing at random. The men of mess number ten then came to pick up their meat. The mess of the booshway himself was included in this arbitrary division, and, presumably, no one was able to claim they consistently got the bad cuts.

Meat was the diet; the mountain men wanted nothing else. The finest of all foods was the hump rib of a fat buffalo cow, though some liked tongue nearly as well. Occasional contests are recorded where two mountain men start at either end of a slippery *boudin*—the buffalo's intestine—and swallow their way to the middle. Like all meat eaters in history, the mountain men knew you have to have plenty of fat with the lean, and the condition of their buckskins testified to the fact that they got it. What with the blood drippings of one sort and another, and a good substantial coat of grease, the color of a mountain man's buckskins was a far cry from the delicate beige-brown of the moving picture. They were black. Dirty black, greasy black, shiny black, bloody black, stinky black. Black.

Sentries were posted for the night, but they were generally stationary. The booshway made rounds of inspection of these, too. The trapper in charge of sentry duty communicated with the posted guard during the night by the customary "All's well!" and if the guard answered in turn "All's well!" all, obviously, was well. If there was no answer, the sentry captain would go to investigate.

Somewhere near sunrise—sometimes much earlier, on forced marches—the little booshway would appear to raise the camp. This he did by shouting. "Levé, levé, levé, levé!" fifteen or twenty times (again a French corruption, of course: levez-vous).

If in country not known to be safer than mother's bosom, two scouts were always sent out to check the surrounding area, "ravines, woods, hills, and other places within striking distance of the camp." While these "spies," as Ashley called them, were out, no man was permitted to leave his protective breastwork. If they reported favorably, the morning preparations began. The horses, having grazed during the night in their thirty-foot circle, were again led out of camp by the horse guard and permitted to graze until the party was ready for saddling and shoving off. The campkeepers would wrestle and curse the packs aboard, and when they had succeeded to some degree or other, the party was ready to start again. (This, naturally, does not allow for the recalcitrants; those feisty animals who would let pack be half lashed on, then stampede and scatter pans and panniers and traps and foo-faraw for a mile before being caught. Nor for the endless arguments on the merits of various forms of the diamond hitch. Nor for the campkeeper who got kicked in the head and was now desperately trying to murder the mule without firing a gun.)

The first mess that found itself ready to go moved up behind the booshway and took its choice of position in the column. As the other messes were ready they came up behind. Each mess marched together during the day.

When in dubious territory there would be scouts ranging on all sides of the party, in addition to the hunters. Those in front would be several miles ahead by midmorning, while the flanking and rear "spies" would be keeping a fairly constant distance of half a mile or more.

It was a ponderous, complex, irritating and grueling ordeal, only the general outlines of which have been suggested here. From the experience of these brigades came the knowledge that was to make the cross-continent epic of the Oregon Trail possible, and supply America with part of her mythos. And this was what Bill Sublette had ahead of him when he set out from St. Louis in the middle of March, 1829.

IV

I enter the next section of this narrative with even greater trepidation than usual. The fact is that I feel more than a little guilty about it, and think some sort of—excuse? explanation?—ought to be offered the unwary reader.

Generally speaking, it is necessary and desirable for a student of history to maintain a decent objectivity toward his material; to observe carefully and set down accurately, without bias. I have tried to do this, or have at least tried to make my bias plain enough so that it can't be confused with the facts.

But all history is comprised of the actions of individuals. This devious probing at documents which we call "research" has the surprising effect of bringing the student very close to the individuals he is studying. He finds them to be human beings, and reacts to them as such. This kind of personal reaction puts considerable strain on the admirable principle of objectivity.

In short, I have here reached a point where I must warn the reader not to expect even the semblance of objectivity. This is by way of explaining my attitude toward a character who is about to make his entrance in this narrative. I confess that I am wholly incapable of exercising even a decent minimum of critical judgment about him because I find him such extraordinarily good company.

Joe Meek is his name, *River of the West* is his book, and Frances Fuller Victor is the woman who wrote it down for him.

Mrs. Victor throws you off, at first. You get the impression of a terribly naïve, romantic woman, somewhat wide-eyed at the adventures of Joseph L. Meek. Recent historians have been more than a little condescending toward Mrs. Victor, picturing her as a gullible fluffhead, sitting at Joe's feet and soaking it all up to her wonderment. A lot of this, I think, is due to her prose style, which was naturally the one of the times (1870 publication). But never has condescension been more wasted. Frances Fuller Victor was an extraordinarily keen, shrewd historian, and the evidence is in *River of the West,* among her other writings.[2] For example, the reader should check her observations on white-Indian relations and her analysis of the social and political position of John McLoughlin in later years. She was nobody's fool, and many of her insights into the forces at work were amazingly perceptive for the time in which she lived. And if she chose not to be exceedingly critical of Joe's anecdotes, maybe she had something else in mind.

You must not understand by this that Joe Meek was a liar. He was more a sort of artist—with the truth. James P.

Beckwourth, now, he was a liar. The only reason he's funny today is through his desperate, naïve attempts at self-aggrandizement. But in Joe's stories, often as not, he himself is the butt of the joke.

There are a lot of inaccuracies in *River of the West*: matters of dating, routes, and what not. Sometimes through the normal lapses that occur in all these later reminiscences, sometimes because Joe had a good story to tell. These errors are absolutely without import. I have to be concerned with them, because a finicky accuracy is essential to what I'm doing, but there's no reason a casual reader should give them a second thought. The actual facts can be had elsewhere, after all, but only in *River of the West* can you find those facts shaped into something that greatly resembles a work of art (a statement Joe would not have tolerated for a minute).

CHAPTER 15

"Craig began to sing,
and I began to laugh;
but Nelson took to swearing"

JOE MEEK was eighteen in the spring of 1829, fresh from Washington County, Virginia. He was one of a number of recruits Bill Sublette picked up that spring; many of whom were to play an important—or at least a recorded—part in the settlement of the Oregon country. Joe's particular friend was Robert Newell, another greenhorn. He was known a little later as Doc Newell, with no more rhyme nor reason than any other mountain epithet. (Joe himself is often called major in the contemporary journals.) Another of these prospective Oregonians was George W. Ebberts; all three of these men left their experiences recorded in some form or another.

Sublette had fifty-four men in the outgoing party, and they left St. Louis in the middle of March. While the column was crossing the barren country between Arkansas and the Platte, the new recruits got their first taste of what became almost standardized as a mountain welcome. ("Arkansas" is on Meek's authority, but it is more likely the South Platte he means.)

Roaring out of the desolate country around them came a huge and howling band of Indians, riding full tilt down on the column of whites, screaming and shooting and generally raising a good quantity of plains dust. Sublette quickly drew his men up into a semblance of a fighting line, though the Indians were estimated at nearly a thousand. Whooping wildly, the band careened headlong to within fifty paces of the waiting whites. The principal chief reined up his horse, leaped off, and put his weapons on the ground, making peace signs.

Sublette went out to talk to him, discovered the party was a conglomerate of friendly Sioux, Arapahoes, Kiowas and Cheyennes. The "attack" was simply their way of making the column welcome. Bill gave them a few presents, and they went away happy. (If this seems a grotesque sort of joke, it was at least the standard mountain humor. Joe himself participated in a good many of these welcoming "attacks" in later years, including a memorable one on the Whitman party. The wonder of it all is that there is no record of anyone's being killed in them.)

Sublette rounded up his sweating greenhorns and they pushed off again, finally reaching what passed for Rendezvous 1829 around the middle of July. (This is the Popo Agie meeting between Campbell's detached brigade and Sublette's supply train.)

Sublette stayed here in the valley of the Popo Agie, selling off some of his merchandise to Campbell's men and the free trappers. Joe reports his wide-eyed appreciation of his first rendezvous: the carousing and brawling; the splendid spectacle of the free trappers' wives decked out in their best; and confesses his shock at seeing four trappers playing cards with the dead body of a friend for the table. (Though chances are that Joe is thinking of some other year, or a story that was told him. Custom was, the old hands would corner a greenhorn and pump him so full of lies and truths about the mountain trade that the poor boy would quake in his boots.)

During the two weeks or so they remained on the Popo Agie, Sublette and Bob Campbell made their arrangements for transporting Bob's 45-pack catch down to St. Louis. After Campbell had gone, Sublette divided the remaining men into two parties. A few new men were on hand this year whose names were going to be more important. Another of Bill's younger brothers appears here for the first time. But Milton Sublette had more experience than the short-lived Pinckney. He'd been working the trade out of Taos for a while; he knew a little more. Milton had been with a party in September, 1826, that had gone up the Colorado to the Mojave villages; probably the same party Jedediah Smith had heard of there. Milton was not working for his brother Bill in the mountains, and his presence is indicative of another trend that was beginning to be apparent. The southern, New Mexico-based brigades were drifting toward the north.

At any rate, the twenty-seven-year-old Milton was good enough by this time to be put at the head of a detached party. He shared his authority with two free trappers; and the association must have been congenial. Henry Fraeb (Old Frapp) was a German; illiterate, as far as I know; had a certain amount of trouble with his spoken English and tended to lapse into a heavy accent when excited. The other was Jean Baptiste Gervais, one of the deserters from Peter Skene Ogden's Snake Country Brigade of '24–'25. (Fraeb, except on rare occasions, is naturally Frapp. Gervais, depending on the orthographic whims of his peers, is Jervy, Jervis, Jarvey, etc. etc. etc., and once in a while even John. "Baptiste" is equally flexible, but "Baptice" is a good average.)

Milton, Fraeb, and Gervais, then, were dispatched from the Popo Agie to work the Bighorn River and its tributaries with a party of about forty men. Robert Campbell's 45-pack season—made in that area and the Powder—was certainly not spectacular. But it was good and solid, and made without the enormous risk involved in Blackfoot country. It could be the unspectacular bread-and-butter hunt for the year.

Meanwhile Bill Sublette still had to find Davey Jackson. There are several conflicting reports as to how this was done. Jackson had returned from the Flathead country with Jedediah Smith and was now camped in the beautiful valley across the divide, Pierre's Hole. He probably sent his clerk, Tom Fitzpatrick,[1] over to the Popo Agie with the good news: Smith was back, and alive; and the bad: he'd lost his party and all he had to show for two years was an HBC draft for less than $2,400.

After he had dispatched Campbell down to St. Louis and brother Milton up the Bighorn, Sublette packed up the remainder of the force and started across the mountains. He followed the Wind River to its head; and from there through To-gwo-tee-a Pass it is only a short distance to Buffalo Fork of the Snake, which would take the party into Jackson's Hole and the Snake proper.[2] They crossed the Tetons and moved down into Pierre's Hole for the second rendezvous of the year 1829; a bonus for the *mangeurs de lard,* who thus had the rare opportunity of being lied to by experts twice in the same month. ("Porkeaters" was the mountain term for newcomers, referring to the fact they still had traces of a civilized—and effete, by implication—diet about them; were not yet exclusive buffalo eaters.)

I half suspect this second Rendezvous 1829 is the one Joe

Meek was describing. There were more men here, about 175 of them, including unattached trappers. Further, the safe return of Smith would have been a pretty good reason to celebrate. Not that an excuse was needed; but if an auspicious event occurred any time around rendezvous it was taken advantage of.

Sublette made contact with the Smith-Jackson party on August 5, and for the first time in two years all three partners were together. A strange trio, these men. Their respective functions in the partnership were radically different, though this was more from imposed circumstance than intent.

Smith, for example, was assuming the role of explorer; his far-flung jaunts assured him of his place in history, and certainly he was able to gather a good deal of information which later proved valuable. But for some reason historians have overlooked the fact that as a partner in a fur company he wasn't doing a hell of a lot. Ever since he joined the partnership his hunts had been absolutely unprofitable to SJ&S, however dramatic. He was losing men at a rate no other brigade leader ever approached. Two of the biggest massacres in the trade happened to him, the Mojave and the Umpqua (third being the first Aricara battle, which was Smith's baptism). He lost money hand over fist. SJ&S would be involved in the estates of Smith's dead men for years to come, and this says nothing of the horses and gear. To be sure, he did some trapping, but he always ended up losing everything. This is not to imply any incompetence on his part; rather he was star-crossed. But he was not even paying his own way, and while this may be of little importance to historians of the present day, it would have been bitterly important at the time.

Bill Sublette had gradually taken over the business end; his was the job of making contact with the outside world; selling the furs, buying the new outfits and conducting them back into the mountains.[3] *Qua* mountain man, Bill Sublette was good; *qua* businessman he was superb. He was far and away the greatest double-threat man of the trade; he handled himself well on both ends. He was the greatest of the Sublette brothers; Milton never came up to him. Partially this was because of Milton's early death, but even had he lived he would not have equaled Bill. Milton had a tragic flaw; he was, on occasion, known to let friendship interfere with profit. Of this error Bill Sublette could never be accused. He was utterly ruthless. I'll have occasion to develop this point in greater detail in connection with the next section of this book. For now, let it suffice to say that Bill Sublette was a sharp and incredibly effective businessman. His was the morality of business; the reader may interpret this statement according to his own views.

The third member of the firm, silent, almost anonymous Davey Jackson was the real backbone. He was the trapper *par excellence*; he didn't make history, he didn't explore terra incognita, he didn't lose men right and left. He wasn't much interested in politics, he had no grandiose ambitions. But season after season after season he quietly brought into rendezvous the furs that kept SJ&S in business. It is to be regretted that there is so abysmally little information on him. From our modern viewpoint he is only a pale wraith beside the colorful figures of Smith and Sublette.

There is a tradition that at this meeting Smith persuaded the other partners to move back east, on the indisputably American side of the divide. This, as the story goes, was to show his appreciation to John McLoughlin and HBC for their generous treatment of him. "Smith's Christian nature would not permit the benevolent McLoughlin to outdo him in generosity," says Chittenden.

This is a nice story and I would like to believe it, but it's too lumpy to swallow. For one thing, any such promise made HBC would have turned up in Simpson's correspondence, or McLoughlin's. But there is more direct evidence to the contrary than that.

Mrs. Victor says: "Sublette's camp commenced moving back to the east side of the Rocky Mountains in October." This is immediately after Sublette had "reluctantly consented" to Smith's proposal. But then, in describing the fall hunt of '29, we discover that they worked the west slope after all; if SJ&S were "moving back to the east side" they were taking an awfully roundabout course. Later in the year—after the fall hunt—they did move east again; but this was by prearrangement. All parties were to be reunited in the valley of the Wind River, where they would winter with the Crows. I have to conclude that Smith's generosity was a fiction.[4]

The second Rendezvous 1829 broke up in early October. As usual, Jackson's departure is obscure, and his Fall '29 hunt shrouded in the customary mystery. (Dale Morgan suggests that Jackson worked the Snake country; but this was not until after the winter camp; Spring '30 hunt. Jackson may have stayed around the Pierre's Hole neighborhood, trapping out its streams, then crossed directly over by the reverse of Sublette's route to the wintering camp on Wind River. This is just a guess.)

Smith and Sublette joined forces, taking a large party north, dead into the Blackfoot grounds. They followed Henry's Fork of the Snake up to the present Montana line and the divide, trapping as they went. They crossed over (via Targhee Pass?) and reached Missouri Lake (present Hegben Lake) in November.

From the beginning they were sporadically harassed by Blackfeet. One morning, just as the call to turn out had sounded, the camp was bounced by a fairly large party of Bug's Boys. They had timed the attack for the moment when the horses were unhobbled for their morning graze, but miscalculated slightly. They came, loudly, firing all their guns, shouting and screaming, trying to stampede the herd. Fortunately for the trappers, the Blackfeet were a few seconds too early. Only a few of the animals had as yet been turned loose, and apparently all the hooraw simply turned them back to camp. Tom Fitzpatrick is credited with mounting immediately, galloping "at headlong speed round and round the camp, to drive back such of the horses as were straying. . . . In this race two horses were shot under him; but he escaped, and the camp-horses were saved."

A six-hour skirmish followed, the Blackfeet lodging themselves in a narrow ravine "from which the camp was forced to dislodge them, at a great disadvantage." A few men were wounded; none killed. The Blackfeet eventually "skulked off."

The party moved north under continual harassment of this sort. It gave Joe a good introduction to the mountain necessity of trapping beaver with one hand on your rifle. Heavy guards were naturally set each night, and the new recruits had to take their turn in the chilling fall mountain nights. The traveling was rough, and "the recruits pretty well worn out." Meek drew sentry duty sometime after their first skirmish, and was put under the care of an old hand named Reese. Reese turned out to be competent at dealing with all kinds of problems, including the embarrassing situation when two sentries are caught asleep on their post.

Sublette, making his nightly check, got no answering "All's

Well!" from the Meek-Reese post (both of whom were snoozing contentedly).

> Sublette came round the horse-pen swearing and snorting. He was powerful mad. Before he got to where Reese was, he made so much noise that he waked him; and Reese, in a loud whisper, called to him, "Down, Billy! Indians!" Sublette got down on his belly mighty quick. "Whar? Whar?" he asked.
>
> "They were right there when you hollered so," said Reese.
>
> "Where is Meek?" whispered Sublette.
>
> "He is trying to shoot one," answered Reese, still in a whisper.
>
> Reese then crawled over to whar I war, and told me what had been said, and informed me what to do. In a few minutes I crept cautiously over to Reese's post, when Sublette asked me how many Indians had been thar, and I told him I couldn't make out thar number. In the morning a pair of moccasins war found whar Reese *saw the Indians,* which I had *taken care to leave there* . . . our story got us the credit of vigilance, instead of receiving our just dues for neglect of duty.

About the same time Joe made the acquaintance of another mountain institution: the bear. He and two other trappers were out on foot one day when they suddenly encountered a bear. Meek and Craig, according to account, "ascended a large pine, which chanced to be nearest." Nelson betook himself to a smaller tree, not being in a position to choose too carefully; one which had another small tree growing just beside it.

> With his back against one of these small trees, and his feet against the other, his bearship succeeded in reaching a point not far below Nelson's perch, when the trees opened with his weight, and down he went, with a shock that fairly shook the ground. But this bad luck only seemed to infuriate the beast, and up he went again.
>
> It took three tries altogether. Then the bear became thoroughly disgusted . . . and turned and ran

at full speed into the woods . . . Then [says Meek]
Craig began to sing, and I began to laugh; but Nelson
took to swearing. . . . (He) damned the wild beast;
and Craig and I laughed, and said he didn't seem wild
a bit.

Joe ends his story with a capsule description of mountain
sympathy; and what he says holds true throughout all these
years in the mountains: "If a man get into trouble he is only
laughed at: 'let him keep out; let him have better luck' is
what we say."

"Let him have better luck." There were few men who
couldn't have used it at one time or another, Jedediah Smith
being the prime example. (Joe was one of the lucky ones;
this is part of his great appeal. Almost everything that happened to him turned out all right in the end, and he made it
funny when he talked about it. Sometimes not; the death of
his deeply loved Snake wife Mountain Lamb cannot be made
funny; the death of his daughter Helen Mar Meek at the
Whitman massacre cannot be made funny. But it was not the
mountain code to dwell on these things; and in relating his
adventures to Mrs. Victor Meek certainly followed the
mountain code all the way down the line, not excluding that
clause which adjures the speaker to take a good story where
he finds it.)

From Hegben Lake Sublette's trappers cut northeast,
crossing the Madison and Gallatin Ranges to the Yellowstone
River. While they were resting men and horses there, a
skirmish with the ubiquitous Blackfeet resulted in Joe's being
separated from the main body. He wandered for five days,
heading generally southeast (and thus through present Yellowstone Park), and on the fifth day came upon some of the
sights that have made the park famous: "behold! the whole
country beyond was smoking with the vapor from boiling
springs, and burning with gasses, issuing from small craters,
each of which was emitting a sharp whistling sound."

It reminded him—that romantic old poet of the mountains
—of Pittsburgh. But bigger. He went down and wandered
around awestruck, noting that "curious thoughts came into
his head, about hell and the day of doom," but his final decision was one of pragmatic simplicity: "if it war hell, it war
a more agreeable climate than [I] had been in for some
time."

Shortly after this Joe was discovered by two trappers

who had been sent to look for him. He rejoined the main party and they made their way away from this "back door to that country which divines preach about" and reached the Bighorn River, probably in early December.

Here they found signs of another trapping party in the near vicinity. Scouts found Milton Sublette's party camped nearby, having made a fairly successful fall hunt, as had Smith and Bill Sublette. After resting for a few days the combined parties turned south and made for the wintering camp in the Wind River valley. They arrived shortly before Christmas, 1829.

II

From this encampment Jedediah Smith wrote the letters quoted in Chapter Five, with all their weight of guilt. Here, too, the partners would have to take stock once more. No arrangements had been made for Outfit 1830; probably because they hadn't been certain whether or not they would stay in business. They had a balance on Ashley's books now, and perhaps it would be wisest to cash in. But the Fall '29 returns were sufficient, if not overwhelming, and it was decided a new outfit for the next year was in order. Payment was not a great problem; their credit with the general amounted to about $28,000, counting the estimated returns from Campbell's trip. Some of it was already dribbled away for wages, but three would be enough.

On Christmas Day—possibly the day after—Bill Sublette and Black Harris put on their snowshoes and started out, very much as they had in the winter of '26–'27, traveling alone across country with pack dogs. There are no records of this trip, but it seems they made about two weeks' better time, arriving in St. Louis before the middle of February. They were beginning to get good at it.

The party at the Wind River winter camp was large. Jackson had apparently been there when the Smith-Sublette party arrived from their fall hunt, from the north. The latter brigade had cached their combined furs (from Milton's hunt on the Bighorn and Sublette's in the Blackfoot country) at the point where the two parties had met; somewhere up the Bighorn. Jackson cached his at Wind River.

There were over two hundred men at this winter camp, with all their animals and gear.[5] This alone would have imposed a strain on the food resources of the valley, and to top it off the winter of '29–'30 was exceptionally hard; game and graze were scarce. A week after Sublette and Black Harris left for St. Louis, Smith and Jackson decided they would have to move.

The process of moving an entire encampment in the dead of winter was not a pleasant one, and the situation must have been fairly critical to force them to such a decision.

They decided on the rich area around the Powder River; good buffalo country, and that was the main thing they would be looking for. They crossed (or skirted) the Bighorn Mountains and took up quarters on the Powder somewhere around the middle of January. Here they stayed until the first of April. (It was probably during this winter camp that Joe Meek attended his first classes in the Rocky Mountain College: he learned to read in this noble institution, from an old Shakespeare and a Bible that were "carried about with the property of the camp.")

The Spring '30 hunt was made by two divisions. Davey Jackson took about half the men back across the divide into the Snake country.[6] There is, inevitably, no scrap of information. (I have a growing conviction that Davey Jackson selected his brigades by showing his men a pen. If they knew what it was for, they were ruthlessly weeded out.)

The remaining half, under Jedediah Smith, set off in the other direction—north. They soon crossed over the range separating the Powder from the Tongue River; trapped on the latter for a while; and moved west to the Bighorn itself. Times were good, according to Meek's report, and the pelts began to mount up. While they were on the Bighorn a heavy spring snow was dumped on them, making traveling hard. When the snow melted, it raised streams to dangerous heights. Trying to cross Bovey's Fork of the Bighorn (present Beauvais Creek, Montana), Smith lost thirty horses and 300 traps. This was a crippling blow to the party, but there was nothing for it but to move on with what they had.

From the time they left the Tongue River they had probably been following a line roughly parallel to the east-west course of the Yellowstone proper, and some miles south of it; intersecting the various named streams and spending a few days or more on each one, trapping up and down from their general line of march.

After the loss on Bovey's Fork, Smith crossed the Pryor Mountains (the northern horn of the Bighorns) through

Pryor's gap, and cut almost due west to Clark's Fork of the Yellowstone; thence to the Rosebud River. (This is not the present Rosebud—which is about 150 miles east—but the Stillwater River.)

While trapping the Rosebud, Meek—again with two others—found himself another bear, or, rather, the bear found him. They had just killed a fat buffalo cow, gorged themselves on it—the mountain manna—and rolled into their blankets for the night. The choice pieces they wanted to save were stuck under their heads, which was a standard way of keeping food away from animals. However, the animal that came hunting was not a skunk, as was frequent, but a large, hungry bear. Joe was wakened near dawn by "something very large and heavy walking over him, and snuffing about him with a most insulting freedom." Joe says:

> You may be sure that I kept very quiet, while that bar helped himself to some of my buffalo meat and went a little way off to eat it. But Mark Head ... raised up, and back came the bear. Down went our heads under the blankets, and I kept mine covered pretty snug, while the beast took another walk over the bed, but finally went off again to a little distance. Mitchel then wanted to shoot; but I said, "no, no; hold on, or the brute will kill us, sure." When the bar heard our voices, back he run again, and jumped on the bed.

Eventually, after a good deal more promenading over the blanket bundles, the grizzly decided "he couldn't quite make out our style," and took off down the mountain. Joe, "wanting to be revenged for his impudence," followed after and killed him. "Then," says he, with a justifiable satisfaction, "I took my turn at running over him awhile!"

Reaching the Yellowstone, which was also in high water, Smith made bullboats to ferry the goods across. Mrs. Victor mentions another system of crossing rivers, which is of some interest:

> The mode . . . was to spread the lodges on the ground, throwing on them the light articles, saddles, etc. A rope was then run through the pin-holes around the edge of each, when it could be drawn up like a reticule. It was then filled with the heavier

camp goods, and being tightly drawn up, formed a
perfect ball. A rope being tied to it, it was launched
on the water, the children of the camp on top, and
the women swimming after and clinging to it, while a
man, who had the rope in his hand, swam ahead
holding on to his horse's mane. In this way, dancing
like a cork . . . the lodge was piloted across. . . . A
large camp of three hundred men, and one hundred
women and children were frequently thus crossed in
one hour's time.

Smith was moving north again; across the Yellowstone and
up to the headwaters of the Musselshell. Now he was in
Blackfoot country again, and the harassing began. He
moved—still north—to the Judith, and things were no better.
However rich the country might be, it was no good unless
you could trap it. And owing to the constant annoyance of
Bug's Boys, Smith found "trapping impracticable."

The spring hunt had been good, however; good enough
that there was no reason to risk another massacre for the
sake of a few more pelts. They turned back, having made
only a halfhearted attempt to penetrate the implacable wall
of violence and hostility that surrounded this rich ground. It
was now late spring anyway, and time to begin thinking
about Rendezvous 1830. Since much of the fur was cached at
Wind River, the rendezvous was scheduled there.

Smith's party wound its way back up the Bighorn to the
valley of the Wind and raised the cache there. Samuel Tulloch took another small party back up to Milton Sublette's
cache on the Bighorn. (Sublette's had been dug into an
overhanging bank the previous December.) Meek was with
this group, and while he and a "Frenchman named Ponto"
were digging out the cache, the bank collapsed on top of
them. Ponto was killed almost instantly, "rolled in a blanket,
and pitched into the river." Meek came out of it alive, but
had to be packed up with the furs and carried back to
Wind River.

Someplace along the line, "Jackson also arrived from the
Snake country with plenty of beaver." Of course.

Now all that remained was the supply train from St. Louis.

III

Bill Sublette and Black Harris reached St. Louis about

February 11, 1830. Chances are Sublette didn't like what he found there. There were ominous storm clouds on the horizon, strangely resembling John Jacob Astor.

Shortly after Sublette's arrival, Pierre Chouteau found an opportunity to chat with him. Chouteau's firm, B. Pratte & Company, had become the Western Department of American Fur in December, 1826 (see Chapter 9). Now, there were a few things Chouteau would like to know, purely in a friendly way. Sublette, like a Hemingway hero, said nothing.

The disgruntled Chouteau finally had to write Astor: *"Je l'ai beaucoup questionne. Je n'ai rien obtenu de satisfaisant. Il me regard toujours comme un opponent."*

It is hard to see how Sublette could have seen Chouteau as anything but an opponent. By now he knew that the Western Department was outfitting an expedition for the mountains on its own. It had signed on two of Pilcher's former partners, Fontenelle and Drips, and one of the Robidoux brothers to lead it. This was bad news, particularly when it came in addition to another threat. The virtual monopoly of SJ&S on the mountain trade was about to be broken; that much was obvious. If not this year, then the next. John Jacob Astor was moving west with all the relentless inevitability of the tide.

Six months after American Fur had absorbed B. Pratte & Company, another merger was negotiated. This time Astor bought up the small—but annoying—Columbia Fur Company. (This was the company based at the Mandan villages, far north on the Missouri, which had been started by a combine of former Nor'westers and some Americans.) This was retitled the Upper Missouri Outfit, or simply UMO.

The Western Department was in virtual control of the lower river (having bought out the last serious competition, Joseph Robidoux; $3,500 cash for his goods, and $1,000 a year for two years to say out of competition). With the establishment of UMO at the Mandans, this made the Missouri—in so far as the fur trade was concerned—the private creek of John Jacob Astor.

When he bought Columbia Fur, Astor got a bargain, because with it he secured the services of Kenneth McKenzie. One of McKenzie's first orders of business was to build the new post at the mouth of the Yellowstone, Fort Floyd. (It became Fort Union—and the greatest of American posts—almost immediately, and will be so called here.)

Sublette certainly knew of Fort Union; Hugh Glass had gone there in the fall of '28 to invite McKenzie to the feast.

Other considerations had prevented, and McKenzie hadn't been able to get a supply party into the mountains for Rendezvous 1829, as desired. But Sublette was perfectly well aware that it was simply a matter of time before SJ&S was caught between two forks of American Fur: the Western Department from St. Louis and the Upper Missouri Outfit from Fort Union. Like the tide, Astor did not destroy, he simply engulfed. If SJ&S was to escape drowning, it was time to scamper for higher ground.

But Bill had come back to St. Louis with some good ideas for a supply caravan; some new ideas, and he proceeded to put them into effect.

Instead of the customary horse-and-mule caravan, Bill had in mind to try a radical innovation—wagons. As a further change he would take along cattle, to provide for the party until they reached good buffalo country. The idea of letting the provisions carry themselves proved to be a good one.

Sublette worked fast. By April 10, two months after his arrival, he was ready to go. It seems highly likely he was hurrying to get back before Western Department's caravan could move; and he succeeded. The party of Fontenelle, Drips, and Robidoux did not get off until May.

Sublette's party consisted of eighty-one men, all of them mounted on mules. There were ten wagons, drawn by five mules each, and two of the lighter Dearborn carriages, which required only one mule. They were driving twelve head of cattle and one milch cow, making up a caravan the likes of which had never been seen in the mountains.

He sent the supply train on ahead, while he remained behind to tie up the loose business ends. Principally he had to get his new license from General Clark and settle up with Ashley. The trading license was issued on April 14, and two days later Sublette went over his accounts with Ashley.

Not so good. Their credit was $28,160, mostly from Campbell's furs of last fall (the previous $6,684 balance made up the balance). But the accumulated debits were a staggering $29,177.15, including $1,000 cash advanced on the day of settlement. SJ&S was back in the red by $1,-017.15.

Still, there had been a pile of furs *en cache* when Sublette left the mountains, and he could reasonably expect a decent spring hunt. This would more than take care of the relatively small debt and probably leave a good deal over, to be divided among the partners. Most important, the outlay for this supply caravan was the last expense; and it would also pay for bringing the cached furs back to St. Louis for final settlement of the business. Anything from here on in was profit.

I am here making an assumption that Sublette decided, on the basis of what he saw of the mounting opposition, to get out of the business before it was too late. Historians have wondered why Smith Jackson & Sublette broke up at the time they did. It seems obvious to me that a man of Bill Sublette's demonstrable shrewdness could have seen the writing on the wall, and drawn the only sensible conclusions. Witness that the business of SJ&S was on an extremely tenuous financial basis, even while the firm held an effective monopoly on supplies. The losses from Indian depredations, accident, and plain mountain attrition were simply too great; even a goodly markup on supplies didn't give enough margin. But this state of affairs was dependent on one condition: that they be actively engaged in taking beaver, because that was where the losses occurred. On the other hand, a company that did nothing but supply—did not directly hunt at all—would completely bypass the stage of the business where loss was heavy. The losses would already have been absorbed by the active hunters before the suppliers even came into the picture.

But that was for another year, and the problem now was to get out from under before John Jacob Astor sat down. Sublette gave Ashley a note for the balance owing, and caught up with his supply train a few days later.

He later described his course:

> Our route from St. Louis was nearly due west to the western limits of the State; and thence along the Santa Fe trail about forty miles; from which the course was some degrees north of west, across the waters of the Kanzas, and up the Great Platte river, to the Rocky Mountains, and to the head of Wind River, where it issues from the mountains.

They fell in with sufficient buffalo to support the train some 350 miles out, on the Platte: "the quantity being infinitely beyond what we needed." They had been obliged to butcher only eight of their meat animals; the remaining four and the milch cow made the trip all the way to Wind River, where they doubtless provoked a good deal of hilarity among the mountain men. A milch cow in the Wind River valley? *Wagh!* That's *some*, now!

The letter to the Secretary of War went on to say that the wagons could have crossed the divide without difficulty—via South Pass—"had it been desirable for them to do so, which it was not." They had made an average of fifteen to twenty-five miles a day, and run into no insuperable obstacles. The worst were ravines and creekbanks, which sometimes had to be cut away to let the wagons pass. But the trip was not only feasible, it was easy, and there were no losses. The conclusion:

> . . . the ease and safety with which it was done prove the facility of communicating over land with the Pacific Ocean. The route from the *Southern Pass,* where the wagons stopped, to the Great Falls of the Columbia, being easier and better than on this side of the mountains, with grass enough for horses and mules, but a scarcity of game for the support of men.

This was a little overoptimistic, but the import is clear enough. Settlers, colonists, families, and wagons can go to Oregon just as soon as their beneficent Uncle takes care of the dragon that guards the gates to that promised land: HBC.

Arriving at Rendezvous 1830, Sublette sat his partners down and told them which way the stick was floating.

Fortunately, there happened to be five buyers on hand.

PART THREE

THE ROCKY MOUNTAIN
FUR COMPANY

1830-1834

CHAPTER 16

"Rushed upon him like so many blood-hounds"

A LEGEND was born at Rendezvous 1830; a legend that went under the name and style of the Rocky Mountain Fur Company. "The greatest name in the mountains," Bernard DeVoto called it, and he was right. Ironically enough, in succeeding years the very greatness of the name created a mythos around RMF that thoroughly obscured the reality. The literature of the trade has dealt, for the most part, with the legend; the actual status of the company has been hidden behind luminous clouds of folklore. The difference is a significant one, for "the greatest name in the mountains" was doomed to failure from the beginning. They committed the unforgivable sin. They put their trust in the wrong people.

RMF was headed by a five-man partnership; all of them superb trappers, the epitome of the breed we know as mountain men. Unfortunately, there was not a politician among them, nor a business mind. Tom Fitzpatrick was their brain, in the sense that he constituted RMF's main liaison with Bill Sublette. The other partners were Jim Bridger ("Old Gabe" to the trappers, "Casapy"—Blanket Chief—to the Indians), Milton Sublette, Henry Fraeb, and Jean Baptiste Gervais. In the increasingly bitter competition of the trade, this combination of practical trappers was at a distinct disadvantage. The RMF partnership probably thought a fur company would be successful if it trapped more furs than anybody else; it would seem a not-unreasonable hope.

But it was the sheerest naïveté; the competition in the field, fierce as it was, was as nothing compared to the financial manipulations these men had to face. The profits of a business that contained such men as William Ashley, Bill Sublette, the Chouteaus, and John Jacob Astor would accrue to the manipulators, not the trappers.

In the pages that follow it will appear that RMF's hardest fight was with American Fur's expansion to the mountains, and this is the traditional view. It is true only in a limited sense. The competition between RMF and the Company produced some of the most dramatic and bitter events of the trade. The fact that American Fur came to be known simply as "the Company" is proof enough of their awe-inspiring power. Invitably, RMF is seen as "the Opposition." Historians have generally followed this line and seen the story of RMF as a process of being "humbled" by the monolithic power of the Company.

The mountain conflict between the two firms was certainly a potent factor in the eventual destruction of RMF. But it was not the only factor, nor was it even—in my opinion—the most important one. The history of RMF is made comprehensible only through a consideration of its relations with one man, who was, ostensibly, on their side. This was Bill Sublette.

Bill Sublette served as midwife at the birth of RMF, as nurse and confidant, and—when the company ceased to serve his own purposes—as executioner.

It is my contention that the Rocky Mountain Fur Company existed almost as the personal instrument of William L. Sublette; that he manipulated its fortunes with a sure and steady hand; that the company served as a pawn in a game being played between Sublette and John Jacob Astor.[1]

Normally I would be better content to let a point of this sort develop gradually, as the narrative proceeded. I mention it here because I feel the events that follow will make a more coherent pattern for the reader if he views them in this light.

The Fall '29 and Spring '30 hunts of Smith Jackson & Sublette had been good ones; part of this no doubt due to Jedediah Smith's good sense in turning back from the Blackfoot country when the going got rough. There must have been around 170 packs of beaver at the Wind River rendezvous. Most of this would be free and clear; SJ&S were indebted to Ashley for only about $1,000. When the beaver was turned into cash, it would amount to nearly $84,500; even after deductions for expenses, commissions, and what not, a very sizable sum would remain to be split among the three partners, netting them better than $17,500 apiece.[2]

Sublette's wagon caravan had arrived at Wind River in the middle of July. Rendezvous 1830 lasted almost three weeks, until August 4. By the 1st of the month the important business of the day had been completed and Smith Jackson & Sublette had ceased to exist. The Rocky Mountain Fur Company had come into being.

Prophetically enough, RMF was born up to its ears in debt. In spite of the impressive trapping power the owners displayed, the company remained in debt throughout the whole of its existence; financially speaking, it never got off the ground. And rather than improving, the situation simply got worse. Gradually, through means that will be discussed later, all the outstanding obligations of RMF came to be concentrated in the hands of Bill Sublette, and this was the main source of his power over the partnership.

However, at Rendezvous 1830 the red figures would not have seemed remarkably ominous. The new partners gave a note in the amount of $15,532.22 which was not to fall due until November 1, 1831. This gave them three full hunting seasons in which to get started: Fall '30 and Spring and Fall '31. Considering that the $85,000 on which SJ&S were retiring constituted only a two-season return, it must have seemed quite reasonable to expect to clear this note easily in three seasons.

The actual document of the transfer of SJ&S's mountain business to RMF hasn't been preserved. The money was certainly payable in beaver, but the price at which beaver was to be valued is in doubt. SJ&S had bought out Ashley in beaver at $3 a pound; but there is some indication that RMF's note could be paid at $4.25 a pound.[3]

With this business out of the way, the retiring partners loaded up the wagons with fur, and departed for St. Louis on August 4. Sublette left the light Dearborns behind in the mountains. He took the ten wagons back to civilization, and four of the oxen. The milch cow, alas, also was returned to the Missouri settlements. Had she remained, she would doubtless have provided the Indians with a good deal of wonderment, augmented by the trappers' poker-faced explanations of how that crazy-looking buffalo got that way. It would have been good for a few wild stories.

II

Bill Sublette's timing had been perfect. He dissolved Smith Jackson & Sublette just as the pressure began to mount. At the time the transactions that resulted in RMF were under way—at Wind River—an American Fur Company party had already taken the field. The Robidoux-Fontenelle-Drips brigade of the Western Department had gotten off from Council Bluffs in May, 1830, about a month after Sublette's wagon train to Rendezvous 1830.

While SJ&S was selling out to the five-man partnership, the Company brigade, somehow misdirected, was looking for the free trappers in the Green River-Cache Valley area. By October they were on the Malade, where they were encountered by an HBC brigade under John Work.

When Rendezvous 1830 broke up the RMF men scattered for the fall hunt. Aside from a few small bands of free trappers, there were two main brigades.

One, under Old Frapp and Gervais, headed over the divide to work the Snake country. Around the mouth of the Salt River they were found by Joseph Robidoux's Company brigade. Robidoux immediately attached his party to the RMF brigade, following them down the Snake to their proposed Fall '30 hunt on the Raft Rver (known to them as Cassia or Casu) and the Malade. Fraeb and Gervais's party consisted of about twenty-two whites and ten Iroquois, plus the usual number of itinerant Crows, Flatheads, and what not, who drifted in and out of camp. RMF and the Company then trapped the same area until December, when they were separated. After this the movements of the RMF brigade become vague. (Our record of this hunt depends on a Company man, Warren Angus Ferris.[4])

Milton Sublette, Jim Bridger, and Tom Fitzpatrick had combined forces for the Fall '30 hunt. And with good reason; they went north into Blackfoot country again. This was a large brigade; according to Doc Newell—who accompanied it—there were over eighty men; enough to make Bug's Boys a little cautious.[5]

They worked up the Bighorn and across the Yellowstone; from there, following about the same pattern Smith had set the previous year, up into the heart of the Blackfoot country around the Great Falls of the Missouri and Three Forks.

This was a good hunt and—following it through Joe

Meek's eyes—a lively one. A couple of Joe's bear stories date from this fall, including one on Milton Sublette. Joe and Milton, it seems, were out on a buffalo hunt:

> at a distance apart of about fifty yards, when a large grizzly bear came out of a thicket and made after Sublette, who, when he perceived the creature, ran for the nearest cotton-wood tree. Meek in the meantime, seeing that Sublette was not likely to escape, had taken sure aim, and fired at the bear, fortunately killing him. On running up to the spot where it laid, Sublette was discovered sitting at the foot of a cotton-wood, with his legs and arms clasped tightly around it.
>
> "Do you always climb a tree in that way?" asked Meek. "I reckon you took the wrong end of it, that time, Milton!"
>
> "I'll be damned, Meek, if I didn't think I was twenty feet up that tree when you shot," answered the frightened Booshway; and from that time the men never tired of alluding to Milton's manner of climbing a tree.

(As they were returning from Three Forks in late fall this brigade had a brush with HBC. According to some reports, this resulted in the loss of a few more of HBC's freemen, due to the superior quantity of whiskey in the American Company's packs. However, the British partisan John Work—though he mentions contact with Americans—says nothing of this, and it may be some confusion with the various encounters had by Americans with Peter Skene Ogden.)

This party took up winter quarters in the good buffalo country around the confluence of the Yellowstone and the Powder. (Fact is, Meek says the Powder and Newell says the Yellowstone. "Around the confluence" is a neat historical compromise intended to tidy up the contradiction.)

When spring opened up the rivers, the partners intended to work south. Fraeb and Gervais had wintered somewhere in the Snake country (Cache Valley?) and would spend their Spring '31 hunt combing the western slope; this party would rake southward along the east slope of the Rockies, and by Rendezvous 1831 both sides of the mountain would have been trapped. This was one of the most thorough hunts ever made in the mountains, covering every good bit of beaver country, including the Blackfoot strongholds. Rocky Mountain Fur Company was starting out with a clean sweep.

Accordingly, Fitzpatrick, Milton Sublette, and Bridger set out in early spring. But they were in Crow country here, and the sight of all that beautiful horseflesh was too much for the happy Absaroka; they had to have some. And they got about sixty.

This was a bad situation; $3,000 bad, at mountain prices, and RMF couldn't afford it. The horses had to be recovered. An impromptu war party was organized under Antoine Godin, including both Meek and Doc Newell.

"This," says Newell, "is the first time I went to war on foot."

The party trailed the Crows for three days with almost no rest. Sometime on the third day they caught up with the band, which amounted to about sixty young braves

> who believed that now they had made a start in life. Alas, for the vanity of human, and especially of Crow expectations! Even then, while they were grouped around their fires, congratulating themselves on the sudden wealth which had descended upon them, as it were from the skies, an envious fate, in the shape of several roguish white trappers, was laughing at them and their hopes, from the overhanging bluff opposite them. [Meek and Mrs. Victor]

During the night Doc Newell and Antoine Godin sneaked into the Crow camp and freed the horses. They stampeded, of course, and wakened the Crows. As the Indians rushed out to the horses, they were met by a volley of rifle fire from the bluff where the rest of the trappers were enforted. It was later reported that seven Indians were killed in this initial fire.

In the confusion the trappers rounded up the horses and started the long drive back to their own camp. This again was a forced march, and the laughing rogues were pretty damn tired when they finally got back to camp. Aside from the simple fatigue and sleeplessness, the traveling was becoming increasingly hard because of melting snow which made the ground a pulpy morass. On the other hand, RMF got its horses and Joe got a story, so it was probably worth it.

Shortly after the episode of the horse theft, Tom Fitzpatrick left the mountains for St. Louis. It is probable that a tentative arrangement had been made at Rendezvous 1830 similar to that between SJ&S and Ashley the year before. That is, an express would be sent from the mountains in early spring to confirm arrangements for supplies. In the spring of '31, then, Fitz departed on this mission.

Milton Sublette and Gabe Bridger each took a brigade for the interrupted Spring '31 hunt. This was a long foray down into the mountains of Colorado; farther south than the usual range. This is the first (recorded) hunt of a mountain-based party in an area that was to play a large and colorful role in years to come: the Parks of Colorado. These grassy, beautiful valleys are strung along a north-south axis through the center of the present state.

(North Park was known to the trappers as New Park; present Middle Park was called Old Park. South Park became famous in the literature of the trade as Bayou Salade; reputed to be the most beautiful place in the mountians. Trappers out of Taos—including Milton Sublette, some say— had gotten up this far, and this southern approach is the reason for designating North Park as New Park; it was the last to be discovered.)

There is no direct record of this hunt, just a casual comment by Newell as to the area worked. The two parties joined again on reaching the Parks, and as spring drew on began to drift up toward Rendezvous 1831. By summer Fraeb and Gervais were back from their Snake River foray, and all the partners were gathered together in Cache Valley, waiting for Fitzpatrick to show up with their supplies.

By now the presence of outlanders was only too thoroughly confirmed. Fraeb and Gervais's encounter with the Robidoux bunch—working out of American's Western Department—had an ominous ring to it. And the Company had several other parties in the mountains that spring. One was under Henry Vanderburgh, and operated out of UMO and its main base, Fort Union. Rashly, his first trip had been to the Madison. Bug's Boys immediately resented this in their characteristic fashion, and it cost him one man and ten horses. Two men and fifty horses were wounded, and Vanderburgh scuttled back to the protection of Fort Union.[6]

This would have been material for chortling over, perhaps. But the partners of RMF would have been shocked had they known what the crafty Kenneth McKenzie was up to now. As they sat at Rendezvous 1831, McKenzie was in the process of performing the impossible: He was negotiating an honest-to-god treaty with the Blackfeet.

Through an intermediary, a brave (or possibly insane) interpreter named Berger, the Blackfeet and the Assiniboines had been persuaded to go to Fort Union for a peaceful visit.

The treaty that was finally negotiated in the fall of 1831 is a kind of minor masterpiece. I quote here only the opening passage:

> We send greeting to all mankind! Be it known unto all nations that the most ancient, most illustrious, and most numerous tribes of the redskins, lords of the soil from the banks of the great waters unto the tops of the mountains, upon which the heavens rest, have entered into a solemn league and covenant to make, preserve and cherish a firm and lasting peace, that so long as the water runs, or the grass grows, they may hail each other as brethren and smoke the calumet in friendship and security.

McKenzie had quite a literary flair when he got carried away. By the actual time of ratification of this flowery document the Blackfeet had gotten bored and gone home. The Assiniboines were of stronger stuff, however, and their principal chiefs duly signed:

> . . . conforming to all ancient customs and ceremonies, and observing the due mystical signs enjoined by the great medicine lodges, a treaty of peace and friendship was entered into by the said high contracting parties.

Since the Blackfeet weren't around, McKenzie signed for them himself, which was thoughtful.

As tender of his good will and sincerity McKenzie established a small trading post, Fort Piegan, at the angle between the Marias and the Missouri. It was an enormous success, in spite of competition from the HBC posts across the border, who, until this time, had enjoyed a monopoly on the Blackfoot trade. Unfortunately, this post lasted only one season. When the trader left to take his furs back to Fort Union at the mouth of the Yellowstone, the Piegans burned it.

Nevertheless, McKenzie had opened trade with the Blackfeet, the first American to do so.

The trappers of RMF waited at Cache Valley in early summer of 1831 until it became obvious that something drastic had gone wrong. Fitzpatrick was long overdue, and the situation would be extremely serious if he didn't make it back. Traps were short, knives were short, all the gear was worn and dwindling. There was no liquor, even, and Rendezvous 1831 was but a pale wraith that nobody would remember with pleasure.

It was apparently Old Frapp's idea to consult a Crow shaman about Fitzpatrick's whereabouts. After the long ritual (some of them lasted nearly a week), which included dancing and drumming and singing that probably livened up the rendezvous considerably, the shaman went into a trance. On reviving he gave Fraeb the benefit of his Vision.

Fitzpatrick, said the Crow, was not dead. "He was on a road; but not the right one." (This, as it worked out, was entirely accurate.)

Fraeb was encouraged by the news of Fitzpatrick to send a party out after him, leading it himself. They set out in early August, first going over to the Wind River on the chance that Fitzpatrick had gone to the location of Rendezvous 1830 by mistake. Nobody there, so down to the Sweetwater and the Laramie Hills. After being in this area for some time they finally found the missing partner. He was coming—not west from St. Louis but from the south. Up from Santa Fe, in fact, having wandered several thousand miles off the track.

III

In order to understand this unlikely occurrence we must backtrack a little better than a year, to Rendezvous 1830. When the RMF brigades set out on the fall '30 hunt, Bill Sublette, Davey Jackson, and Jedediah Smith turned back toward civilization. No longer in the mountain business, they would return to St. Louis and look around for the next venture.

The returning heroes—and so they were received— reached St. Louis on October 10. This rich caravan was just what the people of St. Louis wanted every year; further incontrovertible proof of the enormous personal fortunes to be made in the trade. One newspaper estimated the return as

about $150,000, and this exaggeration—almost double—
was comparatively moderate. Spectacular success in the fur
trade was a great hunger on the frontier; the spirit was optimistic in the extreme.

When Jackson, Smith, and Bill Sublette reached St. Louis
they did not immediately turn their furs over to Ashley. The
former partners had one fairly tenuous contact to be explored first: Robert Campbell's brother Hugh. As Robert had
done a few years earlier, Smith wrote Hugh Campbell asking
him to look into prices on his own. That always-obliging
gentleman did so, in spite of his deep personal hatred of the
mountain life for his brother. However, by the time Hugh's
reply could be received, they had decided to market through
their old friend Ashley after all. Around November 10 they
turned the catch over to him. (A possible factor involved in
the decision to market through Ashley was his willingness to
give the partners an advance on sales. Marketing through
other channels would have cost them much in time, perhaps
six months or more, before the beaver could be turned
into cash. Ashley obligingly advanced them $23,000 at 6 per
cent interest, giving them sufficient capital to embark on a
new venture.)

In the meantime the partners had drafted their letter to
the Secretary of War, proposing the feasibility of land travel
across the continent; plugging, in short, for the route that
later became the Oregon Trail. With its recommendation that
the government do something drastic about the joint-
occupancy convention of 1818, this letter provoked as much
interest as the exaggerated reports of their financial success.
Part of the prevailing optimistic atmosphere on the Missouri
frontier was a conviction that the nation was due for a great
surge of expansion westward. The proponents of this position
naturally took the SJ&S letter to their hearts and, more
effectively, to their presses. The letter to Secretary Eaton was
widely printed in newspapers, evoking such reaction as that
of the former Missouri Fur Company man, Charles Keemle,
in the St. Louis *Beacon*:

> They could have crossed the mountains at the
> *Southern Pass*, which is at the head of Wind River,[7]
> without difficulty. Messrs. Smith, Sublette & Jackson
> are the first that ever took wagons to the Rocky
> Mountains. The ease with which they did it, and could
> have gone on to the mouth of the Columbia, shows

the folly and nonsense of those *"scientific"* characters who talk of the Rocky Mountains as the barrier which is to stop the westward march of the American people.

It would seem that Smith had in mind some kind of partnership with Robert Campbell. Something of the sort is mentioned in Robert's letters to his brother, and it is certain that the two men were close; when Smith left for California he made Bob Campbell executor of his will. But Campbell was still in Ireland; worse yet, his health was bad again, according to his brother. Regretfully, Smith had to abandon the notion and cast about for some other way to invest his capital.

The Mexican trade caught his eye. By this time it was a booming business; the Santa Fe Trail was well open. This year, 1831, it would be traveled by no less than 130 wagons; 320 men under 80 different proprietors, most of them small. The merchandise for this single year would be worth $250,-000.

The Santa Fe trade was organized around wagon caravans. It was a trade of goods: textiles, hardware, and what not, intended for the civilized Mexican communities of Taos and Santa Fe. Occasionally the St. Louis traders would be paid in furs from the southern-based trapping parties, but more frequently in bullion. This trade employed far fewer men per company than the mountain business; just enough to handle the large caravans of wagons. It was also a great deal less hazardous. The only Indians of menace were the Comanches (sometimes known as Hietans) and the Pawnees, with whom they were generally at war. If a white caravan encountered a war party of either of these nations, there might be trouble. However, the Santa Fe caravans generally moved in sufficient strength that Indian attack was unlikely.

During the winter of '30–'31 Smith was busy outfitting this foray into new fields. There was also a good deal of family business to be taken care of; his brothers were congregating in St. Louis. Ira Smith arrived shortly before Christmas of 1830, possibly with some notion of joining his elder brother on one of his far-flung jaunts. If so, he was disappointed, because Jedediah immediately enrolled him in a seminary at Jacksonville, Illinois. Two other brothers, Austin and Peter, Jedediah decided to take with him on the Santa Fe run.

In the meantime Sublette and Jackson had been engaged in

preparation for an expedition, too. They had formed another partnership, called Jackson & Sublette, and were outfitting with merchandise. It would seem most likely that this was originally destined for RMF; contingent, of course, on the spring express in the event business warranted supplies for another year.[8]

But as the spring wore on—the traditional March 1 date for such an express had passed—it began to appear there was going to be no word from the mountains. Jackson & Sublette then shifted plans. They decided to go with Smith to Santa Fe, though not as partners with him. On March 23, through General Ashley, Sublette requested a passport for the Mexican provinces. Ashley comments that Sublette will be with Smith (for whom a passport was previously issued) "to a certain point, Thence they will take different directions."

Whatever the plans for eventual separation, the two groups were combined for the Santa Fe run. In combination they had about twenty-two wagons and seventy-four men. They were later joined by two other wagons of independent traders, and more men to the total of eighty-three.

Ownership of the main body of wagons was divided about equally between Smith and the Jackson-Sublette partnership. Only one of them was owned jointly by the three: an artillery wagon, carrying a six-pounder and ingeniously arranged so that the cannon could be pulled out, using the back wheels of the wagon as a carriage.

Some of the wagons may have gone ahead as early as April 1, but the main caravan got off from St. Louis around the 10th of the month. They put up for some days at Lexington to take on last-minute provisions, supplies, and so forth. (They were there at the end of April; on "April Thirty first" Smith made out a will, naming General Ashley as executor.)

Either during their encampment at Lexington or a few days out on the trail, the Santa Fe-bound caravan was joined by two more men.

Tom Fitzpatrick, unofficial head of the brand-new Rocky Mountain Fur Company, had come down from winter quarters looking for supplies, a little too late.

The sudden appearance of Fitzpatrick here has been confusing to historians and may well have been equally so to Jackson & Sublette. There is little information on this whole year in the trade. (Smith wrote to his brother Ralph that "it is certainly verry far from my wish to have too much publicity given to our business." This policy he followed so assiduously that it is quite difficult to tell what was going on that winter.)

If the sketch I have given is correct, it is difficult to understand why Jackson & Sublette did not then proceed from Lexington to the mountains, leaving the Santa Fe expedition to Jedediah Smith. Possibly they were so far committed that they had no choice; the merchandise required was somewhat different. It is also possible that Sublette, Jackson, and Smith had planned the Santa Fe trip from the beginning and that the encounter with Fitzpatrick was in the nature of an accident.

Whatever the case, Fitzpatrick was persuaded to accompany the caravan to Santa Fe. An arrangement was made for him to be supplied there, with Jackson & Sublette providing two thirds of the outfit, Smith the remaining third.

The last encampment before the march began was at the Big Blue, outside Independence. The caravan left here on the 4th of May, slanting southwest across present Kansas on nearly a direct line toward Santa Fe. There were four distinct phases to the Santa Fe Trail, each providing a different sort of traveling. This first leg ended at Council Grove, 150 miles from Independence. By this time the caravan was shaken down into marching order; and here the final organization was made by most parties. Officers selected, messes organized or reorganized; the whole caravan, in short, whipped into shape for the crossing of the barren country.

Council Grove was the last source of wood along the route, and one of the more important orders of business would have been stocking the party with replacement axletrees and so forth. The wood collected here was generally strapped beneath the wagons.[9]

From Council Grove to the ford of the Arkansas (known as Cimarron Crossing) was another 240 miles; and now the geography began to change. From the fertile prairies the caravan moved into dry, arid plains; the beginning of the desert. Cimarron Crossing was a few miles above Dodge City, and represented the halfway point from Independence to Santa Fe.

Now came the worst section of the entire passage; crossing the Cimarron desert. One man of the party had already been lost, less than two weeks out of Independence. Around Pawnee Fork, Jackson & Sublette's clerk, a man named Minter, was separated from the main body of the caravan while out hunting antelope. A band of roving Pawnees found him and killed him. This was in the relatively safe portion of the passage, and the event was ominous.

Crossing the Arkansas, they entered the desert. This was bleak and forbidding country, bone-dry, scorched, and desolate. There was no telling the wagon road from the interwoven net of buffalo trails. Nothing was here to mark the trail, and the land itself was dead-flat and featureless. This desert was a crossing of fifty or sixty miles (from the Arkansas to the Cimarron River) without water. The caravans moved slowly, perhaps averaging fifteen miles a day, and with luck the crossing could have been made in four days.

But luck was not with them. The way was lost, and the water ran out. When they had been without water for nearly three days, the party divided. In desperation small groups of men scattered in all directions, combing the parched countryside along their route, finding nothing; the season was one of drought.

Smith rode on ahead in the direction the party was traveling, roughly south. One story says Tom Fitzpatrick was with him. According to this version, the two men finally reached a dry hole where water might have been expected. Smith told Fitzpatrick to stay behind there, and wait for the party to come up to them. Alone, he rode on ahead. This was the 27th of May, 1831.

Smith passed over a low ridge of broken ground and passed beyond Fitzpatrick's sight. Some fifteen miles beyond, he topped a bank and stood looking down at the bed of the Cimarron.

"River" by courtesy only; the drought had hit it, too, and there was nothing that might be called a stream. But along the bed were scattered pools of precious water. He scrambled down over the bank, having once more escaped death by thirst through the narrowest of margins. Buffalo trails converged on the minuscule water hole, and had Smith not been in the desperation of thirst the fact might have made him more cautious; buffalo water holes were good hunting.

He and his horse drank from the pool, bathing their seared bodies in the cool water. Finally Smith rose and mounted, returning to bring the caravan up to him; to carry back the good news. He found himself confronted by a band of Comanches.

Riding directly to them, Smith tried to communicate. The Comanches did not understand; or were simply not interested. There were fifteen or twenty of the Indians, and they began to move out to either side as Smith tried to talk to their headman. Smith's gun was at cock and ready; and the Comanches had no desire to look down its muzzle. They concentrated then on Smith's horse, shouting to frighten it. The horse shied, and swung away.

The Comanches fired on him immediately, wounding him in the shoulder. Smith turned back to the headman and shot him through the chest.

Seconds later Smith slid from his horse and died under the Comanche lances.

Surviving the three great massacres of the trade, Jedediah Smith died at last with only his God for comfort in the desert.

The main caravan found its way to the Cimarron some distance from the spot of Jedediah's death. They refreshed themselves there, and, when Smith did not return, set off again. Shortly after this they were attacked by a huge band of Gros Ventres; relatives of the Blackfeet and ranging very far south from their usual grounds.[10] Sublette was able to negotiate with them—possibly through judicious demonstration of his artillery—and the caravan escaped unhurt. That night, not trusting to luck, Sublette had the wagons drawn up in a barricade; and the trouble was well worth it. During the night they were surrounded by the war party again, and Sublette's defensive measures once more preserved them.

From there to Santa Fe they encountered no trouble from the Indians. They reached the Mexican settlement on the 4th of July; and found the relics of Jedediah's death among a recently arrived party of Mexican traders. The Mexicans had traded Smith's rifle and two pistols from the Comanche band. Peter and Austin Smith were able to secure the guns, and also the details of the attack (as given above), which the Comanches had passed on to the Mexicans.

Sublette made a fairly successful trade in Santa Fe, and took his payment in furs: 55 packs of beaver and 800 buffalo robes. But he liked neither the country nor the business. He and Jackson broke up their short-lived partnership there in Santa Fe; Jackson to go on to southern California with Peter Smith and several others, in the mule-trading business. Jackson's partner in Santa Fe was David Waldo, who was given a power of attorney by both Sublette and Jackson for the purpose of collecting their $15,000 note from RMF in beaver at the Santa Fe price: $4.25 a pound.

Tom Fitzpatrick, acting for RMF, was apparently toying with the idea of marketing their furs through Taos and Santa Fe rather than St. Louis; this $4.25 price was contingent on delivery within sixty miles of Taos.

Fitzpatrick was outfitted as agreed, with Smith's part of the agreement (⅓) being handled by his clerk.[11] He set out north toward Taos with a few men, and recruited more as he went along. (One of his more interesting recruits was a young runaway named Christopher Carson.) By now it was late summer; long past rendezvous time and Fitz was almost as far from the mountains as though he had still been in St. Louis. He started a forced march across present Colorado, probably heading almost due north along the eastern base of the Rockies. His outfit was not large—probably thirty men all told, and not more than about $6,000 worth of merchandise—and he was able to make fairly good time.

By September he had reached the Platte. Now it was known territory to him. He would ascend the Platte, the Sweetwater, across South Pass—the familiar last stages of the overland route from St. Louis. Rendezvous 1831 had been set in the old stamping grounds of Cache Valley, and Fitz hoped to be able to locate the RMF brigades near there.

While camped near the mouth of the Laramie, Fitzpatrick was found by the party of his own men under Henry Fraeb (see section ii). They went into camp together for a short time; then set out for winter quarters, trapping as they traveled. There was a lot of news to be exchanged; and it was nearly all bad. The death of Smith, who was genuinely liked by all his compatriots; the small amount of merchandise Fitz had gotten from Jackson & Sublette; Fitz was not bringing very cheerful tidings.

Old Frapp's news was little better. The hunting had been fair, but they were no longer alone in the mountains. During the Fall '30 hunt, Fraeb and Gervais had been joined by a brigade of American Fur men, under the shrewd and competent Joseph Robidoux. This brigade had stuck with them throughout most of the fall hunt, not leaving until December. (Even the small firm of Gant & Blackwell had a party in the mountains now; though the partners did not yet know of it.)

It was absolutely necessary to be sure of a supply train for next spring. Owing to both the competition and the slightness of the present load, RMF could not afford another mistake;

couldn't take the risk of another late arrival of supplies. Accordingly, Fitzpatrick turned his goods over to Fraeb and with three other men set out down the Platte to arrange for the supply outfit for 1832.

Just after he left Fraeb's brigade, Fitzpatrick came on the camped party of Gant & Blackwell, which was trapping the tributaries of the Platte on their way to the mountain country.

This did little to improve Fitzpatrick's disposition; nor was he a particularly gracious man in the best of times. The Gant & Blackwell party received him hospitably, but Fitz was in no mood to encourage the opposition, however feeble.

One of the members of this brigade was Zenas Leonard, a young *mangeur de lard* out on his first trip. He left a record,[12] and says of this meeting with Fitzpatrick:

> He was an old hand at the business and we expected to obtain some useful information from him, but we were disappointed. The selfishness of man is often disgraceful to human nature; and I never saw more striking evidence of this fact, than was presented in the conduct of this man Fitzpatrick. Notwithstanding we had treated him with great friendship and hospitality, merely because we were to engage in the same business with him, which he knew we never could exhaust or even impair—he refused to give us any information whatever, and appeared disposed to treat us as intruders.
>
> On the 3d of September, Captain Blackwell, with two others, joined Fitzpatrick, and started back to the state of Missouri.

Well, Tom had things on his mind. And Leonard would soon become accustomed to the techniques of mountain competition.

Meanwhile Fraeb and his party started back across the divide with the supplies, headed for the Salmon River country in central Idaho, which had been selected as their wintering grounds for '31–'32.

After Fitzpatrick's nonappearance at Rendezvous 1831 the other RMF trappers had made their Fall '31 hunt in small detached brigades. One of them is recorded; Bridger and Sublette were accompanied by that chronicler of few words, Doc Newell: "left for fall hunt from Bear River to Greys

fork of Snake River (a Scrimmage with Black feet)   from
thare to Snake River and on to Psalmon River."

That is: from Cache Valley north to the Snake; then northwest across the Snake River plains to the Salmon. He then
adds a trip due north into Montana to the Flathead River,
and—late in the fall—a final return to the winter quarters on
the Salmon: "and met Mr Freab with Supplies from Mr.
Fitzpatrick and took up winter quarters with the flat heads
and napercies."

What Newell does not mention is that the Flatheads and
Nez Perces were not their only companions this winter of
'31–'32. Joseph Robidoux of the Company was somewhere in
the vicinity. And Henry Vanderburgh had gotten another
party into the mountains from Fort Union; he was making
his winter camp back in Cache Valley (running about a
season behind RMF, who'd been there in the summer).

Well, the Salmon was good wintering country, and RMF
settled down to see in the new year with the customary
festivities: 1832 was upon them, the most eventful year in
the history of the trade. All hell was about to break loose,
and very little of it would do the Rocky Mountain Fur
Company any good.

IV

Two of the Company men, Drips and Fontenelle, had returned
to St. Louis in the early summer of 1831 to make arrangements for supplies. Drips, with a small load, returned in the
late fall, joining the Vanderburgh brigade in Cache Valley
for the winter. (These present Company men had all been
involved in Joshua Pilcher's abortive mountain attempt in
'27–'28.)

As soon as spring made mountain travel feasible again, this
detachment set out north from Cache Valley, hoping to catch
up with an RMF brigade; and they did.

At about the same time that Vanderburgh and Drips were
moving out of Cache Valley RMF was breaking up its winter
camp on the Salmon and dispersing for the Spring '32 hunt.
One brigade, under Milton Sublette and Bridger, worked
across to Henry's Fork—southeast from the winter camp,
across the Idaho lava beds. Then down the Snake to the Salt
River, Gray's Hole, and finally down to Bear River.

But at Gray's Hole, to the enormous disgust of the RMF
partisans, they were found by Vanderburgh. The Company

contingent had apparently not had a very successful spring hunt; but then trapping, for the present, was not their main interest. Vanderburgh promptly latched on to the RMF brigade as Robidoux had done to Fraeb and Gervais; happily turned around and headed back toward Bear River with them.

It was obvious by now what the Company was doing—taking on-the-job training frm RMF. Vanderburgh and Drips were learning their geography by the simple expedient of following the master trappers of RMF. "Whither thou goest, I will go," and a very fine idea it was, probably springing direct from the man at Fort Union who was now beginning to be called the King of the Missouri, Kenneth McKenzie.[13]

Each firm had something the other lacked. RMF had the skills of the best trappers in the mountains; men with years of experience that dated back to Ashley and Henry's first expeditions; but financially they were on the thinnest of ice (their note to SJ&S hadn't yet been paid off—and more debts were being incurred all the time). The Company had as much capital as it needed. If necessary, it could absorb losses for several years, and still end with a profit in the long run. It had, in short, a comfortable margin for error, which RMF had not at all. Further, the Company brigades could, in time, learn to trap effectively, particularly when they took as mentors men like Bridger, Fitzpatrick, and the other partisans. But RMF had no way of making up its disadvantage in capital; there were no resources to call on.

This situation was sufficient to enrage the RMF partners, but there was little they could do about it, except to delay the inevitable outcome as long as possible. And the way to do that was to show the Company their heels as often as they could; it was a solution that would be congenial to these mountain men *par excellence,* proud of their wilderness skills. Accordingly, Bridger and Milton decided to take off.

However, at this Bear River meeting, probably while the rival camps were near each other, Milton ran into trouble. Somewhere along the line, possibly in an unrecorded hunt of early spring, Milton had picked up a band of eight Iroquois trappers in Ogden's Hole.[14] This outfit, now operating semi-attached to RMF, was led by John Gray. (Probably the troublemaker John Gray-Ignace Hatchiorauquasha who had deserted from Peter Skene Ogden.) An altercation came up between Gray and Milton "on account of some indignity, real or fancied, which had been offered to the chief's daughter."

Milton was stabbed in the fight; cut up badly enough that he seemed certain to die shortly. When Bridger and the rest of the party moved off, Milton had to be left behind; Joe Meek was to stay with him and bury him. It must have been an odd sensation for Bridger, remembering how he had been left with the grizzly-mauled Hugh Glass in the same circumstances; and what he had done.

As Old Gabe moved off to tie up the spring hunt, he received another shock. Vanderburgh declined to be lost. He had, of course, decamped immediately behind Bridger, and for the rest of the spring the Company brigade was a persistent, unlosable nuisance. No sooner had Bridger begun to work an area than Vanderburgh appeared and happily dispersed his men.

Worse, Vanderburgh had recently been supplied, and Bridger was in the thin times just before rendezvous. The Company booshway made efficient and annoying use of his little surplus of goods to buy up pelts from some of Bridger's free trappers; and also to buy up a few of the free trappers themselves.

By the time the almost-combined brigades reached rendezvous—this year in Pierre's Hole—Bridger was no longer simply annoyed by Vanderburgh; he was worried. The Company men were sticking too close; they were up to beaver now, and something drastic had to be done in a hurry.

Back at Bear River, Milton Sublette was being stubborn; he refused to die. Day after day he lay in camp, slowly regaining his health; the deep, slashing wounds closing up. Joe tended him carefully for forty days of isolation. "To him," says Mrs. Victor, "Joe Meek was everything,—hands, feet, physician, guard, caterer, hunter, cook, companion, friend."

And at the end of forty days Milton was well enough to ride again. The two men broke camp and set out to find Bridger's party or, failing that, to meet them at Pierre's Hole for Rendezvous 1832. They had set out for the north and hadn't gone far when they stumbled on a Snake encampment. Between them and the village, the bucks of the band were feeding their horses. Seeing the whites, an uproar broke out, and there was a dash for their mounts.

Meek and Sublette realized there was little chance to outride the Snakes, particularly with Milton in his still-weakened condition. They spurred ahead, straight past the band of mounting Indians, and headed full tilt into the encampment itself. They scrambled off their horses in the middle of the village and made a dash for the chief's lodge, identifiable by its gaudy trappings. Once inside they were officially under the hospitality of the chief.

They made it, and stood panting inside the lodge while the angry Snakes began to converge on them. Soon the braves began to file in, and within half an hour the lodge was full. The Snakes didn't speak to either of the whites. They went into a sort of official conference, at which the life or death of the two was discussed. This conference was probably endless; most Indian councils were. (They operated on a perfectly democratic principle; anyone who had anything to say was given his chance, even if the outcome was a foregone conclusion. As was customary with Indian oratory, the speeches were very long, very diffuse, and generally wandered off into a discussion of the feats and achievements of the speaker himself.) This one lasted the rest of the day.

The verdict was, of course, unfavorable. According to Mrs. Victor, a long argument for the defense was conducted by a chief she calls "the good *Gotia*." If this is in fact the Snake chief Mauvais Gauche, he was more frequently known by less complimentary sobriquets; most printable of which was Bad Gocha. (We last met him as he massacred Etienne Provost's party. The present incident is the only thing to his credit in the annals of the trade.)

"Gotia" was the last to leave the tent—everyone else having gone to prepare the ceremonials—and he motioned to Milton and Joe to remain quiet while he was gone. (Not that there was a great deal of choice, but I'm paraphrasing Mrs. Victor here.)

About dusk there was a great noise, and confusion, and clouds of dust, in the south end of the village. Something was going wrong among the Indian horses. Immediately all the village ran to the scene of the disorder, and at the same moment Gotia, the good, appeared at the door of the Medicine Lodge, beckoning the prisoners to follow him. With alacrity they sprang up and after him, and were led across the stream, to a thicket on the opposite side, where their horses stood, ready to mount, in the charge of a young Indian girl.

According to the tradition, this was the first time either Joe or Milton saw the Mountain Lamb: *Umentucken Tukutsey Undewatsey,* as Joe renders it. This was the most beautiful woman in the mountains (also according to tradition and Meek), and the next year Milton brought his brigade down this way and married her. (When he left a couple of years later, Milton bequeathed her to Joe; and there began one of the great romantic stories of the trade, lasting until she was killed by a Bannock arrow.)

But for now she was a holder-of-horses. Joe and Milton hastily departed the Snake camp, rode all night and the next day. Once out of danger, they slowed, and made the rest of the way to Rendezvous 1832 without incident.

Bridger was there before them, and probably also Fraeb and Gervais, though their activities on the Spring '32 hunt are unknown. Fitzpatrick was back in St. Louis with Bill Sublette, making arrangements for the supply caravan.

Camped cozily beside the RMF brigade in Pierre's Hole was Henry Vanderburgh. He, too, was waiting for supplies; Fontenelle was bringing up a caravan from St. Louis, and there was also some expectation that Etienne Provost—now a Company man—would be coming with something from Fort Union. (Provost, however, joined Fontenelle somewhere along the line.) This was interesting, the first time *two* caravans had come to rendezvous. The free trappers were going to have a choice of buyers, perhaps. But as it shaped up, it began to look as though the first supplier to arrive was going to pick up the greater share of the business.

The RMF partners settled down for a hasty consultation. What could be done about the Company? This was the big question of the day, and the answer they came to must have seemed a reasonable one at the time.

CHAPTER 17

"Then began the usual gay carousal"

THERE were roughly a hundred men at Rendezvous 1832 who were directly connected with RMF, by wage or other agreement. The Company brigade under Drips numbered about ninety. The institution of rendezvous was well known in the mountains by now, and always attracted large numbers of Indians who dropped in to see the fun. There were 120 lodges of Nez Perces and 80 lodges of Flatheads camped in Pierre's Hole, far outnumbering the whites.

The number of unattached men—the free trappers—isn't exactly known. But this unnumbered group would be the hub around which the rendezvous would spin. And spin is the appropriate word.

Both the major forces, RMF and the Company brigade, had these free trappers very much in mind. The opposing companies were nearly matched in size. The balance would be swung by the free trappers and where they chose to dispose of their furs. That, in turn, depended on which supply train reached Pierre's Hole first, the one Bill Sublette was bringing up for RMF or Fontenelle's Company caravan.

On July 8 the supply train pulled in, and it looked as though RMF had won this round; Sublette was first. But after the shouting had died down, the partners received a shock. They had been under the impression that Tom Fitzpatrick would be with Sublette's caravan. He was not. Sublette had been hoping to find him at rendezvous.

Fitz was, in effect, RMF's brain, and this was a serious

situation. From what Sublette told them, the chances were good they had lost him to the Indians.

Remember that Fitzpatrick had not remained in the mountains the previous year. After his long—and almost disastrous—detour by way of Santa Fe he had met his partner Henry Fraeb in the summer of 1831. Turning over the year's supplies to Fraeb, Fitzpatrick immediately turned back down the Platte for St. Louis. He was to arrange supplies for Rendezvous 1832 and recruit new men.

By early May a supply party had been outfitted by Bill Sublette, and Fitzpatrick had his new recruits. The two parties, though semiautonomous, were to travel in company to rendezvous. Sublette's party had been swelled by the addition of Nathaniel Wyeth, New England iceman turned explorer, and his company. He was bound for the Oregon country, meaning to investigate the possibilities of colonization there. (Wyeth's activities are of sufficient importance to be treated more fully than I am able to do here. See Appendix B.)

The combined Wyeth-Sublette-Fitzpatrick caravan numbered 86 men and nearly 300 head of pack animals. Under Sublette's leadership they got off from Independence on May 3.

Around the middle of June, somewhere past the Laramie, Fitzpatrick separated from the main party. Taking one of the fastest horses, he set off ahead, the intention being to "discover the disposition of the various Indian tribes through whose dominions we were to travel." He was to meet the rest of the caravan "at a designated point on the head of the Columbia River." (To the trappers "Columbia" meant any of the Columbia waters, and in particular the present Snake.)

When the party arrived at the meeting point on July 2, Fitzpatrick wasn't there. This was an ill omen, indeed. Zenas Leonard was with the caravan, and his journal calls it a "melancholy circumstance . . . (and) perplexing." (Leonard had joined Fitzpatrick's group of recruits after his own employers went bankrupt.) "The most natural conclusion at which to arrive," Leonard continues, "was, that the dull and cloudy weather had caused him to lose his course, and that he had become bewildered."

This may have been the natural conclusion for Leonard, still a relative novice; it would not have been so for Bill Sublette. Men with the experience and mountain technique of Tom Fitzpatrick simply did not become bewildered and lose their course, however "dull" the weather. The number of times mountain men were actually lost—particularly on familiar ground—were vanishingly few. To Bill Sublette, Fitzpatrick's absence would have meant trouble, and the most hopeful view would have been that he had gone on to Pierre's Hole. . . . Bill decided to move on.

Fitzpatrick had been engaging in one of the adventures that became a classic story of the trade: Broken Hand's Escape From the Blackfeet. Very briefly, and without going into alternative versions of the story:

For three or four days after leaving Sublette's caravan, Fitz had made good progress. (He was attacked by a grizzly, thrown off his horse, and "in a fit of desperation" rushed straight at the bear and scared him off; but this is the uneventful part of the trip.) A day or so later, coming down a narrow defile, he blundered directly into a village of Gros Ventres. (This same village shows up several times this spring and summer. It was a band returning from a several-year visit to their cousins, the Arapahoes.)

Nothing for it then but a cross-country chase. No longer able to afford the luxury of a trail, Fitzpatrick set out directly up the side of the mountain through the brush, over the deadfalls, rocks and ditches, with the howling bucks of the village hot after him on foot. It doesn't take much of this kind of activity to exhaust a horse, and Fitz had to abandon the animal halfway up and continue on foot.

As he scrambled up the hillside, he heard behind him the delighted whoops of the Big Bellies as they captured the abandoned horse. The horse was only half the game, however; a free white scalp was the other half, and before long the Gros Ventres began to gain on him. Seeing this, Fitzpatrick gave up the attempt to outrun them, and tucked himself into a hole in the rocks, covering the entrance with leaves and sticks.

For the rest of the day the Indians prowled around his general vicinity, beating the bushes with general good humor and malice. Several times they passed close to his little cave, but somehow missed him. Toward sunset they returned to the valley disappointed, with only the horse to show for their exertion.

Fitz waited until well into the night before he crawled out. He figured the direction least likely to bring him into contact with the Gros Ventres again, and set out. Soon he walked into the outskirts of their sleeping camp; decided it was just not his night and went back to his hole in the hill.

The next morning the hunt was resumed, and the Gros Ventres combed the hillside again; and again without finding the white man. This kind of nonsense was as boring to the Big Bellies as it was frightening to Fitz, and they finally abandoned the search in disgust. The rest of the day they spent giving their new acquisition a tryout; racing Fitzpatrick's horse against the best of the Indian, while the white man watched from up on his hill.

The second night Fitzpatrick sneaked out again, and made his way down to the creek some distance below the Gros Ventre village. He followed this until daylight, and then found another hole to hide in. Several small groups passed him during the day, but were apparently hunters, rather than search teams. He saw his horse under a man he took to be a chief; the animal had done well in the races.

The next night Fitz decided to cross the river, hoping there would be fewer Indians on the other side. (The geography of this escapade is somewhat uncertain; this may or may not be the Snake.) He made a raft, loaded self and goods aboard, and started across. The current broke up the raft, depositing its cargo in the water. Fitz had now been without food for a couple of days, and working hard to boot. He barely made it to shore, and was then without gun, flint, steel, or any of the necessaries except a butcher knife.

There followed a starvation trek, in which he lived on such buds, weeds, and roots as he could scrabble up. It wasn't much. By the time he reached rendezvous—the same afternoon as Sublette, the 8th of July,—he was incoherent from starvation and exhaustion, and barely recognizable. Since the loss of his gun and possibles, he'd been tramping for better than a week. Of the last stages, Leonard has Fitzpatrick say: "I thought of preparing myself for death, and committed my soul to the Almighty. I have no recollection of any thing that occurred after this, until I found myself in the hands of my deliverers."

(The tradition is that his hairs turned white overnight, thus giving him his second Indian sobriquet, White Head [Broken Hand being the first]. But these stories tended to pick up little details like this around the winter camp, and none of the immediate reports mentions anything of the kind.)

But he had gotten through, thanks to a mountain-tempered constitution, and that was all that was important.

II

And so Rendezvous 1832 got off to a roaring start with the customary Indian trouble.

Sublette unpacked his alcohol kegs, watered the stuff down, and maybe threw in a handful of tobacco for color and flavor. (In a different context we find one formula for "Injun trading whiskey," which was what the trappers got. One gallon raw alcohol to three gallons water. A pound of tea or rank black tobacco, some ginger, and a handful of red peppers. Indians mindful of HBC's very fine rum at the northern posts were consoled by the addition of a quart of black molasses.) Camp kettles—the mountain goblet—were passed around cheerily, emptied, and refilled with amazing regularity.

The trappers lied and bragged, challenged each other to horse races, foot races, drinking bouts, card games, shooting contests, or fights; whatever happened to enter their minds first. Every man, to hear him tell it, was the greatest anything-you-want-to-name in the mountains and stood ready to prove it on request. Frequently no request was necessary, in fact; the very presence of newcomers in the mountains was quite enough to fire up the athletic, alcoholic, and amatory pride of the veteran mountain men, and they proceeded to demonstrate their skills on beast, bottle, and brown-skin beauty to the enormous wonderment of the *mangeurs de lard*.

As Mrs. Victor has it, rather conservatively,

> then began the usual gay carousal; and the "fast young men" of the mountains outvied each other in all manner of mad pranks. In the beginning of their spree many feats of horsemanship and personal strength were exhibited, which were regarded with admiring wonder by the sober and inexperienced New Englanders under Mr. Wyeth's command. And as nothing stimulated the vanity of the mountain-men like an audience of this sort, the feats they performed were apt to astonish themselves. In exhibitions of the kind, the free trappers took the lead . . . [but] the manlier sports soon degenerated into . . . a "crazy drunk" condition.

During which time the humor was apt to become a bit

rough, no matter how good-natured. Of another rendezvous, Mrs. Victor reported:

> one of their number seized a kettle of alcohol, and poured it over the head of a tall, lank, red-headed fellow, repeating as he did so the baptismal ceremony. No sooner had he concluded, than another man with a lighted stick, touched him with the blaze, when in an instant he was enveloped in flames ... some of the company ... began beating him with pack-saddles to put out the blaze. But between the burning and the beating, the unhappy wretch nearly lost his life, and never recovered from the effects of his baptism by fire.

About the only thing doubtful in the story is that the prankster knew the baptismal ceremony, and even that is quite possible (Old Bill Williams, for example, one of the meanest and most cantankerous of them all, had once been a preacher.)

The bucks of the various tribes would be wandering around from group to group with wives, sisters, or daughters in tow, haranguing the interested mountain men with their amatory excellences. When the price was agreed on—it always went to the man in charge, never the woman involved— the trapper either bundled his squaw off into the bushes or laid her down where she was.

More independent squaws would be parading around camp on horseback, dressed in their finest white doeskin robes, looking for something more permanent in the way of liaison with the whites; a mountain marriage, with the prestige and comparative wealth and ease it brought a squaw.

And the beaver disappeared magically into Sublette's packs, very much faster than it had come out of the bitter cold streams, and the alcohol got a little weaker as perceptions dulled, and the shooting and shouting got a little wilder. The social event of the year, this week, and everybody who was anybody was there with bells on.

And there was business to be settled, too, and serious business it was this year. Remember that Bridger had not been able to lose the Company brigade under Vanderburgh this spring. And while Vanderburgh was presently looking on and biting his nails until Fontenelle arrived with his supplies, it meant nothing in the long run; it was a temporary embarrassment.

The conference between the partners of RMF resulted in an incredible proposal: an outright admission that their hold on the mountain trade was broken. Sometime during the week of rendezvous, they proposed to divide the mountains with American Fur, each taking its own section to work, avoiding the bitter clashes and the losses that heavy competition would mean to both firms.

No, thank you, said Mr. Henry Vanderburgh. His present course suited him just fine, and he thought he'd just sort of tag along and get some experience in RMF's trail. Fact was, he didn't know enough yet to be sure he—and Mr. Astor—got a fair shake on the division. And it would seem he didn't trust Messrs. Fitzpatrick, Sublette, Bridger, Fraeb, and Gervais very far.

Back went the RMF partners to their lodge, in a nasty mood.

The newcomer to the mountains, Nathaniel Wyeth, was having his troubles, too. Wyeth's men were complete novices—"men of theory," one source calls them—and he had difficulty with them all the way from Boston. Wyeth was himself a resourceful, acute man, despite the fact that he had no more experience than any of his party. He learned fast, this one, and in a year or two would be giving the mountain men some stiff competition at their own game. But now he was in a bad position, and the malcontents in his group took advantage of it.

The main problem was discipline. Some of the men—in particular Wyeth's own nephew, the nineteen-year-old John B. Wyeth—seemed to feel that everything ought to be completely democratic. That before any decisions were made the hired hands ought to be consulted. In their view Wyeth was behaving more like a tyrant than a respectably elected leader. (What this seems to boil down to is that they didn't like the necessary discipline of the trail; in spite of the fact that every other party also operated, of necessity, under conditions of military harshness.)

Accordingly, John Wyeth and some others of like mind broached their leader on the subject of his future plans:

> We wished to have what we had been used to at home—a town meeting—or a parish meeting, where every freeman has a right to speak his sentiments, and

to vote thereon. But Captain Wyeth was by no means
inclined to this democratical procedure. The most he
seemed inclined to was a caucus with a select few, of
which number neither his own brother . . . nor myself
was to be included. After considerable altercation he
concluded to call a meeting of the whole, on business
interesting and applicable to all. We accordingly met,
Captain Wyeth in the chair, or on the stump, I forget
which. Instead of every man speaking his own mind,
the Captain commenced the business by ordering the
roll to be called; and as the names were called the
clerk asked the person if he would go on. The first
name was Nathaniel J. Wyeth, whom we had dubbed
Captain, who answered "I shall go on." The next was
William Nud, who, before he answered, wished to
know what the Captain's plan and intentions were,
whether to try to commence a small colony or trap
and trade for beaver. To which Captain Wyeth replied that *that* was none of our business. Then Mr.
Nud said: "I shall not go on."

The end result of this ludicrous town meeting in Pierre's
Hole was that seven of Wyeth's men decided not to go on.
(This made a total of thirteen he had lost, out of an original
twenty-four.)

Wyeth and the remaining loyal eleven relinquished one of
their tents to the defectors. His situation was now critical—
a party of twelve, and particularly twelve of their limited
experience, was just meat for the Blackfeet, any way you
wanted to look at it.

Wyeth approached the friendly Milton Sublette for help;
he wanted to accompany Milton's Fall '32 brigade as far
as he could toward Oregon, at least out of the Blackfoot
country.

This was all right with Milton, and the two parties were
joined. Milton—possibly anxious to get back to the Mountain
Lamb—got his brigade in order before any of the rest of the
rendezvous was prepared. He started out with Wyeth's men
of theory in tow on July 17. It was probably fairly late in the
day, because they moved only six or eight miles before camping for the night. The next morning they woke early, packed
up, and walked into the battle of Pierre's Hole.

III

Rendezvous 1832 contributed more than its share to the mountain mythos. What with the escape of Fitzpatrick, the share-the-spoils proposition of RMF, and a few other trans-actions, it was probably the most important rendezvous ever held. It seems only fitting that it should have been climaxed by the most famous battle of the Rockies.

Milton Sublette and Wyeth started out of the valley toward the south. As they were getting ready to set out on the morning of July 18 they saw a dust cloud approaching; a large party. Since Fontenelle's supply train was expected hourly, this occasioned no great concern, but the normal precautions were taken. Before long Wyeth's spyglass had revealed that the approaching caravan was not white, after all, but a village of Indians; our old friends, in fact, the migrating Gros Ventres.

When the Indians had come into plain view they stopped, and the parties mutually surveyed each other. There were only about forty-two men in the combined Wyeth-Milton Sublette brigade; and an estimated two hundred Indians. (Inasmuch as this was a migrating village, including women, children, dogs and goods, the fighting force was nothing like this large.)

For their part, the Gros Ventres seemed dubious. Their bucks must have outnumbered the white party or they would have turned around immediately. But it was not an over-whelming superiority or they would have attacked with equal speed. Uncertain, they equivocated.

A flag was raised in the front of the Indian band (some sources say a white flag; some say the Union Jack) and one of the principal chiefs stepped forward. In the white party was the half-breed Antoine Godin, whose father Thierry had been killed by the Blackfeet a couple of years before. Taking with him a Flathead—whose tribe was constantly decimated by the Blackfeet—Godin rode out to meet the Gros Ventre chief.

The chief came forward with a pipe in his hands, and Godin and his Flathead companion met him about halfway between the opposing camps. As the Indian raised the peace pipe, Godin grabbed his hand. The Flathead raised his cocked rifle and shot the Gros Ventre at point-blank range. Godin snatched off the chief's red blanket as he fell, and the two wheeled their horses and made back to the white camp,

Godin waving the red blanket jubilantly, finally avenged in his own mind for his father's murder.

The Gros Ventres raised a howl, fired a few rounds, and scattered into a willow grove; part of a beaver swamp, where they began to build a fortification of deadfalls and limbs.

In the meantime, Milton had sent an express back to the main encampment where the other trapping parties were still in rendezvous. While the Gros Ventres worked on their fortification the greater portion of the combined companies, together with a large force of their Nez Perce and Flathead allies, was pounding along the plain like the cavalry in the last reel.

The astonished Gross Ventres—who had no idea there was a rendezvous around—suddenly found the little valley swarming with armed horsemen. They dug furiously at their fort, making trenches inside where they could be protected from the fire of the trappers.

When all the whites had arrived, Bill Sublette (and/or Tom Fitzpatrick) took over the generalship of the campaign. Sublette and Bob Campbell dictated oral wills to each other as they rode to the fight, and there were doubtless a goodly number of hastily got up wills of the same sort.

It was obvious to Sublette that the Gros Ventres were in a good position. The point of willows in which they were throwing up their breastworks provided ample protection from the white guns, if for no other reason than the lack of visibility.

He proposed that an attack be made on foot, directly through the grove up to the fort, where they could see something to shoot at. This notion met, so to speak, with a mixed response. The Nez Perces and Flatheads, for the most part, considered any direct attack through the woods little short of suicide, and many of the whites agreed. They wanted no part of any such thing.

Sublette volunteered to lead the attack himself. He got support from Bob Campbell and a few others; principally a free trapper named Sinclair and—of all people—the greenhorn Nathaniel Wyeth. Finally they recruited about thirty whites and the same number of Indians. Sublette's own recruits did not engage in the battle, nor did Wyeth's men; by one account Sublette flatly forbade the greenhorns to take a hand.

Wyeth himself, however, led one of the brigades into a circling motion, approaching the Gros Ventre fortification from the opposite side. It is incredible that this quondam ice merchant, fresh from Boston, should take such a part in this fight; but lead he did, and acquitted himself well enough.

Sublette and Bob Campbell and Sinclair led the frontal attack. As they approached the log wall, Sinclair parted some bushes to peek through and was shot through the body. A second later Bill Sublette himself was shot through the shoulder, and another man hit in the head. The Indians' fire from the fort was deadly accurate, and their position strong.

Wyeth's party had meantime arrived behind the fort, only to find themselves caught in both Indian fire and the overshots from Sublette's brigade. One of Wyeth's Indians was killed in this way, and a Gros Ventre ball accounted for another man.

The whites retreated, moving back to their camp to reconsider the situation. They were astonished by the work the Gros Ventres had been able to do on their fortification, and gave up all idea of taking it by storm.

The only thing remaining was to burn them out. The Nez Perce and Flathead allies objected strongly to this notion. While burning the fort would get rid of the Gros Ventres, it would also wipe out any plunder there might be, an unforgivable waste.

Nevertheless, the plan was carried over their objections, and the squaws were set to gathering wood. While this was going on, the stubborn Gros Ventres were hurling taunts out of the fort. A conversation was carried on between the inhabitants of the fort and an interpreter; the gist was apparently that, while the whites might be able to burn out this small fortress, revenge would come soon. There were six or eight hundred warriors not far from here, who would descend on the whites and wipe them out.

In the process of translation, as is customary, something was lost. In this case it was the meaning. When all the interpreters had finished hashing out the threats through two or three Indian languages and English, it was relayed as saying that six or eight hundred warriors were already in Pierre's Hole, wiping up the trappers who had remained behind: the greenhorns, and those otherwise disinclined to fight.

Promptly the white party got into an uproar and, leaving behind a small force to keep the Gros Ventres in their fort, stormed all the way back to the site of the rendezvous, to rescue *that* bunch. They didn't need rescuing, except from each other perhaps, and that didn't count.

By now it was near night, and there wasn't time to get back to the Gros Ventre position before dark. In the morning, when they did return to finish up the job, there was nobody at home in the willow grove.

The survivors had slipped out during the night and were scattering through the woods in retreat. Disconsolate, the Nez Perces and Flatheads discovered that the retreating Gros Ventres had taken all their gear with them; no booty at all. They found only one squaw, some distance from the fort, and immediately butchered her.

(One story is that she sat beside the body of a fallen warrior and made no resistance. Another, less romantic, that she had been shot through the leg.)

The final casualty score on the white side was three whites killed (another died later) and four or five wounded, including Bill Sublette, who had had his wound dressed by Bob Campbell and was carried back to camp on a litter. Eight or ten of their Nez Perce and Flathead allies had been wounded or killed. The Gros Ventres later admitted to a loss of twenty-six men—though when the trappers finally overran the little fortification they did not find that many. (The figures are, of course, those from the battle proper; there were other casualties directly attributable to the Battle of Pierre's Hole, but they did not occur until later.)

So the battle of Pierre's Hole was over. Everybody went back to the rendezvous site to discuss it, have a drink, and get organized for the Fall '32 hunt all over again.

CHAPTER 18

"A dishonest transaction from beginning to end"

BILL SUBLETTE, his supply caravan now loaded with furs, had to remain in Pierre's Hole until his wound healed enough for him to ride. Jacob Wyeth, Nathaniel's doctor-brother, bound it up as best he could; the rest was up to the mountain constitution. The dissenters from Wyeth's party intended to accompany Sublette and Campbell back to St. Louis, and so were forced to remain at rendezvous until Bill was able to travel. The Company brigade under Vanderburgh and Drips was stuck, too; Fontenelle had still not arrived with their supplies. They sent out a scouting party to see if he could be located. The presence of the expected six hundred Gros Ventre warriors somewhere east of the divide made everybody a little nervous. Bill Sublette, of course, was in the worst position. He had to go back that way.

Milton's party (which apparently included Gervais) was scheduled to hunt southwest; on a slant north of the Great Salt Lake and its desert, working the area around the Humboldt River and perhaps the Owyhee. This was starving country for every party that ever went through it, and the beaver not enough to justify the hardship. It is hard to explain this hunt. It may be that Milton veered too far south from his intended grounds or perhaps the idea was to clean off the fringes of the Snake country before HBC had a chance to do it. With Wyeth still in tow, they got off on the 24th of June, about a week after the battle, and headed down the valley of the Snake.

The other principal brigade of RMF, under Tom Fitzpatrick and Bridger, was headed north from Pierre's Hole; back to Three Forks, with all that implied—much beaver, many Blackfeet. (From Fort Union McKenzie was supplying powder, lead, and guns ... Bug's Boys were better armed than they had ever been.)

There is no record of Fraeb's whereabouts on this fall '32 hunt. At a guess, he would be heading down into the valley of the Green again. With the Fitz-Bridger brigade working north along the west slope and Milton working south, also on the west side of the mountain, the only prosperous area not accounted for is the valley of the Green, southeast of Pierre's Hole.

About the time Milton's party got off for the southwest, a violent argument broke out at the camp. Shortly before he rode on ahead of Sublette's supply party, Tom Fitzpatrick had bought 120 pelts from the captain of the Gant & Blackwell trappers and taken men into RMF's service from the now-defunct small firm. (One of these was Zenas Leonard.) The furs had been cached near the mouth of the Laramie. These, of course, belonged to Gant & Blackwell, bankruptcy or no, and their brigade captain had no right whatever to dispose of them to RMF. (This man, one Alfred Stephens, appears to have been a querulous sort, not above a judicious double-cross in time of need; several members of his own trapping party suffered from the captain's duplicity.)

Now, in Pierre's Hole, Stephens decided he had been cheated by Fitzpatrick. The beaver was to be paid for in horses, of which Stephens was short, and he objected to the price set on the horses by Fitz. But the latter held all the cards. In the altercation that ensued (by Zenas Leonard's account):

> No person interfered, for we all knew that it was a dishonest transaction from beginning to end. Fitzpatrick having everything in his own possession, was therefore contented and as independent as any mean man who had it in his power to make his own terms. Stephens, on the contrary, was in a bad situation—having paid beforehand, and not being able to force measures, had to put up with what he could get.

Furious, Stephens decided to leave Pierre's Hole without waiting for the supply train of Bill Sublette. He managed to recruit six men, several of them discontented Wyeth men, and left the day after Milton, the 25th of July. His intention was apparently to get back to the mouth of the Laramie and raise the cache of furs there before Fitz could get it.

One day out of Pierre's Hole they stumbled into an advance party of the rumored Gros Ventre camp. Two of the men were killed immediately, including the ex-Wyeth man, George More, who died a very long way from Boston. Stephens' wound was not considered dangerous at first, being comparatively small. But gangrene makes all wounds the same size; he died a few days later.

I have implied previously that RMF was born with Bill Sublette's hand on its collective throat. Now, as he lay in Pierre's Hole recuperating from his shoulder wound, the man known to Indians as Cut Face began to tighten his grip.

RMF had not been able to get its furs down since the company was formed, and so had two years' hunt on hand. In Pierre's Hole there were 11,246 pounds of fur, and another 2,473 pounds in caches on the Sweetwater and Platte. (Part of this, of course, was the Gant & Blackwell fur, which reverted to Tom Fitzpatrick when Stephens was killed. Or at least there wasn't anybody to object to the proceedings.) Altogether 140 to 150 packs, a respectable catch, and not even counting the castoreum and miscellaneous furs.

With Milton Sublette, Gervais, and probably Fraeb already off on the Fall '32 hunt, Fitzpatrick sat down and drew up an agreement with Bill.

The Articles of Agreement[1] were dated "under the Three Teton mountain this Twenty fifth day of July." It is rather a long document, mainly because it concerns itself with the debts RMF has accumulated in two years. It is also an interesting one, inasmuch as it effectively places control of RMF in the hands of Bill Sublette. Ostensibly it is no more than an agreement for Sublette to sell the RMF catch as best he can and instructions for the disposal of the money.

Disposing of the money was no problem; RMF's debts, when added up, were staggering. For the merchandise Bill Sublette had just brought up they owed him $15,620. They owed back wages amounting to $10,318. The note given to SJ&S had come due the previous November: $15,532. (This was the purchase of the business.) They owed the firm of Jackson & Sublette over $3000 for the merchandise Tom Fitzpatrick had purchased in Santa Fe.

These, together with several other outstanding notes, totaled nearly $47,000. In addition, they would have to pay Sublette 50 cents a pound for transporting the furs back to St. Louis. While the debts are ominous enough in themselves, there are further even more important provisions in these articles: providing the proceeds from the sale of the beaver are not sufficient to cover the above, Sublette is authorized to pay them on his own hook, and is also authorized to pay any other outstanding debts that may turn up.

Sublette is thus placed in this position with respect to RMF: The partners depend wholly on him for supplies (at Sublette's price); they depend wholly on him for the disposal of their catch; he becomes their banker, handling all their money affairs, which will cost them 6–10 per cent interest; and in paying off their outstanding notes he is, in effect, buying the debts for himelf—he becomes their sole creditor.

With this document, then, Bill Sublette assumes effective control of RMF. The risk to himself is that the company will be unable to pay its debt to him. This is minimized by the fact that—since he handles all the money—he is able to see that his share is deducted early in the game.

But the money, however important, is not the only consideration here. The possibility that RMF might necessarily default on its debt is outweighed by another positive advantage given Sublette by assuming control. Being master of RMF's fate gives him an ace in the hole for a game that has not even become manifest as yet.

Bill Sublette is shortly to challenge the monolithic Company. By a several-pronged attack he is going to force American Fur into a position where it must deal with Bill Sublette on his own terms. In his negotiations with the Company, one of Sublette's strongest bargaining points was his position with respect to the Company's toughest opposition; Sublette, very simply, could say whether RMF continued to harass and annoy the Company or left the field to them alone. A very long lever; it would be worth a good deal to the Company to have RMF fold up on request.

Through account books now in the manuscript collections of the Missouri Historical Society we can follow the disposition of this catch of fur. It might be enlightening to do so. Occasionally all of us get to the point of wondering where the money went; and the fur companies were no different, particularly those composed of practical trappers, as was RMF.

The debts enumerated in the Articles of Agreement amount to $46,750 (Rounding off figures for convenience' sake). St. Louis price on furs is down by the fall of 1832; these will bring about $4.25 a pound. Even at that, Sublette will be taking home around $58,000 worth of beaver. On the face of it, this will put RMF about $11,250 to the good.

But, in the way of such things, the debt gets bigger and the net gets smaller. Here are some of the ways:

(1) Sublette had an arrangement with Ashley. (Now Congressman Ashley; he had been elected to a vacant seat in the House of Representatives in the autumn of '31 when the incumbent died.) While Sublette was in the mountains, Ashley had bought trade goods for him in the East. Returning with the furs, the bulk of them were turned over to Ashley to sell. The congressman's fee was $1,500.

(2) Interest at 8 per cent a year mounts up quickly, even over a few months. Sublette had been instructed by Fitz to pay off RMF's debts immediately, if it looked as though there were going to be too long a delay in the final sale of furs; this, of course, to cut down on the interest. Accordingly, Bill paid off the note to Smith Jackson & Sublette in January, 1833. (With interest the note was now worth $16,632.41.) The sale of beaver hadn't been completed by then, so RMF temporarily went into the red in Sublette's books for $13,-445.69. Bill charged them only 6 per cent on the amount of this temporary indebtedness. Obviously, 6 per cent on $13,-000 is less than 8 per cent on $15,000; and so Sublette has done RMF a favor. (And done himself a favor too, it might be noted. The 8 per cent on the original note had to be divided three ways: Smith's estate, Jackson, and Sublette. But this brand-new 6 per cent was all for Bill Sublette; it was a new debt, and he was the sole creditor. As usual, Bill comes out on top.) Altogether, interest charges on the various transactions amounted to better than $2,000; about five full packs of beaver.

(3) The freight charges of $7,069.50 could have been paid for the first sales made in St. Louis, before the 8 per cent began to run on November 1 per the Articles of Agreement. And these charges, by the Articles of Agreement, were to be paid first of all. Instead, Sublette chose to pay off smaller obligations out of these first proceeds. He let the freight

charge go unpaid until it had picked up another hundred dollars in interest, for a total of $7,171.61.

(4) In addition to the above, there were the customary discounts for cash payment—over $1,500; dealers' commissions (including a commission for arranging for insurance)—$820; the insurance for shipping; insurance for fire; handling expenses, barrels, drayage, and so forth.

By these various deductions the value of the furs decreased by about $5,000. Through the various additions, the debits inceased by over $11,000. The last entry I have on this transaction shows RMF $5,400 in the hole, with about three packs of beaver still unsold; not nearly enough to break even. It's a good thing they were expert trappers; one shudders to think what it would have been like if their hunt had been unsuccessful.

II

I've gone into detail on this transaction for two reasons. The first, obviously, is to demonstrate Bill Sublette's relations with RMF; the second is much more general.

It should not be understood that the above is in any way unusual: the expense attending the sale of furs were pretty much the same no matter who was handling it. But it points up a contrast that constantly bemuses me.

The men of the fur trade—the mountain men—were probably the most independent, tough-minded, asocial bunch of nonconformists you are likely to run across. The society in which they lived was virtually anarchic; every man his own conscience, every man assuming the responsibility for his own actions. As a group, they lived more nearly in a rule-less society than any other I can think of. They were aggressively independent as individuals; they knuckled under to no man, and personal freedom was the principal good they sought.

The comment of one can stand for all: "I should like to see the man to make me do what I don't want to—that's all I live for." And for this kind of personal freedom—irresponsibility, if you choose—and for the other intangibles of mountain life they were willing to face the hazards of the trade. Starvin' times, and freezin' times, and Bug's Boys with their brand new Company fusils and all the rest of it.

This fierce independence sometimes ran to a ludicrous extent, naturally; any position carried far enough becomes an absurdity. If a man dropped his possible sack on the trail ahead, chances were the man behind wouldn't pick it up. That's *his* business was the attitude; let him solve his own problems. In Meek's words, "Let him have better luck." And, in turn, you didn't want anybody else fooling around with your business either.

To most of modern America this is not a congenial attitude. We put our faith in the group, in the society, in the state. We organize committees and conduct brainstorming sessions out of some weird conviction that if you get enough third-rate minds working together a first-rate idea is bound to come out of it. The individual impulse is smashed and perverted. Even the normally healthy impulse to freedom becomes converted into a stupidly negative rebellion against society, producing nothing. When the impulse to freedom is thus converted into a purely negative thing, it becomes simple fraudulence; an aping of society, but in reverse. The superficiality of the society is equaled by the superficialty of the grandstanding rebels; and both derive from the same weakness, a lack of any strong sense of individual worth and responsibility.

This was the thing the mountain men had that made it worth while for them to live the kind of life they did; a massively strong sense of the worth of the individual, and his independence. It is one of the main reasons we find them difficult to comprehend today.

They were misfits even in the nineteenth century, when the individual was held in higher esteem than he is today. They were the men who just couldn't get along in town, even the towns of the frontiers. The reasons for it ran all the way from a Thoreau-like impulse to a murder trial if they went back. It was an incredibly varied group, and this added to the conviction of uniqueness most of them shared; no two were alike.

The amazing thing is that, within limits, this structureless society of theirs worked pretty well. To be sure, "Mr. Bray was killed by a blow from the hand of Mr. Tullock," and "Thomas, a half breed, was killed by Williams," and so forth; the physical brutality has certainly been emphasized enough in recent years to make that aspect of the mountain trade familiar to us. But, given the circumstances, it seems to me that the anarchy of the mountains worked out reasonably well; better, I think, than our social theorists would be wont to predict.

The brutality of their life we no longer understand; and hence it becomes interesting to us in a novel, dramatic way. Furthermore, it is against our present laws, and hence unethical.

On the other hand, the business practices of the day were equally brutal; though they seem less so than the mountain life, because our present business structure is much closer to that time than our life is to the mountain man's life. The transactions I have outlined are quite within our present understanding of law; and hence we tend to regard them as automatically ethical. (We have a constitutional weakness for equating that-which-is-legal with that-which-is-ethical.)

The interesting thing is that the anarchic society of the mountain men was absolutely helpless before the organized society of the St. Louis businessmen, and this is the contrast that both attracts and repels me.

For all their pride in their independence, for all their boasting that no man could push them around, they were shoved this way and that every time Bill Sublette's clerk put his quill in ink. Every time he scratched down that "interest at 8 per cent to date," some trapper was pushed into the icy water at dawn, or into a Blackfoot ambush, or into Digger country and starvation.

What with the up-to-2,000 per cent markup on goods and the further manipulations during sale, the trapper didn't have a chance. The point I would like to make is that the two phases of the business are not qualitatively different from each other. We can view this 2,000 per cent markup as vaguely unethical, because it isn't done now. But I doubt that many readers will be aghast at the business dealings I've described in this chapter; and for the simple reason that those dealings are not essentially different from our modern conditions. In short, we are familiar—and comfortable—with the brutality of profit. It does not carry the same emotional charge as the physical brutality.

With the Articles of Agreement—and the Rocky Mountain Fur Company—in his pocket, Sublette got his sixty-man party off from Pierre's Hole on July 30. He had with him a request from Fitz:

> I wish you, should I not here after have an opportunity of writing to Genl. Ashley to let him know the situation of this country and how much it is infested by intruders and bad men . . .

The intruders and bad men were, of course, Wyeth and the Company force of Vanderburgh and Drips, principally the latter; as yet Wyeth was not seen as a threat. The suggestion that Ashley be informed was no mere gesture of communication but an attempt to bring some pressure to bear. With Ashley in the House of Representatives, RMF had a voice to raise against the Astor combine. From the looks of things in the mountains, RMF was going to need help on every front, and Washington was certainly not the least of these.

Sublette's returning party was apprehensive about the reported 600–800 Gros Ventres in the neighborhood; and their apprehension had not been eased by the attack on Stephens' party. Less than a week out of Pierre's Hole, and just after they crossed the divide, the forebodings were realized; they ran into the Gros Ventres. There was simply no avoiding them this summer.

There are no records of the meeting, except the casual notice in Bill Sublette's informative letter to Ashley: "I expected an attack from them daily, as my force was only about 60 men, but from some cause unknown to me, they suffered me to pass unmolested."

He moved on, reached the Sweetwater caches on August 15 and raised the 2,400 pounds of fur there. He was back in St. Louis by the first part of October, turned the catch over to Ashley for disposal, and began to organize his most ambitious project yet: the baiting of the Company.

III

When Milton Sublette's brigade got off on their Fall '32 hunt—for the second time—they left Pierre's Hole by the same route they had tried before. It had now been a week since the battle, and Wyeth made a short side trip to "visit . . . the scene of our conflict."

> . . . the din of arms was now changed into the noise of the vulture and the howling of masterless dogs   the stench was extreme   most of the men in the fort must have perished   I soon retired from the scene of this disgusting butchery.

They made bullboats a day or so later to cross the Snake. They roughly followed the course of the river—while it was going their direction; southwest and west. Finally they struck out overland for the barren plains between the Humboldt and Owyhee rivers. (This, very roughly, is around the juncture of the present Oregon, Idaho, and Nevada state lines.)

Now they got beyond buffalo range, and for the mountain men that was always bad. It was almost the definition of starvin' times. The largest game they had was beaver; and beaver in this part of the country wasn't even safe to eat. From eating poisonous plants (possibly wild hemlock) the meat of the beaver was occasionally poisonous to man. Milton Sublette's party—according to Meek, who with it— had this trouble.[2]

Now they were in Digger country; the most miserable of all the tribes, related to the Shoshones. Mrs. Victor says:

> Nothing can be more abject than the appearance of the Digger Indian, in the fall, as he roams about, without food and without weapons, save perhaps a bow and arrows, with his eyes fixed upon the ground, looking for crickets! So despicable is he, that he has neither enemies nor friends; and the neighboring tribes do not condescend to notice his existence, unless indeed he should come in their way, when they would not think it more than a mirthful act to put an end to his miserable existence.

Nothing more abject, perhaps, except a trapping party of buffalo eaters getting food the same way. When the provisions—meaning game, not carried provisions—gave out, Milton's party was reduced to the same diet as the miserable Digger. Says Joe Meek:

> I have held my hands in an ant-hill until they were covered with the ants, then greedily licked them off. I have taken the soles off my moccasins, crisped them in the fire, and eaten them. In our extremity, the large black crickets which are found in this country were considered game. We used to take a kettle of hot water, catch the crickets and throw them in, and when they stopped kicking, eat them. This was not what we called ... good meat ... but it kept us alive.

Here the party was also faced with an almost classic dilemma: which did they need more, animals-as-transportation or animals-as-food? They reached a sort of compromise by bleeding a mule at night and making soup of the blood. But, since the mules themselves couldn't afford the loss of blood, it was a touchy proposition; usually objected to by the man whose mule was drawn for tonight, whatever his opinion may have been last night. Occasionally a mule was killed for food, but since the only ones they dared kill were the poorest and most famished of the lot, this, too, was no answer to the problem.

Wyeth's little party had separated from Milton's brigade before they reached the real starvation country. He was single-mindedly pushing on toward the west coast and Fort Vancouver, and the trapping route was out of his way. Just before departure, he was given an example of mountain morals.

> Joe Meek one day shot a Digger who was prowling about a stream where his traps were set.
> "Why did you shoot him?" asked Wyeth.
> "To keep him from stealing traps."
> "Had he stolen any?"
> "No: but he *looked as if he was going to!*"
> This recklessness of life very properly distressed the just minded New Englander.

(It is entirely probable that Wyeth had left the party some time before this incident didn't occur. However. Joe is a friend of mine.)

After separating from Milton, Wyeth moved up the valley of the Snake, taking geological specimens, a few beaver, meeting Bannock and Shoshone bands. Of the latter: -

> I found these Indians great thieves in the small line knives ect. Missing mine I went to one of the Sub Chiefs and told him of it   he made enquiry and pointed out the thief who refusing to open his Robe I gently did it for him but instead of finding the knife found a coat of one of the men which he held upon until I drew a pistol on which he gave it up and caught up what he supposed to [be] one of our guns but it happened to be my covered fishing rod   he was then held by the other Indians and sent to the village and I saw him no more.

However great thieves the Snakes might be—in the small line, of course—Wyeth was impressed with their chief:

> [He] is a good sized man and very intelligent and the President would do well if he could preserve the respect of his subjects as well or maintain as much dignity.

And with their acuity:

> [After an exploring trip in the middle of September] I returned where I left the party and feeling in the mood of banter I told the Indians at the mouth of the creek (the party having left) that I had eaten nothing for two days this to see if they would give me anything for charity sake. One of them went and looked at my saddle and pointed me the fresh blood of a beaver I had that morning caught ... I then bought 2 salmon for one awl afterward I told him I had three children at home he brought forward three tawny brats and his squaw who was big I backed out of story telling with Indians.

Wyeth had been gone for ten days on this side exploration, and when he rejoined his camp (near the mouth of the Boise) he discovered he had missed visitors.

Milton Sublette and Fraeb, wearied of cricket eating, had swung north from the Humboldt and were back in southern Idaho. Their first good meal in several weeks of famine and "four days of almost total abstinence" had been when they reached the Snake, improvised some fishing gear, and caught enough to "furnish them a hearty and a most delicious repast." In the morning, says Meek, they went on their way rejoicing.

After their brief meeting with Wyeth's Oregon-bound party, Sublette and Fraeb moved their brigade up the Payette River, heading due north until they reached the Salmon. There was better trapping here; but not good enough. The Fall '32 hunt was working out very slim indeed.

During the late fall this brigade apparently worked down the Salmon to a point near the forks. Here they settled in for the winter, and were joined not long after by the party of Fitzpatrick and Bridger, back from the Blackfoot country.

All the partners were back together again. Fitzpatrick and Bridger had not had any better hunt than Milton, but a more exciting one. Old Gabe had accumulated a couple of arrows in his back—he carried the iron head of one in his shoulder blade for three years—and all the trappers had some stories to tell.

CHAPTER 19

"A bitter and unreasonable commercial strife"

FITZPATRICK and Bridger would have left Rendezvous '32 with a certain sense of satisfaction, if not outright triumph; inasmuch as they left the Company brigade behind twiddling their thumbs and without supplies.

Doc Newell, Joe Meek's confrere, went with this party. His notes of the Fall '32 hunt are brief, as was his custom:

> Into Rondezvous   got our Supplies and Scattered in the following courses to our profession Wm Sublette to the States with the returns   M. Sublette to the west down Snake River   Mr Fitzpatrick to the north i wone of that number   from Piers hole to Psalmon River   crossed the mountain to the 3 forks of Missourie (a scrimmage with Black feet) up to the head of galiton fork . . .

and the heart of Blackfoot country.[1]

Visualize this Three Forks area as three splayed fingers pointing south. The west finger is Jefferson Fork, the central is Madison Fork, and the eastern is Gallatin Fork. They point to the Centennial Mountains (which run east-west), and just across that range is Henry's Fork of the Snake; and down the Snake is the valley known as Pierre's Hole.

The Company supply caravan under Fontenelle never did make it all the way to Pierre's Hole. After the departure of Fitzpatrick and Bridger the Company's field partisans hastily decamped and went in search of the delinquent Fontenelle.

308

They found him, at last, camped in the valley of the Green River. (And camped nearby was yet another newcomer to the mountains, Captain B. L. E. Bonneville. An army officer on leave, Bonneville was making a strictly commercial foray into the fur trade [see Appendix B for the background].)

Vanderburgh and Drips picked up their long-delayed supplies and hastily returned to Pierre's Hole, where they detached a small party to investigate trade with the Flatheads. The main brigade then set out on the now-old trail of the RMF party under Fitz and Bridger.

Near the last of August Vanderburgh crossed fresh trail. He had found them, and in some of the most broken, confused country there is. Putting on a burst of speed, he overtook the RMF brigade on about the 11th of September, just a month after leaving Fontenelle at the Green River. (The directness of Vanderburgh's interception route indicates that he had more than general information of RMF's plans. This would not have been hard to come by, however. The general atmosphere of the rendezvous—camaraderie, good fellowship, and what not, even between competing companies—made it quite likely that a drunken RMF man would confide in a drunken Company man. Not the partisans, of course, though they were genial enough to each other. But there wasn't much the partisans could do about free trappers. There wasn't much anybody could do about free trappers.)

Vanderburgh's brigade was now shaken down into trail order; they were traveling as fast and surely as the best: RMF's men. Now all that remained to be introduced to the best beaver ground, and the Company was in business.

The RMF partners were baffled and disgusted at Vanderburgh's appearance on Jefferson Fork. There was no losing the Company. Hastily Fitz and Bridger switched direction; heading northwest (toward present Missoula) to show the Company a little plain and fancy ridge hopping.

No good. Vanderburgh and Drips stuck right behind them, losing them, catching up again, playing a little game of mountain tag in which the Company was perpetually It.

The RMF brigade confirmed what Bridger had discovered last spring: when the Company wanted to follow, it could follow, and there wasn't a thing to be done about it.

All right, if that was the game, RMF would play it. Let the Company follow, then. But they would follow barren ground. Fitz and Bridger switched back again, but this time there was no attempt to lose the Company brigade or to take beaver. Doggedly RMF marched straight into the worst kind of country; beaver bare and full of Blackfeet. The Company caught up with them (this is the middle of September) on the Missouri itself; southeast of present Great Falls, and north of Three Forks.

By this time the RMF plan was painfully obvious. Both companies were killing the fall '32 hunt in this game of fox and geese. This fur desert was also extremely dangerous; the country of Bloods, nastiest of the Blackfeet.

Now the Company took advantage of its numbers, and split into two groups. One of these, under Drips, could follow RMF around as before. It would either be led into beaver country or, at worst, would completely nullify the Fitzpatrick-Bridger hunt. The remainder of the Company brigade would be taken south by Vanderburgh, to work up the Madison—central branch of the three forks.

But Drips had not Vanderburgh's persistence. He followed RMF south to the forks itself; the actual junction of the three rivers to form the Missouri. Here, on about October 1, the parties were separated. (This is about the time Milton Sublette's brigade got back to the Snake from the starvation march in northern Nevada.) Whether Drips took the wrong fork by mistake or just gave up the race is uncertain. But the Company men moved up the western stream, the Jefferson; the RMF contingent swung up the east branch, the Gallatin.

By a neat division, there was now a party working each of the three branches: Drips on the west, Vanderburgh in the middle, Fitzpatrick and Bridger on the east.

It would seem that the RMF men had not known where Vanderburgh was going when they separated on the Missouri. If they had, they would probably not have taken their next step. On October 6, after ascending the Gallatin some distance, they crossed over to the Madison and—inevitably—ran into Vanderburgh's brigade. Again.

For several days the two camps were near each other, and there must have been some discussion among Vanderburgh, Fitz, and Bridger; discussion with a note of desperation in it. The way things were shaping up this fall, it was not competition but suicide. Both companies were being rendered impotent by their chase; there was no trapping getting done, or not enough. Vanderburgh's ability to follow RMF wherever it chose to lead was obvious. And it may be that he felt secure enough in his knowledge now—they had, after all, covered a great deal of territory in the past year—to abandon his harassing technique and strike out on his own. (All this is conjectural.)

Whatever went on at this meeting, the two camps separated for the last time. Fitzpatrick and Bridger—on October 11—moved out; up the Madison toward the head. Vanderburgh waited another day or so for some small bands of trappers to come in. On the morning of the 14th of October the company brigade moved down to the Ruby River, probably intending to follow it to the Jefferson and make contact again with the detached party of Drips.

They had been picking up Indian sign lately, and a couple of scouts found more that morning. A deserted camp, it was, with the half-butchered carcass of a buffalo cow left to rot. The obvious conclusion: a hunting party, frightened off by the presence of the white camp. Either gone home, or to get reinforcements, or skulking around for an ambush.

Vanderburgh decided to track them down, to allay the nervousness of his trappers. (Sensibly enough, they had promptly refused to move until the disposition of this band of unknowns was established.) About three miles away from this camp was a dense stand of timber, the only one in the area. There, if anywhere, he would find the Indian hunting party. He took six men to set out to investigate.

To reach the woods they had to cross a small gully, full of water at the flood season, but now just a dry ditch, scarcely wider than a horse could jump. As they reached the opposite side, the woods around them exploded; gunfire and the battle screams of Blackfeet.

Vanderburgh's horse was shot out from under him in the first volley. Three of his trappers wheeled their horses and leaped back out of the gully in panic despite Vanderburgh's reported shout, "Boys, don't run." One other was thrown off and left helpless on the ground, where he was butchered. Warren Ferris, himself attempting to vault the ditch, was wounded in the shoulder. The single remaining man, one Nelson, had his horse wounded. Ferris and Nelson joined the headlong flight out of the defile.

When Vanderburgh's horse was killed, he unpinned himself just as the Blackfeet swarmed down out of their hiding places into the gully. He killed one with his rifle, but as he was raising a pistol for a second shot he was cut down.

The Indians chopped off his arms (later displayed as victory tokens at Fort McKenzie) and carried them away. They stripped the flesh from the rest of his bones and threw it in the nearby river; then buried the bones by the bank. (The bones were later recovered by a Flathead party sent out by the survivors.)

The surviving members fled in panic back to their main encampment. Cautiously they made their way out of the area, rejoining Drips and his party a week after Vanderburgh's death, on the 21st of October. Three days later the entire Company brigade deserted the Three Forks area, crossed over the Centennial Range and down onto the water of the Snake.

The death of Vanderburgh is summed up by the historian Chittenden:

> The whole affair was one of the most lamentable tragedies that ever occurred in the mountains, for the principal victim was a man of chivalrous character, high standing, and universally beloved by those who knew him. Its most regrettable feature is the fact that it grew out of a bitter and unreasonable commercial strife in which Vanderburgh was a victim of his own zeal.

It is traditionally held that RMF led Vanderburgh to his death, and that they were directly responsible for it. However, much of the evidence seems to indicate that the game of follow-the-leader had been abandoned some time before Vanderburgh's death. The facts from which I have sketched the above account can also be viewed in another way: that an agreement was reached by the companies at their meeting on the Missouri, whereby the three branches were to be divided among them. This would have resulted in the situation during the first week in October, when Drips was on the Jefferson, Vanderburgh on the Madison, Fitzpatrick and Bridger on the Gallatin. RMF's offer to split the hunting may have been renewed and this time accepted by Vanderburgh. But he was killed before he had time to inform his superiors. The largest factor in this offer was Vanderburgh's field of competence. Thus, after his death, RMF would not be under any necessity to make the same arrangement with his successors.

Further, Vanderburgh was not killed in the fur desert, as usually stated; rather, several weeks later, in good beaver country and at a time when the companies seem to have reached some sort of peaceful settlement of their difficulties.

In short, I think the competitive chase of early fall should be viewed separately from Vanderburgh's death, as an already settled phase of the fall '32 hunt. I don't believe the direct connection usually made between the two events has an adequate basis in fact, since the movements of the various brigades strongly suggest that the marching competition was over a full two weeks previous to the ambush of the Company party.

From this point of view, the event ceases to carry the ethical implications usually assigned it. Vanderburgh's death is just one more example of the mountain man down on his luck, one more scalp to the credit of Bug's Boys and not to RMF.

II

After leaving Vanderburgh on the Madison, Fitzpatrick and Bridger moved on up, trapping as they went. Their course for the rest of the fall is uncertain. They were traveling in hostile country, and took the appropriate measures. As a large brigade, they were relatively safe from direct attack; the danger came at the vulnerable hours of camp. Horses had to be protected at the evening graze, during the night, and at the morning graze. Before setting out a thorough reconnaissance would be made of the area around camp and, particularly, in the direction of their march. When Indian sign was missing, the camp would pick up and go. There were unavoidable risks, of course, brough on by the nature of the trade. The trappers would often be in small parties; the whole brigade couldn't check a trapline together. When separated on what Newell calls "the courses [of] our profession," the trapper ran his greatest risk: "(a scrimmage with Black feet)." "Scrimmage," perhaps, gives a bit too sporty a tone to these encounters; but then the idea of sport was somewhat different. Joe Meek's idea, anyway.[2]

Seems that Joe and a couple of others encountered a small band of Blackfeet—very small, presumably—near a lake, and "thinking the opportunity for sport a good one, commenced firing on them."

The Blackfeet took to the lake for protection, while Joe and the others sportified to their hearts' content by occasionally plugging a half ounce of Galena into the water near them.

Unfortunately, however, these were only stragglers from a

main encampment of Blackfeet. Attracted by the shooting, more Indians showed up. Joe and his partners hightailed it away from the lake. The Blackfeet swarmed after them, howling for blood.

Unfortunately, however, these were only stragglers from a main encampment of white men. Attracted by the shooting, more whites showed up. And before long, both main encampments were drawn up facing each other.

One of Fitzpatrick's trappers, Loretto, had a Blackfoot wife. By one report, she recognized her brother among the opposing force and wandered over to talk to him ("Threw herself on her brother's neck, who clasped his long-lost sister to his heart with a warmth of affection," by Washington Irving's version).

Then, as at the battle of Pierre's Hole, one of the chiefs came forward with a calumet. Bridger rode out to meet him, carrying his rifle across the pommel of his saddle.

At the moment when the chief extended his hand, Bridger saw something in the main throng, "which he took to mean treachery." He clicked back the hammer of his gun to full cock.

This, of course, the Blackfoot dignitary took to mean treachery. He grabbed the muzzle of Bridger's rifle, which exploded into the ground. The chief—"a large and powerful man"—then snatched the gun out of Bridger's hands completely and clubbed the white man out of his saddle with the butt.

All hell broke loose. The chief (pausing only long enough to grab Bridger's horse) went back to his own lines; and Bridger to his, receiving two arrows in the back as he ran.

Loretto's wife was still in the Blackfoot camp. It was a desperate situation; because their baby was still with Loretto. Quoting Mrs. Victor:

> her lamentations and struggles to escape and return to her husband and child so wrought upon the young Mexican ... that he took the babe in his arms, and galloped with it into the heart of the Blackfoot camp, to place it in the arms of the distracted mother. This daring act ... so excited the admiration of the Blackfoot chief, that he gave him permission to return, unharmed, to his own camp. ... Loretta begged to have his wife restored to him, relating how he had rescued her ... from the Crows, who would certainly

have tortured her to death ... but the chief sternly
bade him depart, and as sternly reminded the Blackfoot girl that she belonged to his tribe, and could not
go with his enemies. Loretta was therefore compelled
to abandon his wife and child, and return to camp.

(This incident, wild as it sounds, is pretty well vouched for
in several places. Loretto appears on RMF's account books.
He settled his affairs with them shortly after, and he and his
Blackfoot wife [whether or not the same woman deponent
sayeth not] show up in 1835 as trader and interpreter at
Fort McKenzie. The romantic tradition demands the treatment as above; but it seems to me there may have been
another motive for Loretto's desperate dash with the child.
After all, what in God's name is a squawless mountain man
going to do with a baby?)

The final score on this scrimmage was nine Blackfeet,
three whites and six of their horses.

All contacts with Blackfeet this fall were not hostile, however. The results of McKenzie's grandiose treaty with these
"lords of the soil" were surprisingly in evidence. A band of
Piegans they encountered just before the above battle professed deep and undying friendship for everybody, and implied the state was permanent. (They had a white flag; the
King of the Missouri had told them to display this in token of
their friendship with the whites.) They could, however, speak
only for themselves. The Bloods, for example, were still
mean, and this batch of good-hearted Piegans warned
Bridger to be on his lookout for them.

All this is most likely covered by Doc Newell's cryptic
"(met some Black feet 60 warriors made piece with them
and the next day fought another party)   Returned to Psalmon
River and took up winter quarters."

III

The original winter quarters this year were on the Salmon
near the Forks. I frequently identify these places in modern
terms in hopes it will make a quick survey of movements
easier for the reader. In this case it can't be done. This is still
a primitive area and quite as wild as it was when the
wintering camps of '32–'33 were there. It's about 100 miles
southwest of Butte, Montana, and 140 miles northeast of
Boise, Idaho, in the Salmon National Forest.

The total wintering party was huge, consisting of not only the RMF brigades but Drips' men and assorted concentrations of Nez Perces and Flatheads that came and went.

In addition to these familiar faces there was also an encampment belonging to Captain Bonneville. At the time of Rendezvous 1832 Bonneville had been camped in the valley of the Green River, near Fontenelle's supply caravan. It had been his original intention to build a fort near the mouth of Horse Creek, and this post was in fact begun. (In the history books you will find it as Fort Bonneville or Bonneville's Old Fort. The mountain men called it variously Fort Nonsense or Bonneville's Folly. Four names, and it was never used.)

Information received from Fontenelle had convinced the captain that winters on the high plateau of the Green were too severe for a permanent post, and he moved on across the mountains. In transit he made a sort of grand tour of the summer's battlefields. In Jackson's Hole he found—and "decently interred"—the remains of the two men killed in the Gros Ventre ambush of Alfred Stephens' little party. He moved across the Tetons, camped on the site of the battle of Pierre's Hole, and was duly impressed by the evidences of recent activity there.

By the 26th of September he had reached the upper waters of the Salmon. He put his horses to pasture, threw up a temporary fortification, got out his sextant, and meticulously noted his latitude some fifty miles too far north. (The captain was a handy man with navigational procedure; he had also gotten the longitude of Fort Bonneville wrong by about 125 miles.)

The essentials accomplished, he settled down for his first winter in the mountains and was soon after joined by the wintering camps of RMF and the Company. During the fall his company was broken up into at least four smaller groups, trapping, getting lost, getting robbed, getting starved and shot up. Bonneville himself wandered about a good deal, acquiring, among other mementos of the mountains, a Nez Perce wife: "Not a young, giddy-pated girl, that will think of nothing but flaunting and finery, but a sober, discreet, hard-working squaw."

When Washington Irving was writing his book about Bonneville, he worked directly from Bonneville's journals and notes. Once in a while he quoted verbatim, apparently feeling that Bonneville's style was temporarily adequate. One such case was Bonneville's description of the free trapper's bride, given in connection with his own marriage. With Meek's description of Mountain Lamb in her finery, this forms the classic picture of the white-married squaw:

> The free trapper, while a bachelor, has no greater pet than his horse; but the moment he takes a wife (a sort of brevet rank in matrimony occasionally bestowed upon some Indian fair one, like the heroes of ancient chivalry in the open field), he discovers that he has a still more fanciful and capricious animal on which to lavish his expenses.
>
> No sooner does an Indian belle experience this promotion, than all her notions at once rise and expand to the dignity of her situation, and the purse of her lover, and his credit into the bargain, are taxed to the utmost to fit her out in becoming style. The wife of a free trapper to be equipped and arrayed like any ordinary and undistinguished squaw? Perish the grovelling thought! In the first place, she must have a horse for her own riding; but no jaded, sorry, earth spirited hack, such as is sometimes assigned by an Indian husband for the transportation of his squaw and her pappooses: the wife of a free trader must have the most beautiful animal she can lay her eyes on. And then, as to his decoration: headstall, breastbands, saddle and crupper are lavishly embroidered with beads, and hung with thimbles, hawks' bells, and bunches of ribbons. From each side of the saddle hangs an *esquimoot*, a sort of pocket, in which she bestows the residue of her trinkets and nick-nacks, which cannot be crowded on the decoration of her horse or herself. Over this she folds, with great care, a drapery of scarlet and bright-colored calicoes, and now considers the caparison of her steed complete.
>
> As to her own person, she is even still more extravagant. Her hair, esteemed beautiful in proportion to its length, is carefully plaited, and made to fall with seeming negligence over either breast. Her riding hat is stuck full of parti-colored feathers; her robe, fashioned somewhat after that of the white's is of red, green, and sometimes gray cloth, but always of the finest texture that can be procured. Her leggings and moccasins are of the most beautiful and expensive workmanship, and fitted neatly to the foot and ankle,

which with the Indian woman are generally well formed and delicate. Then as to jewelry: in the way of finger-rings, ear-rings, necklaces, and other female glories, nothing within reach of the trapper's means is omitted that can tend to impress the beholder with an idea of the lady's high estate. To finish the whole, she selects from among her blankets of various dyes one of some glowing color, and throwing it over her shoulders with a native grace, vaults into the saddle of her gay, prancing steed, and is ready to follow her mountaineer "to the last gasp with love and loyalty."

This description is a lot like a Hollywood Indian; a pretty white woman dressed up funny. Still, disregarding the genteelizing tone, the details are among the best we have. It is certainly true that—after liquor—most of the squaw men were kept broke buying foofaraw for their wives and had to get credit from the companies to outfit themselves with traps for the year's hunt. (Joe Meek says he paid for Mountain Lamb's outfitting: horse, $300; saddle, crupper and girths, $150; bridle, $50; "musk-a-moots," $50. But he is lying.)

It was even said that some of the free trappers bought foofaraw *before* liquor at rendezvous. . . .

Before the end of January, 1833, the companies were forced to move. The size of this encampment imposed an impossible drain on the grazing resources of the area. One RMF brigade moved across the Snake River plains to the junction of the Snake and Portneuf, present Pocatello, Idaho, while another moved to the Lemhi valley, not far from the Forks.

Grazing was not the only problem this winter. There were a lot of Blackfeet around who hadn't been listening attentively enough to McKenzie. War parties were on the prod all over eastern Idaho, even in the bitterest winter for many years. This was part of an early form of five-year plan. With the powder, lead, and guns they got from McKenzie's post the Backfeet had entered on a considered campaign to make the world safe for Blackfeet. Practically speaking, this worked out the way most such things have in history; it involved killing everybody that wasn't Blackfeet. First, according to their schedule, the Flatheads, Crows, and other tribes. Last of all, the white men; one can't cut the throat of one's armaments dealer until near the very end.

They made a good stab at it during the winter of '32–'33,

but it was costly. On Godin's River (present Big Lost River, in central Idaho) they attacked a village of Bannocks and Snakes, which turned out to be more than they had bargained for. The Blackfeet retreated to a willow grove; a grave tactical error, because the Snakes promptly fired the grove and butchered Bug's Boys as they were driven out by the flames.

Several other attacks occurred during the winter, and in general things were kept lively. It was late in the spring when the Blackfeet started moving north again, back to their home country. They made a passing swipe at a bunch of Flatheads— killing all but one, but suffering heavy losses themselves. Ammunition was low by that time; some reports said the mountain marauders were down to using stones for balls. So maybe it was time to put on a good heart and go see McKenzie, with a white flag.

There were at least two RMF brigades on the Spring '33 hunt, of which we have information on only one. This one, led by Milton Sublette and Jean Baptiste Gervais, intended to work the Malade River (present Big Wood) in southern Idaho. ("Malade"—I think—from the poison-beaver sickness of Peter Skene Ogden's HBC brigade there.)

On the 6th of April they were on their way south to the Malade, and had holed up from the severe weather in the canyon of Godin's River. There they were discovered by two "spies" who turned out to be from Captain Bonneville's party.

Bonneville was thoroughly disgusted at finding the RMF men moving in the same direction. He had been having troubles enough learning the trade, and this was the last straw. As he aptly evaluated the situation,

> to have to compete there with veteran trappers, perfectly at home among the mountains, and admirably mounted, while [we] were so poorly provided with horses and trappers, and had but one man ... acquainted with the country—it was out of the question.

RMF and Bonneville now camped near each other; "not out of companionship," says Irving, "but to keep an eye upon each other." Both parties were held up here. The extraordinary snows of this winter had blocked all exit from Godin's

River toward the Malade. Several times Milton and Gervais tried to push through and were turned back. In the meantime Bonneville hoped his horses would be gaining strength; the delay was in his favor.

Finally, toward the end of April, they made their way through.

Lucien Fontenelle had begun Bonneville's mountain education by stealing off a couple of the latter's Delaware hunters; RMF now put the polish to this rough learning.

> We shall not [says Irving] follow the captain throughout his trapping campaign, which lasted until the beginning of June, nor detail all the manoeuvres of the rival trapping parties and their various schemes to outwit and out-trap each other . . . after having visited and camped about various streams with varying success, Captain Bonneville set forward early in June for the appointed rendezvous.

Which, freely translated, means it was a massacre. Milton and Gervais mopped up southern Idaho with Bonneville's men. He arrived at Rendezvous 1833 with only twenty-two packs of beaver, having learned just how much "out of the question" it was to compete directly with the RMF brigades.

This is about the only information we have on RMF's Spring '33 hunt. Fitzpatrick, Bridger, and Fraeb are unaccounted for. The one man who might have helped out, Joe Meek, didn't. At the point in *River of the West* where Joe should have been detailing the spring hunt for the benefit of historians he was, instead, telling another story.

This is my favorite, and it happened at the second winter camp (on the Portneuf). Meek, Hawkins, Doughty, and Antoine Claymore[3] were out on a hunting party:

> As they traveled along under a projecting ledge of rocks, they came to a place where there were the impressions in the snow of enormous grizzly bear feet. . . .

At length Doughty proposed to get up on the rocks above the mouth of the cavern and shoot the bear as he came out, if somebody would go in and dislodge him.

"I'm your man," answered Meek.

"And I too," said Claymore.

"I'll be damned if we are not as brave as you are," said Hawkins, as he prepared to follow.

On entering the cave, which was sixteen or twenty feet square, and high enough to stand erect in, instead of one, three bears were discovered. They were standing, the largest one in the middle, with their eyes staring at the entrance, but quite quiet, greeting the hunters only with a low growl. Finding that there was a bear apiece to be disposed of, the hunters kept close to the wall, and out of the stream of light from the entrance while they advanced a little way, cautiously, towards their game, which however, seemed to take no notice of them. After maneuvering a few minutes to get nearer, Meek finally struck the large bear on the head with his wiping-stick, when it immediately moved off and ran out of the cave. As it came out, Doughty shot, but only wounded it, and it came rushing back, snorting and running around in a circle, till the well directed shots from all three killed it on the spot. Two more bears now remained to be disposed of.

The successful shot put Hawkins in high spirits. He began to hallo and laugh, dancing around, and with the others striking the next largest bear to make him run out, which he soon did, and was shot by Doughty. By this time their guns were reloaded, the men growing more and more elated, and Hawkins declaring they were "all Daniels in the lions' den, and no mistake." This, and similar expressions, he constantly vociferated, while they drove out the third and smallest bear. As it reached the cave's mouth, three simultaneous shots put an end to the last one, when Hawkins' excitement knew no bounds. "Daniel was a humbug," said he. "Daniel in the lions' den! Of course it was winter, and the lions were sucking their paws! Tell me no more of Daniel's exploits. We are as good Daniels as he ever dared to be. Hurrah for these Daniels!" With these expressions, and playing many antics by way of rejoicing, the delighted Hawkins finally danced himself out of his "lion's den," and set to work with the others to prepare for a return to camp. . . .

And ever after this singular exploit of the party, Hawkins continued to aver, in language more strong than elegant, that the Scripture Daniel was a humbug compared to himself, and Meek, and Claymore.

CHAPTER 20

"It appears that they make hats of silk"

KENNETH McKENZIE, King of the Missouri, was one of
the most energetic, capable men ever to engage in the trade.
He was a man of extraordinary practical imagination; and I
rather suspect he took the word "impossible" as a personal
affront. We have seen his vigor—and some of his prose
style—in the 1831 treaty with the Blackfeet and Assiniboines.

McKenzie, of course, was behind the various Company
brigades whose movements we have sketched here. And while
Vanderburgh-Fontenelle-Drips-Robidoux were carrying the
battle to RMF in the field, McKenzie was backing them up
with a prodigious show of energy. In order to understand the
mountain situation in this year of 1833, we will have to catch
up on activities Outside.

McKenzie's first major project on taking control of Fort
Union was to dispatch the interpreter Berger to the
Blackfeet; which foray ended in the incredible treaty of
1831. He had, for a starter, opened trade with the most
implacable enemies the whites ever encountered in the mountains.

Even before the treaty had been formally concluded,
McKenzie sent a trader into the heart of Blackfoot country.
On August 25, 1831, James Kipp and twenty-five men set out
from Fort Union to build a permanent post with Bug's Boys.
It was probably in the middle of October that Kipp arrived
at the mouth of the Marias River and Commenced his fort on

the angle between the Marias and the Missouri (roughly fifty miles downstream from present Great Falls, Montana).

This short-lived post was known, appropriately enough, as Fort Piegan. The Piegans were McKenzie's principal contact among the Blackfeet; which was good. They were the least bloodthirsty of the tribal divisions and were also the beaver hunters of the tribe.

McKenzie had no intention whatever of trapping in Blackfoot territory; that simply led to lifted hair and too little beaver. Lost scalps and gained furs ran too close to each other in number. (This is a feature of the fur trade observed by no less a body than the Hudson's Bay Company, whose rather chilling motto was *Pro Pelle Cutem:* For a Pelt, a Skin.)

And when white men set traps on Blackfoot land, the Piegans cheerfully joined in the massacre as a rudimentary conservation measure. This was no bright revelation, of course; the "wave of hostility" of 1823, resulting in the Aricara campaign, was directly attributable to just that. A great many Indians who were perfectly willing to trade their own catch were distinctly unreceptive to the idea of white men skimming off their beaver.

The Piegans were among the most hostile in this respect. The Ashley-Henry innovation of direct trapping on Indian land (which is still illegal, incidentally, by 1833) was regarded as a threat and imposition amounting to war. Beyond their normal aggressiveness, this is the principal reason the Blackfeet were so implacably hostile to the American parties and were yet able to get along, within reason, with the HBC traders across the line.

So, when McKenzie established Fort Piegan, his trader was very well received; according to report, 2,400 skins were brought in during the first ten days of trade. This would have been a good year's catch for twenty men; and gained without the enormous risk and usual loss that twenty men would sustain over a year.

The experiment was successful. Fort Piegan was soon destroyed, true, but it was almost a gesture of affection. When Kipp returned with his furs to Fort Union in the spring of '32, his men were afraid to remain behind. But the Piegans had been most anxious to have the post remain open through the summer; when the whites refused to do so, they got mad and burned it.

In fall '32 McKenzie dispatched another man, David

Mitchell, to take charge of Blackfoot affairs at the Marias. This almost went badly. Mitchell's party was accompanied by a number of Blackfeet, and he was carrying a load of presents for the tribes. On the plodding way up the Missouri from Fort Union, the keelboat *Fora* was broken from her moorings in a storm and lost on a sand bar, together with Mitchell's outfit and all the presents. For some indeterminate reason, the accompanying Blackfeet got it in their minds that the loss of the keelboat was deliberate, and an insult to the Lords of the Soil. This, for a time, made a touchy situation. However, Mitchell was outfitted again, and made his way safely to the Marias, where he found Fort Piegan burned and the surrounding bands in a bad mood.

Mitchell moved the location upriver six miles and began a frantic scurry to build a post before anything could happen to precipitate trouble. Several thousand Blackfeet were present at the beginning of this new post, and the whites lived precariously on their keelboat while the fort was being built. Mitchell somehow managed to maintain the peace, and when the stockade had been erected most of the hostiles drifted away. He named the post Fort McKenzie and settled down. The Company was now permanently enforted in the heart of the Blackfoot country.

McKenzie was not a man to rest on his laurels. No sooner had Fort Piegan been established among the Blackfeet than McKenzie began planning a fort to grab up the trade of the Crows. About the same time that Mitchell was building Fort McKenzie, a post was being constructed at the confluence of the Bighorn and Yellowstone for the Crows. Samuel Tulloch, erstwhile Smith Jackson & Sublette man, built this post, and the official name was Fort Cass, after Lewis Cass, then Secretary of War. (One of Tulloch's first orders of business was to relieve one of Bonneville's parties of their furs, while the surrounding Crows relieved them of their horses; a pattern is being established here.)

This is now the base situation of American Fur: Fort Union, at the mouth of the Yellowstone; principal headquarters for mountain operations, depot, supplier, trader. Fort McKenzie, near the mouth of the Marias; center for the Blackfoot trade. Fort Cass, at the mouth of the Bighorn, center of the Crow trade. In addition to the fixed posts, of course, were the mountain brigades. Ideally, these trapping parties would cover the country not easily available from the

Company forts; which is to say the west side of the divide, the Snake country.

McKenzie has one more innovation to his credit this summer of 1832: the first use of a steamboat on the upper Missouri. Largely through the urging of McKenzie, the Company had a steamboat built to their specifications which was called the *Yellowstone*. McKenzie was convinced—and managed to convince the other senior members of the Company—that the steamboat would be an enormous improvement over the customary keelboat travel up the Missouri.

In the spring of 1832 the *Yellowstone* made her first trip to the river she was named for[1] and demonstrated the "practicability of conquering the obstructions of the Missouri considered till almost the present day insurmountable to steamboats."

She carried as her principal passenger no less a personage than Pierre Chouteau, Jr., head of American's Western Department. Also on this trip was the famous painter of Indians, George Catlin.[2]

The voyage of the *Yellowstone* was very rightly hailed as an epochal achievement, and the enormous enthusiasm which greeted it was by no means restricted to the United States. Writing from France, John Jacob Astor noted (to Chouteau): "Your voyage in the *Yellowstone* attracted much attention in Europe, and has been noted in all the papers here."

(Mr. Astor was also making other observations in Europe during the summer of 1832; from London he comments almost casually: "I very much fear beaver will not sell well very soon unless very fine. It appears that they make hats of silk in place of beaver.")

II

There is a lovely sort of irony in the fact that the Company post on the Bighorn was named Fort Cass. Because in the fall of 1832, when the post was built, Lewis Cass was one of the worst enemies the Company had.

This odd situation came about as the result of the unceasing warfare waged by Congress against the fur trade. So it appeared to the trade, at any rate, though other eyes might see the situation in a less gloomy light.

The problem was liquor. Liquor had always been one of

the major points of difference between the government and the fur trade, and in 1832 it came to a head again.

Very briefly, this was the situation: Congress was deeply and profoundly concerned with the degradation of the Indian that resulted from the use of liquor in trade. One of the principal reasons for the original establishment of the government factory system was to eliminate the tragic impact of liquor on the native races. (This self-imposed prohibition was a major factor in the eventual destruction of the factory system.)

With the overthrow of the factory system in 1822, the government imposed the strictest sort of control on private traders, flatly forbidding the sale of liquor to Indians. It is one thing to forbid, of course, and quite another to enforce such an order. And enforcement was impossible. None of the traders paid any attention whatever. Some, perhaps, did go along with the government to the extent of not selling their liquor; they gave it away instead. This munificent gesture— performed just before trading sessions opened—was not a total loss to the trader.

Liquor thus destined for the Indian trade was nominally for the use of the traveling party. All right, this privilege was being misused, and the government cracked down a little tighter.

No liquor shall be imported into the Indian country at all, except for the specific ration granted boatmen, in recognition of their fantastic labors.

Wonderful. The race of boatmen proliferated at a rate quite amazing. It must have seemed that the world had been full of latent boatmen, only waiting an auspicious time to emerge from their cocoons. And in odd places, for boatmen.

Remember Bill Sublette's supply caravan to Pierre's Hole, Rendezvous 1832? Eighty-six men and three hundred animals? Boatmen all. Not one mile of the journey was made by water. Perhaps the animals were regarded as an experimental form of keelboat, however. On April 25, 1832, when Sublette took out his trading licenses, General Clark authorized him to take along 450 gallons of whiskey:

> Under authority vested in me by the Secretary of War to grant permission to Traders to take whiskey for the boatmen, limiting the quantity according to the time they are to be absent and taking bond that it is not to be used in trade, or barter, or to be given to

the indians ... for the specific use of his boatmen, when employed in the trade with the indians under the licenses granted him this day.

(This was not, strictly speaking, whiskey, but pure alcohol, later to be cut with water 3:1 (at first) making 1,350 gallons of "whiskey." The increase of dilution as the recipients got drunker increased the effective supply even more.)

Obviously, there was no difficulty in obtaining liquor for the trade regardless of government restrictions. General Clark was not deceived; but he was sympathetic to the traders, whose complaints he had to listen to. A few scattered references will show the attitude of the trade:

So violent is the attachment of the Indian for it that he who gives most is sure to obtain the furs ... No bargain is ever made without it.

(Without liquor) we are sure to lose the trade. . . . at all events *we must have it*.

Without it, competition is hopeless.

We must either abandon the trade or be permitted to use it.

Liquor I must have or quit any pretension to trade.

The more I think of it the clearer I see the injury we are going to sustain by being deprived of that article.

The point is sufficiently made. But in spite of the determined opposition of the trade through its lobbyists, Congress, in an act of July 9, 1832, prohibited the importation of liquor into Indian country under any pretext whatever. The "boat-men" would have to go dry. Further, steps were taken to implement the act by setting up inspection posts at Fort Leavenworth and Bellevue. Every boat going upriver had to stop for this liquor inspection.

This act, naturally, threw the trade into a panic. The greatest sufferers were the men of American Fur, inasmuch as they were much more dependent on river transportation (to Fort Union) than the competition. While this act was before Congress, every possible argument was advanced to block it, including the old stand-by of the American trade: the British Menace. Astor wrote in the spring of 1832, before this act was passed:

Wherever the trade is exclusively in the hands of our own citizens, there can be no doubt that the uniform and complete enforcement of such a law will be beneficial both to the Indians and the traders; but at those points where we come in contact with the Hudson's Bay Company we must either abandon the trade or be permitted to use it, to a limited extent at least, in order to counteract ... the influence of our rivals. ...

Our new posts ... must yield to the superior attractions of our opponents, unless the government will permit us like them to use spirituous liquors; and the friendly relations we have at last succeeded in establishing with the Blackfeet (those inveterate enemies of the Americans) at so much expense and personal hazard, must inevitably be destroyed, and the British be restored to the unlimited control they have heretofore exercised over these Indians.

If the Hudson's Bay Company did not employ ardent spirits against us, we would not ask for a single drop.

Interestingly enough, Astor was writing to our old friend, Congressman Ashley, appealing to him as a friend of the trade to throw his weight against passage of the prohibitory act. Ashley certainly had a soft spot in his heart for that good old trade (where he was still making money). But warmer still were his feelings for his political career; and political expediency dictated his enthusiastic acceptance of Administration measures. After the fact, Ramsay Crooks of the Company commented on this rather bitterly:

Had Ashley opposed the bill, his presumed knowledge of Indian trade would probably have been more than a match for the influence of the Secretary of War. But it was got up as one of the government measures of the session, and your representative, as a good Jackson man, gave it his unqualified support, and secured its passage.

After prohibition had gone into effect (in theory—General Clark issued several permits after this, on the grounds he had not been officially notified of the new law) Crooks and Astor still did not give up. Crooks himself went to Washington to present their case before Cass, the moving force behind the act: "I explained fully to Governor Cass. . . . I pointed out the pernicious tendency . . . I also placed before the secretary . . . I pressed upon his attention . . . I showed him. . . ."

Showed him nothing, really, but it was a terribly sad story he had to tell. As Crooks phrased it, the whole thing seemed to become a question of the honor of the United States:

> . . . our sole and only wish for a partial supply was to enable us to cope with our Hudson Bay opponents . . . relinquishing it voluntarily everywhere else. . . . I pointed out the pernicious tendency of its exclusion on our side, while they enjoyed the privilege to an unlimited extent; and the absolute certainty of the country being deluged by a larger supply than usual, purposely to show their superiority over us, degrading us, and with us the government, in the eyes of the Indians, by our withholding from them a gratification which was abundantly and cheerfully furnished by the British. I also placed before the secretary the dangers . . . flowing from this source, when stimulated by disappointment, and excited by our rivals to institute comparisons between themselves and us, which inevitably must lead to conclusions altogether unfavorable to the Americans . . . and lastly, the loss of influence which the government must sustain . . . when contrasted with the affluence and liberality of the British, who supplied every want, while we denied them [the Indians] the greatest of all gratifications. I showed him the entire prostration of all the philanthropic hopes of the government in enacting the late law, and tried to convince him that it would do infinitely more harm than good.

This concern for the national prestige and the philanthropic hopes of the government is really very touching, I think. And Secretary Cass was not unmoved by this appeal to his nobler instincts. It was, said Cass, entirely different if they just wanted to use the liquor in *defense*.

He would speak to the President and the Secretary of State about the matter at once. They would, he was certain, immediately enter into a correspondence with Great Britain, "and do all in their power to induce *that* government to exclude from the trade ... spirituous liquors, as effectually, as by law we have done on our side."

Crooks went home.

"Gov. Cass," he wrote gloomily to Pierre Chouteau, "is a temperance society man in every sense of the word."

Thus, with the act of July 9, 1832, began the craft, art, trade, and practice of smuggling liquor up the Missouri. This brought out the best of the American spirit: our ingenuity. The history of smuggling in succeeding years is fascinating in itself; I must—reluctantly—restrict myself here to very brief notice, since it is legitimately beyond the scope of this narrative. However, one episode I can't forbear. (This is stolen *in toto* from Chittenden's account.)

1843: the Company outfit for the year; steamboat *Omega*, Captain Joseph A. Sire, master. The *Omega* carried a distinguished passenger, the famous John James Audubon, prodigious naturalist and painter, whose reputation was already enviable. She also carried the usual stock of liquor.

The *Omega* safely ran past the inspection at Leavenworth, circumstances not noted, and approached the more critical scrutiny at Bellevue. When they reached there, Captain Sire discovered to his great joy that the agent was absent from the post; no inspection at all. Hastily he debarked his freight and got off again. He made upriver until nine that evening and, feeling himself out of danger, put in to shore for the night.

Next morning the *Omega* was scarcely off her mooring when she was stopped by several rifle shots across her bow. It seems the agent had left orders with a captain of dragoons, who was commanding troops in the area, to make the inspection for him. Captain Sire was handed *"un note polie du Capitaine Burgwin,"* informing him that the captain's duty required him to pay a visit to the boat.

Audubon carried credentials from the government, authorizing himself and party a little liquor, presumably on the basis of his prestige and reliability. These were shown to the lieutenant who had stopped them; he was duly impressed, and Audubon was "immediately settled comfortably." But the great naturalist suddenly developed a terrible urge to study the red-breasted dragoon captain in its natural habitat, and accordingly asked the young officer to take him to their camp, four miles away. (Captain Burgwin would be at the *Omega* shortly, for inspection, but never mind that.)

When they arrived at the dragoon camp, Captain Burgwin was astonished that such a prominent person should desire to visit with him; refused Audubon's credentials, saying his name was too well known throughout the United States to require any such thing.

There followed a pleasant and comradely visit, everyone in fine humor, everyone courteous and kind and obliging. Together, Audubon and Burgwin rode back to the *Omega*, the inspection thus having been delayed for better than two hours.

While Burgwin and Audubon were getting acquainted, the crew of the *Omega* had been scrambling frantically in the hold. The hold of a steamboat was divided by a partition that ran down the length of the boat. The main loading hatch was in the forecastle, near the center of the deck. There was a miniature railway in the hold, U-shaped. The legs ran on either side of the partition, and the curve where they joined was directly beneath the loading hatch. Thus, little tram cars could be loaded from the hatch and pushed along their tracks to the stern of the boat on either side. There was no source of light except that from the hatch and from candles. As a result, the hold was, in effect, pitch dark. In the two-hour delay provided by Audubon, the crew had pushed the train of cars all into one leg of the U, and loaded the kegs of whiskey on them.

Captain Burgwin was treated to lunch aboard the *Omega*. The pleasant company was rendered further amiable by the thoughtfulness of Audubon in providing the captain with some of the liquor authorized by his credentials.

After lunch, Burgwin "was in most excellent temper toward his hosts, and was quite disposed to forego the inspection altogether." Captain Sire insisted; nothing would do but that the captain should make his search, and, according to Sire's log, *"une recherche aussi stricte que possible."*

It was not often an inspector received an open invitation to make the strictest possible search, and the only condition Captain Sire added was that he should do the same with the other traders who came by. Only fair, certainly, and Captain Burgwin—"whose mellow faculties were now in a most accommodating condition"—agreed wholeheartedly.

The whole jolly party made its way down into the black hold; the captain was given a candle and steered into the proper, or empty, side. They moved back to the stern, making a strict search per agreement, and possibly even moving a bale now and then. At the stern they passed through an opening in the partition and began to work forward. The candle cast a limited circle of light. If the captain heard the rumble of little wheels—well, we all hear the rumble of little wheels once in a while, so be our hosts are as generous as Audubon. At the end of the hold the minuscule train was stealthily disappearing around the partition to the side already inspected.

All parted company the very best of friends, and the captain went back to his camp enchanted with the hospitality of John James Fougère Audubon and Joseph A. Sire, master of the *Omega*.

III

We left Nat Wyeth with his tiny band on the Snake River near Boise, Idaho, in the late summer of '32. The details of the remainder of his journey to Fort Vancouver are not essential; he had difficulty getting through the Blue Mountains, and the journal is a daily record of going supperless, traveling rough country, meeting Indians (not hostile), and so forth. He and a small portion of his party were ahead of the main body—a courtesy term only, since it was about seven men—and reached the HBC post at Walla Walla about five o'clock in the evening of October 14. Now he was amongst the dragons that guarded Oregon's gates.

Somewhat to his surprise, he was "received in the most hospitable and gentlemanly manner by Peanbron the agent for this post."[3] Wyeth had now been separated from civilization for a number of months; his present realities were rocks and rivers, buffalo and bear. Thus: "At the post we saw a bull and cow & calf, hen & cock, punkins, potatoes, corn, all of which looked strange and unnatural and like a dream."

It was, Wyeth discovered, not the only dreamlike thing about entering the sphere of influence of HBC. He embarked from Walla Walla five days later, after the rest of his men arrived, on one of the company "barges." When he reached Vancouver on October 29 he discovered not the barbarity he had learned to connect with the fur trade but a civilized outpost, stocked with books, and men who could and did read them.

Wyeth was received in the customary HBC manner; absolute and unlimited hospitality, right up to the point of business.

> I find Doct. McLauchland a fine old gentleman truly philanthropic in his Ideas he is doing much good by introducing fruits into this country which will much facilitate the progress of its settlement. . . . The gentlemen of this Co. do much credit to their country and concern by their education deportment and talents. . . . The Co. seemed disposed to render me all the assistance they can they live well at these posts.

And as for the good doctor, he cordially interviewed Wyeth (mistaking the name for "Dwight") on his journey. Wyeth arrived at Fort Vancouver around noon; before the day was out McLoughlin had a letter on its way to the Governor and Committee:

> He says he came to ascertain if possible to make a business of curing Salmon in this River, & at the same time to supply the American Trappers in the Rocky Mountains, but that from what he has seen on the way here, he thinks the latter would not answer, & that if possible, he will endeavor to go to St. Francisco, & return next Summer from thence across land to Salmon River, where the American Trappers are to assemble, & go home with the party that brings them their supplies. . . . It is impossible for us to say, in the short interview we have had with him, if these are his views or not; & though it may be as he states, still I would not be surprised to find that his views are in connexion with a plan which I see in a Boston paper of March 1831 to colonise the Willamette.

Once again the hospitable McLoughlin had more knowledge of his visitor than the visitor knew. Wyeth soon found himself in difficulty at Vancouver, however. Immediately on his arrival, his remaining eleven men wanted to desert. This was more or less expected, but the Honourable Company objected to the desertions; an interesting variation on this often-repeated theme. On a practical basis, McLoughlin virtually refused to permit Wyeth's men to desert him; watching for HBC's interest, as always, McLoughlin

[did] not wish to engage [them] no[r] to have them in
the country without being attached to some Co. able
to protect them alledging that if any of them are killed
they will be obliged to aveng it at an expense of money
and amicable relations with the Indians.

Obviously, the losses incurred in redeeming Jedediah Smith
still rankled at Fort Vancouver. The four-year-old memory
of Smith was fresh in McLoughlin's mind, and Wyeth came
up against it again, a little later, when he was refused
permission to accompany a party to the Umpqua. (Michel
Laframbois—*coureur du bois par excellence*—had gone on
another of his solitary trips and discovered that an HMC
party had been cut off and a man killed.)

I requested to accompany him but the Gov. would
not consent alledging the[y] would conceive that I
came to avenge the death of Mr. Smiths party ... all
which I interpreted into a jealousy of my motives.

It was a wrong interpretation; McLoughlin simply knew
his people.

The problem of Wyeth's men could not be deferred for-
ever. By the middle of November McLoughlin had finally
agreed to permit them to remain at Vancouver until they
could get passage home. Accordingly, Wyeth released them
from any obligation to his own expedition.

I have therefore now no men ... they were good
men and persevered as long as perseverance would
do good   I am now afloat on the great sea of life
without stay or support but in good hands   i.e. myself
and providence and a few of the H. B. Co. who are
perfect gentlemen.

If Wyeth was afloat, it was more than could be said for his
depended-upon supply · ship, the *Sultana* (see Appendix
B). She had broken up on a reef, and sinking, took with her
the last of Wyeth's hopes. Now he was completely destitute,
without men, without supplies, without prospects, having
"lost largely from a capital at first small."

Being Nathaniel Wyeth, he immediately began devising
plans for a second expedition to the Oregon country. The
salmon business still looked good to him; the resources of the

Willamette valley charmed him. The only problem was finan-cing this second effort, and perhaps this might be done through the kindly gentlemen of HBC.

He wrote Governor Simpson his proposition. (This would have been with McLoughlin's permission, possibly even his encouragement.)

Briefly, it amounted to the notion that HBC should provide Wyeth with goods—and, if possible, men—with which he could prosecute a trading business. The implied intent was to do his trading with the Rocky Mountain hunters; in effect, another supply train at rendezvous. These American furs he would then transport back to Fort Vancouver and sell to HBC. He bound himself "to deliver all Furs and skins of every description of which he may get possession to the Co," and offered to post bond for faithful performance.

But we have seen George Simpson's reluctance to infringe on American territory through the medium of a citizen (in his refusal of Pilcher's proposal). It was probably on this basis that Wyeth's idea was finally rejected. (On Wyeth's second trip, he did make an agreement with McLoughlin—though not the same—and McLoughlin's action was disap-proved by the Governor and Committee.)

The adventurer iceman spent the remainder of the winter of '32–'33 at Fort Vancouver, "eating and drinking the good things to be had there and enjoying much the gentlemanly society of the place." He explored most of the surrounding area, making trips to the coast and some distance down the Willamette valley (to present Salem).

When a nominal spring came—February 3, 1833—Wyeth set off with Francis Ermatinger, HBC partisan bound for the Flathead country. Ermatinger, who was by this time a good friend, had in charge three boats loaded with supplies for HBC's mountain expeditions and twenty-one men. Wyeth himself had been able to hire only two men to accompany him back to the mountains.

By the 7th of April they reached the Flathead post. Er-matinger deposited his goods at the post and then embarked for the south on a trapping expedition toward the Snake country. Wyeth went along, and they were shortly in the area where Fitzpatrick and Bridger had played leapfrog with Henry Vanderburgh the previous fall.

Wyeth now lost one of his men—"he appeared to think that as I had but two he might take libertys under such circumstances I will never yield an inch"—paid him half his wage and kept moving.

They encountered a huge Flathead camp, and Wyeth recorded his impressions. (Since most of the mountain journals are concerned with hostilities, I give some of Wyeth's observations here as a mild antidote.)

> ... upward of 1000 souls with all of which I had to shake hands   the Custom in meeting these indians is for the Coming party to fire their arms then the other does the same   then dismount and form single file both sides and passing each other shake hands with men women and children a tedious job. [Indians invariably accentuated what they took from the white men, whether it be drunkenness or handshaking. Nothing halfway.]
>
> Theft is a thing almost unknown among them and is punished by flogging as I am told but have never known an instance ... the least thing even to a bead or pin is brought you if found and things that we throw away   this is sometimes troublesome   I have never seen an Indian get in anger with each other or strangers. I think you would find among 20 whites as many scoundrels as among 1000 of these Indians they have a mild playful laughing disposition. . . . They are polite and unobtrusive and however poor never beg except as pay for services.

While camped with these genial Flatheads, Wyeth observed a phenomenon that struck very close to home:

> ... there is a new great man no[w] getting up in the Camp and like the rest of the world covers his designs under the great cloak religion ... when he gets enough followers he will branch off and be an independent chief   he is getting up some new form of religion among the Indians more simple than himself   like others of his class he works with the fools women and children first   while ... the men of sense thinking it too foolish to do harm stand by and laugh but they will soon find that women fools and children form so large a majority that with a bad grace they will have to yield. These things make me think of ... New England.[4]

They were now in Blackfoot country, and Wyeth's journal for May and June of 1833 is a running record of scares, skirmishes (reported), and thefts. Thus they worked south across the divide, and by the first of July were just east of Henry's Fork. They found some of Bonneville's men here, and a couple of days later moved over to join camps with the captain.

Now Wyeth's always-flexible plans took another bend. He had received word of Bonneville's presence in the Salmon River country as early as June 22. Wyeth had immediately dispatched an express, inviting Bonneville into a partnership to trap the country south of the Columbia. The plan was—as he had mentioned to McLoughlin—to work as far south as San Francisco.

When he came up with Bonneville on the 4th of July, the latter apparently agreed to the proposition, for Wyeth immediately wrote a spate of letters to the East, giving rough details of the plan. But even before the letters had been dispatched something happened; for unknown reasons—Irving mentions this episode not at all—Bonneville backed out.

The three camps—HBC under Ermatinger, Bonneville, and Wyeth—remained together for four days. A batch of Bonneville's men declined to accompany him any farther, and set out on a trapping expedition for the Nez Perce. Ermatinger and his brigade also departed on the occasions of their trade, leaving Wyeth and the captain to continue together.

They broke camp the 7th of July; down Henry's Fork to Pierre's Hole, across Teton Pass into Jackson's Hole; reversing the route Bonneville had covered getting to the Salmon River country for his fall '32 hunt.

On the 15th of July they came down into the Green River valley to the original site of Bonneville's Fort Nonsense.

> Found here collected Capt. Walker, Bonneville, Cerry, of one Co. Dripps & Fontenelle of the Am. Fur Co. Mr. Campbell just from St. Louis, Mess. Fitzpatric, Gervais, Milton Sublette of the Rocky Mountain Fur Co. and in all the Cos. about 300 whites and a small village of Snakes . . .

gathered at Green River for Rendezvous 1833.

CHAPTER 21

"Float down and see what the world is made of there"

I WANT to recapitulate here, very briefly. There are now so many parties in the mountains—and the years so eventful—that it is difficult for a reader to hold a picture in his mind while following any of the separate movements. I hope a short synopsis of the year will make things a little more comprehensive.

After Rendezvous 1832 in Pierre's Hole:

(1) Rocky Mountain Fur Co. Two main brigades. One, under Milton Sublette, pushed down into the barren, starving country between the Humboldt and Owyhee Rivers; turned back up into Idaho and completed the Fall '32 hunt on the waters of the Salmon River. Winter camp on the Salmon, Spring '33 hunt in southern Idaho, on the Malade, competing with Bonneville.

Second brigade under Fitzpatrick and Bridger. Into Three Forks area by way of Salmon River country, pursued all the way by Henry Vanderburgh of American Fur. After Vanderburgh's death, down to winter quarters with Milton's brigade on the Salmon. Winter camp moved, part of the RMF force going to the Portneuf in January, '33.

(2) American Fur Company. Vanderburgh and Drips pursued the RMF brigade of Bridger and Fitz during the fall. Vanderburgh killed. Drips and the remainder wintered near RMF in central Idaho, and made their Spring '33 hunt on Idaho and Montana streams. Small contingent looked over Flathead trade and found it good. McKenzie building forts to take Blackfoot and Crow trade.

339

(3) Wyeth. Accompanied Milton Sublette out of Pierre's Hole, then separated and continued to Fort Vancouver. His ship had been wrecked and sunk, his men all left him. Returned to Rendezvous 1833 with an HBC brigade under Ermatinger, planning a second expedition.

(4) Bonneville. Not at Rendezvous 1832, but on Green River. Early fall, over into central Idaho and Salmon River country, where his party was split into many scattered brigades with varying degrees of catastrophe. Wintered on Salmon. Spring hunt in competition with RMF on the Malade, which was unsuccessful.

(5) Bill Sublette. Took over banking and supplying RMF on an official basis at Rendezvous 1832. Returned to the settlements with furs collected and began to prepare his assault on the American Fur Company.

It now remains to account in detail for the activities of Bill Sublette in fall of '32 and spring of '33.

The returning caravan reached Lexington by the 21st of September, 1832. Bill sat down and wrote an account to Ashley of the battle of Pierre's Hole, which was later published in the *Missouri Republican*. Along with the story of the fight, the newspaper published a brief editorial comment: "We are gratified to learn that Mr. S. has determined to discontinue his mountain excusions, and locate himself in the immediate vicinity."

It is perhaps uncharitable to conclude that Bill was doing a bit of judicious misdirection; it may have been a rumor, or a misunderstanding of some other comment. Still, it would have been decidedly to his advantage to have it believed he was quitting the mountains.

On the way in, Sublette and Campbell met an august personage in western Missouri, Washington Irving, traveling with a government commission to inspect Indian Lands, and getting background for the two books he was to write about the trade.[1] He described this brigade of Sublette's:

We remember to have seen them with their band. ... Their long cavalcade stretched in single file for nearly half a mile. Sublette still wore his arm in a sling. The mountaineers in their rude hunting dresses, armed with rifles and roughly mounted, and leading their pack-horses down a hill of the forest, looked like banditti returning with plunder. On top of some of the packs were perched several half-breed children, perfect little imps, with wild black eyes glaring from among elf locks. These, I was told, were children of the trappers; pledges of love from their squaw spouses in the wilderness.

The late summer of 1832 had seen a cholera epidemic sweep down the Ohio. When Sublette arrived, the panic and hysteria of the plague were just diminishing.[2]

Sublette arrived in St. Louis on October 3. The next two months were taken up with small business—settling RMF's accounts with their men, for example. The furs themselves he had turned over to Ashley, who in turn had them sold through his own brokers, Frederick Tracy & Company.

By the last part of November Bill and Robert Campbell must have hashed out at least the main outlines of their plan. They did not yet have a formal partnership, but there is no doubt it had been arranged. Together they set out from St. Louis on about the 1st of December, bound for the East this time.

Their first business stop was Washington, D.C., and Congressman Ashley. The ambitious plans they had in mind would require credit; much credit, and Ashley was—as always—"a person of credit." With the moral backing of the congressman, Sublette and Campbell would have little difficulty in obtaining backing of a somewhat more substantial kind from commercial firms. Bob Campbell already had one good contact; brother Hugh, Philadelphia businessman, whose warm affection for his brother was exceeded only by his disapproval of his business "amongst those Black footed Black hearted & Blk headed Savages."

Brother Hugh was high on the list of visits to be made this winter, in spite of the fact that he had written Robert as recently as November 14: "What you have done during your late expedition I neither know nor (in a certain point of view) do I care ... I am disgusted with your late mode of life."

Washington, Philadelphia, New York—with Ashley's letters of introduction in hand, they found most of the firms approached amenable to their ideas. It was a confused and harrying winter for both men, back and forth from merchant to merchant, banker to banker; the only real respite being the genial hospitality of Hugh Campbell. Hugh was immediately taken with Bill Sublette and they became close friends.

Formal arrangements for the partnership had been delayed until they could see Ashley; get his reactions (and, not least important, get an estimate of the available credit). Ashley's approval was wholehearted, and the Articles of Copartnership were drawn up on December 20. Operating "under the name and style of Sublette & Campbell," the company was capitalized at $6,000, half from each of the partners. (This was only a fraction of the amount to be involved in this expedition; witness that Ashley was authorized to buy two fully rigged keelboats for Sublette & Campbell, to be at Pittsburgh by February 20, 1833.)

The keelboats were attached to a steamboat, and on the 22nd they moved out, down the Ohio to Louisville. Sublette stopped there to buy a ton of tobacco and some alcohol. (While in Washington he had examined the new liquor law. Wine seemed to be permissible. Throw in a few grapes with the tobacco and call it wine instead of whiskey, then. But let's get on with it.)

By March 4, 1833, Sublette was back in St. Louis with his keelboats and ready to begin the great project.

There were two phases to the expedition, one overland and one upriver, with basically different ends. Bob Campbell was to conduct the supply party to Rendezvous 1833 by the usual Platte-Sweetwater-South Pass route. Sublette himself was ascending the Missouri in one of the keelboats, his ultimate destination being the mouth of the Yellowstone and Fort Union.

On the way upriver Sublette would drop off a trader and crew to open a post beside every American Fur Company post on the Missouri. Snuggled up to their competition, these Sublette & Campbell posts would compete directly for the river trade. The Sioux, Mandans, Kiowas, Kanzas would all find themselves with a choice of posts.

And the principal fort of Sublette & Campbell was to be built at the mouth of the Yellowstone under Mr. Kenneth McKenzie's nose.

It is unlikely that Sublette & Campbell expected any great returns from these posts. The Company traders had been established along the river for a long time, enjoying a virtual monopoly of trade, and they would doubtless be able to hold their own against the small newcomers. But as a tactic of annoyance Sublette's notion was superb. And what he hoped for was to annoy John Jacob Astor into reaching for his wallet (as he had done before, with the Columbia Fur

Company at the Mandans). A mosquito can't kill a bear, but it might make him react; if Astor held to his usual position, the reaction would be to buy out the opposition.

Campbell and his party went overland from St. Louis to Lexington and took up camp there around the 20th. Sublette, with the two keelboats towed behind the steamboat *Otto*, arrived there about a week later. Goods from one of the keelboats were transferred to Campbell's overland party, completing the final outfitting, and they were ready to go by May 7.

There were some strangers on the Missouri in spring '33; strange people, and even stranger motives.

One of these was a fiery, irascible, toothless German, traveling under the name Baron Braunsberg. This was Maximilian, Prince of Wied-Neuwied. The Prince was also a major general in the Prussian Army (against Napoleon), recipient of the Iron Cross, and gentleman scientist. His military exploits were more or less involuntary; the Napoleonic Wars gave the Prussian nobleman no choice in the matter. At heart he was an ethnologist, (in spite of the fact that the field did not then exist). Maximilian was of a now-defunct breed, the gentleman amateur of science. He had a reasonable background in geology, botany, and zoology—all of which were useful—but his main interest was in the Indians of the Americas. He had made a study of South American indigenes—it had gained him a considerable reputation—and was now embarking on a similar project with the Indians of North America.

He had two traveling companions. Charles Bodmer, an artist who was to do illustrative matter for Maximilian's book (and whose paintings are frequently used today for the same purpose), and one Dreidoppel, manservant. (It was Maximilian's pleasure to bellow angrily for Herr Dreidoppel on any occasion. Owing to the Prince's toothless condition this was a very interesting bellow. He bellowed also at Mr. Bodmer, but the effect was apparently not so impressive.)

Maximilian fell in with the King of the Missouri, who was in St. Louis during the winter. The Company steamboat *Yellowstone* got away from St. Louis on April 10 with Maximilian and entourage aboard, and the Prince of Wied-Neuwied entered Indian country under the auspices of Kenneth McKenzie.

McKenzie got the Prussian; Sublette & Campbell, too, had their nobleman, and several others. Theirs was William

Drummond Stewart, heir to the barony of Grandtully; a Scotsman, soldier (ex), sportsman and hunter, and occasional novelist of the American West he was about to enter. Stewart, to jump ahead a bit, was highly regarded by the mountain men with whom he lived in succeeding years; and their respect is some measure of the man. He is described as being on "a trip of pleasure," an adventure, an outing. He did it up brown and had a enormously good time at it. (Stewart's mountain activities are admirably detailed in Bernard DeVoto's *Across the Wide Missouri*.)

At the Lexington camp preparatory to moving out, Campbell also picked up Benjamin Harrison, physician and alcoholic. Harrison was going—or being sent—to the mountains in hopes of being cured of the latter. He was the son of William Henry Harrison, presently retired but soon to become President of the United States.

The last of the occasionals was Edmund Christy of St. Louis. Information is wanting on this man; about all we know is that he was about to invest in RMF to the tune of $6,600 and become a full partner.

Altogether the overland party consisted of about fifty men and the cavalcade of merchandise—loaded mules. Cattle and sheep—a herd of twenty—were driven with the caravan to provide food until they reached buffalo country. They got off early in May; and Sublette started upriver with his keelboat a little later.

II

Rendezvous 1833: "Saturnalia among the mountains," says the literary Mr. Irving; "powerful drunk," says Joe Meek.

Rendezvous is now a thoroughly established institution in the mountains, and we might pause briefly to survey the changes that have taken place in the structure of the fur trade since the opening of this narrative.

The revolution begun by the first Ashley-Henry expeditions has now come nearly full circle. Their great innovation—taking brigades of white trappers, rather than merely trading with Indians—turns out, on close inspection, to have produced a little less change in the trade than it is given credit for.

The mainstay of the companies is, by now, the free trapper; independent, allied only loosely (and through debt) with any particular company, living his own life in the mountains.

These men would, from year to year, travel in fairly small bands and sometimes even alone, like Bill Williams. Their trapping route for a fall and spring season might take them a round-trip distance of two thousand miles or so, but by rendezvous time they would always be back in western Wyoming or eastern Idaho for Sublette's watered-down alcohol and their two-week spree. For this two weeks there would be coffee and sugar, flour, salt, seasonings—all the amenities. The rest of the year it was meat and water.

They were, in fact, Indians, and this is the point I want to make. The trade has, in the run of this narrative, nearly returned to the state in which we found it: trading at posts from the Indians. The major difference now is that some of the Indians had been born with white skins. And the post from which the trade was carried on was semiportable: the rendezvous.

The free trappers adopted everything about Indian life: dress, morals, attitudes, skills, language frequently, and religion fairly often. And along with the benefits of the Indian good life they also took over some of the disadvantages, the principal of these being the fact that they were thoroughly exploited as economic resources by the whites. (Whites in this particular case being defined as those who still owed their loyalties to the civilized centers: the McKenzies and Sublettes and Chouteaus of the trade.)

Most of the men of this narrative whose names are familiar—Fitzpatrick, Bridger, Carson, Bill Williams—are famous not as trappers but as guides in the years after the collapse of the trade. Piloting immigrant trains to Oregon, leading military reconnaissances and war parties and exploratory teams—steering the civilized through country only the trappers knew. This, traditionally, is the Indian function, and in the narratives of these later journeys we find our quondam mountain men described in terms usually reserved for Indians. Taciturn, dispassionate, unemotional—there was always a qualitative difference between the guides and the men they guided.

The characterization is clichéd and inaccurate, of course. In modern times the ubiquitous vacant grin of the American has given us the reputation in large parts of the world of being somewhat loose-witted. We flatter ourselves that such is not the case, and we may even be right. But the international personality of America is that of our unfailing goodfellowship, tinged with feeble-mindedness; and largely this has come about through our purely ritualistic habit of grinning foolishly at one another when there is nothing to smile about. Our traditional characterization of the stony-faced Indian is based on the same kind of evidence. The lack of emotion is, of course, purely fiction. But it was derived from the fact that this was one of the social graces of many American Indian tribes. The expressionless mask was the trading face, the politic face, the face-with-strangers. And this was quickly assumed by many of the free trappers, along with the other accouterments of Indian life.

The great accomplishment and pride of the mountain man was in being a better Indian than the Indians; a better tracker, hunter, woodsman, warrior—everything. The caption on a popular cartoon of the day—showing two mountain men—was "I tuk ye fur a Injun." This was, in fact, the highest compliment that could be paid, and any greenhorn who came up with it on first meeting was sure to be in the good graces of that trapper from then on.

What the innovation of Ashley and Henry finally produced was, in effect, a new tribe in the West. And through the medium of rendezvous, these new men were dealt with as were the other tribes; and as the Indians had been dealt with before the introduction of white trappers into the country.

The men of the time who were tracking down legends of white Indians would have done well to be at rendezvous come summer; that's where they were.

The companies were congregated around the mouth of Horse Creek when Bonneville and Wyeth pulled in from the north. Bonneville stopped at his Fort Nonsense (about five miles above Horse Creek) while Wyeth and the RMF brigades moved about ten miles downriver. American Fur—Drips—stayed put.

The Company had sent its supply outfit again this year by Lucien Fontenelle; and again he had been beaten, but this time only by a few days. (From the rendezvous Fontenelle wrote miserably to his boss Chouteau: "We have always been too late and our opponents . . . make a great boast of it.")

While Bob Campbell's train was still en route, a few miles above the Laramie, Old Frapp and two other RMF men had ridden out to meet it. They camped together for a couple of days while Campbell and Fraeb negotiated in advance for the Sublette & Campbell goods. Fraeb took, for RMF, everything but a couple of mules and ten barrels of "whiskey." A little later, Tom Fitzpatrick rode out to deliver RMF's catch for the year. For some reason, the major business between Sublette & Campbell and RMF was negotiated this year before Campbell even reached rendezvous.

Major excitement this year came from a rabid wolf—or wolves—prowling the neighborhood. (Wyeth thought there was only one, because when one camp was attacked, the others were not.)

Nine men were bitten at the Company encampment, and three from RMF. For several nights one or the other of the camps would be wakened by the maddened bellowing of frightened animals or the screams of a bitten man.

A Company chronicler relates the eerie disintegration of one of the victims, who constantly asked if they thought he could go mad. When a bull that had been attacked began to bellow constantly, the man became paralyzed with fear and panic. According to report, he developed an inordinate fear of water, and had to be carried across streams rolled up in a blanket (which sounds rather as though the writer were taking the name "hydrophobia" somewhat too literally).

(Several of the wolf-bitten died, by report—but this can't be established. The episode of the attack itself became one of the stories of the trade, and it would be recorded they had died whether it happened or not. At least two deaths seem well documented.)

Joe Meek, of course, was not bitten. He was powerful drunk at the time, though, and would have been easy prey, lying insensible in his blanket roll. Captain Stewart said as much to him later, and Joe cheerfully agreed. However, he figured his alcohol content was high enough that it would either have killed the wolf or cured him; didn't greatly matter which.

Competition for men was stiffer this year than it had ever been. Bonneville—by Fontenelle's report—was paying up to $1,000 a year for trappers; an utterly fantastic sum. He had come into Rendezvous 1833 with only about 22½ packs of beaver. What with the horses and gear he'd lost through the winter, the captain was in the hole. But Bonneville, like others since, had a notion he could get rich in California. (His leave from the army was due to expire in three months; but he'd gotten a taste of "wild scenes and wild adventures, and ... vast and magnificent regions." He wasn't about to go home broke because of a little thing like the United States Army.)

Wyeth sat down and wrote out his impressions of the rendezvous for his new friend Ermatinger, of HBC:

> I found here about 250 whites. A list of the Cos. and their Beaver which I have seen I subjoin. I should have been proud of my countrymen if you could have seen the American Fur Co. or the party of Mr. S. Campbell. For efficiency of goods, men, animals and arms, I do not believe the fur business has afforded a better example of discipline. I have sold my animals and shall make a boat and float down the Yellowstone and Missouri and see what the world is made of there. Mr. Wm Sublette and Mr Campbell have come up the Missouri and established a trading fort at each location of the posts of the Am. Fur. Co. with a view to a strong opposition. Good luck to their quarrels. . . .
>
> In my opinion you would have been Robbed of your goods and Beaver if you had come here altho it is the west side of the Mts. . . . I give you this as an honest opinion which you can communicate to the Co. There is here a great majority of Scoundrels. I should much doubt the personal safety of any one from your side of the house.

Part of the business accomplished at Rendezvous 1833 was the formation of a new company. To my knowledge, this company has never appeared in the histories, and for very good reason, too:

> Articles of Copartnership and agreement Made and entered into this Twentieth day of July in the year of our Lord one thousand Eight Hundred and thirty three by and between thomas Fitzpatrick Milton G. Sublette John B Jervais James Bridger and Henry Freab associated under the name and furm of the rocky Mountain furr Cº of the one part and Edmund T. Christy of the other part
> Witness
> 1 the furm Shall transact business under the name and furm of the rocky Mountain furr Cº & Christy and Shall Continue one year after the date hereof—
> 2ᵈ The said rocky Mountain furr Cº have furnished a certain amount of Merchandize Horses & Mules &c. amounting to per Invoice annexed Six thousand Six

Hundred and Seven dollars and Eighty two & ½ cents besides Twelve Men hired Whose wages are to be paid Jointly.

There are three other articles, providing that RMF be paid in "Beaver furr as it may be caught and Traded for indiscriminately" at $3.25 a pound; losses and profits to be equally distributed among the parties; RMF and Christy both agreeing to "devote personal Services" to conducting the business.

The reason this hasn't appeared in accounts of the time is that this document exists in total isolation. Nothing more is ever heard of the Rocky Mountain Fur Company & Christy. When RMF folded, no mention was made of Christy; his partnership was not bought out, his interest not accounted for. An interesting point for speculation, but until more information turns up I'm afraid any speculation must remain somewhat airy.

When the returns of the year were tallied up, the emerging picture was not bright. In his letter to Ermatinger, Wyeth gave the following account (Wyeth reports number of packs; further calculations mine):

The American Fur Company catch amounted to 51 packs. By the time the returning caravans reached St. Louis, beaver there had dropped to a new low; $3.50 a pound. Figure 5,000 lbs @ $3.50=$17,500. They had 160 men to pay off—some of them at the inflated wages beginning to be prevalent—had suffered the usual losses during the season, and had to pay for new supplies. There would be no profit for the Company this year, not from their field operations.

Bonneville's 22½ packs were worth less than $8,000. In all probability he was unable to pay all his men, much less cover supplies and losses. (Fontenelle to McKenzie: "If he [Bonneville] continues as he has done, $80,000 will not save him.")

Our main interest being RMF, we are pleased to see that their hunt had been slightly better than the others: 61 or 62 packs, say 6,000 pounds, $21,000. If transportation to St. Louis was at the previous rate of 50 cents a pound, this reduces the net to $18,000 on arrival there. Deduct the $5,000 owed Bill Sublette=$13,000. Deduct cost of supplies, roughly $15,000,[3] and they are back in debt by $2,000. There were also 55 men to be paid. Bridger and Fraeb lost all their horses to an Aricara band during the year. The same happened to a small party under Black Harris. While we don't know the number of animals lost, it is sufficient to remember the mountain price of $50–$60 each. The further diminution through handling expenses, interest, and so forth (as seen in the 1832 catch) pushed the deficit up and up.

By reason of the unknown factors, it isn't possible to make an exact estimate of RMF's loss for the season. It could not have been less than $12,000–$15,000—a very conservative estimate—and all of it went into the books of Sublette & Campbell, drawing interest of from 6 to 8 per cent.

But what the hell; it's just money. They still had their hair, and the climate was nice (in the summer).

III

Rendezvous 1833 lasted about ten days, from July 15 to 24. Since the greater part of Bob Campbell's merchandise had been disposed of to RMF, there was little left for him to do but sell off the remaining whiskey and watch the celebration.

When time came to disperse on the Fall '33 hunt, the RMF men, like Caesar's Gaul, were divided into three parts.

Henry Fraeb (and possibly Gervais with him) took about twenty men down the Green into Colorado, probably intending to work southern streams of the Green during the fall of '33, then swing over and come back north through the Colorado Parks for his Spring '34 hunt. He had with him Bill Williams, one of the great legendary figures of the trade. In later years Bill was to become the outstanding loner in the mountains; tough, mean, and independent. It was a mountain byword that a man didn't want to walk in front of Bill Williams in starvin' times.[4]

Edmund Christy, the brand-new partner, had a brigade of about twenty-five men. They were off for the west slope of the Rockies, Snake country, possibly down to touch Digger country, by one report. In any event, they expected to winter somewhere along the Snake. (The Company brigade under Drips also moved west across the divide, but there was no recorded conflict this season. They were probably working north of Christy's men, in the Flathead country.)

The three remaining partners—Milton Sublette, Fitzpatrick, and Bridger—started out from the Green in company with Bob Campbell's returning supply train. Wyeth was also with this group, which was by far the largest. (Even Bonneville was, for a while, their unseen shadow. The competitive tactics had begun to make him rather nervous and he preferred to keep out of sight as long as possible, marching parallel to the main party.)

Campbell was not taking the furs back to St. Louis via the Sweetwater-Platte route this year. Instead, he was to descend the Bighorn and Yellowstone to the Missouri, where he would meet his partner Bill Sublette. Bill, in theory, would have set up the Sublette & Campbell posts in competition with the Company, and be preparing their fort at the mouth of the Yellowstone, near McKenzie's Fort Union.

Fitzpatrick was to accompany Campbell to the Bighorn, where the load of furs could be transferred to bullboats. Fitz, then taking command of the horses for RMF, would work that general area (Crow Country) for his Fall '33 hunt.

The trip was enlivened by mountain sport of several kinds; for one thing, according to Wyeth, the Green River valley was a "Country covered with buffalo." On the second day out one of the hunters fell from his horse while running a bull. The enraged buffalo turned and charged twice—missing both times. The man finally scrambled to his feet, recovered his rifle, and killed the animal; discovering the reason for the inaccurate charges, which was more than a man could reasonably hope for. The bull was blind in one eye, and simple luck had put the hunter on the blind side.

A couple of days later the Scots sportsman Stewart (who was still with Campbell's train) "had some sport with a bear near our camp which he wounded, but did not kill. He represented him as large as a mule."

Nor was Wyeth (whose journal is being quoted) confined to reporting the escapades of others alone. He had his own adventure with a white bear, brought on by an uncharacteristic spasm of sheer idiocy. Shortly after they reached the Sweetwater Wyeth rode on ahead of the camp a bit and came on "a white bear in a thickett."

Our redoubtable iceman got a bit heated at this point, for he fired his pistol into the thicket. This producing no noticeable result, he cheerfully started to heave rocks in, infuriating the bear:

> ... he came as though he meant to fight us [says Wyeth, seeming almost surprised at this turn] but I gave him the shot of my rifle through the body. He then rushed on us and I ran as fast as I could Mr.

Kamel snapped at him Mr Sublette ran also being on a mule.

The bear chased them off a short distance, and then ran up a creek. Several of the party followed him on horseback and finished him off with four more shots.

The next day, this combined Campbell-Wyeth-Fitzpatrick brigade came on four whites in a bad way. These four were from Bridger's party (which seems to have been trapping along their route) and had run afoul of some Shoshones, a roving band of fifteen or so. (This by report, though the valley of the Pop Agie is a little far-flung for Snakes, particularly a band as small as this.) There hadn't been any manifest hostility at their first meeting—the Shoshones were generally friendly to whites—just a little smoke together, and the Indians departed peaceably enough. A couple of days later, however, they returned, for the horses. Thompson had fallen asleep while the other three were out hunting. Hearing a noise among the horses, he figured his partners had come back to water them. He opened his eyes, and found himself staring into the muzzle of an Indian fusil. The Snake fired immediately. Thompson must have jerked his head, because the ball "entered . . . outside the eye and breaking the cheek bone passing downward and lodged behind the ear in the neck this stunned him and while insensible an arrow was shot into him on the top of the shoulder downward which entered about 6 inches, the Inds got 7 horses all there were."

(Wyeth then says that another member of this party— "Charboneau"—chased the Snakes on foot. This may have been one of the most famous half-breeds in American history: Baptiste Charbonneau, the child born to Sacajawea with Lewis and Clark, who appears in Clark's journal as the famous Pomp.)

The four dispirited trappers joined Campbell's caravan, Thompson was patched up, and they moved on again. By the 1st of August, they had discovered Bonneville's presence just behind them and the parties joined together.

Bonneville was still fidgety. He planned to trap the western side of the Bighorn this fall, and was not enthusiastic about competing again with RMF brigades. It had cost him too much last time. While he joined Campbell's party, he secretly dispatched several small trapping brigades to work this area, hoping to beat Fitzpatrick and his men. As it happened, Fitz had no particular designs on this country, so the gesture was wasted. It did, however, enable Bonneville to repeat the mistake he consistently made throughout his career in the mountains; that of breaking up his detachments into such small groups that they were easy game for whatever predators they ran across, brown or white.

With the addition of the main force of Bonneville's men, the total party now numbered nearly a hundred. For two weeks they pushed generally north, now in the Bighorn basin, without notable incident. By August 12 they were far enough down the Bighorn to shift to the water phase of the trip.

A brief diversion is necessary here. One other party of major importance had left Rendezvous 1833 on the same day as the RMF brigades, July 24.

This was a party of men from Bonneville's force, under the tough and hardy partisan Joe Walker. During Rendezvous 1833 Walker had recruited men among the free trappers (including Joe Meek) to supplement his own force, and set out on a trip that became one of the classic stories of the trade.

Bonneville later claimed that he had dispatched Walker to survey and explore the Great Salt Lake. It was, according to the Irving-digested account of Bonneville's journal, the "object of his intense curiosity and ambition." That being the case, it seems rather odd that he didn't go see it for himself.

But Bonneville himself, with the remainder of his party, set off to follow the RMF-Campbell party as described above. Joe Walker, whatever his orders may have been, set out for the West Coast.

There is ample evidence that the intention from the beginning was to go to California. Zenas Leonard, for example, describing his enlistment, says "I was anxious to go to the coast of the Pacific." Another of the expedition's members speaks of finding at Rendezvous 1833 "Captain Walker and company bound for California."

But Bonneville was on leave for the purpose of making various geographical observations (in which he did not show the least interest), and the Great Salt Lake was one of the natural curiosities of the West; in short, it simply sounded better to say Walker was sent to explore the lake. Bonneville's only observable interest in the country was to trap beaver.

Wyeth's proposal to Bonneville, shortly before Rendezvous

1833, had been for such an expedition to California; and he had made it sound very inviting, very prosperous. And, whereas Bonneville was apparently unwilling to undertake such a thing in partnership with Wyeth, he might well have been interested in it as a pure-Bonneville expedition. Bernard DeVoto has suggested that Bonneville "decided to shoot the moon"—deluded by the golden fantasy of California—hoping to make back his losses and a profit in one fell swoop. It seems a likely supposition; it was an expedition of such economic bravado that no explanation will ever quite satisfy.

We shall not follow this party in detail; Irving has done it, and Zenas Leonard, and Joe Meek. When Joe Walker broke camp at the rendezvous and set out, his party numbered around forty men of his own (and a few bands of assorted free trappers who thought they'd see about all that reported aguardiente and hospitality). They marched over to the valley of the Bear, made (not enough) meat; and then straight into the desert desolation of the country north and northwest of Great Salt Lake.

They ran into the same thing every other party in this country had: starvin' times, no beaver, suspicious Indians. Meek knew of it from only last year, when he'd accompanied Milton Sublette's RMF brigade down here. Prescription as before: crickets, roots, and mule-blood soup. On the staggering journey across the Great Basin they skirmished with even the miserably unaggressive Diggers, precipitating a massacre of about twenty-five of the abject creatures.

Meek, reporting this event, quotes Joe Walker as saying, "We must kill a lot of them, boys," as an object lesson to stay away from camp. The trappers accordingly fired point-blank into a mass of curious Indians, which scattered them rapidly. Bonneville later picked this incident as the focus for his dissatisfaction with Walker's conduct of the "Salt Lake" party. Irving reports his "horror and indignation" at Walker's action, and the event has taken its place among the less admirable actions of the trade.

After their starvation passage across the Great American Desert—the first party since Smith—they reached Monterey late in year. Penetrating the Sierras took them three full weeks; but it was worth it. Joe Walker and his brigade were the first whites ever to see Yosemite.) If the expedition was horrifying to Bonneville, it was at least a little less so to the trappers themselves. They happily settled themselves into the California hospitality, and were soon immersed in riding contests, bull-and-bear baiting, and amorous diversions with the lovely and willing señoritas, who consistently took quite a fancy to the mountain men.

As expanded around the winter fire, this fine good fellowship with the Californians (and their women) became a memorable event, and there were more than a few who later decided to float their sticks in the same direction. (Walker himself later led a couple of horse-stealing expeditions to the Golden Land; and this became one of the features of the later mountain trade, a sort of business trip to sunny climes, with expense account courtesy of their California hosts.) As was usual, a certain number declined to return to the mountains, and Walker left six men behind. (Two of these—George Nidever and John Price—were to play recorded roles in the subsequent history of California.)

It was the middle of February, 1834, when Walker's brigade regretfully pulled up stakes in California and "lazily left our camp for the east."

IV

We left the three RMF partners in the middle of August, 1833, camped on the Bighorn. The river here was navigable (for bullboats at least) and Bob Campbell prepared to transfer the year's take to the water. RMF would then take possession of the horses that had brought the fur this far, and make their Fall '33 hunt among the friendly Crows.

Here on the banks of the Bighorn a minor revolution occurred. It would appear that Milton Sublette had his back up by this time; and resented brother Bill's iron fist on RMF. There was no way to break that stranglehold as long as Bill Sublette continued to have a monopoly on supplying goods— at his own prices. So Milton listened with interest as Nathaniel Wyeth expounded a good Yankee proposition.

Wyeth's trip back from Fort Vancouver to the mountains had convinced him that supplies would be infinitely cheaper to transport from here. (He later made a calculation for his backers, comparing costs of the route from St. Louis: to carry $3,000 in goods from Vancouver to the mountains = $4,554; from St. Louis = $11,382.) This would bring goods to RMF at half the price or less than Bill Sublette was charging them. As Wyeth pointed out in a letter written later:

The great difficulty which your concern [RMF] has encountered and the enormous expence in getting your supplies has induced me to suppose that you would avail yourself of any opportunity which on reasonable terms would obviate all the difficulties and much of the expense. Such opportunity is now within your reach. By means of our vessells employed in the salmon trade we can take out goods and bring home furs to any extent to the Columbia. These goods we can purchase cheaper than goods can be purchased to send over the mountains [from St. Louis] ... The packing up from the Columbia is neither difficult nor expensive, horses there are comparatively cheap and in that country there is little danger consequently few men are required. These advantages we are willing to divide with you, in order that by getting your goods on reasonable terms you may be able to monopolise in a great measure the trade of the mountains, and thus, much enlarge the amt. of goods which you will take from us ... One other advantage to be derived from pursuing the business through this route is that if you succeed in breaking up the other companies as you certainly can do, when you get your goods so much cheaper you will prevent the influx [of] small traders and others who by their competition continually injure your business and spoil your men.

That was the plan, and it was a good one. Wyeth probably first outlined it at this August camp on the Bighorn, while the bullboats were being made. First notion was to make a trial run of Wyeth-as-supplier; bring out a small load next year, and see how it worked out. Milton himself would go back to civilization to pick out his own goods and get the best available prices.

On August 14 articles were drawn up providing that Wyeth should deliver merchandise to RMF for the following year. First cost was to be $3,000—about the same as first cost on the shipments Sublette & Campbell had brought up. But in this agreement, Wyeth's profit was established in advance; he was to receive, in addition to cost, $3,521. The total cost to RMF is thus about $6,500, and they have been paying about $15,000 for the same thing from Bill Sublette. (Also, the debt to Wyeth was payable in beaver at $4 a pound, which gives RMF another advantage; remember they had figured it worth only $3.25 in the arrangement with Christy.)

Both parties agreed to a bond of $500 in case of default. Milton and Fitz signed for RMF (Bridger had already separated on his hunt), and Wyeth was now in business as a supplier.

Captain Bonneville sent most of his men (thirty-six) back to St. Louis with their small catch. They made three bullboats, and set off down the Bighorn. Bonneville himself took all the horses from his party, forty-six of them, and the remaining four men. He immediately set out to catch up with his detached trappers for a scattered fall hunt, during which he got all the way to the HBC post at Walla Walla.

Campbell made only two bullboats for the year's catch—though his was by far the largest load—and sent some of his livestock overland with a small party under Louis Vasquez (Old Vaskiss of the literature). The remainder of the horses were taken by Tom Fitzpatrick for RMF, who set out for the Tongue to make the Fall '33 hunt in Crow country. Bridger's brigade was somewhere in the vicinity, but was not with the main party.

Campbell's second party, going overland, encountered a bad omen. Vasquez and his men were stopped by a band of Crows on the prod. This contingent wanted to trade, whether the whites were interested or not. They took what they wanted, in short, but not in an outright raid, which would have been more normal. For the first time the usually friendly Absaroka were surly and belligerent. There was always the thing about the horses, of course, but this was different; a kind of hostility not normal to Crows.

Just around the corner, however, was the reason for it. Fort Cass and Samuel Tulloch of the American Fur Company, who was this fall engaged in a little educational project with the Crows: how to tell RMF men from Company men, and which ones to rob.

Even in his bullboats, Wyeth noticed hostile signs among Crows on the banks as he passed. He was moving slowly downriver, his lack of speed mostly due to the good feeling that existed after signing the contract with Milton. On the first day, for example, he made only three miles: "Too much liquor to proceed therefore stopped."

As any of the mountain men could—and probably did—tell him, the only solution to a problem like that is a hair of the dog. Next day—in the morning, at least—he "found

traveling quite pleasant . . . [but] All feel badly today from
a severe bout of drinking last night."

So they careened down the Bighorn until the 17th, when
they pulled in at Fort Cass, near the mouth of the Yellowstone:

> . . . we were treated with little or no ceremony by Mr.
> Tullock, who was found in charge which I attributed
> to sickness on his part well knowing that a sick man is
> never disposed to be over civil to others.

Tulloch wasn't sick, he was working. And the tactics of
American Fur were stiffening up rapidly. Chouteau's maxim
and aim—*écraser toute opposition*—was being converted
into practical terms by Kenneth McKenzie, and, through
him, Tulloch. It amounted to a very simple program: get all
the furs, and don't worry about how it's done. If the situation
seems to call for bribing a few Crows to pillage the rivals,
fine. If it requires paying five times normal value for pelts—
well, not so fine, but do it anyway.

So Wyeth and Campbell and Milton Sublette enjoyed Mr.
Tulloch's hospitality for only a day. They traded off a few
skins at unpleasing rates, then took to the river again, down
the Yellowstone to its confluence with the Missouri.

About noon on the 24th of August they pulled up to the
residence of the King, Fort Union, where they "were met
with all possible hospitality and politeness by Mr. McKensie
the Am. F. Co. agent in this country."

CHAPTER 22

"The company did authorize experiments"

THE King of the Missouri could afford "all possible politeness and hospitality." He was riding high and happy. When Milton Sublette, Wyeth, and Campbell appeared at the doors of Fort Union on August 24, 1833, McKenzie was at the height of his power. In a few short years he had been able to open permanent posts among both Blackfeet and Crows, and Fort Union itself was far and away the most important single post in the American fur trade.

He greeted his competitors expansively, showed them around, explained everything in detail, and gave them to sample of the "fruits of the country."

At this particular moment McKenzie had every reason for elation, because he thought he had solved the conundrum set him by the government with its pestiferous liquor law. He solved it with characteristic directness (albeit tinged with a somewhat uncharacteristic naïveté.) If it was against the law to import liquor, so be it. He would make it himself, and was able to say: "I believe that no law of the United States is thereby broken." He was sufficiently aware that the government might view his proceedings with a jaundiced eye to admit "though perhaps one [law] may be made to break up my distillery."

The components of the distillery were probably taken up aboard the Company boats *Yellowstone* and *Assiniboine* in the spring of '33. On that occasion, McKenzie had essayed to test the act of July 9, 1832; by taking up his usual supply of liquor, in addition to the still. At Fort Leavenworth he discovered that the government was serious about it after all, and had put teeth into their law. He wrote to Pierre Chouteau, Jr., shortly after, that he had

> been robbed of all our liquors, say seven barrels shrub, one of rum, one of wine and all the fine men and sailors' whiskey which was in two barrels. They kicked and knocked about everything they could find and even cut through our bales of blankets which had never been undone since they were put up in England.

The gentleman-naturalist Maximilian was with McKenzie in the *Yellowstone* (which carried passengers and goods as far as Fort Pierre, where they were transferred to the *Assiniboine*). He, too, notes the severity of the inspection, complaining that he was barely allowed "to take a small portion to preserve our specimens of natural history." (But Maximilian was new to the country; he wouldn't know how familiar—and fanciful—were the evasions used to slip the alcohol past. "Preserving specimens" was comparatively unimaginative.)

But McKenzie had his distillery aboard in addition to the whiskey. At the mouth of the Iowa River he put ashore a crew of laborers to start a corn farm to feed it.

By the time Milton Sublette and the others arrived in August, the distillery was running, and running well. "Our manufactory flourishes admirably," McKenzie wrote a little later. "We want only corn to keep us going. . . . The Mandan corn yields badly but makes a fine, sweet liquor."

This was to Chouteau again, and in a letter to Ramsay Crooks: "It succeeds admirably. I have a good corn mill, a respectable distillery, and can produce as fine a liquor as need be drunk." (These letters are quoted to demonstrate beyond question that the Company officials were well aware of the exact nature of the project.)

So McKenzie showed his visitors around, naïvely elated over his success, and thereby set in motion the events which destroyed his usefulness to the Company and ended his career in the fur trade.

Milton and the others enjoyed the hospitality of the King of the Missouri for three days. Wyeth in particular was much impressed with what he found at Fort Union. McKenzie's second-in-command was James Hamilton Palmer—"a man of

superior education and an Englishman"—who was going under the name James Hamilton; reason unknown. McKenzie
and Hamilton lived in style; there was a sophistication to
them both which Wyeth duly noted. Fort Union was flourish-
ing, a center of civilization by this time, with refinements to
which the roving New Englander was now unaccustomed:
milk, bread, bacon, cheese, butter, and such.

In referring to Hamilton, Wyeth wrote: "I am perhaps
presumptious in saying that I felt able to appreciate his
refined politeness." Refined politeness, indeed! Shades of rendezvous must have flitted before Wyeth's mind.

(While at the fort, Wyeth was shown a memento of his
first expedition: a powder flask belonging to his man More,
killed in Jackson's Hole. Blackfeet had brought it in for
trade.)

Now the bullboats were abandoned. For the trip down the
Missouri proper they were provided with a Blackfoot pirogue, a cottonwood canoe of about twenty feet. On the 27th
of August the three relinquished the hospitality of the Company and put out.

Fort Union was situated on the north bank of the river,
some five or six miles (by water) above the mouth of the
Yellowstone. Milton's pirogue floated down to the confluence, and a few miles beyond. It was early in the evening
when they came to the keelboat lying at anchor, and the
brothers Sublette had a small family reunion.

Bill had just arrived, after planting small Sublette & Campbell posts (at least twelve or thirteen of them) at the Company locations on the river. There now remained the *pièce de
résistance;* the principal fort corresponding to, and competing with, the Company's Fort Union.

The burden of the actual building of Fort William (as it
was called, after the elder Sublette) was to fall on Bob
Campbell. Bill was to continue carrying the war to the
Company from St. Louis. He was also, at this time, very
ill—"at the point of Death," according to Campbell—and
was under the simple physical necessity of getting back to
civilization where he could get medical care of a slightly
more sophisticated nature than was available in the mountains.

The exact nature of Bill Sublette's illness is not specified;
his biographer postulates some respiratory disorder. Milton,
too, had his troubles. He was suffering from a foot injury—
again unspecified—that was more serious than his older

brother's difficulty. This injury may well have been one reason why Milton was leaving the mountains temporarily; in any event it added impetus to his action in going with Wyeth.

In spite of his illness, Sublette received Wyeth "with much politeness," probably because he did not know of Wyeth's arrangement with RMF for supplies. (Though it is true that the heads of all the companies—witness McLoughlin, McKenzie, etc.—received their competitors with the utmost cordiality. Even at rendezvous no one was averse to tapping a keg with the opposition, even while judiciously considering how to tap its profits. These little scenes of conviviality bring strongly to mind Chaucer's "Smyler with the knyf under the cloke.")

Wyeth remained at the anchored keelboat only overnight, departing the next morning. But he lost, for the time being, his most valuable passenger, Milton Sublette. Milton elected to remain behind until Bill took the keelboat back down—again, probably because his foot injury made any kind of traveling difficult. The keelboat would, without doubt, be easier on him than Wyeth's crowded little pirogue. Also, there was an exchange of information required at this point between the two brothers.

It seems clear that Milton Sublette was forced into assuming an active share of command in RMF along with Tom Fitzpatrick. The other partners—Bridger, Fraeb, and Gervais—were not inclined to concern themselves with the business end of RMF's operations. They were trappers, and that was all; they neither wanted to cope with other aspects, nor were they competent to do so.

This fall of '33 Milton began to take things into his own hands, in an attempt to salvage something from the damage that had already been done to the company's finances. The first step was his arrangement with Wyeth for a trial supplying run.[1] If Bill wanted RMF's business, he was going to have to get it on a more equable basis than before. After all, if Wyeth were willing to supply for $6,500 what Bill gave for $15,000, the difference could easily be the difference between solvency and bankruptcy for RMF.

As a token of his newly assumed authority—and his intent to back it up—Milton flatly refused to pay part of Sublette's charges of the previous year; and a rather significant part it was.

According to the document as drawn up, Milton was

acting "for himself and Thos Fitzpatrick H Freab James Bridger J B Jarvie."

> ... there is an Item in the account rendered by said [Bill] Sublette to the party of the second part [Milton & RMF] of Commission paid by Wm L Sublette to Wm H Ashley of Fifteen Hundred dollars for attending to the Sales of the Furs of the party of the Second part and which they ... refuse to settle— the accounts therefore and receipts are passed leaving this charge unpaid.

It must be admitted that denying Ashley his little cut is taking a very hard line, indeed; amounting almost to sacrilege, perhaps. Milton also insisted on having a few other things put in writing; apparently tired of leaving things entirely to the business honor of older brother Bill:

> Having transacted business for The Rocky Mountain Fur Co last season by which a number of their notes and drafts came into my hands and left by me at my House in St. Louis Co M° for safe Keeping I promise and agree to deliver over those Notes and drafts to said Rocky Mountain C° on their arrival there.[2]

An almost unbrotherly distrust would seem indicated; but then, the notes ought to have been turned over to RMF on settlement of accounts. Milton also very prudently refrained from telling Bill anything about the arrangement made between RMF and Wyeth. There was, after all, no point in giving him too much time to combat the move.

It was about the middle of September when Bill Sublette's keelboat, with Milton as passenger, got off in Wyeth's wake, leaving Campbell behind to complete the construction of Fort William and set up business. Campbell had about sixty men all told, some few of them hired under McKenzie's nose, and the work went rapidly. Fort William was finished by the middle of November, with the exception of a few minor buildings. It consisted of eight cabins and a number of supplementary storehouses within a stockade of about 130 by 150 feet. Like its competitor, Fort Union, it was on the north bank of the Missouri on raised ground. One of Campbell's principal clerks was young Charles Larpenteur, a *mangeur de lard* on his first trip. (Larpenteur had received a sort of unofficial promotion at Rendezvous 1833, through his unique personal characteristics. He was a teetotaler; and thus about the only man they could rely on to remain sober enough to distribute the liquor to the other trappers while keeping a clear eye for progressive dilution and profit. Larpenteur later recorded his experiences in a book called *Forty Years a Fur Trader*, which has served as source for some of this material.)

II

Tom Fitzpatrick had taken over Campbell's remaining horses on about the 15th of August. While Milton was making his way down the Bighorn and Yellowstone to Fort Union, Fitz was working overland toward the valley of the Tongue River. Captain Stewart was with him, and Dr. Harrison; both getting their first taste of the gay and carefree trapping life.

About three weeks out, Fitz ran into a large Crow village. He made camp nearby, and rode over for a visit with the principal chief. Captain Stewart, having had considerable military experience, was left in charge of the camp. (This, incidentally, is a remarkable demonstration of the mountain men. To entrust an encampment to a *mangeur de lard*—military or no—was unheard of.)

While Fitz was engaged in friendly concourse with the Crow chief, a band of young Absaroka bucks from the same village swarmed down on the camp. The exact circumstances aren't known; but they can be guessed fairly accurately.

The Crows—happily for the twenty or thirty trappers—remained Crow-like in their reluctance to kill whites. This precludes an outright attack. What is more likely is that the band simply infiltrated the camp in large numbers, joking, trading, wandering around, poking their noses into everything. In the course of time there would inevitably be at least one sturdy Absaroka near every desirable object. (Stewart, remember, was completely unfamiliar with the American Indian; and more, he knew the Crows were traditionally friendly to whites. In all probability he was completely unsuspecting; in the course of this narrative we've seen it happen to booshways of much greater experience than the Scotsman.)

At this point, with their hands on the reins both figuratively and literally, the Crows would have broken the bad news to Stewart and his companions.

Everything went. Horses, traps, guns, ammunition, furs—everything. When the happy Absaroka left the white camp they had cleaned them out in one grand coup, and without bloodshed.

A grand game it was, and they were so happy about it they greeted Fitzpatrick with the utmost affection when they encountered him returning from their village. Fitz himself was persuaded to part with his horse, gun, most of his clothes and even his watch, and that kind of thing is enough to ruin a man's whole day.

The furious Fitzpatrick stormed back to camp and found it, if possible, more destitute than himself. Then, by account (not his own), he went back to the Crow village and demanded restitution from the chief. The chief replied, as expected, that while he hadn't anything to do with the affair, sometimes it was hard to control the young men. However, Fitz somehow managed to get a few horses back, and a few traps; enough that he could at least be moving on.

And by this time he was aware that it was just about time to be moving on. It was perfectly clear to him—and rightly so—that the Crows were not acting entirely independently. They were operating as a semidetached arm of American Fur. In letters recounting the robbery Fitz places full and entire blame on the Company; and there is no doubt he was right.

And here, in a strange and cloudy way, we run into an old friend of ours. There were three agents of American Fur in Crow country this year. Tulloch, of course, at Fort Cass, and two other resident agents among the Crows, who were paid an annual salary by the Company to secure the Absaroka furs. One of these was a man named Winter and the other was no less a personage than James P. Beckwourth.

Beckwourth was getting $800 a year from McKenzie for his good offices among the Crows (which amount he raises in *Life and Adventures* to a preposterous $3,000). James P. was traditionally given his part in this robbery, and he goes to great lengths to refute the accusation, inventing a wildly imaginative story in which he rescues Fitz and party from imminent peril and other such Beckwourthian adventures. Bernard DeVoto wrote about this: "The fantastic yarn he tells in rebuttal is sufficient evidence that those who accused him had the goods on him."

It may be so, though the fantastic yarn isn't much evidence in itself; James P. was accustomed to doing such things up brown anyway. But it is at least certain that Beckwourth was (1) accused of it, and at great pains to deny it (2) perfectly well aware of the proceedings, whether or not he took actual part in them.

Fitz himself, with his small remaining stock of horses, immediately headed out of Crow territory, lucky to have even that to show for it. This was the final demonstration, if any was needed, of the solidity with which American Fur was now entrenched in the mountains. By the middle of November he was in camp on Ham's Fork of the Green River again, and wrote two letters concerning this robbery. One was to Milton Sublette, the other to General Ashley. The one to Ashley was considerably more formal, inasmuch as it was probably intended to be read aloud in Congress. Fitz showed the touching concern for the United States that seemed so often to overwhelm trappers cadging for something from the government. In this case Fitz wanted two things: reparations from the Company for the outrage and, in effect, a law against them.

Fitz tells of escorting Campbell to the Bighorn, and goes on:

> I set out to look for the crow Indians in order to obtain permission of them to make my fall hunt in their cuntery but before I had time for ceremony or form of any Kind they robed me and my men of every thing we possessed save some horsis and a few traps and all this accordingly to the advice of the american furr Co. as they then told me the agent of these people who was there present did not pretend to deny it, in short genl if theire is not Some alteration made in the system of business in this Cuntery Verry Soon it will become a nuisance and disgrace to the U.S. So many different Companies roving a bout from One tribe of Indians to another Pack all telling a different tale [illegible word] Slandering each other to Such a degree as really to disgust the Indians and will evidently all become hostile towards the americans I now appeal to you for redress. ... I ask no More than the laws of the U.S. dictates in Such Cases is it be cause they are More powerful than we are that they are allowed to be instrumental to Such

acts of Violence on people who are licensed and
authorised according to law. They have traping partis
all over the indian Cuntery as well as we have and
still more numerous and yet their Violation of the
laws are over looked So as to allow them to deprive us
of the produce of our dear bought labour   if there is
no room for amendments in this system order us out
of the Cuntery and we shall forthwith obey the command ... or Say we are limited to any Certain part of
the Cuntery and others in like manner then the
indians in each boundary if properly manage Could be
Kept in proper order otherwise they will all be come
hostile in a Short time   So Soon as one party will do
perhaps another will arive next day to undo and in
this Sort of way business is carried on ... I shall
await advice from the honorable Members in Session
... Advice or instructions from you respecting our
Case shall be faithfully attended to by

> Your Most
> Obt Servt
> Thos Fitzpatrick

And to Milton, Fitz added that if they couldn't obtain
redress from the government "we will have to Lick it ourselves."

The redress, such as it-was, was of a rather infuriating
kind. The Company had the furs, all right. And McKenzie
offered the following intelligence to Tulloch at Fort Cass, in
January:

> The 43 Beaver skins traded, marked "R.M.F. Co.,"
> I would in the present instance give up if Mr. Fitzpat-
> rick wishes to have them, on his paying the price the
> articles traded for them were worth on their arrival in
> the Crow village, and the expense of bringing the
> beaver in and securing it. My goods are brought into
> the country to trade and I would as willingly dispose
> of them to Mr. Fitzpatrick as to any one else for
> beaver or beaver's worth, if I get my price. I make
> this proposal as a favor, not as a matter of right, for I
> consider the Indians entitled to trade any beaver in
> their possession to me or any other trader.

And McKenzie was happily able to end his report (to Pierre Chouteau) of Fitzpatrick's misfortune by saying, "That party can consequently make no hunt this fall."

Lucky McKenzie, on top of the heap. Again. But when he wrote those notes of triumph the wheels were already turning, and they had been set in motion by Nathaniel Wyeth, almost as an afterthought.

III

When Wyeth set off on his canoe journey down the Missouri he had with him a half-breed Flathead, age thirteen, and a Nez Perce of around twenty. The Flathead, Baptiste, was the son of François Payette of HBC, one of the principal friends Wyeth had made among that company. Baptiste was going to the States with Wyeth to improve his education, learn a little English and to "read write and cypher tolerably well." The unnamed Nez Perce boy seems to have been a private responsibility of Wyeth's.

The balance of his crew was made up by two "old hands as they call them selves"; Irving gives their blood-line as French Creole, Shawnee and Pottawattomie, which is mountain for white man anyway. These hunters provided Wyeth with a good deal of his amusement and pleasure, both during the bullboat passage to Fort Union and later on the Missouri. The Yankee *mangeur de lard* found them "more conceited than good which I have generally found to be the case with the hunters in this country." He took a good deal of satisfaction in beating the old hands at their own game; and he could do it. (Wyeth was the fastest learner in the mountains, and by the time he got to Rendezvous 1833 from Fort Vancouver he could shine in any company. The only thing he didn't learn fast enough was the business ethic.) He notes complacently that "Our hunters as usual having failed went myself and killed a [buffalo] cow."

He was confident of his own field ability—when Milton left him at the budding Fort William, Wyeth noted that "we are therefore left without any one who has decended the Missouri but I can go downstream."

All the way downriver Wyeth visited the American Fur Company posts, and impartially paid his respects to their new satellites, the Sublette & Campbell agencies.

At Cantonment Leavenworth, which he reached in late September, Wyeth was received hospitably. Baptiste and the

Nez Perce boy were vaccinated, terror-stricken by the military with their uniforms and knives on the end of their guns, and astonished by the women they saw.

The doctor's wife and another were present at the vaccination, and Wyeth records with amusement:

> ... they were really beautiful women but the eyes of the two [Indian boys] were riveted on the White Squaws Baptiste who speaks a little English told the other Boys when he returned to the boat that he had seen a white squaw white as snow and so pretty.

Sometime during the polite wining and dining, Wyeth happened to mention that Kenneth McKenzie had a very nice little distillery going up at Fort Union, very nice. Which doubtless caused a spasm of choking and coughing at table.

It is frequently written that Wyeth informed on McKenzie as a gesture of revenge, and a commercial blow. Chittenden, the great historian of the trade, seems to be the originator of this notion. He says Wyeth was angry at being refused the purchase of liquor, and at the prices McKenzie charged; that he settled up "without a murmur and bided [his] time for revenge."

I don't think this was the case, for several reasons. Wyeth's journal references to McKenzie are all highly favorable:

> ... all possible hospitality and politeness ... we took leave [of] our hospitable entertainers and on the experience of a few days with prepossessions highly in their favor we found Mr. McKensie a most polite host.

Certainly not the words of a revenge-bent man. Wyeth also seemed to be poorly informed (*Wyeth* poorly informed!) on the actual precarious state of the liquor situation. Of the distillery itself he says that "here they are beginning to distil spirits from corn traded from the Inds. below. This owing to some restriction on the introduction of the article into the country."

I doubt that a man familiar with the government's new, hard policy would refer to it as merely "some restriction." I think it much more likely that, since the act of absolute prohibition had been passed while he was in the mountains,

Wyeth simply didn't yet know of it. He certainly thought nothing of his own "introduction of the article into the country"; it was part of the usual run of the business he was learning. It seems most probable that Wyeth was unaware of the potential ruckus he was stirring up.

It's a minor point in any event, since the authorities would soon have learned of McKenzie's project from Bill Sublette. But since it has reflected some discredit on Wyeth for a hundred years, I wanted to clear it up.

So Wyeth proceeded on to Boston, where we will pick him up again shortly. He left behind him a stew and ferment that nearly wrecked American Fur, and did wreck McKenzie personally. In order to follow this we will have to skip a little ahead of our narrative.

When Wyeth left, the Indian agent wrote General Clark in St. Louis, giving the information. Clark forwarded this to Pierre Chouteau, Jr., head of American's Western Department. If Mr. Chouteau thought it proper to explain the matter, General Clark would be very happy to hear it. Chouteau replied late in November. As Chittenden (whose account of this affair I follow here) very properly observes, Chouteau's answer "for ingenuity, surpassed even the distillery scheme itself."

The Company, of course, knew nothing whatever about all this. Further, they most emphatically disclaimed any and all responsibility for unauthorized acts by their personnel (an attitude reminiscent of the Crow chief's position after the robbery of Fitzpatrick). Chouteau did go so far as to admit:

> The company, believing that wild pears and berries might be converted into wine (which they did not understand to be prohibited), did authorize experiments to be made, and if, under color of this, ardent spirits have been distilled and vended, it is without the knowledge, authority, or direction of the company, and I will take measures . . . to arrest the operation complained of, if found to exist.

He forthwith sent an express to McKenzie, complaining that the King had "placed the company in an unpleasant situation." This, of course, annoyed McKenzie considerably, since what he had done had been with the full knowledge of Chouteau and the Company officials. He was a Company man through and through and, if it would help, he was willing to be made the scapegoat (which he was); but he resented the rather high tone Chouteau was taking. (It appears that Chouteau had been so far involved in this as to get a legal opinion on the project in St. Louis; and it was, wildly enough, favorable.) Let's have it understood, said McKenzie, that he was acting for the benefit of the Company, and with their knowledge.

But however annoyed he may have been with Chouteau, McKenzie was still the Company on the upper Missouri, and he presently presented his own explanation. In this he was not less ingenious than Chouteau himself. It seems he was sort of trying the still out for a friend.

This (imaginary) friend of McKenzie's lived over the border, at the Red River settlement of HBC. In a friendly enough spirit, McKenzie had agreed to purchase a distillery in the United States, take it to Fort Union and store it until the friend came to pick it up.

Purely by coincidence, a mechanically inclined American happened to show up at Fort Union about this time, and took an immediate fancy to the marvelous contraption, just sitting there idle. He wanted to try it out on the fruits of the country; fool around a little, make a bit of wine perhaps. McKenzie saw no harm in this, and granted permission. But, as should be obvious, this had nothing at all to do with the Company's affairs; just a passing incident to enliven the slow-moving days on the frontier.

Washington was not happy about these explanations. The Company fell into bad odor, and came very near losing its license to trade. American Fur had, very naturally, a great number of enemies who were happy enough to count coup on this sort of thing. The opposition was hot and heavy for a while, in spite of Senator Benton's efforts on behalf of the Company.

The resolution that came about at last seems to have been due to the personal efforts of Pierre Chouteau in Washington. Two letters indicate what happened. The first, from the St. Louis house to McKenzie in the spring of '34:

> In asking you to stop at once its operation, we now urgently renew the request, and however painful it may be to destroy an establishment which promised such excellent results, it is nevertheless of the most urgent necessity to submit. Otherwise we shall expose ourselves to the greatest embarrassments. It was only

by the assurance of our Mr. Chouteau to the Secretary of War that we would conform to the government regulations pertaining to the Indian trade that the affair has not been followed up. Under these circumstances we think it will be prudent to send the still down or to dispose of it otherwise so that it may give offense to no one.

The second was from Ramsey Crooks, superior of both McKenzie and Chouteau, to the latter:

The General tells me that you had the address to persuade Judge H—— that your distillery at the Yellowstone was only intended to promote the cause of botany. But *prenez-y-garde*. Don't presume too much on your recent escape. . . . The less of this sort of business you do the better, for the time may, and very probably will, come when you will be exposed by the endless number of spies you have around you.

McKenzie was brought down from Fort Union shortly after the conclusion of this affair and sent to Europe for a year. He returned for a short time, but never again assumed his control of Company destinies on the upper river. (When he finally left the Company he went into the wholesale liquor business.)

One other circumstance adds to the confusion this winter of '33–'34; American Fur was in the process of changing its corporate structure; as a man may be said to change his personality by being beheaded. It will be remembered that John Jacob Astor had noted the presence of silk hats in Europe, and Astor was not a man slow to take a hint.

He had not been personally engaged in the trade for some time. Ramsay Crooks of the Northern Department was the effective head of the Company, while Chouteau in St. Louis and McKenzie at Fort Union operated on the western frontier. In spite of this, Astor was always the abiding force—referred to by Crooks as *notre estimable grand-papa*. When McKenzie had medals struck to impress the Indians, it was Astor's profile on them, looking very Roman, very well fed.

But Astor was at the point of retirement. He was seventy years old in the summer of '33; and there were silk hats on the Continent; and it was just about time to get out. While much of the Astor fortune had been accumulated by shrewd investment—depreciated government bonds, and, above all, New York real estate—the fur trade was his first success, the rock on which all that came later was founded: "the business," wrote Crooks, "seems to him like an only child and he can not muster courage to part with it."

But Astor's judgment did not fail him, nor did his courage, and in June of 1833 he wrote from Geneva:

> Wishing to retire from the concern in which I am engaged with your house, you will please to take this as notice thereof, and that the engagement entered into ... between your house and me, on the part of the American Fur Company, will expire with the outfit of the present year.

The Titan of the fur trade was leaving, and it was one more reason for Chouteau and McKenzie to be nervous in the early spring of '34; stepping into John Jacob Astor's boots was going to take some doing.

CHAPTER 23

"Obliged to pay well
for a cessation of hostilities"

THE years 1833 was known in the Sioux calendar as *Wicarpi okicamna:* When the Stars Were Falling. RMF's star had begun its fall, but the signs were not yet clear. Tom Fitzpatrick on the Powder had his troubles—robbery by the Crows—but that was routine; hazards of the trade. The other partners were off about the mountains this fall, trapping beaver, fighting Indians, and telling each other lies about Rendezvous 1833. For them, there was nothing to indicate the sudden, incandescent rush to destruction that would burn out the company as surely—and almost as quickly—as a meteorite is burned out in its passage through atmosphere.

Massive forces were at work this fall, shaping the end of RMF. Ironically enough, they would probably have welcomed the news, because it seemed to be just a little trouble for their old friends, the Company . . .

The preceding chapter took us a little ahead of our narrative. McKenzie's disgrace and Astor's withdrawal were still in the future. The problems facing the King of the Missouri this fall also seemed routine—the challenge of another company, the burgeoning competition of the upstart Sublette & Campbell firm.

By September their posts up and down the river were established and Fort William was well under way, under the direction of Bob Campbell. By the middle of the month Bill Sublette was sufficiently recovered from his illness to leave for St. Louis in company with his brother Milton. Campbell settled down at the spanking-new Fort William to divert the Company trade to himself.

A few miles upriver, at Fort Union, McKenzie was worrying over this new threat, and for the almost inevitable reason: liquor. Somehow or other Bill Sublette had managed to squeeze past the government inspection. McKenzie thought they had around a hundred kegs of alcohol; the flat-curved panniers usually lashed to the sides of mules.

"It is hard," McKenzie wrote, "that new hands and limited means should have such advantages over us . . ." and in a different letter "at the lower post they have an abundance of alcohol and we are destitute, and you know how fond some Indians are of strong water."

The new competition was the sole subject of conversation among the *engagés* at Fort Union, and this, of course, also held true for the Indians. Virtually all the Assiniboine chiefs and some of the Crees from across the border made visits of inspection and curiosity to the new fort.

It was all very exciting during the fall, and things at first looked promising for Sublette & Campbell. They stole away three Company men for interpreters, paying them $500 a year; good wages for a post-based interpreter.

But McKenzie was not one to grumble without action. He immediately lashed out against Sublette & Campbell with the single weapon he possessed over them—cash. If they had the liquor, McKenzie had the money. By January, 1834, McKenzie could look back on the fall of '33 with more than a little satisfaction. He had, in four months, met and demolished the opposition. He outlined the conflict with Sublette & Campbell in a letter to his partisan at Fort McKenzie (this letter is quoted at length in Chittenden, and here reprinted from that source):

> They had, moreover, a full complement of clerks and seemed prepared to carry all before them, nothing doubting but that they would secure at least one half the trade of the country. They abandoned the idea of sending to the Blackfeet this season. They started a small equipment on horses to the Crow village on Wind river. They were expected to return early in December but have not yet been heard of. Mr. Winter and J. Beckwith passed the fall in the Crow camp and traded all their beaver. While Mr. Winter was with the Crows Mr. Fitzpatrick of the R.

M. F. Co. (my friend Captain Stewart was with him) arrived with thirty men, one hundred horses and mules, merchandise, etc., etc., and encamped near the village. He had not been long there before a large party paid him a visit and pillaged everything he had, taking even the watch from his pocket and the capote from his back; also driving off all his horses. This has been a severe blow to Sublette and Campbell. [Meaning that RMF's hunt was probably already committed to Fort William, rather than being taken to St. Louis.] And although on their first start here they made great show and grand promise to the Indians and although among the men nothing was talked about but the new company, they live now at the sign of "The case is altered." Their interpreters have quarreled and left them, and are now working hard for me. The Indians find their promises mere empty words and are applying continually to me to engage them. They have a post near to Riviere au Tremble in opposition to Chardon where they are doing literally nothing. Chardon has it all his own way. They have another post on the Yellowstone in opposition to Pillot and Brazeau and there they get no robes although they offer a blanket of scarlet for a robe.

You must be aware that I have not been asleep this fall. It has cost me something to secure the Indians to me, but being determined to get the peltries, nothing has been neglected that would carry my point. My opponents can not by any means get peltries sufficient to pay the wages of their men. At the Gros Ventres and Mandans they have not even robes to sleep on. At the Mandans my last account states that Picotte has eighty packs of robes and eight beaver, and I hope things are equally promising lower down. [They were. Larpenteur wrote from Fort William: "This post was not the only one that was out of luck for all those along the Missouri proved a failure.] On my return from Fort Pierre, Mr. Campbell called on me. W. Sublette had previously gone down stream on his way to St. Louis and proposed to sell out to me all their interest on the river. I listened to his terms but was by no means disposed to buy out an opposition, when all my old experienced and faithful clerks and tradesmen felt so certain of driving them out; especially on my giving them carte blanche with respect to trade at their respective posts, of course to be used with discretion but with this condition, that all peltries must be secured for the A. F. Co. and thus far I have no reason to complain. The new company is now in bad odor and must sink.

"Carte blanche," says McKenzie, and he was not exaggerating. Fitzpatrick's robbery was part of it, and so was the appalling price of $12 for beaver recorded at the Mandans. This about four times what the pelts would bring in St. Louis. The Company was taking a fantastic loss on furs this season; but they were getting them. It would seem indeed that Sublette & Campbell were out of the running; so badly whipped that McKenzie wouldn't even deign to consider buying them out.

But the above letter of triumph was written on January 21, 1834. Bill Sublette was already en route to New York.

In view of the disastrous failure of Sublette & Campbell's operation, Bill Sublette's achievement in New York this winter is all the more remarkable. In about a week of conferences he managed to undo everything McKenzie had accomplished in the field in four months.

In a series of secret negotiations with American Fur Company officials, Sublette pushed through an agreement which was tantamount to a capitulation by the Company.

The terms of the agreement finally reached were stated in the letter informing McKenzie:

> By the enclosed agreement you will see that we have concluded an arrangement at New York with Mr. Sublette. We take such of his equipment in merchandise, utensils, etc., as remains at the close of the season's trade and we retire from the mountain trade for the ensuing year.

In return for this Sublette was to abandon the posts on the Missouri; not to compete with the Company any longer in their own stronghold.

Bob Campbell's brother Hugh entertained Sublette for some time after his return from New York. His description of the affair to his brother expresses some of Hugh's admiration for the accomplishment:

> As you are deeply interested in the agreement made with the A.F. Co. I may as well give my opinion of that matter. In no instance have I ever known a settlement conducted with more ability—nor has our friend Mr. Sublette ever shown himself to more advantage than in bringing those men to the terms agreed on. It is impossible for me to comprehend the bearings of every question involved—but with regard to the importance of setting at rest all competition (unprofitable to both parties) and receiving payment for useless trumpery I think the compromise is excellent. The article itself looks much like a treaty of peace betwixt soverign potentates— perhaps I might add a little resembling the partition of Poland too—but after all there is something in it which has gratified my pride. That despotic Company have by this document acknowledged your equality (I might say superiority) and been obliged to pay well for a cessation of hostility. You quit your forts with all the honours & some of the spoils of war, to use a military phrase.
>
> Upon the whole my dear Robert I am glad you have resigned the trade on the Missouri. ... If you are still determined on pursuing the trade, other points offer greater inducements. I shall not however allude to them—because doing so ... might be construed into my approval of your present mode of life—a thing that no success can ever reconcile me to under my circumstances.

So Bill Sublette had brought it off, in the face of what appeared to be complete defeat. In the mystery that surrounds these transactions in New York, there is one principal question that calls for answer. What leverage did Sublette have?

There were several elements. First of all, the impending reorganization of the Company put them in a vulnerable position. When John Jacob Astor retired, American Fur would no longer be able to call on his enormous cash reserves in emergency; there would be no more $12 prices to ensure that "all peltries [would] be secured for the A.F.

Co." They would not, in future, be able to afford this kind of competition. (In the letter to McKenzie quoted above, the St. Louis house referred to Astor's withdrawal: "As a consequence of this change we have found it necessary to make an arrangement with Mr. Sublette.")[1]

A second handicap sustained by Astor's retirement was the loss of some of the Company's political influence, which was also expensive. And they could not afford any more trouble with the government. With the robbery of Fitzpatrick, the famous still of McKenzie, and one or two other affairs, they were treading on thin ice indeed. So far, with the assistance of Astor's political influence, they had been able to weather the storms of adverse opinion fairly well; but that could change overnight. Ramsay Crooks himself expressed their jeopardy thus:

> . . . we are looked upon by many as an association determined to engross the trade of the upper Missouri, by fair means if we can, but by foul proceedings if nothing short will ensure our objects. With such a reputation it becomes us to be more than usually circumspect in all we do. Every eye is upon us, and whoever can will annoy us with all his heart.

For this reason Crooks, in New York, had advised against McKenzie's distillery, but, as we have seen, the project went ahead anyway, with results that were eventually embarrassing for the Company and disastrous for McKenzie personally. Thus, in view of the increasing scrutiny to which they were being subjected, the Company would be hamstrung in its competitive tactics.

Thirdly:

> to keep Sublette from purchasing a new equipment and from connecting himself with houses that were making him all sorts of offers. His reputation and that of his patron, Ashley, whatever may be the cause, are far above their worth. Nevertheless such is the fact and it is enough to procure them unlimited credit. It is this which induced us to offer to buy them out.

A fourth factor, and the one with which I am most concerned here, was Sublette's virtual control over RMF. I have previously shown how this control came to exist, through the simple means of picking up all debts outstanding, until the finances of RMF were totally in Sublette's hands. They were deeply in debt to him, and it now remains to see how Sublette used the debt to force them out of business; thus, in Hugh Campbell's words, "setting at rest all competition."

Sublette returned to Philadelphia after his victory in New York. It was about the 4th of February when he arrived, and he stayed there with Hugh Campbell for almost two weeks. On about the 16th he left for St. Louis. His original intent is made clear, again by Hugh Campbell to Robert:

> A few days after Mr. Sublettes departure I wrote you ... At that time I had supposed that he would have proceeded at a very early day up the Missouri to aid you in carrying into effect the late arrangement with the AM. F C°. Believing that his stay in St. Louis would have been very short, I did not forward any more letters ... for I expected both of you would have been (back) in St. Louis in July or Aug^t."

So, at the time of the "partition of Poland," Bill had no plans for returning to the mountains in 1834. However, when he arrived back in St. Louis his plans were abruptly changed.

During the winter an express had arrived in St. Louis from the mountains. Sublette's old traveling companion Black Harris had made another winter overland, this time in company with the alcoholic Dr. Harrison. They carried (at least) two letters from Tom Fitzpatrick, one of them to General Ashley—which was quoted above—and the other to Milton Sublette:

> I am sorry to have to relate to you I unfortunately met with the Crow Vilage, [Fitzpatrick began], and was robed of every thing ... [he then details the company-instigated attack] ... However it is not quite so bad as you may Suppose Bridger and Myself have on hand about twenty three packs of Beaver furr. [Say, 2,200 lbs. = $7,700 St. Louis, not counting any deductions.]

Fitz. goes on to sketch in the whereabouts of the other RMF parties of the fall '33 hunt. Then:

the understanding between you and My Self will have to remain in the Same State you left it until Our Meeting next Summer as the partis are absent I have been uneasy ever Since we parted about Our aramgents with Wyeth however it may terminate well but still I dread it. I have an Idea we will Stand in Need of a large Supply of Madz [Merchandise] at rendezvous as the Spanish companis will meet us there and there is now a party of them with Fraeb I wish you to work Wyeth as advantageous and Secure as possible Studdy well the articles of profit Liquor will be much wanting. I well Know and indeed all groceris come as soon as possible to the rendesvous and look Out for the Crows on your Way up I believe they will be hostile to all partis here after: they have good encouragmt from the A F Co ... dont gou So high up on SeetsKiddee as horse Creek Strike Some where about the Mouth of Sandy and remain until we come.

It was through this letter to his brother that Bill Sublette first learned that he had more competition to meet than American Fur, and it must have been a shock. Milton had been very quiet about it. During the time they were together at Fort William—and on the boat trip downriver—nothing whatever had been said about an agreement with Wyeth. And then again, when they had been together at Hugh Campbell's house in Philadelphia (just after Bill's coup in New York), there was no intimation of any such thing. Milton was wisely keeping his own counsel.

How did Bill have access to a letter intended for his brother? Wyeth's guess is most likely correct: The letter to Milton was "sent by Doctor Harrison who opened it and I presume told Wm Sublette."

In the face of this information, Bill changed his plans suddenly, and decided to get into the mountains as fast as he could, to foreclose the RMF debt.

This is a tricky point. Until now it has always been assumed that Sublette's trip in the spring of '34 was a routine supplying venture; that it was straight competition, as with previous races to rendezvous by supply parties. It has also been assumed that he knew all about Wyeth's arrangement at the time. Sublette's biographer has stated that "The solution was simple: Sublette had to beat him [Wyeth] there; show

him up as second rate." Part of the confusion among scholars
has been caused by the fact that the above letter was thought
to have been addressed to William, rather than Milton. (It is
so labeled in the manuscript collection of the Missouri Historical Society.) This is not the case. (I was under this impression during the original draft of this book. Clearly, had it
been intended for Bill, it would have amounted to outright
betrayal of RMF by Fitzpatrick; and so I originally wrote.
This would have been a bad misevaluation of Fitz.)[2]

The true state of Sublette's knowledge and his motives for
going to the mountains at this crucial time are expressed in
Hugh Campbell's letter to Robert. This was written on April
5, 1834. He states Sublette's original intent to proceed up the
Missouri (as quoted above) and continues:

> Within a few days I have had two letters from Mr.
> S announcing his intention of getting up a small outfit
> with about 20 men & proceeding direct to the moun-
> tains. I am aware that you will receive a full explana-
> tion of his motives for this expedition—yet I cannot
> avoid giving you a brief outline of what I understand
> to be his reasons for the movement. In the first place
> he designs sending up his youngest brother [Solo-
> mon; most certainly not Milton, as stated in *Bill
> Sublette, Mountain Man*] by the Am. F C°. boat
> with letters and papers to you, from which he thinks
> you can carry into effect the settlement entered into,
> as well as if he were personally present. He therefore
> thinks that he will not be required in that direction &
> that his presence is needed elsewhere.
>
> Captain Wyeth has made an arrangement with the
> Rocky Mountain F. C° *the nature of which has not
> fully transpired.* It is believed that he is to furnish
> their supplies at 150 per cent on first cost & take furs
> in payment in the Mountains at $4. [This informa-
> tion Bill Sublette would have gotten from Dr. Har-
> rison, who was present on the Bighorn at the time of
> this supposedly secret agreement between RMF and
> Wyeth.] The R. Mountain F Co are likely to dis-
> solve shortly. This and the arrangement with Captn.
> Wyeth are likely to operate against the goodness of
> the debt due you & Mr. S. by the Company. You will
> now perceive the object of the present expedition—
> *which is got up promptly with the view of collecting*

the debt & perhaps laying the foundation for future operations. [Italics mine.]

It is difficult to see how an arrangement that would put RMF on a much sounder financial basis—by providing them with supplies at half the previous cost—would operate *against* the goodness of the debt. Rather, it would seem to have made payment that much more likely. My own theory of these events is this:

(1) Bill Sublette expected RMF to fold. ("The R. Mountain F Cº are likely to dissolve shortly.")

(2) But with their new, and supposedly secret, arrangement with Wyeth, the company's prospects were much better. (That they had no intention of going out of business is indicated by the plans for future—and expanded—relations with Wyeth, and by the first document of sale (p. 397) which refers to Fraeb as "late of the firm of the Rocky Mountain Fur Company" and to the "remaining partners of said Company." Even after Bill's arrival there was every intention of remaining in business, short-lived though it was.)

(3) When Bill learned of RMF's improved prospects, he was abruptly forced to change his own plans. ("His presence is needed elsewhere.") He had to go into the mountains and ensure the collapse of the firm. He knew from Fitzpatrick's intercepted letter to Milton that the year's catch would not nearly clear the debt, and foreclosing at this time would seem to operate against his own interests. Why the sudden urgency?

(4) It can be explained by the strong possibility that the early collapse of RMF had been promised—or at least intimated—in Bill's agreement with American Fur in New York, and was one of the conditions of that agreement. (". . . setting at rest all competition.") If RMF collapsed on schedule, the company would return to the mountains after their promised year's absence as sole proprietors. This was more desirable than ever in their new, more tenuous position after the reoganization. If Sublette could offer such assurance, it would have been a powerful bargaining point. In view of the failure of Sublette & Campbell's field operations, he needed one.

(5) But if RMF's arrangement with Wyeth worked out, they could remain successfully in competition with American Fur. Bill had to be certain it did not work out, and the surest way was to put the company out of business. By reason of his

financial control he was in a position to do it. Collection of the debt would leave RMF without return for the season and without money to buy supplies for the following year. In short, completely bankrupt, and unable ever again to annoy the American Fur Company.

So it was that in April, 1834, Bill Sublette set out to ring down the curtain on the Rocky Mountain Fur Company. It is my contention that he did so in order to fulfill the terms of his agreement with American Fur, which had been jeopardized by the willingness of a Yankee ice-merchant to give the trappers a fair break on their supplies, and that the action was triggered by information gotten from a rifled letter intended for his brother.

I am painting a dark picture of a highly respected man. I've been forced to do this because it is the only way in which I've been able to read the documents concerned: account books, letters, articles of agreement, and so forth. But it would be grossly unfair not to register a dissenting opinion on Sublette's character from a source contemporary with him. I think most eulogies on public figures—which Sublette certainly was, then and later—may be taken with a good helping of salt. This one, however, is from a man whose judgment cannot be ignored, Hugh Campbell. Reading Campbell's letters raises a vivid and inescapable image of the man. And Campbell is one whose opinions would be well worth listening to, then or now: intelligent, honorable, witty—and, above all, a man of excellent perception. Here from his letters to Robert, are a few of his evaluations of Bill Sublette—and it should be remembered that Campbell detested the business into which Sublette had drawn Robert, and might normally have been expected to hold this against him.

> So long as you do continue in the business, I trust you will be associated with Mr Sublette—a man to whom I have become strongly attached, from his love of truth, high sense of honour, kindness of heart & sound Judgement in every department of y^r business.
>
> [Sublette is here and] his company is so desirable and my time (after business hours) is so pleasantly occupied with him that I deduct from sleeping hours in order [to write you].
>
> You will of course make liberal allowances for my letters written . . . while such society is amongst us.

In fairness, the deep friendship Sublette engendered in Hugh Campbell ought to be placed in the scales against my own evaluation a century and a quarter after the fact.

II

Nathanial Wyeth was back in Cambridge by the first week of November, and started the always-unpleasant job of getting backing for the party. In one proposal he frankly admits that he had no expectation of great profit; the enterprise is a beginning, a tentative step:

> The contract as you will perceive will amt. to little more than carrying me into the Indian country free of expense and procuring the business of a very efficient concern, in this light I hold it to be valuable.

He discovered, somewhat to his dismay, that he had more to contend with than the normally expected inertia of backers. The young deserter John B. Wyeth had, in the manner of travelers before and since, written a book about his adventure in the West. (Or, rather, had it written for him by Dr. Benjamin Waterhouse.) The villain of the piece was, of course, Nat Wyeth, who appears as a sort of drunken, power-mad Nero of the mountains. Other deserters had written defamatory letters which, in the eastern hunger for western news, had been duly published in newspapers.

In the process of justifying their own actions—which included theft of horses from the party—these men painted an extraordinarily black picture of Wyeth himself, and one that has warped historical evaluation of him ever since.

While disproof of many of these unflattering contentions would have been easy enough, Wyeth knew perfectly well that retractions are printed on back pages in smaller type, a practice sufficiently maintained to our own day; the damage was done, and there was little chance of repairing it:

> Had I been in the country at the time the case would have been different. The injury is now done and thousands have read the slander who can never see the answer, even if I should make one.

In the end he made no attempt at personal justification. He simply set out in his persistent way to raise backing for the second expedition, and his energy and persistence were more than a match for the slanders. In spite of the fact that his first expedition had been an unqualified and profitless failure, he had remarkably little difficulty in securing financial backing for the second. (His principal financers were Henry Hall and Messrs. Tucker & Williams of Boston. Wyeth himself engaged for 25 per cent of the profits, if any.)

Two weeks after his arrival in Cambridge—two weeks of frantic activity—Wyeth was able to write Milton: "I am now ready to fulfil the contract made with Mr. Fitzpatric and yourself on ... Big-Horn River and to request that you will as soon as possible come to N. York."

(This letter was sent to Milton through a St. Louis firm with the explicit caution: "I request that you will be careful to avoid passing it through the hands of his brother Wm. L. Sublette.")

The general outline of Wyeth's plan was not much different from his first. He engaged the brig *May Dacre* to carry supplies around the Horn. The notion of the salmon fishing industry still appealed to him, and the *May Dacre* was also to be outfitted for that line of business. He gave his new company the title of Columbia River Fishing and Trading Company.

To the Rev. Clark Perry he outlined the entire business better than I could paraphrase it:

> In regard to what I propose now I answer the same as at first viz. to make money out of the fur trade. So far I have lost some money and have gained some experience and hope yet to make out. Am now fitting out a Bg. to go round the Horn to Bring out some goods and bring home a cargo of Salmon. 1st March next I shall go to St. Louis and start overland again with some goods which I have contracted to deliver to a concern in the mts. with the furs received ... go to the mouth of the Columbia and send them home by my Brig take the goods which she has brought out, and up again to the mountains exchange goods for furs employ residue of year in trapping Beaver until salmon season (having left men making barrels through the winter) This done another vessell comes ... takes the salmon and collections of the year. I take of her more goods and so the same round again.

On this expedition Wyeth was to carry with him a figure who loomed tall in the history of Oregon for the next twenty years. This was the Rev. Jason Lee, Methodist: the first ripple of the tidal wave of missionary activity that soon engulfed the West. This mission, under Lee and his nephew Daniel, was originally destined for the Flatheads, but, when the time came, moved straight on to Oregon and the Willamette valley. (Bernard DeVoto sees Jason Lee as an emissary of "the Continental Mind." It may be so. There is, at least, no more satisfactory explanation for the missionary's behavior. See DeVoto's *Across the Wide Missouri* for an excellent brief survey of conditions leading up to the Methodist Mission to the Flatheads.)

In addition to the missionaries, Wyeth also acquired two other supplemental travelers this winter; these were of a scientific bent.

On his first expedition Wyeth had made natural history collections for his friend Thomas Nuttall, the curator of the Botanical Garden at Harvard College. Now Nuttall wanted to go along, and with him the young John Kirk Townsend (whose *Narrative of a Journey across the Rocky Mountains* is one of the most valuable of sources).

Nuttall was no stranger to the West; he had been there twenty years earlier while Wyeth was still rolling hoops in the streets of Cambridge. He had accompanied Wilson Hunt's overland portion of the Astoria enterprise up the Missouri during Hunt's epic flight from Manuel Lisa, and now he wanted to return. Townsend, twenty-five, was a capable ornithologist, some of whose research on this trip would later be incorporated by Audubon in his works.

Both the religious and scientific detachments were to meet Wyeth at St. Louis, just before jumping off for the mountains, and in the meantime he had enough to do to outfit the new party.

He repeatedly urged Milton to come to New York so they could work out together the merchandise for the trip. He was also concerned that Milton and his backers should get together, hoping to establish by personal contact between them the confidence that would be necessary if the business were to continue in the future: "beside I am desirous of a spree with an old *Mountaineer* these folks here won't do."

But Milton's delay in St. Louis was far from capricious. He

was under daily care of a physician; the mysterious trouble with his leg was not getting any better.

It was early in January, 1834, before Milton was able to join Wyeth in Boston, and together they proceeded to purchase goods for RMF. This was not possible in any one place, and during the month of February they made the rounds of New York, Philadelphia, and Baltimore.

Wyeth had engaged for his second-in-command a Boston sea captain, Joseph Thing. While Milton and Wyeth were buying their goods, Captain Thing was busied making last-minute preparations in Boston. (It appears that one of the captain's most persuasive qualities was his ability to use a sextant. Wyeth covers several pages of his letter book with meticulous notes on taking latitude and longitude, with examples. Presumably he took a long hard look at this involved page, for a little later he wrote: "I have engaged Captain Thing who is well versed in taking observations.")

Thing had also to take care of Wyeth's contemplative afterthoughts: "it has occurred to me that some medicines for the clap and pox may be wanted ... unless there are some remedys the consequences are bad."

Bad consequences were not restricted to the clap and pox, and Wyeth knew it well. In the rush of his energy, one easily loses sight of the fact that he was profoundly aware he was teetering on the edge of chaos; that his plan was so finely balanced it could easily be upset. But only occasionally does his depression get the better of him in these days.

He knew he could not expect "adequate returns until the third year. In the mean time if those concerned fail in confidence or perseverance all is ruin."

And to his wife he admitted: "These things make me melancholy and I half believe I have got the Blues."

But expressions of discouragement are minor facets of Wyeth's character. The single comment in his letter book that best defines the man is this: "If true satisfaction is to be found it must be I think in the success of ones plans against the current of the worlds opinions and the ridicule of fools."

It was with this spirit that Wyeth pushed through his preparations in the face of all the difficulties that arose to plague him. True to his schedule, he was outfitted and at the final jumping-off place, Independence, by April 17, 1834.

There, of course, he found more trouble in the person of his nemesis, Bill Sublette.

III

St. Louis and Independence, the two great centers for departing brigades, were a riot of outfitting this spring of '34. Hugh Campbell was putting it moderately when he observed that St. Louis had

> quite a bustling apparance. There are two or three parties preparing for Santa fe. A party & outfit are getting ready for Captn Bonneville's Co. Another under Captn Wyeth for the R. M. F. C^o.—our friend Mr. S[ublette] has still another,—and to crown all, the dragoons are filling up for either escort or some other purpose.[3]

(There was another that Hugh didn't mention. The Company brigade was outfitting under Lucien—"we are always late"—Fontenelle; and was going to be late again by a few days.)

It was a race to get off first, and if you could throw a log in front of the other runners, so much the better. There, at Independence, Bill made one last attempt to torpedo Wyeth, probably more on general principle than any real hope of stopping the energetic Yankee. It happened like this:

> ...last year Sublette & Campbell took out to the mountains Capt Stewart & Doct. Harrison and authorized Milton Sublettes Company [RMF] to credit them and draw for the amt. These drafts Sublette & Campbell refused to honor . . . as soon as they ascertained that we were to supply Milton Sublettes Company with goods unless Milton Sublette would remain at home. [Wyeth]

The amount in question was about $500; on Bill Sublette's refusal to pay, Wyeth promptly advanced the money himself. Sublette's tactics were clear enough. Milton was now his most serious opposition in RMF. Little brother wasn't sitting still for it any more, and if Bill could get him out of the way everything would go much more smoothly. Wyeth would thus be deprived of his principal ally. However, it isn't likely Bill thought he could actually bring it off; he was probably making trouble simply as a matter of policy, on the principle that it didn't do any harm and might possibly do some good.

All this was taking place, incidentally, against a background of events that cast long shadows into American history. Wyeth's ornithologist passenger, Townsend, mentioned it in passing:

> The little town of Independence has within a few weeks been the scene of a brawl, which at one time threatened to be attended with serious consequences. ... It had been for a considerable time the stronghold of a sect of fanatics, called Mormons, or Mormonites, who, as their numbers increased, and they obtained power, showed an inclination to lord it over the less assuming inhabitants of the town ... accordingly the whole town rose, en masse, and the poor followers of the prophet were forcibly ejected from the community. They took refuge in the little town of Liberty, on the opposite side of the river, and the villagers here are now in a constant state of feverish alarm. Reports circulated that the Mormons are preparing to attack the town, and put the inhabitants to the sword, and they have therefore stationed sentries along the river for several miles, to prevent the landing of the enemy.

It would be thirteen years before the Mormons' epic trek into the wilderness, but here are the seeds of it.

For Wyeth, of course, the unsettled condition at Independence was just one more in a series of minor annoyances. The higher prices were bad enough, but when Bill Sublette showed his hand Wyeth decided he was obliged "to purchase a more expensive kind of animals than I had at first intended in order to be first at the rendesvous which I consider very important."

These eventualities all cut down on his margin for possible error. Everything had to go like clockwork from here on out. There was too much at stake now. Jason Lee and his fellow missionaries had not yet arrived; they were preaching their way out to the jumping-off point:

"There are none of the Dignitaries with me as yet," Wyeth wrote, "and if they 'preach' much longer in the States they will loose their passage for I will not wait a minute for them."

But when all the loose strings were gathered up, it was the relative newcomer Wyeth who was first out of the gate, several days ahead of his nearest competition.

John Townsend records their departure from Independence:

> On the 28th of April, at 10 o'clock in the morning, our caravan, consisting of seventy men, and two hundred and fifty horses began its march; Captain Wyeth and Milton Sublette took the lead, Mr. N[uttall] and myself rode beside them; then the men in double file, each leading, with a line, two horses heavily laden, and Captain Thing (Captain W's assistant) brought up the rear. The band of missionaries, with their horned cattle, rode along the flank.
>
> I frequently sallied out from my station to look at and admire the appearance of the cavalcade, and as we rode out from the encampment, our horses prancing, and neighing, and pawing the ground; it was altogether so exciting that I could scarcely contain myself. Every man in the company seemed to feel a portion of the same kind of enthusiasm; uproarious bursts of merriment, and gay and lively songs, were constantly echoing along the line. We were certainly a most merry and happy company. What cared we for the future? We had reason to expect that ere long difficulties and dangers, in various shapes, would assail us, but no anticipation of reverses could check the happy exuberance of our spirits.

Ten days later this exuberance was sharply dimmed. While only Wyeth was aware of the exact significance—"disastrous significance" might be better—the mood of it caught the whole camp. Townsend:

> 8th [May] This morning Mr. [Milton] Sublette left us to return to the settlements. He has been suffering for a considerable time with a fungus in one of his legs, and it has become so much worse since we started . . . that he finds it impossible to proceed. His departure has thrown a gloom over the whole camp. We all admire him for his amiable qualities, and his kind and obliging disposition. For myself, I had become so much attached to him, that I feel quite melancholy.

This was on Thursday. The following Monday, the 12th of May, Wyeth's plans—and RMF's future—received their sec-

ond serious blow. The camp had stopped for mending hob-
bles, intending to spend the day making the minor repairs
always necessary, and resting horses and men. Jason Lee got
a report that one of the mission cows was missing, and
scrambled out to find her. While ranging about ahead of the
camp the little search party came upon a fresh trail. Bill
Sublette had passed them in the night. Bill was making forced
marches, all the way across the prairie; and he was in better
shape to do it. His party was less than a third the size of
Wyeth's (as he carried no merchandise) and the lack of bulk
and awkwardness told. Townsend remarks the event, not
without a certain naïveté:

> They must have travelled very rapidly to overtake
> us so soon, and no doubt had men ahead watching
> our motions. It seems rather unfriendly, perhaps, to
> run by us in this furtive way, without even stopping to
> say good morning, but Sublette is attached to a rival
> company, and all strategems are deemed allowable
> when interest is concerned.

Wyeth immediately sent an express ahead to Fitzpatrick
and RMF:

> Wm Sublette having passed me here, I am induced
> to write to you. . . . You may expect me by the 1st
> July at the rendesvous named in your letter to Milton
> which which you sent by Dr. Harrison who opened it
> and I presume told Wm Sublette of the place. I am
> not heavily loaded and shall travell as fast as possible
> and have a sufficient equipment of goods for you
> according to contract. . . . Milton left me a few days
> since on account of his leg which is very bad. . . . P.S.
> I have sent a vessell around the Horn with such goods
> as you want and would like to give you a supply for
> winter rendesvous or next year on such terms as I
> know would suit you.

So Wyeth put on speed, and even with his missionaries and
scientists slowing him down managed to keep within two days
of Sublette's party. In view of the comparative sizes of the
two caravans—and Sublette's unquestioned ability and experience with such brigades—Wyeth's achievement is almost

monumental. It was a stacked competition with one of the best.

The rest of the journey is documented as speed, pressure, and more speed. Jason Lee agreeably threw himself into all the camp activities: stood his guard, watched over his mess, kept his cattle and crew in order. Townsend had observed that Lee looked big enough to take well to the trail—and he did. Though he was inclined to attribute to God a rather special interest in the caravan, providing for them in the shape of buffalo and game in plenty. He writes:

> Shot an Elk this P.M., which was very acceptable.
> ... Elk is not considered good meat except very fat.
> Through the goodness and mercy of God we have had
> plenty. O that our gratitude may keep pace with his
> mercies. Bless the Lord I think I do feel thankful for
> his goodness to me. Glory to God in the highest he
> feeds me with both corporeal and spiritual food.
> Amen. Insted of taking a due west course as we
> should have done we followed the River ... [and]
> lost our A.M. march.

But Lee was not a man wholly without humor. He, better than most of the missionaries who followed him, managed to adapt himself quite well to the mountain life. He was vigorous and curious and co-operative, taking the dirty jobs when he had to and entering into the trail procedure as best he could. Fairly early in the trip he and Townsend went out with a hunter named Richardson—"to learn to kill buffaloe," Lee says—and they had a long, hard chase of it. By the time they had brought their buffalo down, all the party was consumed with thirst.

Lee and Townsend, *mangeurs de lard*, wanted to ride back to the Platte at full speed for a little water, but Richardson just laughed. Drink aplenty right here, said he, and obligingly "invited (us) to partake ... of what they called cider but I chose not to participate in their beverage. It consisted of the water drawn from the paunch of the buffalo[4] ... but it was too thick with the excrement to please my fancy."

Lee told his diary only half the story. Richardson offered an alternative refreshment in the form of the fresh blood. While Townsend hadn't been enthusiastic about the cider, his thirst finally overcame his squeamishness. The hunter amiably opened up the buffalo heart, and Townsend "plunged my head into the reeking ventricles." He drank all he could hold, this happy greenhorn, and stood up and:

> turned my ensanguined countenance towards the missionary . . . but I saw no approval there: the good man was evidently attempting to control his risibility, and so I smiled to put him in countenance; the roar could no longer be restrained, and the missionary laughed until the tears rolled down his cheeks. I did not think, until afterwards, of the horrible ghastliness which must have characterized my smile at that particular moment.

And so the pork-eaters were gradually shaken down into mountain shape, and it is to their credit that they did so rapidly and well. The crossing was made in extraordinarily fast time—as was Sublette's, of course—and by the 1st of June they were already at the Laramie. Sublette was feeling the Yankee breath at his heels, for he'd left off thirteen men here. When Wyeth arrived, he camped beside the first cut logs of a post Sublette was establishing at the mouth of the Laramie. Bill called it Fort William—as with the Missouri fort—but it has come down in the texts as Fort Laramie. This group of Sublette's trappers were in the process of planting a little corn; and unknowingly establishing one of the great landmarks of American history, the famous stop-off on the Oregon Trail.

Wyeth reached Independence Rock early on the 9th of June. That evening he sat down and sent off another express to RMF, saying he was only two days behind Sublette and "shall continue to come on at a good rate. . . . I wish that you would defer making any contract for carrying home any surplus furs . . . or for a further supply of goods until I come."

It was the sheerest optimism, and Wyeth probably knew it. By the time he reached Rendezvous 1834, Sublette had been there for two days.

RMF had no surplus of furs at all. They didn't even have a company.

IV

Rendezvous 1834, observer John Kirk Townsend:

22nd. [June]—We are now lying at the rendez-vous. W. Sublette, Captains Serre, Fitzpatrick, and the other leaders, with their companies, are encamped about a mile from us, on the same plain, and our own camp is crowded with a heterogeneous assemblage of visitors. The principal of these are Indians, of the Nez Perce, Banneck and Shoshone tribes, who come with the furs and peltries which they have been collecting at the risk of their lives during the past winter and spring, to trade for ammunition, trinkets, and "fire water." There is, in addition to these, a great variety of personages among us; most of them calling them-selves white men, French Canadians, half-breeds, &c., their color nearly as dark, and their manners wholly as wild, as the Indians with whom they constantly associate. These people, with their obstreperous mirth, their whooping and howling and quarreling . . . their dashing into and through our camp, yelling like fiends, the barking and baying of savage wolf-dogs, and the insistent crackling of rifles and carbines, ren-der our camp a perfect bedlam. . . . I am confined closely to the tent with illness, and am compelled all day to listen to the hiccoughing jargon of drunken traders, the *sacré* and *foutre* of Frenchmen run wild, and the swearing and screaming of our own men, who are scarcely less savage than the rest, being heated by the detestable liquor which circulates freely among them.

Rendezvous 1834, observer the Rev. Jason Lee:

Some of the companies . . . threatened that when we came they would give them Missionaries "hell" and Capt. W[yeth] informed us and advised us to be on our guard and give them no offense and if molested to show no symptoms of fear and if difficul-ty did arise we might depend upon his aid for he never forsook any one who had put himself under his protection.

I replied . . . I *feared* no man and apprehended no danger from them when sober and when drunk we would endeavor to [keep] out of their way. . . .

another drunken crazy hooting quarreling fighting

frolic. . . . My God My God is there nothing that will have any effect on them?

Rendezvous 1834, observer Nathaniel Jarvis Wyeth:

. . . much to my astonishment the goods which I had contracted to bring up to the Rocky Mountain fur Co. were refused by those honorable gentlemen. Latt. 41°30'.

A figure of speech. Wyeth was not astonished; no more than any of us are astonished when our bleakest forebodings are realized.

From the rendezvous Wyeth wrote to Milton Sublette, informing him that Fitzpatrick had refused to abide by the contract:

I do not accuse you or him of any intention of injuring me in this manner when you made the contract but I think he has been bribed to sacrifice my interests by better offers from your brother. Now, Milton, business is closed between us, but you will find that you have only bound yourself over to receive your supplies at such price as may be inflicted and that all that you will ever make in the country will go to pay for your goods, you will be kept as you have been a mere slave to catch Beaver for others.

I sincerely wish you well and believe had you been here these things would not have been done. I hope that your leg is better and that you will be able to go whole footed in all respects.

I am Yr Obt. Servt N. J. Wyeth

In this Wyeth did Fitzpatrick an injustice. It does not seem likely that there was any bribe involved. Rather, Fitz and the other partners of RMF were helpless in the face of their debt to Bill Sublette.

It had been a miserable year for furs.[5] Tom Fitzpatrick had with him twenty-five packs when he wrote Milton the previous November. At that time he had high hopes that Fraeb and Gervais's brigades, which were still absent, would do well. It didn't work out that way. When Bill Sublette returned to the States, he took with him only about forty packs of furs. This is not all RMF fur; part of it would have been what Bill was able to trade at rendezvous from unattached—or treasonous—trappers. (Fontenelle complained of losing eight or ten packs by "the rascality of a few men.")

Even if thirty-five of the packs had been RMF's—a generous estimate—they would have been worth (maximum figures again) about $12,250 St. Louis; with deduction for freight only (50 cents a pound), $10,500. I haven't been able to establish the exact amount of debt; but it is beyond doubt that this year's catch fell far short of paying it, much less leaving anything for a new outfit.

Bill collected, and RMF was finished. The firm repudiated Wyeth's contract when he arrived at Ham's Fork on June 19; and on the 20th the breakup started.

There must have been an enormous confusion attending this collapse. Some of it is indicated by the fact that it apparently went on piecemeal throughout the day.

Old Frapp was the first to go:

> [Know] all men by these present that I Henry Fraeb late of the firm of the Rocky Mountain Fur Company ... in consideration of forty head of horse beast, forty beaver traps, eight guns and one thousand dollars worth of merchandise ...

He sold out, according to this document, to "Thomas Fitzpatrick, Milton G. Sublette, James Bridger and John Baptiste Jervey, remaining partners of said Company." But RMF was broke, as I have said. The above-named items were obligingly furnished by Bill Sublette, and he got an official one-fifth interest.

A little later in the day Gervais decided he, too, had had enough:

> Know all men by these present that I Jean Baptist Jervait late of the Firm of the rocky Mountain furr Co ... in consideration of twenty Head of Horse beast, thirty beaver traps and five Hundred dollars Worth of Merchandize ...

Bill Sublette must have provided the goods, as with Fraeb, but I have no written record of it. Whatever had gone on between the sale of Fraeb's interest and Gervais's decision, there was no longer any hope that "the greatest name in the mountains" would keep going. When Fitzpatrick signed Gervais's bill of sale it was not as a representative of RMF, but for "Fitzpatrick Sublette & Bridger."

The last nails in the coffin were a series of public notices, all worded about the same, which were probably circulated or posted at the other camps. This, then, is the end:

Whereas a dissolution of partnership having taken place by mutual consent between Thos Fitzpatrick, Milton G. Sublette, John Baptiste [Gervai]t and James Bridger members of the rocky mountain fur company all persons having demands against said company are requested to come forward and receive payment, those indebted to said firm are desired to call & make immediate payment as they are anxious to close the business of the concern

Ham's Fork June 20th 1834   Thos Fitzpatrick
test   M G Sublette
Wm L Sublette for   Henry Fraeb
Bridger & Fitzpatrick   J B Gervais
                 Witness (?) Ristey
                 for Fraeb & Gervais

                                               his
                                         James x Bridger
                                               mark

The Public are hereby notified that the business will in future be conducted by Thos Fitzpatrick, Milton G. Sublette & James Bridger under the style & firm of Fitzpatrick Sublette & Bridger

Hams fork June 20th 1834   Thos Fitzpatrick
test   M G Sublette
                                               his
Wm L Sublette   James x Bridger
                                               mark

End of an era. The competition now well and truly set at rest.

Afterword

The company that rose out of RMF's ashes—Fitzpatrick, Sublette & Bridger—was not a company at all. Milton Sublette, of course, was not even present, being in St. Louis. His leg was amputated there, and for a few years he used one of cork. But the amputation had come too late, and he died of his mysterious "fungus infection" on April 5, 1837. It is not certain who signed for Milton in the transactions described above; the signature is similar to Bill's in some respects, different in others. In any case Milton himself was not involved in the new company in any way.

That Fitzpatrick, Sublette & Bridger was a paper company is best indicated in a letter from Lucien Fontenelle to Pierre Chouteau. Fontenelle, leading the Company caravan, had arrived at Rendezvous 1834 late, as usual; but this time the timing was fortuitous, since he was able to pick up the shattered pieces. The pieces, in this case, constituted some of the best trappers in the mountains, and the Company emerged from Rendezvous 1834 in good odor indeed. On his way down the Missouri with the year's take, Fontenelle wrote his boss. He mentions the previous situation of RMF with respect to Bill Sublette, and continues:

> . . . they have concluded not to have anything more to do with William Sublette and it will surprise me much if he takes more than ten packs down next year. I have entered into partnership with the others and the whole of the beaver caught by them is to be

turned over to us by agreement made with them in concluding the arrangement.

So the Company got them in the end. Shortly after this, all pretense of an independent firm of Fitzpatrick, Sublette, & Bridger was given up and both Bridger and Fitz went officially on the payroll of American Fur.

Wyeth was doomed to see another of his grand notions explode into nothing. Joe Meek reports him as saying—after the contract had been repudiated: "Gentlemen, I will roll a stone into your garden that you will never be able to get out." It rings true—the stone in the garden is a New England-oriented threat, certainly. From rendezvous Wyeth proceeded to the Portneuf River, near the Snake, and built a fort. He christened it with "a bale of liquor" on August 6, and named it Fort Hall (after Henry Hall, his principal backer).

Fort Hall was Wyeth's stone in the garden. He left some of his men and goods there and went directly down to Fort Vancouver, still driving hard, trying to salvage something. His main hope now was his brig, the *May Dacre*. If he could establish her in the salmon trade, and set his men trapping south of the Columbia, and make an arrangement with Hudson's Bay on supplies, and perhaps carry goods back to next rendezvous . . .

Columbia River Oct 5th 1834
Dear Wife
   I am here but have had no good luck. The vessell was struck by lightening on her way out and detained so long that the salmon season was past.

Struck by lightning. (Guthrie, a man in Fraeb's brigade, had been struck by lightning in the fall of '33. Fraeb rushed out of his tent shouting "Py gott, who did shoot Guttery!" The answer, as reported by Meek, was "Gawd a' Mighty, I expect: He's a firing into camp.") It looked very much as if Somebody was firing into Wyeth's camp too, and with amazing accuracy.

Fort Hall was soon after sold to HBC and played a large part in the trapping history of the next few years. But it brought Wyeth about the same as all his other ventures—nothing at all.

He eventually returned to the ice business with his friend

and mentor Frederick Tudor. He did well there, developing tools and techniques and making a fine business success of his career; it was only in the mountains that he was unlucky. But one wonders if he did not, sitting in Cambridge, occasionally think back on what it would have been like without the reef that sank his first ship, or the lightning strike. "Let him have better luck," says Meek. And Wyeth did. But while it was going on he certainly had a sufficiently long run of the bad.

In spite of rumors to the contrary, Sublette & Campbell never again engaged to any extent in the fur trade. Shortly after the great breakup, they converted the firm into a mercantile outlet, wholesale-retail, and went through the economic vicissitudes of the late thirties in civilization. Sublette became active in politics—as had his mountain predecessor Ashley—but never achieved the stature of the worthy congressman-general.

Jason Lee, the Methodist mission to the Flatheads, startles us. For reasons best known to himself, he went on to Oregon. Several of the Flatheads and Nez Perces visited him at Rendezvous 1834, anxious to have the missionary or some of his party stay. Lee politely shook hands with them, said he might be back in two or three years, and promptly set out for the Willamette valley with Wyeth. He opened a famous mission in Oregon, and one which played an influential part in the history of that future state.

Why the mission to the Flatheads moved on so quickly is still something of a mystery. Lee says nothing about it in his diary, simply recording the hospitable way in which the Flatheads received him. Bernard DeVoto suggested that Lee was made fidgety by the *Zeitgeist;* which DeVoto takes to mean what he calls the Continental Mind. It may be so.

And so, with the documents quoted in the preceding chapter, the mountain trade has become the exclusive property of American Fur Company. It remained so for another nine years, until 1843. This date—which marks the establishment of Bridger's famous fort—is generally taken to mark the end of the trade, and rightly so.

American Fur had occasional squabbles with other small companies during this period, but nothing that compared with the terrible competition of '30–'34. The Company was never seriously threatened.

The chronicles of the years from 1834 to 1843 are chronicles of decay. The vigor has gone out of the trade, pushed by steadily sinking prices for beaver. More and more, the important fur was the coarse: buffalo robes. In the prime days—if one can really say such a time ever existed—most trappers wouldn't bother with coarse fur. The decline of beaver hats and the rise of silk killed the trade as we have seen it develop in the course of this narrative.

The emphasis after '34 came to be somewhat removed from the trade itself. The most important people in the mountains were not the fur hunters but the transients. Missionaries, visionaries, potential settlers; all of them people just passing through (usually to the enormous disgust of the old-time mountaineers). By 1840 some of the trappers were leaving the mountains for good. To Oregon and the Williamette valley, taking up the uncongenial and dissatisfying pursuit of farming. Most of them succeeded only poorly at it; they didn't take to steady cultivation any more than have most American Indians. The lives of some were complicated by the puritanical moral code of the pioneer; their Indian wives and half-breed children had a hard time of it in civilization, even when the civilization was no more than Oregon City.

In a period of decay we find the eccentricities more emphasized. In the late thirties and the forties the eccentric is the norm; Bill Williams is perhaps the classic example. The trappers had always had a jargon more or less their own, but now it became a complicated language of metaphor and symbol which, whatever else it may have accomplished, further separated the mountain man from the *mangeur de lard*.

It was during the forties that the mountain man fell into bad repute as a useless, evil-smelling old eccentric. The men that were left were being squeezed out of existence, and were just too damn cantankerous to admit it.

It seems to be incontrovertible fact that the mountain men who died happiest were those who finally gave up all pretensions to being white men. Who became Indians in name as well as fact: became Crows, Utes, Bannocks, Nez Perces. Who lived out the balance of their fading lives watching, with Indian eyes, the relentless progress of the American nation toward the west, hoping they would die before it could kill them with civilization.

Brief Calendar of Events
in the Fur Trade Preceding 1822

1796. Congress appropriates funds for the establishment of government factories to trade with Indians. All but one of these posts east of the Mississuppi.

1804. Louisiana Purchase; an area greater in extent than the United States as it then existed.

1804–1806. Lewis and Clark Expedition to the mouth of the Columbia River gives first information on vastness of the new territory. Called "incomparably the most perfect achievement of its kind in the history of the world."

1807. Manuel Lisa establishes first trading fort deep in the mountains, Fort Lisa, at the mouth of the Bighorn. Intention to open trade with Crows and Blackfeet, hitherto untouched tribes.

1809. Lisa's report on upriver prospects so favorable a new company formed to exploit these fields. Called Missouri Fur Company and containing "nearly all the prominent businessmen in the city [St. Louis]," including Pierre Chouteau, Sr., and Andrew Henry, later partner of General Ashley.

1810. One of Lisa's trapping parties, operating from Fort Lisa, moves into Blackfoot territory around the Three Forks of the Missouri. This party, under Andrew Henry, was equipped to trap beaver for itself, as well as trade with Indians; the first introduction of white trapping on a large scale into Indian country. Blackfeet savagely resisted the white intrusion, driving Henry across the divide to the waters of the Snake, where he made winter camp 1810–11.

1811. Bighorn post of Missouri Fur abandoned and all parties north of the Mandan villages pulled back. World trade situation steadily worsening, building to War of 1812. Beaver bringing a sad $2.50 a pound in St. Louis, making Lisa conservative.

1811. John Jacob Astor's great concept of a cross-continent-China trade. The Astoria enterprise organized with two parties. One traveled overland, roughly following the route pioneered by Lewis and Clark. Second traveled around the Horn on the ship *Tonquin*.

1812–1813. Astoria established. War of 1812 breaks out. Astoria surrendered to members of the British Northwest Company.

1813–1822. Interregnum. Trade depressed and virtually inactive due to economic slump following War of 1812. Manuel Lisa dies 1820, leaving control of Missouri Fur Company in hands of Joshua Pilcher. Joint-occupation treaty between Great Britain and United States signed in 1818, allowing each nation free access to "disputed area" between the continental divide and the Pacific, and between latitudes 42° and 49° N. After a bitter struggle resembling open warfare, the two Canada-based companies, Hudson's Bay and the Northwest Company, were amalgamated in 1821, taking the name Hudson's Bay Company.

1822. Government factory system overthrown in Congress. Economy of frontier coming to life. Many new enterprises being devised in St. Louis regarding fur trade on the upper Missouri, including Ashley-Henry venture.

APPENDIX A:

The Government Factory System

The career of the United States government as a fur-trading company is an ironic one. The credit—or blame—for its eventual ignominious failure has generally been laid to the fur trade's unofficial lobbyist, Senator Thomas Hart Benton, and to the more private and aggressive attacks of the American Fur Company's general agent, Ramsay Crooks. Benton, particularly, since it was he who conducted the campaign in Congress that led to the eventual overthrow of the government-conducted system. With the American Fur Company bitterly contesting the field and Benton in Congress, the government was indeed facing rugged and determined opposition, but it is probable that this opposition might eventually have been overcome. The deeper reasons for the failure of the factory system lay in inherent weaknesses in the system itself; it was virtually self-defeating as established. Acting through a mixture of irreconcilable motives, Congress evolved a plan of operation so contradictory in its elements that its chance of survival were, from birth, nil.

It was all conceived with admirable intent: benefit to the people of the country, meaning the frontier territory. But they tried to benefit too many people at the same time, and were incapable, when faced with a choice, of deciding which particular group was most important. The government system also fell between the two stools of public and private enterprise, and this uncomfortable arrangement was never settled to anyone's satisfaction until the system was abandoned.

In 1796 Congress appropriated funds for the establishment of factories—trading houses—to be located in Indian country. These establishments were not considered a commercial venture, but more a tool to be used in the increasingly difficult relations with the native inhabitants of the country. No profit was expected; the only monetary requirement was that the posts be self-sustaining. It was hoped that these factories would benefit the Indian in several ways: his furs would be bought at a fair price; his goods supplied likewise; he would gradually be familiarized with the white way of life, "so that, when the tide of settlement should have swallowed up his domains and have destroyed his ancient means of subsistence, he would accept his new situation without deep reluctance." By conducting its trade without liquor, the government hoped to save its charges from the already familiar disaster.

Considering the date, this was a remarkably farsighted plan. It involved an attempt to face the problem squarely, rather than postpone dealing with it. With the relentless westward pressure of the nation, it was seemingly clear to the initiators of this plan that a time would come when the Indian could be pushed ahead no longer, and would have to be dealt with. W. H. Crawford, Secretary of War, to this effect: "These views are substantially founded upon the conviction that it is the true policy and earnest desire of the government to draw its savage neighbors within the pale of civilization."

The government factories were duly established and stocked with the usual trade goods. Of these posts all but one were east of the Mississippi. The single exception was Fort Osage, or Fort Clark, on the Missouri about forty miles below the site of present Kansas City. This, the outlying post, was unstable. It was established in 1808, evacuated five years later, and only spasmodically occupied thereafter until it was formally abandoned on the founding of Fort Leavenworth.

It was a noble project, this attempt to soften the impact of white expansion on the Indian. Had it worked, the ensuing century of Indian relations might well have followed a different course. The fur trade, as envisioned under government management, would have been more a sociological instrument than a commercial enterprise. However, Congress was apparently reluctant to infringe on private enterprise to the extent of making the entire trade a government monopoly. Permits to trade continued to be issued to private concerns, thus bringing government policy into direct conflict with the commercial interest of individuals. By issuing trading licenses the government, in effect, created its own competition, and it was a competition motovated by entirely different desires than those of the government which licensed it.

The traders were, of course, concerned with only one thing: a profitable trade. Ethical matters did not weigh heavily in the balance against the pure aesthetic pleasure of a satisfactory account book. And, while the government factories were forced to operate under self-imposed limitations, the private trader was relatively free of these restrictions. There were naturally regulations governing the conduct of private trade, particularly with respect to liquor, but these were circumvented with great regularity and ingenuity.

The government posts had the advantage that they were under no obligation to make a profit, but they were handicapped in ways that far overbalanced this initial leverage in their favor. By refusing to supply liquor to the Indians they denied themselves, from the beginning, the most potent weapon in the trading arsenal. By securing their trade goods exclusively from American industry—not highly developed— what they offered for trade was often distinctly inferior to that provided by private traders, who commonly used British goods. Theirs was a "no credit" policy with the Indian, presumably in order to establish a sound sense of thrift. Trading was a passive affair; the government factors simply sat and waited until an Indian came in with his furs.

The private trader: used as much alcohol as he could smuggle in; used high-quality imported trade goods; allowed advance credit as desired, outfitting the Indian trapper before he began the hunt and thus, in effect, mortgaged his furs ahead of time. While the government factory waited for the Indian to volunteer his catch, the private trader developed the policy of accompanying his customers on their annual hunts. By collecting the pelts as they were taken, he guaranteed payment of the debt and, presumably, ensured that the Indian's credit rating would not be impaired by any oversight on his part.

The government simply could not compete on the same level as its own licensees. The very reasons for setting up a government trade prohibited the use of such tactics. This is not to imply, however, that the factory system was an immediate or unqualified failure. The wonder is that it succeeded as well as it did, for despite the advantages held by private concerns the government remained in the field for twenty-six years. During this time its share of the trade was great enough to incur the substantial hatred of the private traders who, for their part, believed the factories held an unfair advantage, and fought for their overthrow with persistent vigor.

Unofficial spokesman for the commercial traders was Ramsay Crooks, who, as general agent for John Jacob Astor's American Fur Company, was probably the most important critic of government policy. The intensity of his opposition and, by implication, the opposition of all the St. Louis traders is indicated in the letter of congratulations he sent Senator Benton on the final overthrow of the system in March, 1822. In it he refers to the "unqualified thanks of the community for destroying the pious monster ... the country is indebted for its deliverance from so gross and unholy an imposition."

Bonneville and Wyeth

In the spring of 1832 there were in the mountains two new parties of major importance. The activities of one of them, Captain Bonneville, were peripheral to the affairs of the Rocky Mountain Fur Company. Nathaniel Wyeth, however, became deeply involved in the affairs of RMF and was a major character in the remaining two years of the company's existence.

The historical importance of both these men warrants giving their background in somewhat greater detail than was possible in the narrative text.

I

Benjamin Louis Eulalie de Bonneville (known to the Indians less euphonically as Bald Head) was a captain of the 7th Infantry. French born, he had come to the United States as a child, a fugitive from the Napoleonic Wars. He graduated from West Point in 1815 and subsequently served tours of duty in such frontier posts as Fort Gibson, Oklahoma, and Fort Smith, Arkansas. On these tours he was brought into contact with various Indian traders, pioneers, trappers, and other assorted wilderness wanderers. Bonneville was not the first to have his imagination fired by their stories, nor certainly the last. As Washington Irving later described it:

> (He) became so excited by their tales of wild scenes and wild adventures, and their accounts of vast and magnificent regions as yet unexplored, that an expedition to the Rocky Mountains became the ardent desire of his heart, and an enterprise to ex-

plore untrodden tracts the leading object of his ambition.

There is a moderately intriguing air of mystery about this
1832 junket of Bonneville's. For one thing, it has been
suggested that he was serving the government in some capacity as a spy; ferreting out the secrets of British infiltration in
the disputed area, and what not.

(The argument for this seems to me flimsy. It is summed
up by Bernard DeVoto in *Across the Wide Missouri* thus:
"One can hardly believe that in the late autumn of 1831 the
Army, under the Secretary of War, would grant a two-year
leave of absence to an officer who was going to Oregon
without considering what he might accomplish there and
briefing him accordingly. . . . Finally when Bonneville over-
stayed his leave . . . he was dismissed [from] the service—
only to be reinstated by the commander-in-chief, Andrew
Jackson . . . even an admiration for maps would hardly have
justified a full pardon for a grave military offense." But when
Bonneville returned to civilization he didn't report to Washington, as might have been expected; he went directly to
Astor's house as a guest [where he met Irving]. With the
mountain parties anxious enough to give all the information
they could on British activities [which were no secret any-
way] such an undercover assignment seems unnecessary.
However, this is the army, and the military mind is passing
strange. It may have been so.)

Whatever the actual case, Bonneville was officially on a
26-month leave, running from August, 1831, to October,
1833. In granting him leave, the War Department authorized
it

for the purpose . . . of exploring the country to the
Rocky mountains and beyond, with a view to ascer-
taining the nature and character of the several tribes
inhabiting those regions; the trade which might be
profitably carried on with them; the quality of the
soil, the productions, the minerals, the natural history,
the climate, the geography and topography, as well as
the geology of the various parts of the country.

As far as it is possible to tell, however, Bonneville was
simply intending to engage in the fur trade. The army gave
him no money; expenses were contributed by private individ-

uals, and there is some kind of connection with John Jacob Astor in the background. While he did make two maps, there was very little in them that had not appeared on the map of Albert Gallatin a year previous (and which was, in turn, based on information from Ashley and the Smith Jackson & Sublette parties). He seemed to have a really massive enjoyment of the mountain life with all its little freedoms from civilized conventions. Certainly he made no great effort to get back to the army.

(Hubert Howe Bancroft, who vilifies both Irving and Bonneville up one side and down the other, claims Bonneville "was in his coarse way a *bon vivant* and voluptuary . . . [and] preferred lording it in the forest with a troop of white and red savages at his heels, and every fortnight a new unmarried wife flaunting her brave finery, to sitting in satin sackcloth of conventional parlors and simpering silly nothings . . . [to Bonneville] men were the nobler game, whom to search out in their retreat and slaughter and scalp were glorious. What were the far-off natives . . . doing, that this reckless, bloodthirsty and cruel Frenchman should . . . kill them?" They just don't make historians like Bancroft any more.)

Bonneville's principal backing came from Alfred Seton, one of the original Astorians, and a group of more or less anonymous gentlemen associated with him. (There is a strong presumption that one of these was Astor himself.) For his field lieutenants he picked Michael Cerré and Joe Walker. Both were tough, experienced partisans and good men for the job. Both had been involved in the Santa Fe trade, and Cerré had worked around the upper Missouri.

One of Bonneville's notions was to prove the contention Bill Sublette had made in 1830; that wagons could be taken across the divide at South Pass. At the final tally, before leaving civilized settlements, Bonneville had a party of 110 men and 20 wagons. Walker and Cerré had recruited the party, and it was as motley as most:

> Their very appearance and equipment exhibited a piebald mixture, half civilized and half savage. Many of them looked more like Indians than white men, in their garbs and accoutrements, and their very horses were caparisoned in barbaric style, with fantastic trappings. The outset of a band of adventurers on one of these expeditions is always animated and joyous.

The welkin rang with their shouts and yelps, after the manner of the savages; and with boisterous jokes and light-hearted laughter. As they passed the straggling hamlets and solitary cabins that fringe the skirts of the frontier, they would startle their inmates by Indian yells and war-whoops, or regale them with grotesque feats of horsemanship well suited to their half savage appearance.

Bonneville's jumping-off place had been Fort Osage (ten miles from Independence) and he got off on the 1st of May, 1832. His wagons traveled in two columns in the center; the rest of the party was about equally divided into a van and rearguard. By now the route up the Platte and Sweetwater to South Pass was well known, and Bonneville's passage was not novel, though too much has been made of his wagons. (It is, of course, quite true that they were the first actually to cross the divide, with the exception of Ashley's small artillery piece). Bill Sublette's spring '30 caravan had preceded him all the way; and the crossing of the vast plateau called South Pass presented no particular problems.

By July 20 Bonneville was in sight of the Wind River range, and the succeeding week saw him over South Pass and into the basin of the Green River. Toward noon on the 26th the caravan was alarmed by a cloud of dust rising directly on their trail.

The party halted and drew up; held a brief council of war; and dispatched scouts while the wagons were drawn into defensive position. (They had previously crossed Indian trail, and the consensus was that a war party had hidden until Bonneville's caravan was in the open plain, and without natural protection.)

However, the scouts soon returned with the news that the dust was being made by a party of whites; fifty or sixty Company men and a supply train headed for Pierre's Hole and Rendezvous 1832. This was the supply caravan for which Vanderburgh and Drips were waiting at rendezvous; the Company opposition to Bill Sublette. Lucien Fontenelle was the partisan, and he was late. Rendezvous 1832 was, by this time, already over: Bill Sublette, bullet wound and all, was preparing to leave for St. Louis.

In an attempt to make up time, the party was making forced marches. After a brief conversation with Bonneville, Fontenelle scooted on ahead to the Green, which he hoped to reach by nightfall. The main body of his party made it, but at the cost of extreme exhaustion for men and horses.

Bonneville came up next morning, the 27th, and the two parties camped near each other. Here Fontenelle amiably lifted a few of Bonneville's best trappers—a band of Delaware Indians—by offering them $400 for the fall hunt. The Delawares picked up their gear and left Bonneville for the padded embrace of the solvent Company, which could not expect to get enough beaver from them to pay their salaries.

Shortly after this both camps moved upriver to the vicinity of Horse Creek. This seemed to Bonneville an excellent location for a permanent establishment. Accordingly, he took its position (getting the longitude wrong by about 125 miles) and began to build the post you will find in history books as Bonneville's Old Fort, or Fort Bonneville. It was known among the mountain men as Fort Nonsense, or Bonneville's Folly. At this point, while camped near Fontenelle, Bonneville entered our narrative for the first time.

II

Nathaniel Jarvis Wyeth, ice merchant of Cambridge, Massachusetts; a man whose intelligence, perseverance, and adaptability have often been underrated.

Properly speaking, Wyeth's story begins with another man, the feverish Prophet of Oregon, Hall J. Kelley. Kelley, a Boston teacher, had been enamored—impassioned might be a better word—with the idea of Oregon for fifteen years before Wyeth's entrance on the scene. Kelley's was one of the higher-pitched voices of Manifest Destiny, and he brought to his chosen task the dedication and passion of the fanatic; and also the fanatic's unwillingness to let facts influence his position.

Beginning in about 1817, shortly after the failure of the Astoria enterprise, Kelley became obsessed by the notion of American expansion to Oregon. He saw this distant country (figuratively speaking; he'd never been there) as a sort of Elysian Field, which it was the duty and necessity of the United States to claim. "I foresaw," he said, "that Oregon must, eventually, become a favorite field of modern enterprise, and the abode of civilization."

This is a most moderate statement from Kelley; more frequently his perorations were laced with a religious fervor. All his knowledge of Oregon was based, of course, on reading the journals of Lewis and Clark and the various documents of sea captains who had visited the coast. He believed every word of praise, stoutly ignored any slight hint that Oregon might not be heaven-on-earth, and based his exhortations on the resulting view. After a while it seemed to him that the actual visitors had missed the true glories, and he began to make things up.

This was all very wild and interesting, and Kelley eventually came to conclude that he was the chosen leader of the colonization; the Boston Moses, as it were, who would lead his flock to the promised land.

In 1829 he organized the American Society for Encouraging the Settlement of the Oregon Territory. His notion was simple enough, if a little difficult to put into practice: he wanted to transplant a Massachusetts town to Oregon, as the nucleus of the western civilization. In 1831 the organization was incorporated as the Oregon Colonization Society, with its headquarters in Boston, and Kelley began to organize an expedition.

This was the state of things when Nathaniel Wyeth, then twenty-nine, became involved in Kelley's great scheme. But for Kelley's hot mysticism, Wyeth substituted a rock-hard, Yankee practical sense. Wyeth was more interested in commercial and practical questions than in the visionary fulfillments foreseen by Kelley.

It wasn't long before Wyeth was disillusioned with the Oregon Colonization Society. He intended to accompany them—if the great migration ever took place—but he was also hedging his bets. If the wavering and insubstantial leadership of Hall Kelley was not sufficient, then Wyeth would organize a party of his own; which he proceeded to do. In November, 1831, he wrote:

> As time passes on the project of emigration assumes form and shape, and a nearer approach toward certainty. I think there is little doubt of my going, for I find that I can get good men who will follow me on a trading project, on the basis of division of profits, and this thing I will do (if I can) if the emigration fails.

Wyeth conducted an intensive campaign of research, involving himself with the accumulation of any and all knowledge he thought might be useful. He wrote query after query: detailed questions, for example, on the cultivation of tobacco. With tobacco an important part of the fur trade, what would be the chances of cultivating it in Oregon? And how? To his brother, in the same letter quoted above:

> Will you have the goodness to collect the information required for answering the questions below and as soon as practicable forward me answers to them ... be pleased to give your answers as definite as possible and be certain that it is correct as ... a mistake would be bad business.
>
> 1st Should it be planted as early in the season as to be entirely out of the reach of Frost, or will it bear a slight degree of it.
>
> 2nd How should the seed be planted in the field where it is intended to grow? or in beds to be transplanted?
>
> 3rd In what scituations and soil? with manure or without? in a dry or wet place?
>
> 4th How thick will it thrive
>
> 5th what mode of culture is required weeding? training, gathering at what time
>
> 6th method is used to cure it and how kept after it is cured
>
> 7th How is the seed obtained at what time gathered How treated and kept and what is the ordinary quantity required per cwt. of the product usually
>
> Beside these queries be good enough to make any remark which you think will be usefull in the culture of the plant.

Wyeth applied the same persistent attack to all phases of the expedition. Letters to fishermen—there were salmon on the west coast; how caught? how preserved? what is the market?—letters to merchants, government officials, bankers. He wallowed in information as Kelley wallowed in inspiration.

Above all, he wanted to keep his plans as flexible as possible. He was profoundly aware that his knowledge was wanting; and planned to guard against evils arising from this lack. In December 1831, he wrote that his expedition would go "without positively settling the particular business in which they will engage but to be dictated by circumstances when there (probably the fur business will be selected)."

By January: "We have no connection with Mr. Kelleys enterprise further than accident and circumstances may indicate."

Inevitably, aspects of the ludicrous crept in; bugles and amphibiums coming first to mind. Apropos of the wonderful notion of bugles:

> [They] should be of the plainest kind and the most simple to use and the least liable to get out of repair or broken . . . sometimes in marching a little music will enliven us. We propose that one should learn it well and then teach all the rest. We shall have as much as ten and to be used alternately so as not to be tedious to any one. I am utterly ignorant of all kinds and uses of music but have thought that we could march by a number of bugles but if we cannot they will at least do for signals. . . . If Thomas will make himself master of the bugle . . . please write immediately . . . as in case that he does not I must engage some other person to do it.

The amphibiums were the Wyeth answer to plains and river crossings; thirteen-foot boat-wagons, resembling a cross between a canoe and a gondola. Wagons on land, barges on rivers; the Harvard students—even then notoriously easy to amuse—lined up to jeer them as they went by. In Independence somebody convinced Wyeth they were impracticable and he abandoned them; sold them for half what they'd cost him and went over to the more traditional type of travel.

The scheme finally resulting from all this meticulous study was one very similar to that of John Jacob Astor twenty years earlier. As Wyeth saw it, and quite correctly, the major deterrent for a trading company operating in Oregon was the enormous risk and expense of overland supplying. He proposed to cut this expense by having the major portion of his supplies sent around the Horn by ship; the captain undertaking the job on shares. On its return from the Pacific, the supply ship could bring a cargo not only of furs, but of salmon. (The previous spring the brig *Owyhee*, operating in the northwest coast trade, had brought some fifty-three barrels of salted salmon from the Columbia. Fourteen dollars a barrel—$754; with a larger load the expenses of the whole trip might be paid by this profitable sideline.)

(Wyeth's mind brimmed over with such supplementary

money-making ideas; as he wrote an inquirer, "as to giving you every particular of this business it is quite impossible. Two days would not suffice to write such a letter.")

After a couple of false starts, Wyeth finally made arrangements with Captain Lambert of the brig *Sultana* for the sea half of the expedition. When he gave up hope that Kelley's party would ever get off, Wyeth had set as his own approximate date of departure March 1, 1832. In spite of endless difficulties with his financing—his only backing was what he could scrape up from friends, relatives, etc.—he came very close to this date, leaving Boston on March 10.

He had more than a little trouble with recruiting. He agreed to take along a few of Kelley's adherents, but was obviously not enthusiastic about the idea. He was in no position to be nursemaiding the visionaries, and this was clearly what he feared. He engaged in a voluminous correspondence with prospective recruits, all of whom were consumed with detailed curiosity, and toward the end his patience was growing a little short. (I also suspect he was somewhat tired of the pleading position he was often forced into when asking for money. The role of humble petitioner was not one he enjoyed, nor was he well suited to it. His requests are occasionally almost curt with embarrassment.)

To one of his prospectives he wrote:

> As to difficulties in the undertaking each man must judge for himself and also what his prospect of gain. What my own opinion is on the subject may be judged of by my giving up for it a salary of 1200 per year and a buisness that brought me as much more. My own opinion of this thing must be good or I am an errant fool. To say more on this head would be useless. Examine for yourself, look about.

When he left Boston on March 10, Wyeth had a twenty-man party, and in Baltimore picked up four more. Among the recruits were his older brother Jacob, as company surgeon, and a nephew (or cousin), John B. Wyeth. (Wyeth wryly informed Jacob that "the amt. of salary which you will receive is not worth the trouble of asking about.") John B. was eighteen and unruly; he later deserted the party with much bad feeling. Jacob, too, eventually deserted, but apparently without John B.'s malice. This party of twenty-four was only about half Wyeth's original intention; but he said March, and by God March it was going to be.

When he finally arrived at St. Louis, Wyeth had his first in-the-flesh contact with men of the trade; men who knew what they were doing as thoroughly as Wyeth hoped *he* knew. The novice could have had no better introduction than the two men he did meet, and who helped him. Kenneth McKenzie, King of the Missouri, gave Wyeth himself and a portion of his party a lift up to Independence on the Company steamboat *Otter*, McKenzie being on his way back to Fort Union.

Three of the recruits got no farther than Independence; three more dropped out along the Platte. The party was characterized as being "men of theory, not of practice," and their inexperience began to show at this early stage.

While camped at Independence preparatory to moving out, Wyeth made the acquaintance of Bill Sublette. Sublette's supply party was shaping up to head for Pierre's Hole and Rendezvous 1832; Bob Campbell was back from Ireland and going up, too. Sublette took the Yankee under his wing, and it seems reasonable to suppose that Wyeth's party would not have reached the mountains at all had it not been for Bill's help and guidance. Consensus among historians is that one glance showed Sublette he had nothing to fear from the little party of theorists, and so he took them on. If so, Sublette underestimated their leader, if not the party. He was to regret his generous gesture in the future, but for now—he played the gentleman.

The first pages of Wyeth's journal of this trip have been lost, and it opens abruptly—and appropriately—about thirty-five days out of Independence:

> . . . gray and my face like a plumb pudding the skin is entirely bare [?] of skin is entirely off one of my ears On the blufs the ghnats are equally troublesome but they do not annoy us much except in the day.

Wyeth and his crew were now getting their first taste of cross-country travel; and found it less than congenial: "21st (June) . . . Some of my men talk of turning back and I give them all free liberty many of my horses have given out and the rest are failing fast and unless we soon come to better grass they will all die and leave me on foot."

For Sublette, Fitzpatrick, and Bob Campbell this was all routine, of course, and it must have been with some amusement that they watched the tribulations of the *mangeurs de lard.*

They pushed steadily on, fifteen to twenty-five miles a day, and even found the occasion to turn a bit of profit. While engaged in crossing the Laramie there was an Indian scare, which proved to be a false alarm. The party that joined them was a contingent of the little Gant & Blackwell firm; the former firm is more accurate, since, as Tom Fitzpatrick informed their leader, Gant & Blackwell had gone bankrupt. Their booshway promptly sold 120 skins to Fitzpatrick, which were put *en cache.* The nineteen men then joined Fitzpatrick's party of RMF recruits and went the rest of the way to the mountains in company with them. (Fitz was apparently bring up some new trapping hands; and was leading a semi-autonomous party of his own. It has generally been stated that Fitz rode out from Rendezvous 1832 to hurry Sublette up. This is not the case. Zenas Leonard [of the Gant & Blackwell party], Wyeth's journal, and Newell's jottings make it sufficiently clear that Fitz had been in St. Louis during the winter and accompanied Sublette's party back up. Leonard saw him twice; going in to St. Louis and coming back.)

Shortly after this negotiation with the ex-Gant & Blackwell men, Fitzpatrick (according to Zenas Leonard)

> took one of the fleetest and most hardy horses in his train, and set out in advance of the main body, in order to discover the disposition of the various Indian tribes through whose dominions we were to travel, and to meet us at a designated point of the head of the Columbia river.

(This was the foray that led Fitz into his encounter with the Gros Ventres, described in Chapter 17 of the text.)

A couple of weeks after this, Sublette's supply train, with Wyeth still in attendance, was joined by a nineteen-man brigade from American Fur, who were also on their way to Pierre's Hole for the rendezvous. They were, by this time, on uncertain ground. Fitzpatrick had not been at the appointed meeting place, and Sublette was worried.

Trouble materialized quickly enough. About midnight on the same night they met the American Fur Company brigade: "We were awoke from our slumbers by a furious attack by a large party of Blackfeet." (Gros Ventres, actually, as determined later; but the trappers very rarely made a distinction between Big Bellies and their close confreres, the Blackfeet.)

It was a horse raid, naturally, and the Gros Ventres stood off about fifty yards and poured forty or so shots from their smooth-bore fusils into camp; and a few arrows. Three horses were wounded and they got off with five from Sublette's party, one from a free trapper, and four from Wyeth. (Wyeth observed with some satisfaction: "mine were all poor and sore backed and useless.")

From this skirmish they moved on toward Pierre's Hole with the company of the Company; the detached brigade from American Fur went along for mutual protection. On the 4th of July, appropriately enough, they crossed the divide and were in Oregon; the waters now flowed west. A symbolic gesture was in order for Wyeth, now officially in the promised land, so "drank to my friends with mingled feelings from the waters of the Columbia mixed with alcohol and eat of a Buffaloe cow."

Water and straight alcohol and fat cow; he was well on his way to being a mountain man.

On the 8th they pulled into Pierre's Hole for Rendezvous 1832.

> ... here we found about 120 Lodges of Nez Perces and about 80 of the Flatheads a company of trappers of about 90 under Mr Dripps ... connected with the American Fur Co. Many independent Hunters and about 100 men of the Rocky Mountain Fur Co under Mess Milton Sublette and Mr Frapp.

APPENDIX C:

Notes on the Sources

As a matter of course, many hundreds of books, articles, journals, state historical quarterlies, government documents, letters, account books, and what not were used in making this book. To list them all would be fatuous and misleading. For one thing, the reader would receive an exaggerated—though flattering—impression of my own assiduity. A great many of the sources were read simply for pleasure, because I enjoyed them. Others—and this is true of most historical bibliographies, I think—were useful mainly as confirmations of points found elsewhere or as sources for one disputed event. I have always objected to the fact that bibliographies in the academic tradition are badly out of perspective. They don't tell you what is important and what is of minor value. As a result, the novice can spend months searching for a rare document only to find that it is an inadequate paraphrase of something he can find more accurately somewhere else.

You can't learn the history of the fur trade from this book or any other modern book. You can learn a good deal of what I think about the trade (possibly—as with the little girl and her penguin book—more than you really care to know), but it ought to be understood that this is of secondary importance. The only way in which a really accurate picture can be gained is to return to the contemporary sources. A reader who wants to go into the history of the trade thoroughly should use a book like this as a starting wedge only; a detailed introduction; an outline. I've tried to add to its value by the practice of quoting extensively when possible, hoping to give the reader something of the flavor and accuracy of the original documents.

These notes, then, are not a bibliography at all, in the

usual sense. They are an attempt to hammer the wedge in a little farther, with a minimum of confusion. They do not by any means account for all statements in the text, but they would, I think, be a good start for a reader inclined to go on in the literature of the trade.

The immediate handicap facing the student is that many of the important sources are more or less rare. Several publishers—the Champoeg Press of Portland, Oregon, and the University of Oklahoma Press come first to mind—are steadily bringing important works back into print. Nevertheless, there is a great body of material which will probably never be published at all, and must be gotten in the original form. In the list that follows I have tried to concentrate on works which might reasonably be expected to be available through a good book dealer or a good library.

Any study of the American fur trade begins with *A History of the American Fur Trade of the Far West,* by Hiram Martin Chittenden ($12.50). This was first published in 1902. In 1954 a two-volume reprint edition was brought out by Academic Reprints, Stanford, California. This edition has since been remaindered, but should be available through a book dealer at a reasonable price.

Chittenden is the only complete and useful study of the trade made to date. It is time for another, since a good deal of material has come to light since Chittenden wrote, but as yet no one has attempted it. With this newly available information, it appears that Chittenden needs a certain amount of modification on points of detail. As an over-all outline of the trade, however, he is unequaled, and will certainly provide the standard against which any new work must be measured.

The sources for the story of the early phases of RMF—the Ashley-Henry enterprises and Smith Jackson & Sublette—are widely scattered in government documents, manuscripts, etc. The best starting point for a modern reader will be in two comparatively recent books.

The first of these, in point of time, is *The Ashley-Smith Explorations and the Discovery of a Central Route to the Pacific, 1822—1829,* by Harrison Dale (Chicago, 1918; $35.00; O.P.). Mr. Dale's interest, as indicated by his title, is principally geographic; his emphasis is on the exploratory work done by the mountain men. As a consequence, he admirably details routes followed, discoveries made, and so forth. Probably the greatest value of this book is the fact that he reprints in full several documents of first importance. Ashley's narrative of his expedition of 1825 is one (a letter written to Henry Atkinson of Dec. 1, 1825). Dale also reprints several documents pertaining to Jedediah Smith's California expeditions, including the two journals of his clerk, Harrison Rogers. (A reprint of this work is sometimes found at about $25.00.)

Except for the reprinted documents, this book has largely been supplanted by a more recent study, *Jedediah Smith and the Opening of the West,* Dale Morgan (New York, 1953); $7.50–$10.00; O.P.). Mr. Morgan is a scholar of the first order whose care and thoroughness provide the mere amateur of history, like myself, with a standard of precision not easily equaled. My own book is the more carefully researched for having the example of Dale Morgan before me; and greater praise hath no student. . . . My debt to him is obvious throughout, and I hope my comments on his work are adequately tempered with the respect due one's betters.

While his book is nominally concerned with Smith, it is in actuality a meticulous chronicle of the trade during the years 1822–1831. His bibliographic work is a virtually inexhaustible supply of leads, clues, and sources for the serious student. Two Appendices—"Letters by Jedediah S. Smith Relating to His Explorations" and "Personal Letters by Jedediah S. Smith and His Family"—are invaluable source material. It is a shame that this book has been allowed to go out of print.

Among the original sources for the early period, *James Clyman, American Frontiersman* is important. Edited by Charles L. Camp—another fine scholar of the trade—this book consists of Clyman's reminiscences. The edition of 1928, published in San Francisco, is now very rare and expensive; I worked largely from a microfilm copy provided by the Library of Congress. A completely new edition, published by Champoeg, should be in print by the time this book is published (about $25.00).

The history of the Aricara campaign is best approached through a series of government documents, the principal one being *18th Congress, 1st Session, Senate Document 1, Serial 89.* Several other government publications cast a good deal of light on these years: *18th Cong., 1st Sess., Sen. Doc. 56, Serial 89* contains Pilcher's answers to questions put him by the Congressional Committee under Thomas Hart Benton. See also *20th Cong., 2nd Sess., Sen. Doc. 67;*

21st Cong., 2nd Sess., Sen. Doc. 39, and *22nd Cong., 1st Sess., Sen. Executive Doc. 90.* These government publications may be found in some libraries, though the fact that they are so old makes even this uncertain.

The Travels of Jedediah Smith, Maurice S. Sullivan, ed. (Santa Ana, 1934; $75.00), contains an excellent treatment of Smith and—more important—the surviving portions of his journals. Out of print and expensive.

British activities are best followed through the magnificent publications of the Hudson's Bay Record Society. These books, publications from the HBC archives, are unfortunately available only through subscription, but any library with a good collection of western Americana should have them. On occasion isolated volumes may be available through antiquarian book dealers. In the course of this narrative I have used a number of them, most important being *Ogden's Snake Country Journals, 1824–1826,* E. E. Rich, ed. ($25.00), and *McLoughlin's Fort Vancouver Letters, First Series, 1825–1838,* same editor ($10.00). (McLoughlin's letters are generally found only in the complete three-volume set at about $35.00.) This series is quite essential to any student of western history. Also necessary is *Fur Trade and Empire,* Frederick Merk, ed. (Cambridge 1931; $12.50), which contains George Simpson's Journal for 1824–1925 and other valuable supplementary material, some of which is quoted in my text. All quotations from their publications are with the kind permission of Hudson's Bay Record Society.

I think my feelings about Joe Meek's narrative, *River of the West,* Frances Fuller Victor ($7.50), are made sufficiently clear in the body of this book. For historical accuracy it ought to be used with care; for pleasurable reading it ought to be used with complete abandon. A reprint edition was issued in 1950 by Long's College Book Company, and should still be available from that source.

The Champoeg Press, Portland, Oregon, has several volumes of interest to students of the trade. *Journal of a Trapper,* Osborne Russell ($20–25), is a little later than this narrative. (Russell came out for the first time with Wyeth's second expedition.) But as a record of mountain life it is irreplaceable and should be consulted for much detail of the trapper's life. It is now out of print.

Champoeg has also recently published *Robert Newell's Memoranda,* the brief notes of Joe Meek's companion. Only a part of this book deals with Newell's mountain experience, but it forms a valuable cross-check and, in some cases, the only authority for the movements of various brigades. The Champoeg books are superbly made by Lawton Kennedy of San Francisco, and *Robert Newell's Memoranda* is one of the most beautiful of a series of fine volumes. Unfortunately it is marred by the appearance of several typographical errors which seem to me unforgivable in a book of this quality. (Though one of them is the funniest in recent remembrance: the identification of the famous battleground of Pierre's Hole as "Pierre's Hotel.") The main purpose and importance of the book, however, is to present Newell's own material, which it does most beautifully. The book will probably be out of print by the time this is read, and I cannot even guess the price.

The University of Oklahoma Press, Norman, Oklahoma, has preserved the language of the mountain men in two books. *Life in the Far West*, Frederick Ruxton ($3.75), is a novel—only semifictional, however—originally printed in *Blackwood's Edinburgh Magazine* in 1848. Edited in book form by LeRoy R. Hafen in 1951, it is one of the best—and certainly the most flavorful—records of mountain life. Here are all the eccentricities of dress, language, behavior and thought of the mountain men, and there is no other source half so good. *Wah-To-Yah and the Taos Trail*, Lewis Garrard ($2.00), is another contemporary narrative, but deals with the trade somewhat south of the area covered in this book. It, too, has a good record of language and habits and includes several fine stories which have become part of the mountain tradition. Oklahoma is regularly adding titles to its excellent American Exploration and Travel Series, the latest (at this writing) being *Adventures of Zenas Leonard, Fur Trader*, John Ewers, ed. ($4.00). Leonard, too, must be used with some caution and frequent cross-checking. These books are all in print.

Washington Irving's two narratives, *Astoria* and *Captain Bonneville*, are available in a number of editions, and should be considered primary source material in spite of the disrepute in which Irving has been held lately. His shadowed reputation seems to be solely a result of the dislike Hubert Howe Bancroft took to his work.

For the years in which RMF operated officially under the name, *Life in the Rocky Mountains*, Warren Angus Ferris; Paul C. Phillips, ed. ($25.00), is one of the best sources. There are two available editions, of which the one published in Denver in 1940, under the above editor, is the better. Ferris was a Company man, with Vanderburgh's brigade at the time of the latter's death. The book was originally published as a series of the *Western Literary Messenger,* which eventually caused "the readers . . . to beseech the editor to give them no more of it." Mr. Ferris' literary style is not the best in the world. (Most of these mountain records, including Beckwourth's, are at their worst when a professional writer has gotten hold of them and given them the florid style of the day. In their raw, half-literate form they are much more acceptable and accurate.)

Wyeth's correspondence and journals pertaining to his two expeditions are printed in *Sources of the History of Oregon,* F. G. Young, ed. (Eugene, 1889; $15–$20). These are extremely valuable, and I've found them among the most pleasurable of the contemporary writings.

For the history of the trade after the collapse of RMF, Bernard DeVoto's epic study *Across the Wide Missouri* makes an excellent introduction (Boston, 1947; $10.00).

For the flavor of the times, I think Meek's *River of the West,* Russell's *Journal of a Trapper,* the DeVoto, and the A. B. Guthrie, Jr. modern novel *The Big Sky* are excellent, and should give a good, broad picture. The Guthrie book, aside from being an excellent novel, is dependably accurate with respect to the trade. Many of the incidents recounted are taken directly from the literature of the trade, or only slightly modified. The story of Boone Caudill is about as close to being the story of a typical mountain man as is possible. Meek's record provides the humor that was also an important aspect and which Guthrie, for sufficient reason, touches on only briefly. These four books, with the addition of Ruxton's *Life in the Far West,* provide an excellent introduction to the daily life of the mountain men.

The West of Alfred Jacob Miller (Norman, 1951; $10.00) is the pictorial equivalent of all the writing, and further contains Miller's own comments, which adds to its value. It contains reproductions of two hundred of Miller's paintings; by far the best pictorial record of the mountain trade we have.

For those interested in deeper digging, there is an excellent bibliography, *The Mountains and the Plains,* Wagner and Camp ($25.00), which should be available in a good library.

The prices given in the above are as of January, 1960.

Those of books in print are list price. Those of books not in print are given as an approximate market value in the antiquarian trade. The book trade being what it is, any of these volumes might be found at lower or higher prices than those listed. For these—and much bibliographic help in research—I am indebted to Preston McMann of the Old Oregon Bookstore in Portland.

I have worked very largely in the great mine of fur trade information, the Missouri Historical Society. Mrs. Frances Stadler of that organization was very helpful, providing me with the microfilms of manuscripts in their collections. Without these documents this book would have been quite impossible to write, and I am grateful for this help in proportion to its usefulness. With respect to manuscript material, it ought to be mentioned that reprinted versions are never entirely satisfactory; one is always slightly uncertain about them. There is no substitute for going directly to the material itself. It is *always* better to work from the original documents, or from photographic reproductions. No matter how frequently material may be printed, collections like those in the Missouri Historical Society will be absolutely essential to a serious student.

A special note of thanks is due Tamara West, who helped enormously in the preparation of the book by taking most of the mechanical burden herself. Her cheerful, steady help in research and preparation of the manuscript was invaluable.

APPENDIX D:

Synopsis

Among writers of books fashions come and go. One device I'm sorry has gone out of style: the old, long chapter headings. (The ones that started out "Chapter Ten: In Which our Hero ..." and went on to detail the action.) This seems quaint to us, but it was considerably more than a mere archaism. It was a way of making the mass of information in a book more easily accessible, by providing a bridge between the overgenerality of a Table of Contents and the overspecificity of an Index.

Since I would like the present book to be as useful as possible, I have a notion to revive the old custom, in a slightly altered form. Consequently, there is here printed a kind of Synopsis of the book, by Chapter and Section. This is taken more or less directly from my working journal and ought to make the material easier to get at. It will also serve as a running chronology of the years covered.

PART ONE

ASHLEY AND HIS MEN—*1822–1826*

Chapter 1
   I—Ashley and Henry and St. Louis
   II—First expedition prepared
   III—The river
   IV—Henry to Yellowstone
   V—Second boat

Notes

CHAPTER 1

1. Henry had been one of Manuel Lisa's partners in the Missouri Fur Company. As a brigade leader he had taken the first party of white trappers into the rich Three Forks area as early as 1809. Driven out by savage Blackfoot attacks, Henry crossed the Centennial Range and wintered on what is now known as Henry's Fork of the Snake, becoming the first American to trap on the Pacific slope of the Rockies. His party was also one of the first recorded in which the members went specifically as trappers, and not for trading purposes. In view of the historical emphasis that has been given Ashley's "great innovation" of white trappers, this earlier experience of Henry's seems pertinent.

2. Astor had made gestures in this direction in 1809, only a year after the incorporation of his American Fur Company in the East. The St. Louis trading clique, always hostile to "outsiders" in general—and Astor in particular—had forestalled his attempts to establish a connection with one of the St. Louis houses. Their opposition, plus the disastrous and expensive collapse of his Astoria enterprise, caused Astor to relinquish, temporarily, his plans for a western expansion of American Fur. Now, however, he was casting about again.

3. I entertain some doubt as to the number of horses lost in this foray. Minimum valuation of a horse in the mountains was $60, yet the total claim laid later for horses and merchandise lost was under $2,000. It should have been $2,500–$3,000, and traders were not accustomed to underestimating their losses when making a claim to the Office of Indian Affairs.

CHAPTER 2

1. DeVoto, in *Across the Wide Missouri,* says up to ten, but that would be high. The traps had to be spaced well apart, and it would be difficult to check that long a line.

2. Since this book is not written principally for the professional historian, I rarely cite sources in the academic convention. From time to time it will be necessary; when making a debatable point or expressing a view contrary to that generally held by students of the trade. In order to give the serious student an opportunity to check my reasoning on such points, I will append a list of relevant sources consulted in reaching my conclusions.

In this case, see: Extract of Calhoun to Clark, July 1, 1822; O'Fallon to Atkinson, July 3, 1822; Gaines to Calhoun, July 28, 1823; Gaines to Brown, July 26, 1823; Gaines to Atkinson, July 26, 1823; Atkinson to Brown, July 15, 1823, and Keemle's *Statement,* all quoted in *18th Congress, 1st Session, Senate Document 1, Serial 89.* Hempstead to Pilcher, April 3, 1822, quoted in *Jedediah Smith* by Dale Morgan, pp. 28-29. See also the report of the Congressional Committee on Indian Affairs in *18th Cong., 1st Sess., Sen. Doc. 56, Serial 91,* in particular *Questions 5* and *9;* and Pilcher's answers thereto. And: Chittenden, *American Fur Trade of the Far West,* vol. 1, p. 15 (on factory system). Pilcher's answers to Congressional questioning in *18th Cong., 1st Sess., Sen. Doc. 1,* are all particularly illuminating in this matter, even though he was trying to put a different face on the matter entirely.

CHAPTER 3

1. Both were given the nominal rank of captain. Lieutenants: Allen and Jackson. Ensigns: Cunningham and (Edward) Rose. Surgeon: Fleming. Tom Fitzpatrick was quartermaster and Bill Sublette sergeant major.

CHAPTER 4

1. This was a Canadian-American firm, made up of former Nor'westers from Montreal and some independent Americans. While all other traders operating on the river were St. Louis-based, Columbia came overland from the east.

2. Fitzgerald, of course, was gone by this time. Ironically, Glass had probably passed his canoe on the river somewhere

before the Mandan villages. Fitzgerald was at the Mandans before Langevin's party was attacked, which means he was on his way to Fort Atkinson while Glass was still coming up-river.

3. This name, Burnt Woods, was later applied to the half-breed *métis* who worked the Red River trade. The group of Bois Brulés encountered by the Smith party was a band of Teton Sioux.

4. This version accounts better for expended time and for the subsequent meeting of Smith with the Missouri Fur brigade under Keemle and Gordon.

CHAPTER 5

1. For the final and standard version, see Ruxton, *Life in the Far West* (Norman, 1951), where it's put in the mouth of Black Harris.

CHAPTER 6

1. This estimate of size is based on a report received by Peter Skene Ogden from a band of Shoshones the next year.

2. Dale, *Ashley-Smith Explorations,* and Morgan, *The Great Salt Lake,* both include more detailed information on what Morgan calls the "semi-mythical geography of the early West."

3. Kittson's journal of this expedition is a valuable counterpoint to Ogden, often providing information—particularly on the Americans—omitted by the partisan himself. Both journals have been published in a single volume by the Hudson's Bay Record Society, under the editorship of E. E. Rich.

4. "John Grey" appears several times in the literature. The scattered references may all be to this man, whose name was Ignace Hatchiorauquasha, or it may have been something of a generic term for an Iroquois whose name you didn't feel like pronouncing. I am inclined to the former view.

5. Though in another few years HBC's customary 70 per cent would seem small indeed. By the early thirties the mountain men, being supplied from St. Louis by their own compatriots, were paying an estimated *average* of 2000 per cent above prime cost. On many staple items it rose higher than that. A gallon of raw alcohol, costing about 20 cents in St. Louis, was diluted with plain water at about a 3:1 ratio. The four gallons of "whiskey" thus obtained went at Rendez-

vous for the traditional price of "a plew a pint." With a plew (Fr. *plus* = one prime beaver skin) averaging out around $5, this parlays the 20-cent gallon into a respectable $160.

CHAPTER 7

1. This McKay should not be confused with John McLoughlin's more famous stepson, Thomas McKay, who was not on this expedition. He arrived in the Snake Country for the first time with the 1825–26 expedition.

2. I'm not carping at Ashley here, but rather at the semi-mythical image of Ashley that has become part of the folklore and, more unfortunate, part of history. Historians have given him the character of master mountain man, which he eminently was not and never pretended to be. This fairly consistent misrepresentation of Ashley's function has led to a warped evaluation of these early years on the part of many historians and caused much difficulty for students, including myself.

3. There are two sources of information on this journey of Ashley's. The first is a letter to General Atkinson of December, 1825, written at the latter's request and containing specific geographic information. Harrison Dale quotes this in full and edits meticulously with respect to route. The second is a diary kept by Ashley from March 25 to June 27, 1825, newly identified as such by Dale Morgan in connection with his book *Jedediah Smith and the Opening of the West* (which also gives an excellent account of this party). Quotations in the text relating to Ashley's journey down to the Green are from this diary.

CHAPTER 8

1. Dale Morgan identifies the party that wintered near the mouth of the Bear as being Smith's; which is puzzling, inasmuch as it allows Smith only two months or so for a journey that took Ashley six, and does not jibe with Smith's own (admittedly vague) statement.

2. Ogden's journal does not mention the name of the leader of this brigade, nor indeed that of any member. We do know that Thierry Godin was in it, he being one of last year's deserters. At that time he had been "mortified at his Son not going with him," according to Kittson's record. This mortification was eased when his son joined him on this occasion.

CHAPTER 9

1. Ashley to Pierre Chouteau, Oct. 14, 1826. In the collection of the Missouri Historical Society, Ashley Papers, Chouteau Collection.

2. The note does not remain. Ashley's discharge of this balance due him is in the collection of the Missouri Historical Society in the Sublette Papers. It reads:

"Whereas Messrs. Smith Jackson & Sublette are under the impression that in a Settlement with them near the grand lake west of the Rocky mountains in the month of July in the year one thousand Eight hundred & twenty six, they gave a note in my favour for the sum of Seven thousand Eight hundred & twenty one dollars or there abouts which appeared a ballance due by them to me now therefore if any such note is given it is to be considered entirely void as they the said Smith Jackson & Sublette have since paid such amount.
October 1st 1827 *Wm H Ashley*"

3. This is *not* the document of sale of Ashley's interest, though it has sometimes been misidentified as such. The Articles state that Smith Jackson & Sublette are "now engaged in the fur trade and contemplate renewing their stock of Merchandise for the ensuing year," making it clear that the formal arrangements for transfer of Ashley's interest had been concluded at some time *before* the Articles of Agreement.

4. The casualty list of 1831 lists a LeClerc killed "on Head Waters Kansa River by Indians not known" in 1825; this may have been Provost's partner, but not certainly.

5. A letter from Crooks to Astor of April 18, 1827, says that *"you will have learned* that we hold a half interest in Ashley's expedition." (Italics mine.) If word had to come from American Fur, it was not from Astor himself but from his capable agent, Crooks, who made most of the field decisions.

6. Identifications of him as the Jackson who was a (nominal) lieutenant at the Aricara battle are probably mistaken. Leavenworth names that one definitely as George C. Jackson.

7. Weber himself is no more mentioned; where he went is as mysterious as where Davey Jackson came from. His family tradition has it that he returned from the mountains in 1827, but if so there is no record of his last year.

CHAPTER 10

1. Peter Skene Ogden had reference to it in his own journal, June 2, 1826, shortly before Smith left Rendezvous 1826. ". . . there is," said Ogden, "certainly some fine Streams in that quarter that discharges into the Gulph of California." He was of the opinion that a well-outfitted expedition should be dispatched there; and also noted the difficulty in crossing areas where a poorly equipped party would "perish for want of water."

2. Rogers' combination account book-journal is our principal source for activities in California. For the journey, Smith's letter to Wm. Clark, written at the 1827 rendezvous, July 12. Rogers' journal was forwarded to the governor of California as evidence of Smith's nonpolitical intention in invading the region. Both documents are reprinted in Dale, *Ashley-Smith Explorations.* Mr. Dale also examines the route of this party more carefully than I can hope to do here.

Since this expedition is one of the most famous in the annals of the trade, and is the first overland journey of Americans to California, it is worth noting the personnel we can be sure of: James Reed, Silas Gobel, Arthur Black, John Gaiter, Robert Evans, Manuel Lazarus, John Hanna, John Wilson, Martin McCoy, Daniel Ferguson, Peter Ranne (who bears the distinction of being the first Negro in California), and Abraham Laplant. Two other men flit in and out of the journal references, John Reubascan and a "Neppasang," meaning an Indian of the Canadian Nipissing tribe. These last two, however, apparently did not complete the trip; possibly deserted, since none of the casualty lists mention them. Rogers' journal last mentions them around the Virgin River.

3. Echeandia's ambitions are epitomized by his action when a successor was appointed to his post a few years later. Echeandia organized an insurrection, and held tenaciously to his authority for another three years. He was the polar opposite of the "fair and fat" Father Sanchez; and the two men were not friends. Echeandia favored the immediate secularization of the California missions and had already set in motion measures designed to accomplish this end. Father Sanchez fought bitterly against it and, in the end, lost out; but Echeandia was made to know he was opposed by a capable man. Sanchez—for all his "lively disposition" and inclination toward the more comfortable pursuits of life—was a man of very considerable ability.

4. The letter is worth reprinting:

"We, the undersigned, having been requested by Capt. Jedediah S Smith, to state our opinions regarding his entering the province of California do not hesitate to say that we have no doubt but that he was compelled to for want of provisions and water, having entered so far into the barren country that lies between the latitudes of forty-two and forty-three ... that he found it impossible to return by the route he came, as his horses had most of them perished from want of food and water, he was therefore under the necessity of pushing forward to California—it being the nearest place where he could procure supplies to enable him to return.

"We further state as our opinion that the account given by him is circumstantially correct, and that his sole object was the hunting and trapping of beaver and other furs. We have also examined the passports provided by him from the Superintendent of Indian Affairs for the Government of the United States of America, and do not hesitate to say we believe them perfectly correct.

"We also state that, in our opinion, his motives for wishing to pass by a different route to the Columbia River on his return is solely because he feels convinced that he and his companions run great risks of perishing if they return by the route they came.

"In testimony whereof we have herewith set our hands and seals this 20th day of December, 1826.

> *Wm G Dana, Capt. Schooner, Waverly*
> *Wm H Cunningham, Capt. Ship, Courier*
> *Wm. Henderson, Capt. Brig, Olive Branch*
> *James Scott.*
> *Thomas M Robinson, Mate, Schooner, Waverly*
> *Thomas Shaw, Supercargo, Ship, Courier.*"

5. Captain Cunningham wrote his own impressions of Smith on December 26, in a letter which was later published in the *Missouri Republican:*

"There has arrived at this place (San Diego) Capt. Jedediah Smith with a company of hunters, from St. Louis, on the Missouri. These hardy adventurers have been 13 months travelling their route, and have suffered numerous hardships. They have often had death staring them in the face, sometimes owing to the want of sustenance; at others to the numerous savages which they have been obliged to contend with. Out of 50 horses which they started with, they brought only 18 in with them; the others having died on the road for want of food and water.

"Does it not seem incredible that a party of fourteen men, depending entirely upon their rifles and traps for subsistence, will explore this vast continent, and call themselves happy when they can obtain the tail of a beaver to dine upon? Captain Smith is now on board the Courier, and is going with me to St. Pedro to meet his men: from thence he intends to proceed northward in quest of beaver, and to return, afterwards, to his deposits in the Rocky Mountains.

"(St. Diego and St. Pedro are ports in California, W. Coast of America, near 3,000 miles from Boston.)"

It might be noted that Captain Cunningham's own profession—as all who consumed *Two Years before the Mast* at an early age will recall—was not the easiest in the world. His admiration has the ring of a man who cannot comprehend the insanity—or courage—that would lead a man to walk somewhere the wind might take him.

6. The route of this return is conjectural all the way to the Great Salt Lake. Here it depends on the identification of the river on which he left his men. If it was in fact the Stanislaus, then Smith probably crossed by Ebbert Pass and descended the eastern slope somewhere between Mono Lake, California, and Walker Lake, Nevada. This is Dale Morgan's estimate, and I have generally followed him. Mr. Morgan thinks it most likely that Smith and his men crossed Nevada by a route roughly parallel to US 6, but some thirty or forty miles to the north of that highway. These geographical identifications are frequently very tenuous in Smith's case, owing to his tendency to let one word stand where a dozen might have provided information.

CHAPTER 11

1. The irascible Joshua Pilcher had notions of his own that summer. His Missouri Fur Company had folded in 1825; they had gambled for high stakes with the Immel-Jones expedition to the Yellowstone, and lost. Their ablest partisans went under in that defeat, and the loss of capital finally proved fatal. After several attempts to find other work, Pilcher had at last organized a company in his own name, a partnership which included names to be heard from again: Lucien B. Fontenelle, William Henry Vanderburgh, Charles Bent, and Andrew Drips. The new company—J. Pilcher & Company—was never a strong one. There was simply getting

to be too much powerful competition for a company capitalized at a mere $7,000 to make its way. The entry of John Jacob Astor's American Fur Company on the western scene—through their arrangement with B. Pratte & Company—was discouraging news to a man contemplating a successful small scale mountain operation. Caught between the enormous financial resources of American Fur, on the one hand, and the mountain successes of Smith Jackson & Sublette on the other, Pilcher & Company had virtually been born half strangled.

Now, in the summer of 1827, Pilcher once again decided to take his cue from Ashley. In September he set out for the mountains with a supply caravan (which gave him, incidentally, better than a month's head start over Ashley's). Unhappily, the bad luck that had been dogging him since the Aricara campaign caught up with him again.

To summarize his entire project briefly:

Somewhere around South Pass he lost all his horses, probably to the Kicked-in-Their-Bellies band of Crows. By this time the winter was beginning to make itself felt, and he had no choice but to cache the goods that were left. He and his men were forced into winter camp in the valley of the Green, without ever reaching the trappers. (In the spring of '28, when he sent back a party to raise the cache, Pilcher discovered that the greater part of the supplies had been ruined by water during the winter. Discouraged, he picked up what little was left and moved over to Bear Lake, where it was traded off in a more or less desultory fashion at Rendezvous 1828; Ashley's caravan had been there since November. Nobody needed much.)

2. Godin is noted in this journal as "Henry" Godin. This is probably an error of transcription. The journals were kept on beaver skin, often poorly tanned, and tied up with thong. They were quill-written in haste, in bad weather, frequently by men who hated to write. Often quite indecipherable. This has to be Thierry, as he was still in debt to HBC. His son Antoine had paid up.

3. The exchange also gave Ogden cause to ruminate on the American system. His information, presumably, comes from Tulloch:

"Altho' our [HBC] trappers have their goods on moderate terms, the price of their beaver is certainly low compared to Americans. With them, beaver large and small are averaged @ $5 each; with us $2 for large and $1 for small. Here is a wide difference. . . . It is optional with them to take furs to St. Louis where they obtain $5½. One third of the American trappers followed this plan. Goods are sold to them at 150#Pc. dearer than we do but they have the advantage of receiving them in the waters of the Snake country. An American trapper from the short distance he has to travel is not obliged to transport provisions requires only ½ the number of horses and is very moderate in his advances. For 3 years prior to the last ones, General Ashley transported supplies to this country and in that period has cleared $80,-000 and retired, selling the remainder of his goods in hand at an advance of 150 P cent, payable in 5-years in beaver @ $5 P beaver, or in cash optional with the purchasers. Three young men Smith, Jackson and Subletz purchased them, who have in this first year made $20,000. It is to be observed, finding themselves alone, they sold their goods 1-3 dearer than Ashley did, but have held out a promise of a reduction in prices this year. What a contrast between these young men and myself. They have been only 6 yrs. in the country and without a doubt in as many more will be independent men. The state of uncertainty I am now in regarding . . . the gloomy prospects for a spring hunt make me wretched and unhappy."

(The $20,000 figure is, of course, untrue.)

4. Pierre Tevanitagon. He was killed, according to Warren Ferris, on the sources of the Jefferson River. This is the Three Forks area, so it can be assumed that Old Pierre was with Sublette's party. It is also possible that Ferris, who is usually reliable, places this death wrongly. Tradition has it that the beautiful and important valley of Pierre's Hole— now known as Teton Basin—was so named for the death of an Iroquois trapper there, which may have been Pierre Tevanitagon.

5. This quotation is from the manuscript draft of the letter, now at the Missouri Historical Society. The figures on the amount lost differ greatly from Ogden's account of this party's poverty. I'm inclined to accept Ogden's version as more accurate, since Ashley was grinding his own ax in this letter to Senator Benton.

CHAPTER 12

1. Henry "Bosun" Brown, John Relle, John Turner, Thomas Virgin, Charles Swift, one Robiseau, John Ratelle, Joseph

Palmer, Toussaint Marechal (Marrishal, Marshall), William Campbell, David Cunningham, Isaac Galbraith, Thomas Daws, Polette (Potette) Labross, Joseph Lapoint, Silas Gobel, François Deromme, Gregory Ortago.

2. David Cunningham, Silas Gobel, François Deromme, William Campbell, Henry Brown, Gregory Ortago, John Ratelle, Potette Labross, Robiseau, John Relle.

3. Henry Virmond. A well-known merchant trading out of Mexico City and Acapulco. According to Harrison Dale, he was "a skillful intriguer," and hence probably enjoyed this situation, which certainly called for one.

CHAPTER 13

1. Though rather in the line of gesture: Smith had only four men, counting himself. McLeod's total party, aside from the Americans, consisted of fourteen Indians and twenty-two *engagés*.

2. An instance of this had occurred the previous spring, with Samuel Tulloch's suspicion that Ogden had set the Blackfeet on him. Simpson, though probably unaware of this particular incident, is doubtless considering other similar accusations.

3. *Sic*. For 30d/sight=30 days/sight. Probably an error of transcription by Frederick Merk, whose *Fur Trade and Empire*, (Cambridge, 1931), contains Simpson's journals for 1824–25 and many other valuable documents from the HBC archives, including the letters I am quoting here.

4. The final prices were:
"Beaver at 3$ p Skin Land Otters at 2$ pr Skin and Sea Otters at 10$ pr Skin which from their damaged state I conceive to be their utmost value here, fully as much as they will net to us in England; and after making a fair deduction for risk and expence of transport hence to St. Louis, more than they would yield you if taken to and sold in the States."

5. Halifax currency was slightly lower in value than sterling: £541. 0s. 6d. Halifax = £486. 18s. 5d. Sterling = $2,369.60. (Dale Morgan)

6. Simpson was amused by some of the geographical misinformations then current in the United States. He wrote:
"In the American Charts this River, (The Wilhamot or Moltnomah) is laid down, as taking its rise in the Rocky Mountains. . . . But it now turns out, that the Sources of the Wilhamot are not 150 Miles distant from Fort Vancouver, in Mountains which even Hunters cannot attempt to pass, be-

yond which is a Sandy desert of about 200 miles, likewise impassable, and from thence a rugged barren country . . . where Smith and his party were nearly staved to Death. . . . I am of opinion we have little to apprehend from Settlers in this quarter."

CHAPTER 14

1. This is in part a surmise based on two entries of "Smith Jackson & Sublette in account with Wm. Ashley," documents in the Missouri Historical Society, Sublette Papers. On October 26, 1828, the balance was $16,000; under date of "Jan 7 1829": "Ballance due Smith Jackson & Sublette on Settlement this day $6684"; in the interim the difference of $9,316 must have gone toward outfitting the 1829 party and paying some back wages.

2. She was responsible, among other things, for a large part of the Oregon volume in the massive 39-volume history of the West by Hubert Howe Bancroft.

CHAPTER 15

1. Fitz was definitely the clerk of Jackson's party at the Flatheads; and one source puts him at the Popo Agie Rendezvous 1829. Thus he must have come across the mountains as an express from Jackson. Sublette's direct movement across to Pierre's Hole indicates he knew where he was going, though tradition has it that he had no idea where Jackson was and joined him almost by accident.

2. In establishing the most probable routes for parties in this area, I have used throughout this book the maps accompanying the Twelfth Annual Report of the United States Geological and Geographical Survey of the Territories; these were made in 1877 under the direction of F. V. Hayden, and have never been surpassed.

3. Most of the furs went direct to Ashley, who took his commission and sold them to Frederick A. Tracy & Company (usually), who took their commission and passed them on down the line. As might be expected, quite a remarkable amount ended up on the books of John Jacob Astor.

4. The letter from SJ&S to the Secretary of War is further evidence. While Smith appreciated and acknowledged HBC's good offices, he certainly didn't let it interfere with his opinion of them as serious competition; and competition to be met in any possible way.

5. Based on Milton's party of forty and the statement of

175 present in Pierre's Hole before they split up for the fall hunt.

6. His route may be: by ascending the Powder to the head; overland to the Sweetwater; South Pass; across Bridger Basin and the valley of the Green. Or perhaps back via Wind River again. If you have a topographical map of the area your guess is as good as mine.

CHAPTER 16

1. It isn't customary for a student to state his conclusions quite as abruptly as this, particularly when they contradict the generally accepted historical view. But before scholars take to the historical journals to reprimand me, I wish they would study the cited documents. In arriving at these notions I have worked principally from the account books and documents now in the manuscript collections of the Missouri Historical Society; in particular those preserved in the Sublette Papers, the Campbell Estate Papers, and the Ashley collection in the Chouteau Papers.

2. As it worked out in detail: Ashley completed sales for $84,499.14. He had advanced SJ&S $23,314.60 before sale, charging them 6 per cent interest for 148 days: $574.93. Ashley's commission at 2½ per cent = $2,114.90. Expenses = $2,573.79. Discounts for cash payment amounted to over $1,110. Another advance of $2,000 was made, of which Smith alone received $1,798.66. I don't fully understand this payment, but it may have had something to do with redeeming the HBC draft given Smith by Simpson. The three partners, in the final accounting, ended with a share of $17,-604.33 each.

It is interesting to note by Ashley's account books the disposal he made of these furs. Of the total $84,500, John Jacob Astor bought $82,000 worth. Seemed as though no matter which company you *thought* you were trapping for, it turned out to be John Jacob Astor in the end.

3. Jackson and Sublette later gave a power of attorney to David Waldo, in Taos, for the purpose of collecting on this note at $4.25 a pound. But this was contingent on delivery of the furs within sixty miles of Taos—and the arrangement wasn't made until a year later. (This could not have been agreed upon at the Rendezvous 1830, since it was made necessary by a complex of factors unknown at the time.) The delivered price, of course, would have been higher than mountain price; the only question is how much. The reasons

for the provision of delivery to Taos—rather than St. Louis—
are suggested in the text.

4. Ferris came out with the Robidoux-Vanderburgh-Drips
party. (His account of the next few years—*Life in the Rocky
Mountains*—is one of the best sources, and sometimes the
only one, for the events of these years. If it is occasionally
contradictory and differs from other records, they all do, they
all do.)

5. A rough total at Rendezvous 1830 would be about 200.
Fraeb and Gervais have 32; Fitz, Sublette, and Bridger, 81.
This leaves around thirty men unaccounted for; these were
probably dispersed in small, detached parties of ten or fifteen
free trappers, who would not appear again until Rendezvous
1831.

6. Apparently the mountain operations of the Company's
1830 brigade had been left mainly in the hands of Joseph
Robidoux. Vanderburgh must have returned to Fort Union
about the time Robidoux was trailing Fraeb and Gervais.

7. Keemle, of course, is basing his remarks on the letter
itself, which is ambiguous; SJ&S probably meant the Popo
Agie, but the letter's phrasing makes it seem that the pass is
at the same place where Rendezvous 1830 was held, which is
given as the Wind. I think the partners were deliberately
oversimplifying the geography of the area to make their
point more emphatic.

8. This is a conjecture by Dale Morgan. It seems borne
out by future events and serves to make some sense out of a
rather confusing situation. It is not really clear who initiated
the Santa Fe expedition. I'm going by the fact that Smith
requested a passport in early February, Sublette not until late
March.

9. This is a general account; not one specifically of this
party. However, by this time the procedure along the Santa
Fe Trail was far more standard than on any other route
beyond the frontier. Chittenden's *American Fur Trade of the
Far West* gives a good account of the route with all its
landmarks, and I generally follow him here.

10. Not relatives by blood or language, however. The
Gros Ventres lived with Bug's Boys and most contemporary
accounts do not distinguish between the tribes, lumping them
all under the generic term "Blackfeet."

11. As it worked out, Smith's estate went almost half;
Jackson & Sublette supplied $3,032; Smith, about $2,800.

12. *The Adventures of Zenas Leonard,* recently reprinted by the University of Oklahoma Press.

13. It should be remembered that John Jacob Astor did not personally involve himself in the trade. When he satisfied himself that he had the best men in the right positions he wisely allowed them to work as they saw fit. Thus the actual mountain operation of American Fur was largely in the hands of McKenzie at Fort Union (UMO) and Chouteau at St. Louis (Western Department). Ramsay Crooks of the Northern Department was general agent and effective head of the Company. He had been with Astor for twenty years and more; ever since the Astoria enterprise.

14. Mrs. Victor, writing from Meek's dictation, here renders "Iroquois" as "Rockway." This has occasioned a lot of wild speculation on the part of historians as to what this mysterious "Rockway" tribe might be, since it never appears in any other place.

CHAPTER 18

1. Since this document is critically important in establishing the relationship between Bill Sublette and RMF, I reprint it here in full:

"Articles of Agreement made and entered into on the Teton Fork of the Columbia River and under the Three Teton mountain this Twenty fifth day of July in the Year One Thousand Eight Hundred and Thirty Two, by and between William L Sublette of the first part and Thomas Fitzpatrick Milton G Sublette John Baptice Jarvie James Bridger and Henry Freab trading under the name and Style of The Rockey Mountain Furr C° of the Second part Witnesseth

"That whereas the said William L Sublette has delivered as per contract a certain Invoice of Merchandize to said Rockey Mountain Furr C° and is now about to return to St Louis missouri The said Rockey Mountain Furr C° have bargained with said William L Sublette to transport on their account to St Louis all their Beaver Furr Beaver Castors, Otter, Musk Rat &c to St Louis Missouri at their risk and to pay said William L. Sublette for so doing Fifty cents per pound with the following undersanding Viz

"The said Rockey Mountain Furr C° owe said William L Sublette for the merchandize above alluded to the sum of Fifteen Thousand Six Hundred and Twenty dollars. also one note due June first for One Thousand Four Hundred and

Thirty Eight Dollars and one Note for Five Hundred Dollars due July 29*th* [I am unable to identify these obligations] besides a settled account [an *un*settled account is meant] of Two Hundred and Six Dollars $^{44}/_{100}$ and also a note to the late firm of Smith Jackson & Sublette amounting to Fifteen Thousand Five Hundred and Thirty Two Dollars $^{22}/_{100}$ and to the late firm of Jackson & Sublette a Note of Three Thousand and Thirty Two Dollars $^{75}/_{100}$ [this for the merchandise picked up by Fitzpatrick in Taos] and also another Note of One Hundred and Three Dollars   and also an amount of their orders and notes to men now going to St Louis which orders are accepted by said William L Sublette and to be paid by him on the arrival of this Beaver Furr in St Louis Missouri They amount to Ten Thousand Three Hundred and Eighteen Dollars $?/_{100}$ —And the said Rockey Mountain Furr C^o have delivered to said William L Sublette Eleven Thousand Two Hundred and Forty Six pounds Beaver Furr (including Two Hundred Musk rats Skins and Fifty Seven otter Skins) and they have also delivered Two Hundred and Forty Seven pounds Beaver Castors all of which together with Three Thousand pounds or thereabouts in caches on the river Platte, which the said William L Sublette is to weigh and transport with the Furrs &c Recvd at this place to St Louis Missouri on their account and risk they paying him at the rate of Fifty cents per pound for same   And on his arrival in St Louis Missouri should he deem it advisable and to the advantage of said Rockey Mountain Furr C^o he is authorized to dispose of it there on their account or should he deem it more to their advantage to Ship it to another market he is then authorized to do so and when sold the Nett proceeds are to be appropriated as follows   Viz

"The said William L Sublette in the first place is to pay himself the before mentioned sum of Fifteen Thousand Six Hundred and Twenty Dollars and also for the transportation of this Beaver &c to St Louis at the Rate of Fifty cents per pound with interest at the rate of Eight per cen per annum from first november next until paid   Secondly—The before mentioned drafts and notes to be paid to men now going to St Louis amounting to Ten Thousand Three Hundred and Eighteen Dollars $^{44}/_{100}$ is to be next taken out of the Nett proceeds The said Rockey Mountain Furr C^o paying whatever interest the said William L Sublette may have to pay on the money he borrowed to pay these drafts and notes on his arrival

"Thirdly Their notes payable 1st June for Fourteen Hundred and Thirty Eight Dollars and Note payable 29th July for Five Hundred Dollars bearing interest at Ten per cent per annum until paid

"Fourthly The balance on their open account amounting to Two Hundred and Six Dollars $^{44}/_{100}$

"Fifthly Their note to Smith Jackson & Sublette due first day of November 1831 for Fifteen Thousand five Hundred and Thirty Two Dollars $^{22}/_{100}$ with interest until paid[1]

"Sixtly one note to the late firm of Jackson & Sublette due first of December Eighteen Hundred and Thirty One for Three Thousand and Thirty Two Dollars $^{75}/_{100}$ and one note for One Hundred and Three Dollars due July 23 Eighteen Hundred & Thirty One with interest until paid   And there is a perfect understanding that all expenses attending the Furrs &c after their arrival in St Louis are to be paid by the said Rockey mountain Furr C^o

"And as there is an uncertainty as to the price Beaver Furr &c may sell for an understanding exists between the parties before mentioned that should the Nett proceeds of the Beaver amount to more than will pay off the foregoing obligations the said William L Sublette is to pay off any of their just notes now in St Louis or that may be taken there as far as money remains in his hands and should a surplus still remain it is to be Subject to the order of the said Rockey Mountn Furr C^o. But should the nett proceeds of the Beaver not more than discharge the foregoing obligations— then should the said William L Sublette pay out money in taking up their notes now in St Louis then the said Rockey Mountane Furr C^o are to pay the said William L Sublette at the Rate of Eight per cent per annum until paid

"In witness whereof the parties have hereunto set their hands and seals the day and [?] before written

Witness   *Wm L Sublette* (Seal)
R Campbell   *Thos Fitzpatrick* (Seal)
A. W. Sublette   for
                             Rockey Mont^n fur Co.

"After signing the above articles of agreement the said Rockey Mountain Furr C^o have drawn in favour Robert Campbell for five Hundred and Sixty Dollars payable when the beaver Furr is sold which draft is accepted by said W^m L Sublette

                         W^m L Sublette (Seal)

>   *Thos Fitzpatrick*
>   for
>   *Rockey Mot^n fur Co* (Seal)

"We the undersigned hereby certify that we have weighed and marked a certain quantity of Beaver Furr belonging to The Rockey mountain Furr C^o which was raised by their directions by W^m L Sublette out of Caches on Sweet Water & River Platte which Beaver weighed Two Thousand Four Hundred and Seventy Three pounds, and Ten otter Skins weighing Fifteen pounds, and Forty five pounds Beaver Castors.

>   "Given under our hands this fifteenth day of August
>   Eighteen Hundred and Thirty Two
>
>   *Robert Campbell*
>   *Louis Vasquez*"

2. A discussion of poisoned meat can be found in Ogden's *Snake Country Journals, 1824–1826.* E. E. Rich, the editor, prints several medical opinions which are most helpful.

CHAPTER 19

1. Which is to say: from Pierre's Hole west across the Snake River plains, then a northeast reversal to the Big Hole River, southwest of present Butte, Montana. (The Big Hole, looping north, then east, joins with the Beaverhead River from the south to form Jefferson Fork.) Down the valley of the Big Hole, then, Fitz and Bridger's brigade began their fall hunt in the Three Forks area.

2. Somewhere along the line Joe had joined the Fitzpatrick-Bridger brigade. Mrs. Victor says the camps were joined at Salmon River in early fall; which is not possible. Newell says "Up to the head of the galiton fork met craig and some of our hunters we parted with at the Randezvous," which is probably it. Joe must have been with a small, detached party from the Salmon.

3. This was most probably Antoine Clement, HBC deserter, mountain man, hunter, half-breed, trapper extraordinaire, who ended up, of all things, a valet on a Scotch baronial estate. See DeVoto's *Across the Wide Missouri.*

CHAPTER 20

1. The *Yellowstone's* maiden trip in 1831 was only to Fort Tecumseh, near the mouth of the Teton (Bad) River; present Pierre, South Dakota. On the trip the name of the

fort was changed to Fort Pierre, in honor of Pierre Chouteau.

2. Catlin's reputation rests largely on place and time, rather than ability; he was the first artist to make a systematic record of the western American Indian. His work is notable for its accuracy of detail. He could not draw.

3. This was Pierre Pambrun, lifelong HBC man. "An active, steady dapper little fellow," by Simpson's Character Book.

4. Wyeth's letter book contains certain tantalizing suggestions. A letter to his brother says: "I should not much regret leaving the land of religious freedom as you call it ... it is not so to me, finding in it none of that freedom... I mean the exercise and avowal of ones ideas without harm accruing therefrom. Can anyone say that my opinions have been exercised in freedom and that no harm has accrued to me [?] Can any one assert that I have not been lowered in the estimation of my fellows thereby? ... And yet you call this a land of civil and religious liberty. I repeat I have not found it such." This is a long letter, and the entire last portion of it has been cut out of the letter book. It suggests possible motivations for Wyeth's Oregon expeditions that have not been investigated.

CHAPTER 21

1. *Astoria*, published in 1836, and *Captain Bonneville* in 1837. (The original title of the latter is more accurate: *The Rocky Mountains, or, Scenes, Incidents and Adventures in the Far West: Digested from the Journal of Captain B. L. E. Bonneville ...*)

2. Cholera provided one of the strongest motivations for Oregon emigration; the diseases of the Mississippi valley were absent on the Willamette. The dreamers saw it as a land without sickness; but Wyeth found "much sickness among the people here ... which I think arises from low diet and moist weather ... the main disorder is an intermittent fever which has carried off all or nearly all the Indians." The Indians called it the "cole-sick-waum-sick," or just the "Boston sick." The descriptions fit malaria, one form of which is endemic to the Columbia Basin. The Indian cure killed more than the disease itself. Most Oregon Indians—all the coastal tribes—had one standard remedy (outside of magic). This was a sweat bath, in a steam hut by a river. When the temperature was well up, the patient dashed from the hut and plunged

into the cold water (coast tribes sometimes into the ocean). Malaria, if that is what the cole-sick-waum-sick was, does not respond well to this treatment. Most of the patients died.

3. Wyeth states that RMF had accepted two supply trains, for which they had paid about $30,000. Definite figures for 1832 show that one to have been about $15,000. Hence the above deduced figure.

4. Bill took to signing himself "William S. Williams, M.T.," meaning Master Trapper. Preacher Bill, Old Bill, Parson Bill, Old Solitaire, were some of his other cognomens. Bill was convinced (among other things) that his soul would migrate into an elk, and he used to sit greenhorns down and warn them against shooting him if they ever saw him in that form. A fictionalized, but fairly accurate, version of Williams plays a major role in Lieutenant Frederick Ruxton's *Life in the Far West*, published by the University of Oklahoma Press.

CHAPTER 22

1. The experimental nature of this first year's expedition is shown by a letter of Wyeth's to Milton, requesting that he come to meet the men who were backing Wyeth in the project: "I have no doubt you will see of how much importance it is that parties who *in the course of events may have such large engagements with each other* should meet and establish a mutual confidence which will afterward facilitate all business." (Italics mine.)

2. During the spring Bill had picked up the last of RMF's obligations for himself—Davey Jackson's share of the moneys due Smith Jackson & Sublette. Bill bought Jackson's share of this remaining debt for half price ($783.93). The understanding was that, if the debt were paid, Jackson would leave the other half with Sublette "to indemnify him for any damage he may sustain on my part of Law suits against [RMF]." And if the debt were *not* collected, Jackson would pay back the $783 with interest.

CHAPTER 23

1. Ramsay Crooks "and associates" bought the Northern Department and retained the name American Fur. The St. Louis house of B. Pratte bought the Western Department (which they had been operating) and continued under the name Pratte, Chouteau & Company.

2. Wyeth's letter book makes it clear that Fitzpatrick's

letter was addressed to Milton Sublette, rather than Bill. Letter CXCIII, March 13, 1834, refers to Fitzpatrick's robbery by the Crows—information Wyeth could only have had from Milton, through Tom's letter. Letter CCVII, to Fitzpatrick himself, says: "You may expect me by the 1st July at the rendesvous named in your letter to Milton which which you sent by Dr. Harrison who opened it and I presume told Wm Sublette of the place." Hugh Campbell's statement that "the nature [of RMF's agreement with Wyeth] has not fully transpired" is further evidence of the secrecy with which Milton was handling the arrangments. All Bill Sublette had was Fitzpatrick's reference to "our aramgents with Wyeth" from the rifled letter.

3. The Santa Fe parties were indeed to be officially escorted; that trade was rapidly growing in importance. In 1822, the year our narrative opened, it had amounted to $15,000. This year of '34 would see ten times that amount: $150,000, and involving only 160 men. The Santa Fe trade was operating more efficiently from the point of view of wages. Only eleven men had been lost, while the mountain trade had accounted for around 150 in the same period. But men, were, after all, only men. The thing that kept the mountain trade going was that rosy possibility of a really big killing; that unqualifiedly successful season of which every trader dreamed. The average margin of profit in Santa Fe was only 15 per cent to 20 per cent, and it was estimated that the B. Pratte-Ashley mountain venture of '27 had netted around 70 per cent on their investment.

4. The stomach was opened, and a tin pan lowered into the belly juices. The most recent water the animal had drunk would be near the top, and flow over the edges of the pan.

5. Wyeth himself noted: "The companies here have all failed of making hunts, some from quarreling among themselves some from having been defeated by the Indians and some from want of horses and what few furs have been taken have been paid to the men."

The great California expedition of Joe Walker—presumably for the benefit of Captain Bonneville—had been a pathetic and total loss. Bonneville sent back to civilization "about 10 pack"—a maximum of $3,500 St. Louis, without deductions—"and men going down to whom there is due 10,000$." (Wyeth's figures. Lucien Fontenelle reported twelve to fourteen pack for Bonneville, but added "it is not enough to pay their retiring hands. . . . I think by next year he will be at an end with the mountains." Which was correct.)

American Fur had not done too badly—not, in any event, as badly as the others. While eight or ten packs had been lost through mountain attrition (and another eight or ten "by the rascality of a few men"), they would still return almost 8,000 pounds of beaver with Fontenelle.

Index

455

About the Author

Don Berry's first novel, TRASK, brought him immediate recognition as a powerful and original storyteller of the American past. MOONTRAP, his second novel, received the accolade of the Western Writers of America, who honored it with their Spur Award as the best western historical novel of the year. Mr. Berry, now in his mid-thirties, grew up in Oregon and still makes it his home. In addition to his writing, he is currently directing and producing television documentaries on the Northwest.

Comstock Editions

HAVE THE BEST OF THE WEST AGAIN ON YOUR BOOKSHELF